Based on true stories of my life living as an
immigrant in the USA.
A story about boxing, romance, surviving on the edge
of lethal disease infections, and much more...

BRIDGE

OF

HOW MY LIFE BECAME A
ROLLER COASTER

DIMITRY SALCHEV

ISBN: 979-8-9865719-3-5 (Hardcover)
       979-8-9865719-4-2 (Paperback)
       979-8-9865719-5-9 (eBook)

Preface

This is not a guidebook. I am not trying to tell you what to do or what not to do. I am not trying to be your father or to look like I am a wise man or some sort of that by expressing my thoughts. This book does not sink in nostalgia either. There are some insights lined up in this memorial. My only goal is to ensure you are having fun while reading this book and not falling asleep between the pages. I hope you will enjoy reading this.

This book is my confession to God. I am not afraid to tell the truth of how messed up my life became. That is just an emotional frame in my perspective while I was walking through a bridge of pain.

Part of the profits from this book will go to foster homes.

Acknowledgments

First of all, I would like to thank my mother who has always supported me and given me all the love that I can ask for. I also would like to thank my father who shows me the right directions in life and to my sister who made me so proud because she never stops revealing her success and ability to become a better person. I must thank all my friends for supporting me and being next to me when I need them. I can firmly say that without my friends, I would never be the man I am today. I believe there is an unhuman power among us that shows us the inspiration of energy to create and perform a platform of art. You will be witnesses of my life experience precisely the way I felt it and saw it.

Most of the names mentioned in this book had been changed for safety purposes. God gave me blessing, honor, and opportunity to write this book, and I feel so thankful to be able to do it. You will be a witness of a story that would shake your mindset.

Chapter 1

Sunday, July 3, 2011, was one of those sweltering days when you were off work, hanging out with your buddies, flipping Italian sausages and juicy steaks on a George Foreman grill in the corner of your mowed yard. You were getting hammered by slurping tons of ice-cold beers and using your buddies as a wall of protection against your cranky wife. Or maybe you were trying to sunbathe while chilling on the beach, laughing out loud, surrounded by many friends.

Around noon, two ambulances rushed, whipping through the residential vehicles over the main boulevards in one of the most notorious cities of Bulgaria christened Plovdiv. The paramedics had an urgent call for a car collision a few miles out of town. When the medical vehicles approached, the paramedics surveyed the countryside where there was a disastrous view.

They saw a huge commercial truck hauling a flatbed trailer that crashed into the ditch and a tomato-red sedan that had struck into that truck. The picture was grotesque and dreadful. It was like when you passed by, operating your car, and you saw a collision between two vehicles that looked so bad that you couldn't recognize the make of the automobile. You noncommittally ponder, Oh Lord, I hope the passengers are still alive!

Many residents were crowding around as if they were a flock of crows gazing at the horrendous carcass. The paramedics pulled out the gurney and rushed toward the smashed vehicles. They drew two male bodies from the tomato-red car. The males were comatose. A young gal was weeping, frightened and buried in emotional shock. She crept from the rear seats of the tomato-red automobile, which looked more like slashed metal.

The truck driver was blabbering in a foreign language incomprehensible to the Bulgarian bluebottles. The paramedics placed meticulously one of the unconscious males into the ambulance that abruptly roared toward the infirmary. A female EMT in her early thirties had placed an oxygen mask on one of the injured males. She fumbled a medical report that laid out details as follows:

Name: Dimitry Salchev. Sex: Male Height: 6.00. Eyes: Blue. Age of 22. Address: JK. Trakya, Block 97 Unit 7. Third floor. Region of Plovdiv. City of Plovdiv, Bulgaria.

Chapter 2

On Friday, the first day of July in 2011, my phone rang instantaneously. The name of Peter popped up on the screen of my blueberry-colored Nokia 3310. Peter was a nutjob. He could come up with an absolutely unforeseen proposal. Something flaky always happened when I was palling around with this fella. It could lead both ways, bad or good. It wasn't necessarily his mistake. It was his karma stamped as a tattoo on his ass. We had known each other since grade school. Peter could be described as a tornado bellowing erratically, and wherever he went, he would drag you away from your routine life. Uncertain, I picked up the phone. What does this bloke want? I thought.

"Hey, Dimitry, what are you up to this weekend?" he exclaimed. His voice was as thrilled as a man who had just won a one-week vacation to the Caribbean.

"Nothing particularly. What's on your mind?"

"I am having a huge party at my house in the outskirts. You wanna come?" He was so hyped that I hardly grasped his words.

"Sure, dude! I'm in," I blurted out, magnetized by his proposal. Later the same day, I picked up Mike and his girlfriend Greta.

We rolled to Peter's house which was around twenty miles away from

Plovdiv. When we arrived, his house was surrounded by many cars parked into the driveway. The party was reaching its climax.

Peter's house had a huge hedged lawn; you could easily get married there. The dooryard had a capacity for around 150 guests. Peter's stronghold was constructed from solid bricks. It was an old house but quite comfy. The backyard patio was packed. A lot of party hunters were swigging booze, jumping into animated conversations. The amplifiers blasted out so loudly that you needed to scream if you wanted someone to hear you. We all had a blast.

I toked a Jamaican grass as a frigging pothead. The revelers didn't stop all night long, including the next day. Some of them passed out for a few hours and then got back at the starting line. There was so much booze that I could take a bath filled with any type of alcohol.

Early in the morning on Sunday, July 3, 2011, Mike stepped closer and asked me,

"Bro, let's roll to Plovdiv." I stared at him and replied,

"Dude, I need to take a nap for a few hours, then we'll head up to the city." There was something that popped in my mind, like those icons prompted on JavaScript. My inner voice declared. You have been drinking actively for the past twelve hours. Hold your horses and take a quick break. Mike didn't like my answer. Regardless, he had to accept my decision if he wanted a ride to his place. Knackered by guzzling a plethora of bevy, I hit the sack. Five hours later, I instantaneously awoke as if I was a frightened squaddie on his first day in the military camp. In the next fifteen minutes, the three of us hopped into my tomato-red compact hatchback of a Mazda model 323F.

"Buckle up," I told Mike. He peered at me, flashing a grimace.

"I don't need any frigging belts," Mike said, annoyed by my suggestion.

Monitoring at him, I shrugged off. It's your call, dude! Then, I fired up the engine, and the Mazda howled. We cruised through a desolate pathway somewhere at the boondocks. As we rolled on the interstate road, a ghostly silence filled my car. Mike and Greta were bushed. They didn't sleep for the past twenty-four hours whereas, I felt an overflow of energy like a large industrial transformer. It shouldn't had been longer than five minutes, and we spotted the Plovdiv's sign. Holding the steering wheel, I saw a blind turn around two hundred feet ahead. I switched the manual gears to reduce the speed. All of a sudden, the sun's reflection dazzled my vision. Then my eyes widened like a startled lemur. What the duck is this?

For a second, my body froze as a mannequin in front of the Gucci's store. What I saw gave me goosebumps. There was a semi-truck traveling in the opposite direction, which had missed that blind turn and merged straight onto the same lane as my Mazda. Come on, hit the brake! The voice in my head cried out. Pressing the brake pedal occurred to be a bad idea. The truck accelerated and swiftly cut the distance. My heart pumped above 150 beats. For a moment, I thought I would spit out my liver from my mouth. Hurry up! Make up your mind! Left or right, for Christ's sake. Nah, can't go at the left side. Perhaps someone from ongoing direction will ram on me. Turn right. Right. Roll this frigging steering wheel on right! Dammit!

KABOOM! It all blacked out as if an electric fuse blew all the circuits of a sumptuous basement.

When my eyelids rolled up, a female emergency medical technician stared at me. Her countenance looked as if she was saying, "Man, you are messed up!"

As I judged her expression, the voice of my subconscious bawled. Why am I in the ambulance? Why does this chick look at me like I am in critical condition? What happened? My last memory was when I drive and…the truck…yeah, the big-arse frigging truck. Oh my God, we've been in a car accident. Holy-shmoly! Where are Mike and Greta? They must be transported with a different ambulance. All of those questions bumped in my head. I had been taken into the intensive care department at St. George Hospital in Plovdiv. The transportation team parked the gurney, where Mike was lying. He was motionless as a frightened mutt beat up by two hoodrats.

"Dimitry, what the hell happened? Why are we at the hospital? I don't frigging remember anything," Mike grumbled, encircled by a swarm of doctors.

"Don't worry, Mike, everything will be fine." My words came out reassuringly, even though I hadn't any idea what was going on.

A male emergency physician in his early forties stepped closer. He started talking, using his agitated voice. "Dimitry, how you feeling? Do you have any pain?" he questioned while he was checking my eyeballs.

"My chin hurts," I said.

"Let me take a look." A pause of a second elapsed, then he cried out,

"Yeah! I think it's broken. We will take care of it. Do you feel pain elsewhere?" the physician enthusiastically exclaimed.

"Nah, I don't think so."

"Well, I guess that's it. See you later," the man wearing a green robe blurted out, then he immediately left.

That's it? I have only a broken chin after this destructive car crash? That was the moment when I comprehended how lucky I had been. The Master of the Universe had interfered and saved our lives in that calamity. A grateful thought whizzed out. Thank you, Lord.

A few minutes later, a transportation man took me into another compartment, where they set me up for the immediate arch-bar procedure. The surgery lasted no longer than twenty minutes. Then, another orderly rolled me down to the non-intensive care unit. As soon as I was left alone, I instantaneously crashed.

The next day, I called my grandma, Tanya. My parents were on vacation in Athene. They rarely could afford to jump on a trip, especially out of the country. My medical report wasn't critical, and I decided not to bother them. Grandma rushed over after an hour. When she burst in at the medical unit, her face got pallid.

"What the doctors' sed?" she asked, appalled. She was peering at me incessantly.

"I only have a broken chin. I will be discharged after two days." No matter what I had told her, grandma couldn't slip into a calm state.

"Call me when you are ready to leave. I will pick you up," she exclaimed. Leaving the medical unit, grandma was doing the sign of the cross and praying to God.

A few hours later, an unfamiliar man stepped into the room. He was in his fifties. His face looked careworn. The man tromped to the medical stretcher. Oh, God. Who is this man! What does he want? I thought.

"Hello, Dimitry! I am Marco, Greta's father. How you feeling, son?" His friendly demeanor quelled my concerns. I had never met him before, but he knew about me. I was dating his daughter before Mike dug it out that she ever existed.

"Doing fine. I got lucky; the doctors found a broken chin, that's all. How is Greta?" When I asked about his daughter, a sip of nuisance crawled over my body. Perhaps he wouldn't know she had lost her virginity while we were dating. The voice in my head said.

"Her collarbone has been broken. She is devastated. Anyway, you need to rest, kiddo. Everything will be fine." Those were his last words before he evaporated from the medical unit.

A couple of hours later, an attending nurse scuttled over. She reported the results from the blood test. There wasn't any trace of alcohol in my blood cells. A plethora of load lifted off my shoulders. Although, there was a severe compunction of my driving accountability, which nagged my mind as a child hailing the arm of his father, screaming, "I want those shoes! Please, Daddy, I want those shoes!" The remorse of guilt hovered over my head like an annoying fly.

Two days later, I cruised to Mike's room to see how he was doing. His medical report wasn't looking as good as mine. At the moment of the crash, he bumped his forehead on the windshield. A load shred of glass crept in his eyebrow. Mike wouldn't have slammed into the front windshield if he had buckled up the passenger belt. As I slunk through his unit, Mike's face was bandaged, resembling a mummy.

"I don't remember anything. What the heck happened?" Mike asked. His anger could be noticed from miles away.

After my brief narration, I quizzed him.

"What the doctors said, Mike?"

"I will stay here for another week. A few cosmetic procedures were required and recommended by the doctors. Where is Greta? Have you talked to her?"

"Nah, her father came by, but I didn't speak with her. She hasn't talked to you yet?" I asked, bemused.

"No, that's why I'm asking you."

That's weird. Why hasn't she checked her boyfriend? She must be appalled. My mind said. The next day, Tanya picked me up from the infirmary.

*****

The truck driver happened to be an Iranian citizen. He was passing through Bulgaria and headed south to Turkey. His business was commercial transportation. He had been apprehended by the police department in Plovdiv. Two days after the car accident had occurred, he paid off his bond, and the police let him go as if they had released a sparrow from a birdcage.

I couldn't munch anything, only drinking liquids. The arch bar had clung to both of my jaws. The physicians declared that I needed to stay like that for a month until they could remove the arch bar. I had lost more than forty-five pounds in the past twenty-six days. The hunger was chasing my ass around like a shadow. A lump of meat could be sensed from a range of five feet. The starvation metamorphosed me into a carnivore. Just picture yourself being unable to gobble any food for twenty-six days. It would be hugely unpleasant, right? I was about to freak out as a wild ape, protesting while being locked in a cage at a zoo. On the fifteenth day of my urgent diet, a friend of mine revealed that I could drink fitness protein shakes. It turned out to be a beneficial choice, same as you play Texas hold'em and the dealer handed you a pair of aces. The malnutrition sucked all of my energy. When I walked with my father on the sidewalk, I couldn't catch his pace. The nutrition deficiency slowed down my walking speed. When the doctors removed the arch bars, I scoffed some snacks at the nearest fast-food booth like a ravenous vagrant, eating food after he was starving for a few weeks. Oh God, I can eat! I can eat! I thought. At that moment, I had learned how to praise the food, and if I had to throw any stale food, I implored the Lord.

A month after the mishap, Greta ghosted Mike. She dumped him without any explanation. They had been dating for two years, and she just left him. Mike truly loved that gal, and she ignored him out of the blue. Her demeanor became ruthless. It was a tough moment for him. He had two more plastic surgeries, which cost him an arm and a leg. He revealed that his family had to give up on their property to pay the bills of those surgeries.

Sometimes, we have to go through hardships in life. That is how we become stronger emotionally and spiritually. No one has mentally prepared for the unpleasant surprises furnished by the kismet. Regardless, we need to suck it up and keep moving forward.

*****

Mike, Greta, and I decided to file a lawsuit against the Iranian truck driver. All three of us had separate requirements. For that reason, we hired three different injury attorneys. My father sent me to meet his friend. His name was Vance. He had been practicing law for ten-plus years. When I met him, Vance looked like a witty weasel. His countenance was vulpine. My thoughts were. This lawyer knows his business. He will easily win this case. It should be piece of a cake! There wasn't any alcohol in my blood. Evidently, the truck driver had snoozed, causing him to drive onto the wrong side of the road.

For the following eight months, we had three trials. Prosecutors, judges, and lawyers were chitchatting as if they were on a convention meeting event organized by a big corporation. It was ludicrous. The Iranian driver had never shown up in the courtroom. The government appointed a public defender to protect the legal rights of this Iranian gentleman. His defender was a young bloke in his early thirties. He was ambitious, and his zeal was to chase the big shot, which would post his name into a media spotlight. And guess what? The defender won the trial in the second instance. It was ridiculous, a total farce. I had been trying to contact Vance multiple times. There were no answers and no callbacks either. A few days before the lawsuit took place, I went to Vance's office. The clerk working for him revealed that he was on vacation. A vacation! This frigging jagoff! Vance, the friend of my father, spending dough on a trip God knows where. That's awesome. Hope you were having a lotta fun, Vance! My mind said. I couldn't afford another attorney, so I went to the courtroom, willing to represent myself at the age twenty-two. My father's expression was, "Do whatever you want to do, son!" My thoughts were. What am I supposed to do there? What the duck I know about law and constitution. I hadn't any choice left on the table. The judges in the court were disgraceful. One of them, a man in his late fifties with a snow-white beard like Sean Connery, was pretty active. The other two were yawning, trying to stay awake and not doze off in the courtroom. After fifteen minutes of wishy-washy palavers, the verdict implied that we lost the case. The legislature system in the Republic of Bulgaria was burlesque, unfair. There was no justice, and no one gave a damn about it. I had been treated as an alien in my country of birth. Matter of fact, the foreigners had more rights than the citizens. How fucked up was that? Overwhelmed by the verdict, I needed time to freshen up my mind. The insurance adjusters proclaimed that they would agree to the decision of the court. They sent an agent to file an estimate. It amused me. Why are you sending an agent to provide an appraisal? Isn't it obvious! The photos of the car are not clear enough? The vehicle is a total loss. You can't even guess what make the car is. Koko (my father) had called his mate Jonny and asked him to keep the tomato-red Mazda in his garage. When we met the insurance agent, I was leering at the piled metal of what had been left from my car. Suddenly, something brightened in my mind. The brake and gas area had been totally smashed. At the time of the collision, I had stuck my chin at the steering wheel. Then the driver's seat (which had been broken as well) had kicked back and pulled out my legs from the smashed area where the gas and the brake pedal were. Holy-shmoly, it's a miracle! My legs are untouched. Oh, Lord Almighty, you had protected me from this destructive menace. Later, a police expert had confirmed my theory as accurate. My thoughts were concentrated on the fact of how lucky I was. God granted me a second chance. It was part of his plan to survive and to continue living my life. Pondering about it, I had started to appreciate my second chance given as a gift. I had learned to be grateful for what I had. We wouldn't know what God had planned for us.

The duration of the lifetime had metamorphosed into one of our best teachers.

I was on cloud nine. I could succumb out there or might have become disabled, grounded on a wheelchair for the rest of my life. Imagine how messed up it would be, a man in his early twenties to suffer the loss of his legs till his last breath.

Mike was pretty salty. He couldn't unravel the reason why his ex had dumped him. He focused on undergoing cosmetic surgeries on his eyebrow. Unfortunately, he hadn't enough financial resources to wrap up those medical procedures. His expression was systematically inclined to depression and disappointment. No matter what, he brazened it out. The quicksand didn't break him up. The rapid change of his soul forced my compunction. I was feeling guilty about the whole tragedy. Regardless, of the fact that it wasn't my fault. This car accident had changed our lives drastically. That was part of God's plan.

My mindset was emotionally twisted. I couldn't hop on the front passenger seat in any vehicle for the following year and a half. The intolerable truth was that the court didn't give a damn about how we felt and what dreadful fear all of us had sensed. We had never gotten any financial support, not even a penny (at least, not me). It was unfair. Thinking of it made me sick. The bitterness slumped on my head like a brick of concrete. That was the horrible feeling when I realized how unjust life could be.

The thought of it was giving me nausea and severe headaches. My Mazda was history. I loved that car. I had been enjoying my ride at every moment since I had bought it. I had busted my ass saving dough to purchase that ride. Koko had found the Mazda for a remarkable deal. I still recalled the first time when we headed to an unknown garage where an old-fart taxi driver pulled out the cover. The Mazda shone in my eyes like a suitcase of pearls. I could not erase my memories of how many girls I banged in that vehicle, and now it was gone.

The most outrageous fact was that I didn't receive any issued economic indemnification for the loss of the Mazda. In Bulgaria, it was tough to own a vehicle. There was no credit score. It was up to the bank whether you could get money or not. It meant you needed to cover a few debts linked to any bank entity, then someone could give you a loan for purchasing a used automobile. Unless you were a drug supplier smuggling loads of extra cash or you were the son of some prominent kingpin who had excelled in society as a political leader.

*****

It was forenoon on Sunday. Mom gave me orders to grab some groceries at the closest deli. I walked toward the tenement where we had been living since 2001. That tenement where my family lived was built in the late 1960s. It was an old dwelling, sharing multiple entries. My father worked his ass off to renovate our condo. He made it look neat and comfortable, nothing too crazy. As I climbed to the third floor, a man named Gus crept through the next door. Gus was our neighbor. He had a mustache like Freddie Mercury and a face of a Russian refugee. Often, my father and Gus got stoned while scoffing a Bulgarian moonshine liquor called 'Rakia'.

"Hey, Dimitry, how are you feeling, bud?" Gus asked, grinning.

"Ah…doing fine."

"Hey, I want to show you something. Check this out." Gus pulled out a local journal.

"What's that? Holy cow!" I exclaimed, puzzled by the headline on the right corner of the paper. A brief article described the malignant collision where we had almost died. It had been eight months since the tragedy occurred, and my neighbor just decided to expose a newspaper held for months. Jeez! Thank God there weren't any names mentioned. That article brought horrifying memories that I tried to remove from my mind.

"How long have you held this journal?" I asked, showing a puzzled countenance.

"A day or two after the car accident. I forgot where I had left it. I've just thought you might want to keep it for yourself," Gus said

"Yeah, thanks!" My thoughts were. What the heck am I supposed to do? I guess it will be beneficial to wipe my arse using it. I didn't judge him. Gus had always been polite to me. He had taught me a lot. Gus and I had many great conversations.

*****

It was Saturday in June 2013. The sky was clear, as if the clouds didn't exist. My family and I headed to a monastery called Bachkovo located a few miles away from Plovdiv. Bachkovo's beauty took my breath out. Once you approached that sanctified structure, you would be mesmerized by one of the most relieving and divine architectures on Earth. My father rolled his silver-colored Mercedes C124 coupé. That was the strongest model you could find in central and southern Europe. He worshipped that car as an art of the century. It was a time to roll back to Plovdiv. Koko gazed at me. His countenance was saying, "Do you want to drive?"

"You mind driving?" he asked kindly, waiting for a straight answer.

"Nah, not at all." I said. It had been two years since the collision happened, and I was extremely twitchy, although, I knew the day of facing my fear would come to pass. My mom and my sister sat on the rear seats. They were quiet as if they hadn't been in the vehicle. I hopped on the driver's seat and fired up the engine. Koko didn't avert his eyeballs from me. He constantly observed my motions. A minute later, the Mercedes started to roll. A spooky silence hovered upon the coupé. My family exchanged glances from one to another.

"Come on, Dimitry! Doncha think you should be driving faster?" Koko said. The Mercedes's rims rolled as slow as five miles per hour. My grandma would be hauling the bumper of her car much faster. When someone was giving a ride to Koko, he became a real piece of work. He quickly tossed orders and guidance to my driving, such as, "Don't go too fast"; "Don't go too slow"; "Watch for this guy"; "Look for the guy behind you"; "Keep checking the side mirrors"; "Don't speed up"; and "Watch out for police. They might be hiding beyond the knoll."

His voice rumbled louder and louder as if any second, he would wallop my ass. My father used to be a time-attack racer in his late twenties. He participated in pro division leagues. He had won a few medals and trophies at some racing competitions. I had several faded memories as a nipper watching how Koko sped his car in racing events. Unfortunately, he hadn't enough financial stacks or any backers throwing him a bone to proceed with his pro career as a racer. Koko was the most skilled chauffeur I had ever known, no question about that, and the worst driving mentor. I hated when he hectored me as if he was a general or a backseat driver. Listening to him was getting obnoxious. I craved to stop the Mercedes in the middle of the interstate road and let him operate the steering wheel. Stop busting my chops. Here, you drive! I thought. This was how he was. Koko would never change. It was tough for me to bite the bullet. The only rational resolution was to accept his personality.

Chapter 3

By the end of March 2012, Koko came home with his friend. Usually, he invited a plethora of friends to come over. They slurped shots of Rakia. The name of that folk was Kyle. He had long hair like Steven Tyler and the lanky body of an NBA player. He was in his forties. His body looked as emaciated as a crackhead's. His pupils were as big as a horse. He worked as a foreman of a construction company specializing in stucco construction. Kyle enthusiastically talked about his job. He was persuasive. He offered me to join his crew. He assured me decent money, and that drew my attention. At that time, I was unemployed and desperately seeking a job. With no other option, I decided to give it a shot.

Three days later, I slogged through a massive scaffolding frame covering the entire front side of a huge condominium complex. Six fellas were working in his crew. They were all cool guys. We joked and chuckled while working. Doing stucco was fun, and I enjoyed it. Two weeks passed, and I started hearing bad stories from my coworkers. They were fussing and complaining about money. One of them revealed that he had been waiting money for five months. They all protested to get paid. At first, I thought they were joking, but it wasn't a prank. I started getting worried. Kyle's boss loomed as if he was a phantom. His silhouette popped up for a few minutes, then he mysteriously disappeared. Kyle was trying to soothe my agitation. He ad-libbed.

"Relax, kid. Don't listen to these guys. You will get your money next week." Week after week, I heard the same crap. "You will get your money next week." The state of being deceived made me nauseous. It was the same horrible feeling as if someone had stolen my wallet. I was forced to speak with Kyle because his boss had never shown up as if he had never existed.

"Kyle, I can't work anymore. It had been a month since I've started, and if I don't get any money, I can't afford to come at work." I said. Kyle apathetically shrugged, projecting a countenance saying, "It is it what it is, kid." That was my last day at work. I had never seen Kyle ever since. I walked out angry and at the same time joyful. I worked pro bono for about a month, spending dough for carfare and lunch. It was unfair. Regardless, I had to cope with those unforeseen circumstances and kept moving forward.

*****

Back in the summer of 2010, I started working at a print house called Nova Print located on the south side of Plovdiv. A man named Blaine, who was working as a chauffeur hooked me up there. Blaine and Koko were close friends. Often, they goofed around, watching a local soccer team at the ballpark. I started the job as an assistant to an offset pressman.

There were over 150 employees in that print house, and most of them were either loony or grouchy. It was one of the most stressful jobs I had ever worked. I was toiling from eight to five, but often, the print house was getting extremely busy and we were urged to work extra hours. The press machine on which I worked was named Heidelberg Speedmaster. That was a big machine with eight colored sections established in Germany. I loved that machine. The crew of technicians didn't support the Heidelberg the way they should have, and that caused a lot of problems. They tinkered, swiftly putting that machine in order. They were saving money on maintenance expenses. My job was to check the ink in each colored section. This ink pussyfooted through sixty-five roll bars, then slunk to a big press cylinder. When I set up the ink, I must be extremely cautious to keep my hands away from the ink rolls. If I was careless, the rolls could yank my fingers. If that happened, only the Lord could save me from a broken or amputated hand. The Heidelberg press required lots of attention. I needed to constantly check the tank containing a specific type of alcohol, used to clean the machine after every single process.

When the printed job had been completed, I had to take off the print frames and clean the printing cylinders by hand. At the front side of Heidelberg, a bunch of clips delivered the paper production. Those clips were holding the paper and releasing it at a specific time during the printing process. I had to be cautious of what I was doing because a single mistake could cause Heidelberg to stop. When the machines stopped, the print operators got mean and persistently displayed a derogatory demeanor, and they expressed offensive phrases directed at me.

I worked at Nova for about two years. During this period, I had been mentally harassed. I wanted to be retrained and start working as an offset pressman. That meant I had to work harder and bust my ass rushing back and forth through the entire press machine. As I mentioned before, the Heidelberg broke down, regularly. Many times, the machine demanded painstaking repair.

The owner of the print house was a stingy man. He refused to pay for anything additionally. Zillion times, he had sent his mechanics working on regular wage to fix whatever they could to run that machine. After a year and a half of grinding, my dream became true and I was appointed to work as an offset operator. The job became much more stressful.

I held accountability for printed production. One weekday, the Heidelberg was completely wrecked. I left the print house incensed. The next day, I resigned my contract from Nova Print. Later, I bumped into a chap; he also worked at Nova Print. He blew the gaff that other pressmen sued the print house. He filed a claim that Nova Print owed him money. On the other hand, the print house countersued this guy for negligence. It was a frigging hodgepodge. I was relieved that a massive freight was lifted from my shoulders. I would rather pursue another job than goof off in some print house where they always had vacant job positions because the employees had always voluntarily walked away. I was sick and tired of the medieval equipment and repulsive treatment.

*****

In February of 2013, I bumped into my neighbor named Zack. He told me to check a print house called Ideal Ltd, located at the industrial park in the same residential district. The print house of Ideal popped up on the web browser showing a bunch of positive reviews. Without hesitation, I burst straight into Ideal's office. The clerk scheduled an appointment with the president of the print house. Fortunately, I had met the president on the same day. Thrilled, I stepped into his office by portraying composure. The name of the president was Anthony. He was a short and bald man in his late fifties. His corporate suit looked flashy. Anthony was a well-educated businessman. His pupils imposed his sharp intelligence. We had a delightful conversation. When I hopped onto the public transportation on the way home, I was thinking. They wouldn't call me back. No frigging way!

Two days later, I got a call from an unknown number. When I picked up the phone, a polite female voice proclaimed, "Dimitry, you've got the job!" I was in awe. My forehead got warm as if I had a high temperature.

My first day at Ideal Ltd was exciting. I looked around like a gleeful kid. Anthony showed his printing manufactory that was as long as a football field. He had two offset printing presses in outstanding condition. The next day, the whistle was blown, and I kicked off my first day at Ideal as an assistant to the offset pressman. Ideal Ltd was the highest-paying job I had ever labored in Bulgaria. I was hauling my ass, toiling like a donkey and running back and forth through the printing press machine like a bumblebee floating over flowers. This is dope! I found the job that I have been looking for, and it's close to home. How cool is that? The voice in my head exclaimed. It was a miracle. I knew how lucky I was to have a job like that.

*****

Ideal Ltd, like most of the print houses, had several warehouses. Sometimes, printing manufactory wasn't demanding enough workers. Then most of the employees were transferred to the next warehouse where the products had been packed and readied for shipment. On one particular day, the shift manager sent me to the packing warehouse to help in folding cardboard boxes.

I worked with two cute gals; one of them was persistently grinning at me. She was playful and charming. Her gorgeous brunette hair was outstanding. Her body wasn't athletic, but it still drew my attention. I didn't know what kind of cologne she sprinkled; it smelled like a fresh watermelon. She said her name was Maria. Ten minutes later, I zoomed to the restroom. On the way back, a man in his forties, as tall as LeBron James, stopped me and asked,

"Hey, buddy, listen up. Do you know this chick, the one that was talking to you?"

"Uh…you mean Maria?"

"Yeah. I think she has a crush on you." He said. I leered at him, grimacing.

"How come? Are you for real?" I questioned, standing as still as the statue of Buddha in Bamyan. To tell someone that a particular broad liked him was a common joke among Bulgarians.

"Nah, bud. I am serious. She hasn't stopped talking about you."

Wait, what? She was talking about me!

"What she said?"

"I don't know, man. You have to find out by yourself," the tall man had claimed. I rubbernecked, confused as if someone was speaking Chinese to me. When I tramped back to the working table where Maria worked, I was baffled. She was looking at me intermittently. I thought. I'll be dipped. She is checking me out! The man was right.

Maria and I had long conversations. She was sharing different stories while I was joking with her. No matter what I said, she always smiled at me. Holy-shmoly! That's freaky-dicky. She really likes me! Initially, Maria didn't draw my attention as a big deal. Although since we had been communicating, I changed my mind. The following week, I didn't stop thinking about her. Dude, you must get her number. You need to take her out. The voice in my head said.

The summer season kicked in. It was a sweltering day. People were hiding in their homes like rats in sewers. At work, I was yawning at the offset printing press. It would be too suspicious if I bumped straight into Maria. At lunch break, I crawled over the pergola where everyone at Ideal could rest. I wanted to meet Maria. I trudged to the pergola. Then I scanned Maria and sat next to her. As we chitchatted, I faltered, thinking how to make my move. At the next moment, I asked for her phone number. There was a pause, and Maria didn't answer. She is hesitating! Ah, man! How dumb can you be to ask her in front of other coworkers? The voice in my head blurted out. A sound of splash occurred. I smacked my forehead, looking at the ground. You, frigging dumbass!

"Write it down," she uttered quietly. It was loud around us. The other employees were babbling enthusiastically. Dude, it's not a joke. She wants you! A few days later, I rang her. Maria picked up the phone almost immediately. She had been waiting for that call. We set up something like a casual tryst. Two hours later, we were rubbing elbows at a joint located in the same neighborhood.

Maria narrated stories about her life. Her stories sounded as if I was listening to a romantic audiobook. She kept exposing her heart by jumping from topic to topic as a locust in a muddy swamp. Maria wasn't married, although she disclosed her frustration living with her beau. We wound up our date, almost kissing each other. On the next date, I had already reached out to the first base. Maria was mesmerized. She almost stabbed my mind by asking, "Dimitry, do you know how old I am?" KABOOM! Where does that come from? Puzzled, I raised my eyebrows.

"I can't tell. I guess you might be in your late twenties or early thirties?"

"I am thirty-nine," Maria said. What? Did she say thirty-nine? Whoa! I've just fished a MILF! My mind cried out.

"Does that bother you?" she asked, regretting her question.

"Are you kidding? Of course not. Just because you are older, it doesn't mean that we shouldn't hang out." Her countenance looked calm. She was joyful to hear my declaration. Maria talked most of the time. She couldn't conceal the lust of boning. If she could, she would hop on my prick straight away. David DeAngelo said, "Attraction isn't a choice; it's nature." As I was growing older, I dug out that he was absolutely correct.

Thirty minutes later, we headed to my place. My parents were out, and the condo was abandoned. As soon as we burst into my parent's condo, we were bumping uglies. The night was amazing. It was the first time when I shagged an older woman, and it was magnificent. The next day, I went to work, exposing an exhilarated demeanor. The employees at the printing press were surveying me questionably. One of them, a hillbilly straw chewer, hollered, "Hey, Dimitry, what are you laughing at?" His dagger eyes were scanning me as if he was a detective.

"Nothing particularly. Just happy to be at work." Picking up my lyrics, he darted closer.

"Listen up, boy. We don't like guys smiling without reason. Just keep in mind." He tapped my shoulder and glided back to his workplace. Many employees working in big print houses were backstabbers and hypocrites. The stories about what kind of people worked in print houses were not confidential. Maria and I tried to keep a low profile when we were in the print house. The two of us avoided each other on purpose. There were around two hundred employees at Ideal. Gossips would spread faster than bullets of AK-47.

*****

It had been around five months since I had been working at Ideal. The foreman of press operators had a diaper butt. His name was Nick. He had a huge beer gut. His head was as big as a fourteen-pound bowling ball. Initially, I started working with Nick. For some reason, Nick and I didn't get along. Nick had a close relationship with the board of directors. Nick didn't eclipse his hatred toward me, and by the middle of the summer, I was transferred to work at a rusty UV varnishing machine, which was older than my grandpa.

The craftsman operating that machine was named Ivan. He needed an additional machinist. Ivan was in his mid-thirties, a chunky and stout redneck. He looked like a ferocious wrestler. Also, he was a hilarious yokel. His jokes cracked me up. Ivan taught me to work on this UV, and two weeks later, we worked in two different shifts. The next month came quickly. I felt comfy while toiling at that UV machine. Frankly, I wouldn't mind if I had to get stuck at that machine till the age of seventy-five. The work at that machine was less stressful. Ivan was a great craftsman, but the amount of production delivered between us was almost equal.

It was a day in the first week of September. The shift manager was a girly bald man wearing specs that resembled the glasses of Peter Parker. He was walking uneasily. He came to me and announced,

"Dimitry, Philip, the director wants to have a word with you. He is expecting you at his office."

"Philip? Why? What is it all about?" I grilled, puzzled.

"I don't have any idea," the shift manager responded, staring at my shoes. Cut the crap. Of course, you know. The truth is, you don't have the balls to tell me by looking straight into my eyes. I thought. After lunch, I headed to the office. When I knocked on the door, a hoarse voice roared beyond the door.

"Come in!" When I entered through the door, there must be at least ten men wearing tuxedos, blabbering in a perky manner. Philip sat on his chair. His body resembled a sumo-wrestling contender. His countenance was always dead serious. Philip gazed at me disdainfully as if I had a bite of his lunch without asking. A few wordless seconds occurred. I thought. Gosh! Hopefully, I didn't mess up some of the productions.

"What's up, boss?" I asked. At print houses, we always spoke in informal language. The nuisance of what was about to happen kept fretting me consistently.

"Your six months contract has expired. You are not qualified for this job. Unfortunately, you are being laid off. That's all. I am sorry, kid." Suddenly, my body became weightless. Goggling at Philip, I couldn't believe what I had just heard. I was busting my ass, working for the past six months, and he easily revoked my contract. They've just kicked me out! What the heck is that? My mind asked.

"May I ask why I've been laid off?"

"You are not qualified for this job. That's all. It is what it is, kid." Philip's expression was grandiloquent. His face was saying something like, "If you don't leave my office at the next minute, I will crack your head up."

That wasn't very nice! It didn't make any sense why I wasn't qualified. Ivan and I were completing almost equal amounts of productions. Philip didn't divulge any reasons. His judgment was entirely unjust. Later, on the same day, I stormed at home as a raging bull. Mom scanned my sulky countenance. She walked to my room and asked, "What is it? What happened?"

Then, I expressed my disappointment and frustration. I felt angry at how unfair I had been treated in my country. A nasty feeling like having nausea bothered me. Koko burst through the door. He sniffed that something awful had happened. He thought it was my fault to be kicked out from Ideal. A bitter strife occurred between us. Koko didn't guide or furnish any tips as a father. Instead, he expressed sullen behavior. Bummed out of my father's accusations, I put my shoes on and scuttled to the entry.

"Where are you going? It's almost midnight!" Mom inquired, portraying her concern.

"I will be back in a minute," I said grumpily through my shoulder.

I strolled to a renovated park district on the rear side of the tenement. I roamed on the trail way, peering at the midnight sky, inquiring the Lord for answers like a young Skywalker glared at the universe and waiting for any response from Obi-Wan Kenobi. Why is this happening to me? It feels like my life has gone downhill. Please, God, help me to find the right answers! The voice in my head asked. The sky was clear and exquisite, it looked like a picturesque sketch of a prominent draftsmen. Light wind patted my beard. I wandered through the park for about an hour. My anger evaporated like the smoke of a cigar. The quiet night soothed my frustration, and I streaked into the condo. Everybody was nodding off. Koko snored like a sleeping ogre. We had to make sure the door of his bedroom was closed; otherwise, we wouldn't be able to doze off. Not too long, I crawled over my bed and slumbered at once.

The next day was my last at Ideal. At lunch break, Maria came to the pergola and sat next to me.

"That's BS. I don't know why Philip had acted like that," she declared. Staggered, I was peering at her.

"You have known already. Who told you?"

"Dimitry, don't be silly. The news here spreads faster than your jokes," Maria said. She tried to bear me up by giving me suggestions regarding my future. She expressed a codependent feeling. Maria was a phenomenal woman. No matter what would happen, she would cover my back.

*****

It had been a week since I was unemployed, and my mind was stuck at an impasse. I didn't know what to do. Maria called me on Friday.

"Dimitry, can you come to my place? I need to talk with you."

Holy cow, what she is up to? Does she have a bun in the oven? Nah, it's impossible. We had used a rubber-jonny most of the time. Besides, it's been…oh crap! Two weeks since we had been doing the boning, I thought. An hour later, I was already knocking on her door.

"Come in, silly. It's open!" she howled, chuckling. When I burst into her condo, Maria was waiting on the balcony. She was puffing a cigarette.

"You want one?" she asked politely.

"Yeah, thanks." I puffed a gob of cigarettes, especially when I was overwhelmed.

"I know why you have been laid off from Ideal," she announced. Listening to her, I had almost dropped the cigarette on the floor.

"What?"

"Philip assigned another man on your working spot. That man is Nick's cousin, the offset operator. Dimitry, they set you up!"

"Well, now that makes sense." Suddenly, everything cleared out. The reason wasn't about the crap that Philip talked about qualification or whatever he was saying. It was all about adjusting an insider into the facility. Thank God she isn't pregnant! She would tell me if she was. Is she? Maria stabbed her cigarette in the ashtray and hopped on my lap. She kissed me fervently like tomorrow would be the end of the human race. Later in the evening, I headed home. My parents were dining and gawking at the fifty-five-inch TV. Koko was gulping the moonshine Rakia. He leered at me as he was saying, "Where the heck have you been?"

Apathetically, I zoomed to my room. Grabbing the swivel chair tucked under my computer desk, I started to mull over. I'm sick and tired of this republic. I don't want to stay here anymore. It is time to FedEx myself in another country. A strong wanderlust had occurred in my mind. This night, I am sowing a seed, which will blossom into a flawless project.

My idea was to set up a journey where I could start over. My target was to make luxury wristwatches. I had never had anything to do with watches, but that didn't mean that I should quit. During the unemployment, I had loads of time to research watches, cases, tools, etc. I was thrilled to explore this industry. My subconscious voice echoed. Keep working on your projects. Don't underrate your potential, and never stop following your dreams.

Albert Einstein said, "If you have a problem, there is always a solution. If there is no solution, there is no problem."

*****

Maria and I kept hanging out pretty often. We had a blast at a resort located in a town sprawled up on the high hills. The name of that town was Hisar.

In Plovdiv, we crept into a bunch of guesthouses, cheap fleabag hotels continuing our physical lust. One day, we strode to a flophouse in downtown Plovdiv. After the boning, Maria peered at me persistently. A minute later, she stately proclaimed,

"Dimitry, I love you." There was a pause. I drew a deep breath.

What should be my answer? I am not head over heels in love with her. I like her, but I am in the blossom of my youth. I am not ready to vow into a serious relationship. The voice in my head said.

You need to be honest to anyone, especially to those who adore you.

Maria worshipped me. She would do anything for us to be together. I couldn't play with her feelings. Getting a full array of composure, I decided to expose my intentions for the future before it would be too late. There were no reasons why I should throw wishy-washy answers and being disrespectful to her. When Maria heard about my purpose, tears filled her eyes.

"Where are you going?" she grilled. Her pupils mirrored trepidation. Maria didn't get straight answers because I didn't have any. One of the greatest ministers, speakers, and authors, Joel Osteen, wrote, "People don't determine your destiny. God does."

My purpose was to work in a different country, and I felt that God had already issued a plane ticket with my name. Maria was a golden woman. When I walked to her place, Maria had always cooked food, and the taste was incredible, even better than my mom's. Maria was one of a kind. I couldn't easily find a female like her. Alas, our paths were crossed over and had to split into separate destinations.

*****

On Saturday, somewhere in October 2013, Maria and I wandered to a restaurant that provided a great selection of Mediterranean food in the hood. We had a long conversation, jumping through different subjects. A cheap vodka was pouring, repeatedly. Then an unsurmountable lust for intercourse transpired. The condos of both were occupied. Great, now what?

I rang my boy Peter. He could always come up with something. Peter was a pimp, a frigging philanderer. He always popped up from nowhere, holding the hand of an unknown hottie. I had never figured out how he did it. He wasn't someone who had deep pockets. In his early twenties, I had seen him dragging over thirty chicks. A frigging Casanova. I thought he might be handy. When I dialed him, Peter had already figured why I was calling.

"Dimitry, you are a frigging nuthead! Okay, listen up, one of my cousins is getting married tonight. The condo will be empty. I will leave the keys under the doormat. Call me if something comes up."

Peter's condo was located within a ten minute walking distance. At the restaurant, we were chuckling, goofing around. An hour later, we rambled up to Peter's crib.

"You are out of your mind! I don't know what I am doing here," Maria exclaimed while she was giggling. We burst into Peter's condo as if we were greedy thugs plundering jewelry that cost a bundle. The condo was abandoned. A plethora of food and booze were left haphazardly. I took Maria to one of the bedrooms. We turned the lights off and fifteen minutes later, a noise rumbled out of the dining room. Someone is in the apartment! I thought. My stomach shrank to the size of a ping-pong ball.

"What the heck are we going to do?" Maria whispered. She was entirely naked. What should I do? Now what? We can't just disappear. I thought. I got dressed and tiptoed to the door. Man, I'm screwed! I crept to the hallway, jittery like a cat. From the dining room, I saw a silhouette of something jerking around. Who is there? Oh God, this is so embarrassing! My mind whispered. At that moment, I thought I was going to puke. I felt sick, like I had eaten a whole bucket filled with hot chilli sauce.

"Oh man, that's Rocco, Peter's dog!" Rocco was wagging his tail playfully. A huge burden fell off from my chest. I had known Rocco since he was a puppy. I had no idea that Rocco was there.

"Let's get out of here," I blurted out. Maria couldn't stop giggling. She found that scene extremely entertaining. Rambling through the pathways, she was cackling as if she was in a stand-up comedy event.

"What are you laughing at?"

"You," she continued. "You are a crazy-arse goofball, and I don't know why I came with you."

"Probably 'cuz you are crazy too," I countered.

"Nah, I'm not," she answered, and we both burst into laughter.

Chapter 4

A few days later, I enthusiastically signed up to study at the Agrarian University of Plovdiv. My bachelor's degree specialized in agricultural engineering. The Agrarian University of Plovdiv had many aesthetic buildings. A lot of the students were out-of-hand yokels; the majority of them travelled from the outskirts. Anyhow, we had a blast out there. Most of the professors were cool. My aunt Vera had been working as an assistant lab technician at the same university. She was one of the loveliest and most amiable people I had ever met in my life. Multiple times, Vera helped me out completing my student work. Her heart had always melted when I bumped into her. Her enthralling grin was like the smile of an infant. Her figure was stunning. She only ate healthy food. Vera used to take care of me when I was a toddler.

*****

In November 2013, I trundled back home from college. Mom was vacuuming in the den.

"Dimitry! I have something that you might be interested in," she proclaimed. I looked at her nonplussed. Mom talked about a guy who arranged university academic training programs in foreign countries.

Her statement drew my attention and I abruptly dialed the number of the website.

I spoke to a guy named Julian. He was in charge of those types of exchange internship programs. Julian suggested meeting him in person at his headquarters positioned in the city of Sliven. An eventual trip to Sliven was a terrific idea. My grandparents had been living in that town before my mother was born. I had a place to stay.

Immediately, I bought a bus ticket, and the next week, I bumped into a bus that looked old as an ancient landmark. When I saw the vehicle, my thought was. Is this thing going to roll? I sprawled my ass on the seat of that bus. The bus was making weird noises. I thought we might get stuck on the turnpike. The bus was rolling unpleasantly. It croaked when turning, and it jolted as if we were bouncing on the beat in a hip-hop video of 2000s where Snoop Dogg rapped. The trip to Sliven took around two hours. During the trip, I was twitchy and restless, contemplating the impending interview. What would this guy want? Is he a shyster? I hope he won't hoodwink me. I thought.

There was a gob of gossips about frauds related to business companies working on internship student programs. The people working in those companies schmoozed about traveling, but they only want to snatch your money. When you file a lawsuit against them, they never existed as a company. It was like you wanted money from Casper.

Sliven was a gorgeous city, located by the longest mountain in Bulgaria called Stara Planina. The entire town had a delightful infrastructure. The history and culture in this city were unique. My grandparents' apartment was about twenty minutes walking distance from the bus station. It was a scorcher day, and I strolled quickly, trying to beat the clock. Around noon, I popped into my grandparents' apartment.

My grandma Elena was a little overweight. Her hairstyle resembled Cruella Deville. She was much shorter than me. Her eyes looked like a hungry bulldog. I hope she would never have access to this page; otherwise, I would be in trouble. Elena's hospitality was flowing in her veins. The smell of food lured me to walk to the kitchen. Elena had an amazing cooking repertoire. She made the greatest meatballs on the entire globe.

A few minutes later, my grandpa walked through the entry.

"Hey, what up, kiddo! I think you are at the wrong address!" He cried out softly. He always cracked me up by saying funny jokes. Grandpa had been proud of me since I had known him. I was carrying his name and he adored me. We were best buddies. As a kid, he used to drag me all around the city and introduced me to everyone. My grandpa's love was bigger than the Earth and could not be described with a few words. He was a happy man. He always joked around. I had never heard him complaining or grouching about anything. When he was in pain, he had never portrayed a grievance. He would keep the affliction inside him. Nobody ever mentioned anything negative addressed to grandpa.

On the next day, I aroused early in the morning. My uncle Millen and his son, my cousin Oliver, came over to pick me up. Millen worked at the police department of Sliven as a criminal investigator. He was a stout and tall man. His crew cut resembled a superior officer in the army. Millen was an acuminous dictator. When he spoke, everyone around was listening. Oliver looked a smidgen like Leonardo DiCaprio. He was in his senior year in high school. Oliver was a chatterbox; his piehole had never zipped up. It was around half-past nine in the morning when we rolled to meet Julian. The streets were clear, and we arrived to Julian's office unexpectedly fast.

"Good luck. I'll talk to you later," Millen said, and he abruptly dissipated. His time was shortened. That was why they couldn't come along. Julian's suite was on the third floor of a newly constructed building. His office was immaculate. The design matched the colors of the walls and furniture. I thought. This man is doing well up here!

When I marched through the door, Julian was sitting on his computer chair like Prince Charles. He was in his mid-fifties, a big and bald man. He stood up, wearing a mesmerizing grin, and we shook hands. Julian presented his internship student programs available in countries like the USA, France, Denmark, and Italy. He had been in that business since 1990.

Julian blathered persuasively. Listening to him, I rubbernecked as a dippy donkey. I chose Denmark. Julian wasn't completely sure if he had any vacant programs linked to Denmark. However, he described all the required documents that I needed to file to participate in a training student program in that Scandinavian country. He made it clear that I could go there for three months.

Julian wound up our forty-minute conversation by saying,

"After you are done with all of my instructions, by next January, you will have to come back here at my office and complete all the paperwork."

"Gotcha," I exclaimed. On cloud nine, I was pondering. Finally, I made a step close to my goals. We had a productive chitchat. God, I hope he isn't a grifter or some kind of deceiver. Taking the local bus, I couldn't stop thinking about my recent conversation with Julian. A feeling that something good was about to happen had incessantly held my grin. At forenoon, I was at my grandparent's apartment, ready to chew down whatever Elena had cooked. Around afterglow, Millen stopped by and enthusiastically announced,

"He's clean. I've checked him out."

My grin broadened. Hell yeah. I was waiting for that. Millen was devoted to criminal justice. He was a man whom I could rely on. Furthermore, Sliven wasn't a big town. The swindlers living in that city would be well known. I pictured what it would be to work in a foreign country as an internship student.

At home, my mom was exuberating over the news from Julian. She shared the joyful updates with my father. Koko wasn't excited; he disliked the idea. It was not easy for him to expose his emotions. My guess was that he wanted to reflect on us as the toughest man whom we had ever known. Three weeks later, my cellular phone shrilled. It was Julian.

"Hello, Dimitry. I don't have anything for Denmark, but I can send you to the USA. What do you think?" Julian was an incredible man. He had not wasted a second on pointless chatter; always straight to the point.

Bemused by his statement, I contemplated for a moment. God, what should I do? The United States of America is not the option I've been thinking about. Anyway, lotta Bulgarians had been bragging about the United States.

"Julian, I can't make up my mind. May I call you later?" That was the only rational answer I could think of.

"Well, I will be at my office till five. Otherwise, you could reach me out tomorrow from nine to five."

"Yeah, sure. Thank you." I hung up on the phone, still pondering. What should I do?

Thirty minutes had passed, and we were back talking on the phone.

"Julian, I am down for the United States," I announced boldly as if Bruce Wayne saying, I am batman!

"Great! According to your bachelor's degree, I have a vacant spot on a farm called Todd Greiner located nearby the city of Hart in Michigan."

"That sounds terrific!" I asserted, not having any idea where the state of Michigan was. Julian gave me instructions on the required paperwork and advised me to study hard at school. We wrapped up our conversation, wishing all the crap two formal businessmen would usually say to finish up a meeting.

As Julian recommended, I concentrated my mind on school. In the meantime, I walked over to the community facilities to complete all the paperwork required by Julian. It was a hassle. Attempting to catch bus after bus through the entire city. Stampeding to different district buildings and then waiting in long lines of people was such a pain in the ass. Some of the clerks, schlepping at those union facilities, had to send me back because they required additional documents.

Annoyed, I had to cool my jets and bite the bullet. I had never stopped chasing my dreams. I didn't stay at home whining how tough it was or getting a chip on my shoulder. The next question was, how I could collect the $3,500 required for service fees, plane tickets, etc.

The trip to the States would cost me a bundle. Also, speaking with a consulate at the American embassy in Sofia wasn't free. The plane tickets cost an arm and a leg. Moreover, when I touch down in Michigan, I would need some cash. While I was toiling at Ideal, I decided to play it smart and saved most of the gross given by the boss. I had around $1,500 in the nest egg.

My family wasn't wealthy, and Koko refused the idea of cruising in the U.S. His behavior could be interpreted as, "If you want to go, it's on your own ass." Mom was willing to help, but she didn't have any resources. The question was, how the heck would I get the rest of the money? At that point, I was unemployed. Even if I was working somewhere, it would be impossible to collect two grand in a few months.

At that time, the currency exchange displayed $1.00 to 1.7 in Bulgarian lev, which meant the dollar was valuable in Bulgaria. Wrapping my head around, I found myself trapped in a deadlock. My friends couldn't loan me any money even though some had the funds. I don't judge them. It is tough to trust somebody these days.

People are like sharks; they are trying to gulp all of your dough. Nowadays, many get ripped off by close friends or even relatives. I was diligent, looking for a resolution, but my options shortened. Again, I was stuck in an impasse. There wasn't any light at the end of the tunnel. Did that mean I should stop chasing my dreams? Hell NO! Excuses were not acceptable. Nobody said it would be easy. I didn't complain about feeling self-pity or weeping on the shoulder of my mom.

One of the most successful hip-hop rappers in the industry, Kanye West, said this in one of his songs, "Now that don't kill me, can only make me stronger." That was what precisely happened under my nameplate. I almost passed away at the smashup where the Iranian truck driver almost killed me, but later, I became stronger spiritually and mentally. At the age of twenty-two, I had learned to value and worship what God gave me and to NOT grumble about what I didn't have. God had blessed my soul, and I was healthy as a brand-new dozer inspired to fish new opportunities at any part of the globe.

*****

It was early in the morning, on a business day in the last week of February 2014. My parents went to work, and my sister Sunny waddled to school. The condo was mine till noon. Maria cruised over for the usual wild mambo. She didn't have any clue about my game plan to trek in the USA. When she saw me, her visage portrayed exuberance. After the boning, we chatted and drank coffee. All of a sudden, she sighed.

"Dimitry, did I tell you how much I want a boy?" Maria said. Wait What? I almost spilled the coffee on the tablecloth. That was her subtle way of uttering, "Dimitry, I want a baby!" Dude, now is the right time to reveal your intentions. Cutting to the chase, I explained her my future goals about flying to the US. Instantly, Maria burst into tears. She was in shock. Dude, give her a hug, she is sobbing! After we cuddled, she relaxed. A few moments later, Maria said,

"How long will you be working out there?" She rubbed the tears of her eyelashes.

"Not sure yet, couple of months," I declared by smacking her fanny. She grinned for an instant, and I walked her to the door. There was no question about how much I adored her. Maria was looking for a father and a second baby. She already had a twenty-year-old daughter who crept out from her first marriage, which apparently was unsuccessful. At that time, Maria was in her late thirties, and I was in my middle twenties. My purpose was aimed to elaborate luxury wristwatches. I didn't have time to sow a seed of a baby in her crop (womb). Maria was a pure angel, but I couldn't let that angel sway me away from my goals. All she wanted was to be hitched and to have a family. She deserved it. Unlike her, my attention was focused on school and the trip to the US. I was too tight. My time became shorter, and I couldn't give her what she needed.

*****

A few days later, something clicked in my mind, and I dialed grandma, Tanya (Koko's mom). She had always welcomed our family, expressing her buoyancy. Tanya could only radiate love, but if you grossed her out, she would never talk to you again. I intended to speak with her in person. That was why I didn't mention anything over the phone. Tanya lived in a lovely and small town named Stamboliiski. An excursion to Stamboliiski could cause me to refresh my mind. It was the same as when you would restart your Mac laptop. I choose to visit Grandma Tanya using the cheapest transportation method via train. I needed to save those greenbacks. Tanya dwelled on the first floor of a brick house built on the north side of the city. She lived with a man named Miro, who owned the residential unit along with his brother. Tanya and Miro had been living together since I knew how to brush my teeth. The first and only husband of Tanya (my genuine grandpa) named George was killed by an unknown hoodlum. (No one had ever found out why or who was the murderer.) I wasn't even born when Grandpa George was executed. He hadn't been a bootlegger, drug dealer, or had anything to do with illicit entities against the government. Grandpa George was a man of integrity. He was a prosperous bricklayer. I had never heard any bad or indecent comments about him. RIP, Grandpa.

When I pussyfooted through the entry, the table in the living room had been served with a variety of food, as it was Christmas. Tanya wanted to make sure my tummy would be filled. After we wound up munching, I appealed Tanya if I could borrow some money.

Nana didn't flinch. She went into the bedroom, then tiptoed back, carrying a bundle of bankrolls.

"Here, I wantcha to take this money. Go and seek your luck. God bless you," Tanya uttered, mirroring her enthralling smile. She handed me five hundred dollars of her savings. That was a gob of money. Grandma's name would never be forgotten.

On the next day, after I gained a few extra pounds, I left Stamboliiski and headed to Plovdiv. For the past few weeks, I was looking forward getting the rest of the thousand bucks. The agenda of how to collect that money had harassed my mind incessantly for days and nights. I was getting frustrated. The deadline was merely two months ahead. An unexpected revoke of the intern program would cause me to lose a significant amount of money. There were no refunds, and I couldn't afford any mistakes. It was a knife-edged situation. I was asking the highest God for answers or directions. I didn't know what to do. I was seeking an opportunity to pick someone's brain, but alas, I couldn't find anyone.

My father didn't provide any hope, and I didn't blame him. It was just the way he was. He would not amend his character. You cannot change people's minds unless they open their hearts to learn more. The only option I had was to accept Koko's character. Everyone had already chosen their pathway. It was astonishing when people whom you had barely known would help you out, and in the meantime, your relatives had never backed you up.

I was pondering on how to eke out the required dough. One day, something popped in my mind as those short, random commercials when you were watching a video on YouTube. Mom had been developing a good bank creditability over the years. Perhaps she could be my holy grail. I thought. The next day, Mom and I had an essential conversation.

She would do anything to protect my ass. She would give up on her life to save mine. Koko would get het up if he found out about our furtive chitchat. He disliked the idea of having bank loans. Thus, we decided to keep our conversation confidential. The next morning, Mom and I wandered to a local bank positioned in the hood.

Every step taken to the bank made me more anxious. In Bulgaria, it didn't matter how good your credit score was. It became a subject of the bank whether to determine if you would qualify or not. A few seconds before we burst into the bank, Mom gave instructions to keep my mouth shut when she would be chatting with the financial associate. The banker blabbered for about thirty minutes while we were filling out the paperwork. Mom got approved, and the bank issued a loan for a thousand bucks. My plan flourished unpredictably fine. As soon as we headed out from the bank, mom glared at me as if she wanted to ask me something.

"What's wrong?" I blurted tersely.

"Are you going to pay off this loan?" she exclaimed, giving me a weird look.

"Mother, of course, I will. What have you been thinking? I am gonna dupe you and leave you here buried in debt? Are you out of your mind? What type of guy do you think I am? Cool your jets. I will be sending you money after I get my first paycheck." I yearned to soothe her by expressing reassuring statements. Mom insulted me a smidgen, but I condoned her attitude. Mom deserved the best version of me. She had been loyal and indulgent since I knew how to speak in general. She would always be next to me and bear me up no matter what I had done. How could I ever do anything to harm her heart?

Nowadays, the price of pretty much everything is ramping up drastically. A financial breakdown could damage any relationship. Trust between people has gotten brittle. That means sometimes we could slip into some sort of suspicion to those we absolutely loved. Some people change. But others stay on the same track, or as they say, "Different strokes for a different folk." It all depends on what mindset you have programmed or what type of quality of life and upbringing you had. Regardless of who you are and where you come from, if you planted a seed of faith in God, sooner or later, in your yard will blossom with plants of answers.

*****

By the first week of March, I rang Julian to report the updates.

"Great work, Dimitry! You need to visit my office and wrap up the last commission, and I will explain you all the details about your appointment with an American consulate at the embassy in Sofia," Julian explained. Inspired by what I had been doing for the past few months, I purchased a ticket to Sliven. This time, the transportation was made by train.

I needed silence to count my blessings. Using the bus wasn't an appropriate option; too tight for a two-and-a-half-hour ride. The conversation with Julian didn't take longer than half an hour. We ended the chat by shaking hands, and he snapped his shark's grin. I left his office and headed to my grandparents. I hadn't much time to linger out in Sliven. I decided to run back to Plovdiv on the same day. Grandpa walked me to the train station. Usually, we jibber-jabbered while strolling, but not that time. That time, we were quiet. It was the hardest walk I had alongside Papaw. As we stood at the edge of the tracks, suddenly, a train's horn rumbled.

"There he is. That's my guy," I uttered, attempting to cheer him up. At the next moment, I was entirely baffled. He was sad. Tears dripped from his eyes. I had never seen Grandpa wailing. Even now, writing this sentence is making me weep.

"We will miss you...a lot!" Papaw said.

"Ah, Grandpa, don't talk like that. You'll see me when I get back. I promise," I asserted boldly. Grandpa merely nodded. We hugged, and I uneasily hopped into the train. That was the last time I saw my grandpa. He passed away a few years later from natural causes. Have you experienced the loss of someone close to you? If you have, then you know how I feel. When you lose a relative, your love on them would grow bigger than the city of Tokyo. I didn't keep my promise, and I have missed him every day since. God bless his heart. He wasn't only my grandpa; he was also my friend. RIP.

*****

The appointment at the American embassy had been scheduled by the end of March. Meanwhile, I decided to retrain my English. Learning English was a mandatory subject at Bulgarian schools. I had been studying English at school for eight years, although, I didn't feel comfy enough speaking and understanding it.

Additional lessons provided by private entities had cost tons of money. I couldn't afford that option. For that reason, I set up my way of learning. You might be asking, what do you mean by that?

At that time, I was a goofball who loved watching movies. Thus, I had started to gawk at movies that were broadcasting English subtitles. In that way, I could listen to pronunciations and, at the same time, explore more treasures. That was how I killed two birds with one stone by entertaining myself and learning English. Also, I spent hours and hours learning English grammar as if I was a rocket scientist.

*****

Two weeks before the impending appointment with the American consulate in Sofia, I had to run into a few errands through the downtown Plovdiv. Early in the morning, I hopped on the carfare, rolling to the city. After thirty-minute ride, I hopped out of the bus. As I ambled through the crammed of people sidewalk, an unknown woman in her late forties called out to me. She wore black cloths resembling a witch.

"Hey, boy, yeah, yeah, you. Your name is Dimitry, right?"

What the duck? How does she know my name? I thought. Mesmerized, I couldn't get the memo of what had just happened.

"How do you know my name? Who are you?" I asked, grimacing. The woman replied that her name was Kate. She expressed her sorrow of the calamitous car crash, in which I had been involved in July, 2011.

My mind asked. How the heck does she know about the car accident? The article written in the local journal wasn't a headline. Furthermore, there weren't any photos or names.

"How do you know about the car accident?" I questioned, startled as if I was thrown into a deep maze.

"I can't tell you how. I've just sensed it in you," Kate uttered. The awkward encounter made me nervous.

Still trying to understand her yammers, I asked,

"Are we related or some sort of…?"

"Naw, there is something else. I see something really bad will happen to you," Kate proclaimed. Her eyes widened as she had just seen the death.

"What do you mean by that? What are you talking about?"

"Let me see your palms," Kate appealed. I exposed my hand, unconfidently.

"Yeah, I see something evil in those hands. You need to be careful. This is what I can tell. I got to go. Have a good day." Kate swiftly turned and trudged through the sidewalk.

"Wait!" I hollered and tried to catch her.

"Take it." I expressed my kindness by handing her five bucks. Kate grabbed the dough and dissipated out of sight. It was one of the most bizarre encounters that I had experienced. Who was this woman? Was she just a swindler or a scoundrel willing to steal some money from deluded people like me? Those questions were spinning in my head while I was peering through the window of the public transportation. Later, I queried my parents if they knew a woman named Kate. As you might guess, the answer was no. The following days, my top alternative was to focus on the interview at the American embassy in Sofia. Eventual disapproval would put me in an unpleasant plight. Failure was not an option, and I would refuse to accept it.

Chapter 5

Angelo, the son of Miro, had lived in Sofia since he was a nipper. Angelo was around five or six years older than me, and he already had his own business dedicated to teaching foreign languages. Angelo's career was thriving, his company had continued to grow over the years. We goofed around as kids in Stamboliiski. He always made me laugh. It was a blast from the past.

Unfortunately, as grown-ups, we hadn't much time to hang out. Angelo was a savvy man. Let me explain what I meant. Let's say, for instance, you kidnapped Angelo and expelled him into any foreign country. Left alone, even if he couldn't speak the local language, he would still find the right path to survive, and on top of it, he would chalk up a fortune. His brain had been designed to be successful. Give him a few apples, and he would develop a farm for apples, which would bring him an abundance. I had learned a lot from him. A week before the appointment, I rang Angelo and revealed the student program and the whole nine yards. Angelo sounded elated. He invited me to sleep over in his apartment the night before the interview at the embassy. I hung up the phone as happy as a little kid. Everything is working just how I have planned. The question now is, what will I do at the embassy? What would happen if I do a faux pas? I don't want to look gawky in front of the American consul. God, please give me your wisdom. I thought.

In the following days, those questions aggravated my mind. Night after night, I snuggled to my bed, eyeing at the ceiling and chewing over. What will you do if you fail? Long nights of incessant ponder caused me trouble with sleeping. Some of my friends had failed to obtain student visas. A fear of eventual downfall had brought me distress. Thus, I looked around and created a plan B.

Finally, the anticipated day came. Carrying a backpack filled with ump-teen pages of paperwork, I slunk onto a train rolling to Sofia. The trip took around two hours, but it felt like it had been two days. I sat on the seat feeling uptight and nervous. The angelic meadows and lands of Bulgaria had loosened me up a little.

Sofia was the biggest among the highest level of population and the most influential city in Bulgaria. Sofia had aesthetic architecture buildings and landmarks such as the National Place of Culture, National Theater, Saint Alexander Nevsky Cathedral, the high hills in the mountain of Vitosha, etc. In my early twenties, I had worked as an electrician at a huge con-dominium building for a few months, traveling each day back and forth from Plovdiv. Alas, I hadn't been screwing around out in the capital Sofia as much as I should.

Leaping off the train, I saw Angelo holding the hand of his daughter, Bojidara. They waited for me at the end of the train station. Angelo was a tall man, around six feet two. His eyes were insightful, resembling an eagle. He had a long beard as a Bulgarian bishop.

Bojidara was the sweetest and most enthralling girl I had seen in my life. Her age was around ten. She was cute and lovable. Her beauty portrayed why people were toiling so hard to have a family. Grinning, Angelo greeted me as if I was his brother. I was gleeful to meet him and, at the same time, nervous. I attempted to conceal my anxiety. However, Angelo had already scanned my uncertain demeanor. Uneasily, I went in his dark-colored Audi. On the way to his apartment, Angelo incessantly talked about a variety of subjects. His purpose was to cheer me up, and at some point, he brought me into a serene statement. In the meantime, Bojidara attempted to show her doodles and drawings.

Angelo had lived in an upscale and peaceful neighborhood. His condo was on the sixteenth floor of a newly renovated swank condominium. When we slid through the entry, Mariana, his wife, gave me a friendly hug. Angelo revealed that he had recently bought that stylish condo.

He had three cheerful kids. All of them were genuine and kind. Mariana had served yummy appetizers, and later, she totted a juicy steak. Angelo gibbered hilarious stories about soccer. He cracked me up multiple times. He knew every player in the local league and all the rumors related to players, trainers, teams, etc. After supper, Angelo and I had a private conversation at his balcony. He craved to know more details associated with the student program in the U.S. When I explained him pretty much everything, he tapped my arm and said,

"Boy, be aware, lotta work is waiting for you."

Speechless, I merely nodded. As I mentioned before, Angelo was a sly man. Despite the fact, we had six years of difference, he was wise enough to be my grandpa. It was essential to listen to what Angelo declared. The odds of learning precious information were pretty high. My life experience taught me that every human is capable of learning from another. If you crave to sponge what others know, you won't stop growing. For many years, I had been using this method, and in most cases, it turned out to be beneficial.

We chitchatted for a while, and around ten thirty, I went to bed. I looked around to make sure I was alone and checked out for the plan B. Then, I passed out. The whole night, I couldn't pull myself together. The consequences of the essential interview gnawed my subconscious. Around seven in the morning, I bundled up. Angelo insisted giving me a ride to the embassy, and a few minutes later, we left the condo. Initially, he dropped his kids at school, then he sat back in his vehicle and alleged,

"Here is the scenario. At quarter to eight, we will stop at a bakery to have a quick breakfast. At half-past eight, you will be at the embassy. Just lie back and watch." Angelo grinned charmingly like Jay Leno at his guests. Traffic in Sofia was horrible, especially in the mornings. There were stalled cars everywhere. A few intersections had been blocked. There is no frigging way! He won't do what he had just said. Not a chance! I thought. A few minutes later, I was stunned. Angelo drove fiercely and safely. He sneaked through the flow of cars and beat up the whole traffic like a freaky cabbie. Unbelievable! Angelo did whatever he said, and by half-past eight, he dropped me at the embassy.

"Good luck! Take care of yourself," he stated. That was his way of saying, "Goodbye". We wouldn't see each other. Right after the interview, I had to jump on the train back to Plovdiv. Angelo did whatever he could to help me out. He took care of me as if I was a member of his household. God bless him and his whole family. Walking over the lavish pathway of the embassy, I was thrilled as a geeky lad ambling to meet his first date.

I marched through the swanky lawn over to the US's embassy. The architecture of the building caught my eye. Then I glanced at the long line of people which started from outside. There were so many people out there it was as if they were giving out free food. Holy shmoly, there are so many people here! It will take all day.

Waiting in the line, I was anxious like a cat on a hot tin roof. My jacket had gotten warm that I was forced to peel it off. After thirty minutes, I crawled a few feet inside of the embassy. Then a horrible discomfort in my stomach occurred. It's the breakfast from the bakery. Shoot! Gotta use the restroom. Sometimes, my digestive system worked on urgent calls, and I couldn't hold it any longer. I tapped on the shoulder of an unknown man in front of me. Abruptly, the man averted. He was scowling. His eyes were saying, "What the fuck you want, Punk?"

"Sir, may I ask you for a quick favor? I need to go to the restroom really bad. Please, would you mind watching my baggage? I don't want to lose my spot in the line." I burst out uncomfortably. It was an emergency. The man was in his late sixties. He shot at me with a sullen glimpse, then switched down to my baggage, then back up at me, and exclaimed,

"Ya, whatever. Go ahead."

I thanked him and hurried to the last room on the right side. After finishing my business at the toilet, I fumbled and pulled out the plan B, which was a baggie containing cheap amphetamine. Then, there was a raspy sound of snorting two thick rails while the toilet was still flushing. Hooray! After blinking a few times, I took a deep breath and wiped out the marble countertop of the sink.

This is very important. Let me be clear. Whatever I did there was totally wrong, and I don't want anybody to use it as an example. Obviously, I am not expecting any kudos and I am not happy to share that story either. I am not afraid to tell the truth because that truth gave me the hope to live again. Please, don't consider that I am trying to encourage you. This is the worst example you could read. Furthermore, I needed to take this detail off my chest to purify my soul.

Back at the embassy, I opened the door and walk, carrying equanimity. The anxiety and insecurities flew away. I returned to the line, and kindly thanked the old man. For the next twenty-five minutes, I stood confidently and anticipated the conversation with the American consul. I had control over my mind that was provided by the white garbage.

I felt like I had been in that embassy a zillion times already. Around fifteen minutes later, someone called out my name. I stepped closer to a wooden booth, which was up to my waist. A well-dressed yuppie popped up from the other side. He looked like an Irish chappie. He had a blond quiff. His tux was snappy as if he was going to a wedding.

Here he comes! The American consulate spoke in an absolute formal manner and questioned tersely without wasting time. As the routine inter-rogation began, the American consulate ejected a few questions. My inner voice stately whispered in my eardrums. Whatever he is saying, do not allow him to put you into the wrong impression. Don't give him a chance to sway you from your purpose.

My answers were as short and insightful as Hannibal Lecter would have spoken. Some of his questions were trappy, although, I remained relaxed. The conversation was brief. That was my first genuine dialogue using English as a communication option. The plan B panned out to be very successful, and I did a flawless performance.

After the interview, they told me that the decision would be mailed after five business days. Regardless, I was assured of my victory. Straight away, I hotfooted out of the embassy and headed to the subway. That was the easiest way to dissipate into the train station of the city. The cab drivers would have ripped me off. When I jumped onto the first available boxcar, locals were staring at me as if I was an alien who had just come from Mars.

That didn't matter. I couldn't conceal my broadened smile, and why should I have to? Butterflies in my stomach were bobbing up and down as corn seeds were bouncing in a popcorn-making machine. It was a rejoicing feeling when everything you had planned worked out. It was afterglow when I jumped out of the train in Plovdiv.

At home, mom was exultant. She portrayed elated emotions, whereas Koko was apathetically speechless. He cast down the same disapproving statement. After all, he couldn't stop me from following my dreams. At that time, I was twenty-four, mature enough to make my own decisions. The rapper Eminem mentioned in one of his songs, "You only get one shot. Do not miss your chance to blow. This opportunity comes once in a lifetime."

I was convinced that was my shot and certainly wouldn't blow up the opportunity. I invested a plethora of time to achieve my goals. Sick and tired from rushing through the whole city, my thoughts were. Dude, you deserve a break. Loosen up a bit. That was how I decided to complicate my life. In the next chapter, you will find out what exactly I am talking about.

Chapter 6

My people from Bulgaria are well-known as party animals. We party like rock stars. Everybody drinks, dances, and has a good time. Male or female it doesn't matter. Just call us—Eastern-European.

Partying till sunrise doesn't make us halfwits or frenzied rednecks. It is just the way we are. Two weeks before my flight to the U.S., I made a few phone calls and hung out with some buddies from different neighborhoods. The first week of April, a few friends and I headed to a club that played house music. The name of this club was Plaza. Habitually, we trekked out there at midnight, and around seven in the morning, we left the club with dragon's eyes. Usually, we had fun up there. Intermittently, we could bump into any kind of ravers or some junk people. The odds might vary. When we passed through the security, I stepped inside, looking around; and most of the faces were the same as usual. That night, a DJ named Joseph Capriati from Italy was taking care of the music. His work was decent.

Plaza had two separate bars placed like the letter L. The VIP area was at the right corner next to the DJ stage. There was a second floor that had a narrow corridor often crammed by the worst ravers. We always had beers at that club. Hard liquor wasn't a good option. If you quaffed liquor, the next day, you would retch as if you ate moldy food. I could speak from firsthand experience.

Those barrelhouses were making tons of dough by selling fugazi alcohol. It was ridiculous. As we were screwing around, gulping booze, I was looking around to spot familiar chums. It wasn't too long when I scanned a chappie named Shawn. I swiftly approached him. Shawn was a short, overweight mate. He was always grinning, especially when he was stoned. We called him the Pancake because his face was as round as a pancake. Anyway, I approached the Pancake and questioned him,

"Yo, whatcha got?" I asked. The Pancake studied me for a moment, then grinned.

"Ya, I got Diamonds. You want some?" he exclaimed.

"Gimme three!" I said.

"You want three?" The Pancake repeated to make sure he heard me. The music was loud, and we had to shout to understand each other.

"Ya, three!"

When you are in your early twenties, you push the envelope and you think nothing can stop you, no matter how much you drink or what you have taken. That was why I gulped three pieces of MDMA substances ciphered as a diamond, all at once. Then, I lay back my spine on the bar and peered at the chicks on the dance floor.

Half an hour later, I goggled with my mouth agape. I couldn't believe in my eyes. I had never seen anything like that in my whole life. Unbelievable! What the duck is happening here! Oh God, What have I done! The voice in my head screamed. People's faces changed drastically. A man looked literally like a mummy was blabbering something to someone. Some of the ravers had a pair of devil's horns attached to their heads. The same went for my buddies. The DJ had metamorphosed into the guise of something like a satanic creature. It was like we had a Halloween party. Unfortunately, that wasn't the type of Halloween party that you would like to be involved. I was perplexed. They all looked so genuine as if they were born like that. Holy smokes! What a bum trip. I thought this crap could be seen only in the movies. I had heard tales about hallucinations as a side effect of popping pills narrated by some jailbirds, but I had never believed it till that night.

All of them were realistic as the fictional character Venom released from the movie Venom in 2018 or all of the nonhuman creatures in the franchise sequel of Avengers. It was similar but still not precisely equal. What I saw that night was beyond the higher quality of 4D cinema software. The bottom line was, there was no reason to panic or to seek medical first responders. I was feeling fine. The only exception was that a bunch of demons, devils, and a mummy had tripped into my eyes.

Who cares? I was chilling out, resting my back at the bar, and enjoying the incredible cinema production. The only thing that I needed was popcorn. Dude! Just don't go to the washroom! I wouldn't crave to see my face in the mirror at that particular moment. Thank God I hadn't any emergency calls for wee-wee. Man, you are such a ding-dong dimwit! How could you have messed up like that a week before your flight to the US? My inner voice cried out.

After a few hours, the power of diamonds ebbed, and the spectacular Saturday night of raving cinema finished. Immediately, I decamped from Plaza and snatched a cab heading to Trakya. At home, no one suspected anything. I was bushed from the Halloween 3D cinema party. I decided to draw a quick shower, then I crashed.

Whatever I saw that night didn't have any influence on me, such as nightmares or flashbacks. However, I considered that should be my last Saturday night show. As a man carrying common sense, I had to concentrate on my purpose and not screw around in similar shindigs.

Everyone does mistakes in their life. We should learn from those blunders and should not repeat them. You might think. Ah, this guy is exaggerating for the sake of his book. Alas, if you took more than two barbiturate substances such as molly or MDMA, you would have all of your answers in front of your eyes, literally. Once again, do not use my story as inspiration or motivation to do something silly like I did. It may harm your sanity for a long time. Stay away from this crap. It's not worth it.

*****

The next morning, I couldn't stop pondering about the imminent trip to Michigan and the entire internship program in general. I had traveled to

France and Macedonia just for a week. The student program would be up to six months. Moreover, I had never been able to fly on an airplane. I was thinking about the fact that I would be the only one Bulgarian out there. There would be two students from Ukraine and four from Moldova. I hadn't encountered any people from those countries before. I heard gossips about Ukrainians that gulped vodka as much as I drink water. Regardless, that was merely rumors podcasted by unknown sources. I couldn't count on that.

Therefore, I attempted to cyberstalk those countries. Unfortunately, I couldn't find anything useful. The plan was to elaborate a friendship along with alpha males, if any. That was the basic structure of my game plan. Dude! Keep your pecker up. You will figure out what to do once you touch down there.

If you want to win the game, you need to play the cards in the right way. You may ask, which way is the right? The right way is the most beneficial, the one that works the best for you. And if it doesn't, it means that wasn't your game.

*****

My next step was to say goodbye to Nana Tanya. She had treated me like a king. Thus, I longed to express my veneration by visiting her in person. When I walked through the entry of the house in Stamboliiski, Tanya served food as if it was Thanksgiving. The food was delicious even Graham Elliot would approve Tanya's skills. I nibbled as much as I could. I knew I would grieve for her cooking craftsmanship. Nana hugged me and wished me the best of luck. Gained a few extra pounds, I scuttled to the train station to catch the train wheeling to Plovdiv.

For the next couple of days, the premonition of what could happen when I touched down to the US nagged my mind. Questions such as, who would I meet there and how would that student internship program affect me were whirling incessantly in my mind.

On Monday, April 21, three days before I had to fly from Bulgaria, Koko invited his friend Kane in our home. Kane was notorious via the moniker the Loco. Trust me, it was not a coincidence. Sometimes, when Kane got drunk, he got out of hand. Once we shuffled to his apartment, Kane glugged a large amount of whiskey. He grabbed his firearm, scuttled to the balcony, and shot a few times in the air just for fun.

He was a whackjob. Despite his craziness, Kane was amusing and funny. He had cracked me up a bazillion times. Kane had long curly hair that resembled a Jamaican rapper. He was over six feet tall and about 250 pounds. Kane used to be a gifted soccer player. Unfortunately, he missed his window. He loved listening to Greek music, eat salads, and drink hardcore liquor. Kane and Koko worked as cabbies in Plovdiv. Both hit it off very well. Often, they slurped moonshine bevy together. That particular evening, Kane popped up around eight, and we all kicked off the drinking contest.

Kane chugged Rakia like a Russian bacchanal. An hour later, he became a stand-up comedy actor jabbering multiple funny stories. We all guffawed a bunch. I crawled on the floor and kicked my legs in the air. We had a ball. I was laughing so hard that, for a moment, I became breathless. Then, out of the blue, Mom woke me up. The clock indicated around forenoon on the next day. A severe feeling of remorse stung me. What happened? I must have been in a complete blackout. I hope I didn't screw somethin' up.

When I interrogated Mom, she quipped,

"Nah, dear, you were fine. As we were chatting, you passed out unexpectedly. You were so stoned that I had to drag you out into your room. Other than that, you were fine. You shouldn't drink like that," Mom exclaimed by expressing dry humor just by the skin of her teeth.

For the following hours, I had to fight back with unpleasant hangover. In the afternoon, my cell rang. It was Maria. She longed to get together, and we made plans to meet up at the park in the hood around four. I came to the park five minutes earlier, and she had already been waiting for me. When she noticed my presence, Maria stepped closer and hugged me tightly. She was blubbering. That was our last date, and she knew it.

Maria sank in an unconditional sob. I attempted to console her by talking about how much I adored her. Regardless, she didn't stop weeping. She couldn't allow me to leave. Alas, it was too late. Maria was one of the fewest people in my life who really loved and cared about me. She didn't care how much money I made, what kind of job I had, or what I did in general. Maria had cooked, cleaned, and did whatever she could to keep me close. She loved me genuinely. Maria gave me tons of kisses and hugs, and that was how we split. We broke up with love. We took different paths. She wanted a second child and a family, whereas I was pursuing my target in developing a business regarding luxury watches.

Chapter 7

On Friday, April 25, 2014, Koko, Sunny, and I headed to the airport in Sofia. Mom couldn't make it. She sent us off from home. She couldn't stop weeping. Mom wouldn't resist the idea of her child traveling somewhere around eight thousand miles away from the condo in Trakya. Her heart had been torn apart.

Early in the morning, we left Plovdiv, trying to be on time at the airport. The chart was from Bulgaria with a layover to Amsterdam, then a seven-hour flight to Detroit, then another layover to Grand Rapids where the manager of the Todd Greiner's Farm would be waiting for me.

After an hour and a half ride to Sofia, Koko and Sunny ushered me to the terminal where we separated. Koko mirrored a mute and tranquil countenance, whereas Sunny reflected pure joy. She wished me best of luck. An hour later, I was on the plane. I swiftly looked around left and right like a squirrel, feeling nervous. Dude! Take the chill pill. You will be fine. The turbulence made me hesitant for a moment. Then I managed to clear my mind and calm myself.

*****

The airport in Amsterdam was crammed as if it was beehive filled with swarm of bees. Everyone was rushing around to catch their flight. Instantly, the tobacco addiction coaxed me to light a cigarette. That was why I pattered to a designated smoking area, which was the size of a shoebox. When I slunk through the entry, there was a fog of smoke hovering inside. Nonetheless, that didn't stop me from lighting a few coffin nails (cigarettes). I was a heavy smoker. One pack was cast out easily per day. My cigarette addiction was getting problematic. When I didn't have any money to buy tobacco, I swiped cigarettes from my parents. Mom knew about it. Koko had no clue.

It was a long, tiresome day. I pussyfooted through all of those airships. In Grand Rapids, I bumped into a peanut guy named Peter. He was the farm manager. He was a short and slender man in his late thirties carrying a charming smile. He was a Wonder Bread white guy who looked like a grown-up version of the fictional character Peter Pan.

Initially, I thought that Peter Pan was a typical white American. It turned out that he came as an immigrant from Africa. I was eager to communicate with Peter Pan. At that time, my English was horrible. Regardless, I was obstinate and valiant to learn it. We stopped at Burger King to get fat whoppers and salty fries. Then, Peter Pan dropped me off at some sort of a Boy Scout cottage.

It looked like a wooden camp where all students would sleep due to the entire program. It was a neat camp. In my country, people would pay decent money to stay in that camp. The farm didn't charge us for sleeping out there, which was kind and amiable. The Boy Scout camp had been divided by a vertical wooden wall built of plywood to separate the cottage into equal sides. The Boy Scout camp was located in the middle of nowhere. There were only crops and meadows around. I saw an old house anchored by twenty feet away and occupied by Mexican wetbacks. My first night in America was boring. I was alone. I was the first student there. I couldn't crash because of the eight hours of difference in the time zones between Bulgaria and the USA.

Peter Pan revealed that more students would trek over in the next few days. The tobacco addiction was killing me. I was jonesing to light a cigarette. In my carry bag were buried ten packs of cigarettes. The only hindrance was that my lighter was missing. I was dumb enough not to think about using the fire of the gas stove.

That particular night, a voice whispered in my mind. Dimitry! Now is the time to quit that crap. Say it… say… I am done with this garbage! The scent of the tobacco was dragging my ass to open the pack. My mind was fighting against the addiction.

Your mind is stronger than any addiction. All you need to do is to allow your faith to fight for you. Reading that, you may think, "Yeah, man, it's easy to say it". That's true, and it's wrong if you really took credit for it.

The entire night, I didn't smoke. I couldn't sleep either. Instead, I gazed at the ceiling, pondering what the next few months would be. The next day, Peter Pan screeched the tires of his truck to pick me up. He wanted to introduce me the farm. There were a few factories, barns, and a load of enormous harvest spread around the perimeter of five miles. Peter stopped near one of those crops. He introduced me to the owner of the farm, Todd Greiner. Todd was a big, tall, stocky man. He was hitting his late thirties. Also, he was very kind and levelheaded. His attitude was of an educated businessman craving to reap tons of dosh. We didn't talk much just because my English didn't allow it. I could understand what he was saying, only up to a point.

When we wrapped up the induction trip, Peter Pan dropped me at the Boy Scout camp. Before I grabbed the door handle noise from inside drew my attention. Someone is in there! Slowly, I crept through the entrance, and suddenly, a young man loomed in front of my eyes.

"Hello! My name is Anton. I've just come here. What's your name?" Anton was a student from Ukraine. He was taller than me and much stronger. His body was as athletic as an Olympic swimming champion. Anton had a blond sweet-corn haircut, same as Dolph Lundgren acting in Rocky III. Anton spoke proper English. Somehow, we managed to understand each other.

Anton wasn't a wino or a smoker; he was a friendly guy. We had fun, talking throughout the entire night. The moment before I hit the sack, the tobacco addiction was bugging me. No matter what I did or where I went, it was there 24-7. I had built up a tremendous mental stronghold to resist the attacks from the abstinence. It had been working out well. Those ten packs of tobacco became problematic. I couldn't throw them in the trash bin. The yearning to light up a cigarette had disturbed me, same as when you lose your passport while visiting a foreign country.

If you want to achieve your goals, you need to keep fighting (working) every single moment. How long is it going to take? Nobody can't predict.

The next morning, Peter Pan scurried to the Boy Scout camp.

"The season hasn't started yet. However, we need two guys to work at the factory. Is anybody interested?" His question sounded like an announcement. We both nodded. They tried to keep us busy, which the two of us looked for.

Anton and I, along with some wetbacks, were working at one of the farm warehouses. Around four in the afternoon, a brand-new Ford Edge rolled over. All of the doors in that vehicle opened at the same time. The chauffer was Sarah, Todd's wife. She was in her mid-thirties, her blond hair glittered like sunrays. Sarah had blue eyes, a polite smile, and acrobatic body. You could tell she frequently visited a gym.

Besides Sarah, four young guys jumped out of the SUV. It must be the Moldavians. Those faces looked 100 percent European. Sarah had introduced us, and we all exchanged a repulsive glimpse. It was a stare that portrayed an attitude that says, "Who the duck are you?" Suddenly, Anton and the Moldavians started talking in fluent Russian. My thoughts were. Cripes! If those guys don't speak English, I am screwed.

The names of these Moldavians were Michael, Victor, Sergio, and Alex. Michael had an owlish countenance, blue eyes, and a blond hair that looked like pumpkin pie. He had the thickest type of body. He was one of those guys who was continually a step ahead of you as if he was beating you in a chess game. His body was naturally potent. His hands were as solid as a mallet. His beer gut looked like he was saying, "Gimme food and drinks". He was a quiet guy, but when he would speak, everybody would listen.

Victor was a shorter mate, around five feet seven. He had a small-size tummy, perhaps from fooling around among his buddies, and drinking tons of alcohol. Victor had impressive communication skills. Also, his mind was like a sharp razor. He had a life experience that you couldn't learn easily. Sergio had a blondish quiff and blue eyes colored like the Pacific Ocean. Sergio had an athletic body. He used to play soccer for a long time. Sergio was a friendly and funny guy.

Alex had a ripped and muscular body. He was jacked up and looked like he had lived in the gym. Alex had a goofy face, resembling Chuck E. Cheese because he was always smiling. He was like those Miami-lifestyle boys who always mumbled about beaches, nightclubs, parties, and wearing flashy clothes and pricey colognes. I couldn't comprehend why this guy had anything to do with working on farms.

Every Sunday, some of the farm managers drove us to the nearest Walmart in Muskegon for groceries. It was forty miles away. After the first week passed, Peter Pan brought the last student of the internship program. His name was Max. He flew from Ukraine too. Max had hay-colored hair and was rated as a highly educated highbrow among us. His proficiency in English was beyond and above. We were impressed. Even the Americans complimented him.

*****

For the first few weeks, we seeded cherries. Seeding cherries was a fun task. It made me feel loosened and comfortable, which was essential at that time. Exuding confidence and speaking English poorly, I successfully established good communication between the Mexican wetbacks and the students.

Everything looked cool, except for one thing. The farm management couldn't provide us with a home internet despite the promises that they had given. When we were off, which was mostly on Sundays, we rambled a half mile to Peter's house to use his Wi-Fi to speak with our families. After two months, we were eligible to obtain some cheap smartphones providing a data service.

Chapter 8

After we finished planting cherry trees, the season kicked off at maximum speed. It was showtime. The season of asparagus started. The asparagus was one of the toughest assignments on the farm. What was so special about picking asparagus? We started picking asparagus from six in the morning until nine in the evening.

We were seated in a specific car designated to pick asparagus. The asparagus car was operated oppositely as automobiles. The speed was adjusted by hand, and wheels were controlled by using legs. Five to six guys could work on the same car. Those cars looked a tad like a plane from the 1920s. It had two wings on each side that gave me the impression that we might fly for a moment. When we sat in the car, we needed to bow down to pick the vegetable. Every time I bent, my spine had a stabbing pain. We sat in that car like the letter L for fifteen to sixteen hours a day. The asparagus season continued for over a month and a half.

We didn't have a day off due to the asparagus season. It was tiresome to schlep every day. On the other hand, we were making good gross wages. After work, we were jaded. The only things we could do were eat, shower, and doze off. The following morning, the same picture rolled. Each day, we picked asparagus at exactly the same field. Once we finished our field, Peter Pan sent us to help others.

The size of asparagus that we were supposed to pluck was between eight and eleven inches. What baffled me was the fact that when I would pick eight-inch asparagus, the next day, it would grow up to an equal size. I was puzzled. The process had initiated so swiftly. How come? When the season of asparagus wound up, we all were on cloud nine. After long labored days working under the surveillance of the sun, we were able to take a break. The asparagus continued to grow, and two months later, it metamorphosed into some sort of shrubbery. Unbelievable!

*****

The next stage was the season of sweet cherries. It was significantly easier picking cherries. We climbed on the fifteen-foot-high trees to collect those cherries like we were apes. I had never eaten that many cherries in my entire life.

When we were at the Boy Scout camp, I befriended the Moldavians, more specifically Victor, Sergio, and Michael. We became good buddies. We drank, worked, ate, laughed, went to laundry together, and always helped one another. Alex was the leper sheep. He had never stopped grouching about the work on the farm. Alex perpetually mumbled about going to beaches, restaurants, nightclubs, and yada yada. At first, it was fine listening to what he yelped. Then, it turned to become annoying. He wanted to leave the farm. Everyone out there jeered and messed around with him.

The Ukrainians separated from us. Max took control of Anton. He was quite persuasive, and Anton followed him whatever he went. Moreover, they spoke in Ukrainian language on purpose, and no one couldn't understand them. The Ukrainian Cossacks had turned against us for no reason.

Max was a weirdo. One day, I pussyfooted through the door of the Boy Scout camp, and my eyes widened. I couldn't believe what I saw. Max kneeled on the floor. His eyes were closed, and he was mumbling something that I couldn't comprehend. God, I wished I had a camera to capture that moment. I had attempted to chat with him, but it was useless.

At first, I thought he was meditating or something like that. Later, I perused some verse left on the table written by him in English, which was related to Satan. Sometimes, Max talked about Satan like he worshipped him. To me, that didn't look appropriate. It was peculiar and abnormal. Max was a nice guy, although his quirky demeanor compelled us to keep distance from him. He had some insecurities carved on his face. Max talked too much. He pissed a lot of people from the farm, including Peter Pan, Todd, and Sarah. They almost booted him out of the farm.

*****

It had been two months since I stopped smoking. Undeniably, the addiction still aggravated me and I had been struggling much since. The addiction's voice had whispered in my eardrums. Dude! Smoke a cigarette. Just one. Nothing is going to change. That's wrong. Don't smoke any cigarettes. Do not smoke! You're done! Keep moving on. You are stronger than this garbage. You can do it. You knew it would be onerous, especially in the beginning. That was the price I needed to pay to reach desirable success. Once in a blue moon, when we imbibed bevy, I had tried to light a cigarette; and after two tokes, I tore the tobacco apart. It's not worth it, dude! You aren't putting in tremendous effort to end up buried in that addiction. The voice of the willpower was speaking in my head.

It had been three months since I quit smoking, and I started feeling better. The voice of the addiction gradually faded. That was how I beat up the tobacco abstention. I didn't use any additional patches or something like that. I merely quit by using the strength of my mind. No one could believe it, not even my mom.

*****

Since the asparagus season finished, we were off on Sundays. Normally, they drove us to the closest town called Pentwater to goof around on the beach. Alex was blown away in total awe. Staring through the windows of the transportation van, I was bewildered. The breathtaking beauty of that town drew my attention. The view mesmerized me. God! I don't know how, but I will find a way to stay here. My inner voice said.

Emily and Vinny had currently dwelled in Chicago. They had known my parents since I learned how to walk. After I purchased my first smartphone, which wasn't that smart, I rang Emily. We chitchatted formally, as we had never been introduced to each other. Then, I switched straight to the point and asked her if she could help me out to find a job and to extend my visa. Emily was a loyal and righteous child of God. She loved helping others. Back in Plovdiv, she was giving food to homeless drifters. Emily agreed to assist, which sparked the flame of my dream and I started visualizing about living in Chicago.

My buddy Mike also touched down in the USA as a student attending a similar internship program initiated in Maine. Both kept us posted intermittently. Normally, we shared stories related to the student programs. Mike hankered to live in the land of Lincoln as well. Thus, we set up a game plan to meet up in Chicago at the end of the summer. The two of us were exuberant as we took a step closer to the target.

*****

The season on the farm ran madly. The next task was picking sweet corn. It was tough, like a dentist pulling my teeth without injecting Novocain. There was a huge John Deere tractor that carried a long platform attached to the front. On that platform were placed four gigantic containers. Those containers were so immense that four guys could easily jump into them.

There was an old-fart farmer who operated that John Deere. We were picking the sweet corn and tossing it in those containers, which were behind us. The old gaffer shoved us by operating the John Deere. You might ask, what is so difficult of picking sweet corn? The issue was breaking the stem. It had been two hours since we commenced picking the sweet corn, and my thumbs and forefingers were bruised already. Even wearing gloves didn't help. Imagine someone pushing you by operating a tractor holding a huge platform while you tried to pick sweet corn with injured fingers. After work, my thoughts were. Angelo was right. There is a lot of work here.

Three months since the season on the farm had kicked off, Peter Pan drove us to the secretary of state. We appealed to take the test for a driver's license. A few students and I passed the test successfully. Then, Peter Pan permitted us to use the transportation van on Sundays. Pentwater was our hot spot. I became infatuated with that city. It was love at first sight.

Everywhere in that town was green and clean. The locals were friendly and kind to us. The beach there was legit. We played volleyball, gulped beers, grilled steaks, and tried to pick up some chicks. We had a ball. On September 1, Sergio had a birthday. We decided to celebrate it in Pentwater. Alex was our driver just because he was a teetotaler.

We burst straight at the first bar and got a few shots of vodka, then Alex had new orders. At midnight, the van parked close to the pier. A reflection of the moon glittered on the lake. It was quiet by the beach. Sergio, Victor, and I plunged into the lake for a night shower. The alcohol made us look like goofy animals. We giggled as boisterous teens. Just a few European nimrods having fun at the lake around midnight. We became goofy because all of us worked hard on the farm throughout the entire summer.

Five minutes later, a few flashlights appeared through the darkness. I thought. Yikes, I hope that is not the cops! A couple of police officers stepped closer and warned us to get off the water. Damn, we are in trouble. We obeyed, following the deputy's instructions and walked to the van. The three of us exchanged perplexed looks like we were listening to the jury in a courtroom, announcing the state's decision. The officers asked questions such as, "What are you guys doing here at midnight? Doncha know that the beach is closed at 10 p.m.? Why were you drinking? What are you doing in America in the first place?" In broken English and with strong European accents, we attempted to explain how hard the work on the farm was. Victor showed his injured hands to prove his confession. Despite our dumb testimonies, the police deputies let us go without any fines. That was a huge favor. It was incredible how lucky we were. God bless the hearts of those police officers. Later the same night, we blacked out from swigging bevy at the Boy Scout camp. The following morning, a severe hangover struck my head. I managed somehow to work. It was the season of peaches, which were easy to pick, and the trees were nearly the human size. We didn't need ladders. It was an advantage, especially when I was tipsy the day before.

Later same day, I had been hiding behind those trees. My vision got hazy. Regardless, I was still productive enough to pile up a sufficient number of peaches among other students. Victor and Sergio were on the same page. They tittered and laughed while wobbling through the trees. Victor grimaced at me and stated,

"No more drinking. I quit." Hearing his statement, I burst into laughter.

"Yeah right. Till we finish work," I said. Victor grinned as if I just called him a cocksucker. I didn't know how, but we made it by the end of the day.

*****

On September 3, I purchased a bus ticket to Chicago, and then I called Emily to tell her the updates. She agreed to meet me at Union Station in downtown Chicago. Later the same night, the Moldavians and I got hammered for a zillionth time. It was my last night at the farm. What else were we supposed to do in the middle of nowhere?

I miss those guys. Without them, it would be different and mundane. They made my time on the farm unforgettable. God bless them all. The next day, I packed my baggage and said goodbye to those Moldavian lushes. A few minutes later, Sarah roared over. She had agreed to give me a lift to the bus stop in Grand Rapids.

What she didn't know was that I had a spare day to waste in Grand Rapids. As soon as she dropped me off, I looked around and booked a hotel room somewhere in the city. I was a slump buster. I wanted to hang out with a few hookers. Unfortunately, my broken English wasn't good enough to hook up with any harlots.

That night, I didn't get laid as I wanted. A bottle of Jack knocked me out. In the morning, a brown bottle of flu (hangover) thudded in my head. I felt like someone had beat me up using a football helmet. I bundled up as fast as I could and called a cabbie. Around ten minutes later, I hopped in the cab. When I uttered the street address, the driver shook his head and said.

"Man, I don't think we can make it by twelve-thirty out there."

What the duck is this bozo talking about? I thought.

"Just drive. I'll tip you good." While the man was driving, my thoughts were. You airhead goofball, look what you've done. Now you will miss the bus. The cab approached the street, and the Greyhound bus was closing the doors. Swiftly, I opened the door and waved at the bus, showing signals to hold it. In the blink of an eye, I passed ten bucks extra to the cabhole driver and slunk into the bus. I couldn't believe it. I literally made it at the last moment, like they do in the movies. I thought it was God's will to catch that bus. With extra time such as waiting at a red light longer, the bus wouldn't be there.

Chapter 9

Two hours later, I woke up from a hangover nap. The bus hit the Turnpike 90 toward downtown Chicago. All of those enormous skyscrapers, Soldier Field, and all the museums baffled me. I fell in love with the architecture and blueprint of the Windy City. Honestly, I had never seen the downtown of Chicago even in a photo till that moment. I did it on purpose. Why? I wanted to explore the city in person, and the result was astonishing. Those moments of how I explored Chicago for the first time were sealed as pictures into my mental scrapbook and would never be erased.

Emily rolled up over forty-five minutes later. She couldn't avoid the traffic jam. After she picked me up, we didn't stop talking throughout the trip. Emily had beautiful blonde hair and a charming smile. Her eyes were asking questions. She was gregarious, talking about any topics.

The house that Emily and Vinny rented was located somewhere in Schaumburg. The atmosphere in this neighborhood was delightful. When we burst in through the door, Vinny stepped closer to say Hi. Vinny looked like a Russian mob boss; his eyes were insightful. You couldn't easily outwit this man. Vinny worked at a construction company as a highly experienced foreman. He was a creative beaver. Vinny and Emily allowed me to sleep at the house until I would find my place. They also helped me to open a bank account.

It had been three days since I moved in with Emily and Vinny. Vinny advised me that buying a car should be my primary step. Listening to his advice, I pulled my socks up and started looking for vehicles using all the time I had. Several days later, an offer drew my attention. It was a peculiar car, a Chevrolet Geo Prizm. This model had been manufactured in the year 1993. The condition of that vehicle was decent, and the price was reasonable. Thrilled, I waited until Vinny roared back from his job. When he stepped through the entrance, I couldn't hide my eagerness and showed him the bid. Vinny bit his lip and said,

"Make sure the car is still available, and let's roll."

Vinny drove about twenty miles. It was around half-past ten when he stopped by a creepy old house. A Mexican chappie loomed from the dark. He pulled up the garage door, and a blue-colored Geo Prizm glittered in front of us. We looked around for any severe body damages.

"What do you think, Vinny?" I asked him, speaking Bulgarian.

"Looks fine to me. Let's shrink the price."

We lapsed into the negotiating stage. Despite our poor English, Vinny and I successfully dropped the price by two hundred dollars. I couldn't sit on the top of the fence any longer and decided to take the vehicle. The cash was passed over. We shook hands, wearing a shark's grin, and in the next instant, I was driving my new ride behind Vinny's truck. It had been three years since the devastating mishap occurred with the Iranian truck. The fear of driving paled, and I felt a little more confident while operating an automobile.

*****

On the second week of September 2014, Vinny took me to work with him. The owner of the construction company was a Chinese man. He was a creative dwarf, thinking only about money. His mind always compelled him to do something. The Chinese patron dwelled in a large mansion. I merely spotted him a few times.

There must be dozens of Bulgarians laboring along with Vinny. All of them came from different cities in Bulgaria. They communicated in funky parlances. It was hilarious to listen how they talked. Working with those Bulgarians was a tad of a hassle. They didn't give you any proper instructions on how to do your job. When you did something wrong, they would break your balls and treat you disrespectfully. Presumably, they acted like that because some pigheaded supervisors had treated them the same way in the past.

Most of those Bulgarian employees puffed cigarettes throughout the working day. It reminded me of how I was hooked on cigarettes. I hadn't been smoking for five months, and I was feeling great. The statement of quitting smoking made me feel proud of myself. The smoking addiction stopped chasing me. I annihilated that awful habit.

On the last week of September, Vinny and I came back from work. Emily made a wonderful traditional Bulgarian food. She smiled at me and said,

"Dimitry, I've got good news for you!" Hearing her words, my sleepy countenance changed. Emily continued. "I've recently contacted a Bulgarian lady. She works as a realtor. She has an apartment. You wanna check it tomorrow?" Emily questioned even if she had already known the answer.

Around a quarter to ten in the following morning, Emily drove inbound toward downtown Chicago. She parked her Hyundai Accent in the parking lot of a big building. When we jumped out of the vehicle, a lady popped up from the side entrance of that building. She was in her fifties and resembled the female version of a vampire. She could easily take on a role in a movie playing the slut of Dracula. She didn't need any extra makeup.

Her name was Natasha. She was dressed all in black like she was going to a funeral. Despite her bizarre look, Natasha was a kind person. The apartment was a one-bedroom and was lodged on the garden level. There was a heater installed under the floor, covered with gray tiles. At the drop of a hat, I signed the lease for one year. Natasha allowed me to live in that apartment for two weeks rent free. It was a generous gesture. God bless her heart. On that day, I took a step closer to my goal. The day of freedom finally came.

Freedom costs an arm and a leg; you had to work hard to have it.

I had been dreaming of freedom since I was a teen. You might ask yourself why. My father had been mistreating me since my early childhood. Almost every night, he dashed back from work complaining about everything in general. Often, he became upset and grouchy, especially when I asked him for money. He had never encouraged me to attend school or college. Koko was a hothead. Sometimes, he exploded, expressing severe anger and wrath. He beat me up many times when I was a kid. He wanted to make me tough. That was his way of preparing me to be a strong man. I had never felt comfortable living with my family. I grew up with a bunch of insecurities and fear. Stephen King wrote, "Love didn't grow very well in a place, where there was only fear, just as plants didn't grow very well in place, where it was always dark."

Koko's behavior muscled me out of my family. I had never heard words like "I'm proud of you" or "I love you" burst out from him. I couldn't imagine living with him around. Don't get me wrong, I loved my father. He was a good man, but he failed at being a parent that I had always missed. When you feel uncomfortable living around your own family, you start looking around for freedom.

Later the same day, Vinny helped me out to move my stuff into the apartment. He asked me a fundamental question that I would never forget. He said,

"Dimitry, how much does it cost you to buy freedom?"

My response was, "There is no amount of money. It's priceless." Vinny couldn't cover his grin. His expression portrayed, "You got it". Vinny and Emily helped me a lot. Without them, I wouldn't be able to process my ambitions in the USA. I believe we should be thankful and NOT take for granted what others do for us because nobody has any obligation or commitment to help us whatsoever.

Chapter 10

Mike completed his student internship program. He was traveling to Chicago on the Greyhound Lines from Maine. We tried to stick to the primary target by sharing the one-bedroom apartment and all utilities. He had sent the location where he would be dropped.

When the day came, I drove through the downtown area. I was constantly gazing at the GPS. At that time, I wasn't confident enough to roll over downtown. It was a disaster, driving on the wrong ways and dashing slower than a turtle. Somehow, I managed to get to the bus station.

When I approached the bus stop, Mike waved, having a twenty-four-inch smile. He hopped in the Geo. Both of us were joyful to meet as we were talking months ago. We were on cloud nine like two inmates who escaped from a penitentiary. What we had been planning in Plovdiv did happen.

It was a great financial option for the two of us to share a dorm room. We trusted each other and still do to this day. It was vital for us to live as roommates. We split every single payment and bill. It is a significant point to choose who you are going to live with. Nowadays, it's tough to find somebody you can count on. Mike had some friends in Chicago. At the beginning of October, he started a job in construction as a plumber. It was his first time working as a dunny diver (plumber).

*****

It had been three months since I had started working in construction as a roustabout. I managed to pay back the money that my mom loaned from the bank in Bulgaria. Her credit accountability drastically improved. I was feeling proud of myself for keeping my promise.

The apartment building where Mike and I lived was on Denley Street in Schiller Park. The whole building was filled with Bulgarians. We met a bunch of those Bulgarian sodbusters.

*****

Emily tried to sign me up for English tuition at private colleges to extend my student visa. She alleged that those education entities required a bank statement displaying a bank account that had over ten grand. That was a gob of money, which we couldn't afford. Thus, my immigration status became undefined.

The failure of getting back to school didn't stop the zeal I had to improve my English. I decided to study in some education facility and also to hook up with some chicks. I did my research and bumped into a student facility named Triton College located in the same district.

The next day, I drove to Triton to check the information in person. A Mexican lady at the front desk was very kind. She claimed that I could enroll in a program named ESL (English as a Second Language). Triton College was positioned a few miles southeast of O'Hare and had fourteen campuses spread around as a Lego City. There was a bunch of extra space in the parking lot, which was quite convenient.

The ESL program was free, and in a blink of an eye, I signed up. I was eager to start classes. The first week of June 2015 was my first day in Triton. Zooming through the classroom in one of the campuses, I scanned five drop-dead gorgeous gals and four guys. A few seconds later, a woman in her late thirties walked into the schoolroom. That must be the teacher. Holy cow! Look at those balconies. They are huge! (I think you know what I mean).

Her hair was fascinating. She said her name was Christina. Her parents emigrated from Romania when she was ten. Christina attended high school in Illinois and had a bachelor's degree from the University of Chicago. Christina was dope. She was the coolest teacher I have ever met. I walked around in the classroom and noticed a cute European chick who sat alone. Exuding strong equanimity, I approached and questioned,

"May I sit next to you?"

The girl leered at me, wondering, "What the heck does this guy want from me on the first day in school?"

Her name was Alexandra. She was a breathtaking bonny lass who looked like the American actress Anne Hathaway. Alexandra just landed from Ukraine. She was in her early twenties. She loved to party, which was quite common for her age.

Christina asked each person in the class to introduce themselves. A beautiful girl sitting at the right corner said, "Hello, everyone! My name is Diana, and I came from Bulgaria." Bingo! This is Gucci! This broad is from my country. How cool is that? The voice in my head said. Diana was a sweet girl. She had charming black eyes and precious Havana-brown hair. After she finished talking about herself, I asked her by speaking Bulgarian.

"Diana, are you really Bulgarian or you're fooling us around?"

Diana turned over, and her eyes were shocked. Grinning, she replied, "I'm so happy that you are Bulgarian too. Let's talk after class."

Behind Diana, I scanned another broad. Her name was Nim. She trekked from Taiwan. Nim was my crush; her body was topnotch like a fashion model. She had a sweet Asian visage. Nim had a great personality, and it was fun being around her. Unfortunately, she was hitched, although we remain good friends.

Most of the boys had never shown up, only a guy named Miguel. He was a cool chappie. He was a religious man, something that I highly honored. At Triton, every day was like we had a free food tray and everyone could say hooray. Often, we played songs without delay. We all had a blast, bantering and completing many school tasks. I became the most active student in the classroom. Christina gave us intriguing subjects to study.

By the end of June 2015, the ESL courses reached the final stage. Diana divulged that she had a fiancé, although we were still friends until she got pregnant and became less available. Alexandra sent me some intimate sparks. But for whatever reason, she had always walked away. Alexandra was playing around. She was checking me out and sprinkling some compliments. But she had never given me permission to sneak beyond her curtains and look at what she was hiding there. That was fine. For gentlemen who have questions about ladies, I highly recommend a book called Attraction Isn't a Choice by David DeAngelo. He had some interesting topics.

On the last day in class, I asked Christina if she could write a referral about my student work at Triton. She suggested exchanging phone numbers and touching base in the following week. My thoughts were. Is she hitting on me, or I'm driving on a wrong-way street? Christina hadn't spoken anything about her personal life. This woman was surreptitious. Around a week ahead, I contacted her. She suggested meeting up at her place. Her address was around two miles away from my residence. Christina rented a studio on the first floor of a moldy house that had a decent dooryard. When I parked on the driveway, Christina was waiting on the porch. She was chilling out and puffing a cigarette.

As soon as I hopped out from the Geo, she stepped closer and hugged me tightly as if we had known each other since early childhood. We sat on the bench in the dooryard. Christina offered something to drink, but I politely refused. Christina and I had a brief conversation for around fifteen minutes. We were talking about school, future goals, and comedy. Gee, those balconies! Don't look at her balconies. Show some respect, would ya! Just focus. Dadgummit! Christina was dressed casually; her bosom bulged through her sports T-shirt. It was hard to concentrate. While we were swimming in a sea of delightful dialogue, I questioned Christina about where her husband was.

"I've never been married," she blurted. Her eyes were staring at me incessantly. Her statement left me bemused. What the heck is up with this broad? A few seconds of silence passed. Christina pulled up the referral paper and handed it to me. She smiled at me most of the time. What a nice person. I didn't want to bother her anymore.

Led by a foolish impulse, I stood up and stated,

"Christina, if you need anything, give me a call, okay?" She hugged me as if she was saying, "Thank you".

On Sunday, my buddy Evan invited me for a cup of coffee. It was around noon. I was off work and had nothing else to do, so I decided to kill some time. We goofed around and hashed over some funny stories and pickup lines for chicks. Then instantly, my phone jingled. It was Christina! What? Why is she calling? We've just met a few days ago!

"Hey, Christina. How you doing?"

"I'm fine. Need to talk to you. Can you come to my house?"

"When? Right now?" I asked.

"Yes, I guess, unless you're not busy!" Christina exclaimed.

"Well, give me thirty minutes, and I'll be at your place," I asserted and hung up the phone. Now, I'm sure what is going on.

"Evan, I got to split, buddy."

"Where are you going?" he questioned.

"I will explain it later, bud," I declared and rushed out of the cafeteria.

When I pussyfooted through her studio, I was shocked. Wow! Christina leaned on the doorframe, wearing a nightgown. My eyes popped out, staring at her bosoms. What the heck? Does she want a boom, boom or what? Is that for real? Why is she showing up like that? Well, soon you will find out, smart-ass.

"Come in. Don't stay at the door like a frightened raccoon," Christina uttered gleefully. There was a cheap bourbon left on the table. It was three in the afternoon.

"Do you want a drink?" she kindly offered, holding the bottle of bourbon.

"Water, please! I'm driving." Back home, when I was a young punk, I used to drive after draining a half bottle of whiskey just to prove what man I was. Thank God nothing had ever happened. Since I had landed in the USA, I had become more mature.

Christina revealed her controversial relationship with her parents. She continued sharing stories related to her family. It was sad. Everybody has gone through a dark side in their lives. A few minutes later, we decided to change the atmosphere by playing some Eastern European folk music, especially from Bulgaria and Romania. The alcohol took action, and I couldn't avoid her balconies anymore.

I chugged a shot of bourbon, which burned my throat; and I started kissing her. In the next scene, we had America's Got Talent in a special edition for adults only. After we finished the late night show, I wasn't sober enough to drive. I decided to spend the night at her place. The following few months, we started seeing each other pretty often. Normally, I cruised to her place. We couldn't have privacy at Denley Building.

It was summertime, one of those days in Chi-town when you wouldn't want to travel anywhere because the sun's heat could lead to a stroke. Christina didn't work at that time of the year, so she was available throughout the day. We had a splendid time together, visiting diverse places such as restaurants and stand-up comedy events.

One particular night in August of 2015, I scuttled over to Christina's studio. As usual, we got some whiskey and had fun by telling jokes. An hour later, Christina got tipsy. She revealed that she was barren due to three abortions. What? Why would she do that? She didn't give me any rational explanation. She wallowed, feeling remorse for her deeds, and mostly, she was mournful because she couldn't have kids. I tried to soothe her by changing the subject. Around two hours later, I grabbed her hands and announced,

"Christina, look me in the eyes." She had no idea what would happen next. Stoned like a junkie, I bent on my knee and proceeded, "Christina, would you marry me?" She stared at me, speechless.

"Are you for real?" she asked.

We discussed a potential engagement a month ago. She gave me the YES, holding a second of hesitation. My words came like a gunshot aimed at nowhere, but I spoke genuinely from the bottom of my heart. I had never proposed to anyone till that moment, and it wasn't completely romantic like what they did in the movies. But the sequence of love was there, and that mattered. Dating Christina enhanced the level of my English. I have never stopped learning English till the present day.

You should keep searching for your passions to work in a field that makes you happy every moment of your life. That is the key to success.

The end of September came through, but the summer didn't go away. It was just another day after work. I visited my fiancée's studio. It was around six in the afternoon, and Christina was already gulping bevy. Is this broad a rummy? She had been drinking until she blacked out. Often, I had to walk her to the bathroom just because she couldn't stay on her feet. The picture wasn't looking good.

Everybody has some issues with parents or something else, but you have to keep fighting and be strong. You cannot just quit. That is not a solution. God didn't create you to quit. Using alcohol would not erase the pain; it could temporarily blind it. I kept trying to support and encourage by being next to her. My efforts were useless. Christina was an intelligent person. She spoke four languages. It was frustrating to watch how she struggled.

Christina didn't accept my help. She kept diving deeper into her blinded world by consuming hard liquor. It was one particular night when Christina and I watched a movie at her place. We started slugging large amounts of alcohol. It was getting wild. We were both laughing and being goofy throughout the night. Christina divulged her talent of belly dancing and hopped on the table. An hour later, my battery ran low. I had to work on the next day, and my decision was to shut off my internal software.

I left Christina to drink on her own as usual, and I hit the rack, passing out. A few hours later, an unknown noise woke me up. Automatically, I turned over, and my eyes widened. My whole body was frozen. What I saw had me mesmerized. What the duck! I couldn't believe at my eyes. Christina stood right next to the bed, holding a twelve-inch kitchen knife pointed at me. She looked daggers at me. At that moment, I went bananas, hollering, "Get this knife away from me. What is wrong with you? Are you insane?"

It was like Lorena almost Bobbitted me. Christina was zonked of alcohol. She could barely stay on her feet. I snuck around, grabbed my stuff, and left the house. She tried to stop me, but her effort was unsuccessful. Bitter as if someone kicked me in the nut sacks, I sped up my car so fast as if cops were chasing me for a brutal felony.

How was that possible? We hadn't had any altercations earlier in the same evening. I thought that could happen only in James Bond movies, but in real life, it was much more terrifying. The woman to whom I was supposed to get married had attempted to kill me without any specific reason. Drinking was no excuse.

Christina tried to reach out to me over the phone for a bazillion times. Regardless, I couldn't speak to her anymore, especially after that unacceptable scenario. Our nooky was marvelous. Nonetheless, I would not be able to sleep next to her again. Just imagine what would happen if I didn't wake up.

Alcohol could lead humans to unpredictable actions, and Christina proved it. She was a stubborn feline, refusing to accept the reality. I learned my lesson, and next time I would be more careful and aware when choosing a bride. The bizarre relationship with Christina made me praise the Lord even more. God had thwarted that horrible manslaughter.

Life is unfair, but God is fair. Sometimes, the kismet could cause you to lapse into unforeseen situations. No matter what, you need to be focused and keep moving on.

Chapter 11

It had been a year and a half since I touched down in the U.S. My dream of making luxury watches was gradually buried in my subconscious. My mind was too tight. There were a plethora of other fishes waiting to be fried.

One of them was to acquire a driving license issued by the state of Illinois. The one from Michigan expired a long time ago. I drove without any legal permission. Thus, I followed the rules strictly. It was frustrating. I was constantly looking out for the state troopers. The anxiety about being pulled over gnawed my mind.

In January 2016, some Bulgarian chappie revealed that the secretary of state provided an option called TVDL (temporary visitor driver's license) which allowed foreign individuals to drive legally in the state of Illinois. Fired up with sparks of hope, I scheduled an appointment in the second week of March 2016.

The appointment was at the secretary of state located 250 miles west of the Denley Building. Why that far? Mike had already gotten his TVDL in a location far away from Windy City. I thought it would be easier to pass the driving test at the secretary of state located far from the city of Chicago.

When the day came, I prepared all of the required documents and hit the highway. The weather was awful. Flurries were floating over the turnpike. Ah gee! What a luck! Screw it! I can't afford to cancel the appointment. I have been waiting two months for this day. Can't just go back. Thank God there wasn't any jammed traffic westbound.

Heading up somewhere to Springfield, my thoughts were.

Dude! Just watch your exit. Don't miss the exit. A few minutes later, I got distorted by insufficient visibility over the floating flurries, and I missed the exit. Cripes! Duck! Cool your jets. There must be another one in a few miles. I thought. The next exit was twenty miles ahead and twenty more to go back. That made forty extra miles. Screw it!

The main target was to get the license. It didn't matter if I drove an extra forty miles. The appointment was scheduled at twelve, and I pulled Geo into Jessie White's parking lot at around a quarter to twelve. Perfect timing! I grabbed the bag with all the documents and hopped out of the Geo. I pressed the button on the door to lock the car and slammed the door happily.

Okay. Now I need my key, and I am all set. The key? Where is the key? I looked through the window on the driver's side and saw the key stuck in the ignition. What the…you knucklehead. How could you forget the frigging key? Dammit! There was a spare key left on the nightstand in Denley around 250 miles away. What a luck! Dude! Pull yourself together. Go inside. Take the writing test, which you've been studying so hard for the past two months. Then, you will think about this problem.

The Secretary of state was crammed as usual. A young gal at the front desk was hollering names. She smiled at me kindly. When I explained to her what the reason for my appointment was, she looked at me as if I was speaking Vietnamese to her.

"I am sorry, sir, but here, we don't issue those types of driving licenses. You have to pick another location."

Is she for real? I drove 250 miles just to hear that? Not to mention I left the car key in my Geo. Ah, the car. Now what, Mr. Hotshot?

"Excuse me, miss, can you call the police department to send someone? I locked out my car by accident, please."

The gal gazed at me like I was some kind of hophead who had just escaped from a nuthouse. She made the phone call, and I strolled outside in the parking lot. Someone told me that the police could help in similar situations. That was why I decided to give it a whack. Otherwise, I had to break the window of my car.

Less than five minutes later, a police vehicle approached. I waved urgently. My careworn face was expressing the word, "Help". A stocky man of Mexican descent in his thirties hopped out of the police car. He pulled out something like a plastic crowbar. He pressed the glass of the door enough to slink his hand in, and unlocked the door in less than fifteen seconds. I was bemused by how swiftly he opened the door. Amazing! Is he a real cop or a car thief? It was like we were making a reboot of Gone in 60 Seconds.

I thanked the police carjacker and hopped in the Geo. I was happy, as if I had just won a jackpot of megamillion. That trip had been welded in my mind as one of the most bizarre experiences since I touched down in the U.S. The next month, I drove to Jessie White in Deerfield. I passed the test, nailing a perfect score. After fourteen business days, they mailed the TVDL and I could take a deep breath.

*****

In December 2015, Vinny formed his own construction business and I started working for him. I had always been faithful and loyal as an employee. As the days went by, the stress at work had boosted fundamentally. Some Bulgarian coworkers were treating me indecently, and I couldn't stand it anymore. Sometimes they mocked me, throwing some foolish jeers. That riled me up. I worked hard, doing everything I could, and they were snarky to me. God knows why.

Vinny took care of me as if I was his son. He had always been covering my back. Regardless, I wasn't satisfied by working as a roustabout. My intentions were to work as an electrician. Unfortunately, Vinny didn't have any positions related to sparky boys.

Back in Plovdiv, in 2009, I worked as an electrician, and I loved it. Doing electrical tasks became my passion. Alas, after a year of toiling, the financial crisis started. The Great Recession hit my country tremendously bad, and the electrical company that had hired me had some banking issues. Thereby, they laid me off. It was frustrating. The money was acceptable. After that, I was unemployed for a year until the print house Nova hired me.

For the next few weeks in a row, I was looking around to find a job as an electrician. Month after month passed by, and nothing changed. It was the first week of April 2016, we worked on a house in Des Plaines. There were some issues relating to the electrical panel at that house. It required a licensed electrician.

A man in his early forties cruised over. He had the insightful eyes and a plump body of a Whopper lover. His name was Nik. He was born and raised in the USA. His family migrated from Greece. Nik was the licensed electrician. We had a long chitchat about work. Nik did a phenomenal job. He was done by afternoon; and before he left, he handed me a paper with his phone number. He said,

"Give me a call if you need a job. See you later, kid." For the next couple of days, I was thinking about Nik's offer.

There wasn't anything to think about. God had handed the chance. In the blink of an eye, I grabbed my smartphone and dialed Nik. The Greek electrician told me that he worked as full-time maintenance at O'Hare Airport, and he did side jobs when he was off work. He texted me the phone number of another electrical contractor. His name was Pete.

Without wasting a second, I called Pete. He wasn't surprised by my call. Nik had told him already. Pete spelled some address, and the next day, I drove to meet him. It was a huge commercial factory. Pete was waiting at the dock platform. He had a thin type of body. He was in his early seventies, and walked faster than an average man at the age of forty.

Pete was a wise man. He survived a bad terminal cancer. Pete migrated to the USA a long time ago. A lot of people had known and honored him. He was a very faithful and generous man. All of a sudden, a big, tall man popped up from the rear side. He was gibbering something in Greek language. It seemed like Pete knew that voice.

That man was as tall as a volleyball player. His long hair resembled Bono's in the 1990s. His age was around sixty, and his face looked like a pure European. His name was Jim. Pete always laughed at Jim's jokes. Jim was a foreman working for Pete. He controlled and managed the business when Pete wasn't available, which was most of the time. Regardless, Pete always showed up to check the work process.

Jim was a slipshod electrician. Whatever he touched, it would either break or had to be redone. Everybody knew how bad Jim was, even Pete. Despite that, Jim had a beneficial ability to save time. He was very organized. Jim would give you a proper task intended merely for you. Usually, he purchased materials for the jobs. Presumably, that was why Pete liked him so much. At the next moment, someone yelled, expressing a strong Mexican accent, "Jim, are you ready?"

Jim replied, "Poppa, come over. The coffee is here!" Instantly, the door opened, and bright light tore up the darkness. A strong burly Mexican man bobbed from the entry. The Mexican man looked to be in his fifties. He took off his pouch and stepped closer. His name was Ventura. He had a mustache like Joaquin "El Chapo" Guzman and shaggy, curly hair. His glamourous smile was always streaming.

Ventura had a bullish body. He was the man. Ventura was doing most of the work. He had more than twenty years of experience in the electrical field. If there was something that could not be done, we called Ventura. He was creative, and at the same time, he worked incredibly fast. Ventura was a typical Mexican beaver; if we would give him tacos and burritos, he would work all day long. Also, Ventura was a delightful man. He loved to talk about any topic. His personality was extremely friendly. I had never seen anyone working so hard and, at the same time, having casual chitchats.

Ventura was a professional employee. Regularly, he was the man who restored Jim's "magic" touch. His guidance taught me how to draw more attention at work. Behind Ventura, another man strolled. He was bald, wearing specs, and had a body as big as the Mexican bull. His name was Perry, the son-in-law of Pete.

Perry was an electrical engineer, expressing a plethora of acknowledgement. He portrayed delightful behavior. We had a gob of chats on diverse topics. Perry was a good man; he had helped me a bunch. Pete called all of us for a short coffee break. He often bought us coffee. Also, he took us to restaurants for lunch, especially when we had to work extremely hard.

Pete was an amazing man, and I wanted to maintain my association with him. Working for him sometimes was extremely difficult and sophisticated. On some days, we had to connect fixture lights at huge storage freezers with temperatures below zero, standing on slippery twelve-foot ladders. The toughest part was when we had to connect lights powered by 277 volts when the electrical power was on. That meant we couldn't afford to make any slipups, not even one.

Occasionally, we had to work in uncomfortable places and conditions such as attics or foundation levels, digging dirt a few feet underground by using shovels. Furthermore, we labored on electric scissors lifts, drivable one-man lifts, and push-around lifts on streetlights and high industrial ceilings. We installed huge pipes.

In those pipes were pulled the main electrical wires to the panels which connect electrical meters powered by street transformers. The bottom line was that we did everything related to the electrical industry, such as commercial, residential, and industrial jobs.

Often, the city had to send a certified electrical inspector to examine a specific part of the job. Many particular methods and rules had to be followed by the national electrical code. If you messed up something, the inspector would not accept your work, which meant you had to reschedule another appointment. Then, the city had to charge the owner of the particular project an additional fee for sending back the inspector. It was a hassle.

If you didn't pass inspection, the work took longer, people were losing money, and everyone got pissed. It was essential to avoid those hindrances. That was why Pete counted on Jim. He was a union employee. He was the man responsible for ushering the electrical inspectors and making sure he would pass the inspection. Jim was persuasive. I didn't know what he talked to those inspectors about, but he had always passed those inspections.

The game plan was to ask Vinny for permission to work at a different construction company. I couldn't just leave Vinny without calling. It would be rude and disrespectful. When we spoke over the phone, Vinny told me, "Boy, if you want to work for this Greek man, that's fine with me. Just come tomorrow for your last day, and we'll be cool."

We made an easy consensus, and the following morning, I drove to the address that Vinny had provided. It was a gorgeous house located in the outskirts. He gave me instructions to wait for him inside. I parked on the driveway and walked to the main door. It's so loud. The others must have already been laboring. I stepped through the door, and BOOM! Holy cow! What the heck! A sledgehammer dropped in front of my feet. Completely bemused, I looked upon the second floor, and someone shouted,

"Sorry, watch out!" Frenzied, I hollered at the top of my lungs.

"What's the matter with you? Be careful out there. Jesus!" It was eight in the morning, and I was already bummed out. Just think about it. What would happen if that hammer had fallen on my head? On that day, I didn't wear any safety construction helmet. Later, I found out that the man who had dropped that frigging hammer was a Polish guy who worked for a heating service company. Often, those guys showed up plastered at work. It was very immature and irresponsible to be drunk at work. Thank God nothing worse happened. Don't get me wrong; I don't mind those Polish guys. I had met a bunch of Polish friends in my life. My last day working for Vinny was abnormal. At the end of the working day, we wished each other good luck and took different directions. I would always be thankful for what Vinny did for me.

*****

Working for Pete was a fascinating and dynamic. Although when I drifted back from work, I was bored and suppressed. My mind hollered. What the heck am I gonna do now? Can't just go to bed at seven. I'm a spring chicken at the age of twenty-six, not an old fart in his eighties.

Often, I drove over to the package store to grab some bevy. Then, I gulped booze till the alcohol knocked me out cold. Drinking alcohol turned into my usual routine. That was an awful lifestyle. I gained over forty pounds. I had never been that heavy. It made me feel vexed. Week after week, the amount of alcohol consumption doubled. I metamorphosed into a pure alky.

Nah, I can't live like that. This ain't my thing. I need to figure out doing something like a hobby. But what? Mike passed out early in the evenings.

He loved to sleep. His boss forced him to work harder. When Mike crashed, I listened to music with my headphones. It cheered me up, reminding me of the path to success. As I roamed through the kitchen, I accidentally threw a punch in the air. Whoa! This is cool. Do it again!

I started throwing punches again and again. That's it. I got it. I'm going to learn boxing. After a quick cyber research, I bumped into a few boxing gyms in Schaumburg, Addison, etc. Unfortunately, they were too far. Then, someone told me about a gym named Hyper, located in the same neighborhood around two miles away.

At the drop of a hat, I went to this gym and signed up for boxing classes for beginners. Those classes were held twice a week. Hyper was a Polish American gym. I had met a bunch of great trainers and members out there. Two guys owned that gym. One of them was the notorious Andrzej Fonfara. His name was engraved in boxing history, with thirty-five pro fights in the light heavyweight division. He was a hardworking boxer. He was busy and rarely appeared at Hyper. The other owner was Bill. He was in his early thirties, tall and strong like a hammer. He wasn't a professional boxer, but he trained like a pro. Bill devoted most of his life to martial arts. He was a vital member in Fonfara's corner. Bill knew how to train and prepare you to be a successful fighter.

Another coach from Puerto Rico trained us. His name was Joe. He guided us through general boxing techniques. He had a big beard and long hair that looked like Bin Laden. His body was ripped, almost like Bruce Lee. Joe tutored us in diverse exercises on how to develop a naturally stronger body. His training philosophy was interesting, and his friendly sense of humor put colors in his lessons.

Joe's methods of training drew my attention drastically. The following six months of those training sessions were extremely intense and tough for my two-hundred-pound body. Sometimes, it felt like I was going to spit my kidneys out (you know what I mean). Nonetheless, I didn't quit. It motivated me to train harder.

One of my favorite stages in boxing was punching the bags. It helped me to release the stress from work. A year later, I switched the classes up to five times per week. Thereby, I built some advanced boxing skills and piled up enough composure. I decided to attempt sparring sessions. My enthusiasm in learning boxing had enhanced with every other week. I lost more than thirty pounds.

On my first sparring day, I was scared to death. My thoughts were. Dude, what if you get seriously hit? Is this the right thing to do? Another voice yelled. Stop crying like a little girl. If they hit you, so what? Protect yourself and try to hit back. Usually, those sparring sessions at Hyper were on Friday night. The first months of sparring, they walloped my ass. The only way to learn boxing was by practicing through sparring. The experience of sparring was unique. Once, a well-known man in boxing history had told me, "You can't teach experience." That is absolutely true.

The boxing coaches could only show you the door, but you had to be bold enough to go through that door. At that time, I was astonished how a man could acquire acknowledgment by a genuine fight. In my opinion, you need to have your heart in boxing before committing a fight.

It was a regular Friday night. I hopped into the ring to spar against an unfamiliar American man. He was a strong whitey. His equipment cost a bundle. After we finished, the American guy quipped, "What's your nationality?" (Apparently, my accent slapped him on the face).

"Bulgaria. Do you know this country?" I questioned him. Then, the American whitey started speaking in a broken

Bulgarian. He sounded like a gypsy version of Bulgarian. Wait, what? Who is this guy? He is not Bulgarian. That was how I bumped into Erik Sobczak. He was around 175 pounds. Erik was six years older than me, but he trained as if he was six years younger. Erik knew so much about my country because he was hitched by a Bulgarian woman. He had been traveling in cities and places in Bulgaria that I had never been.

Erik had a good sense of humor and a great personality. We became good friends. He enjoyed listening to Bulgarian folk music, something that I thought was hilarious. A few weeks later, he got a controversial diss with a Bulgarian gal. She had recently started working at the front desk. Erik was frustrated. He moved to train into another boxing club located in Franklin Park.

It had been several months since I started sparring sessions, and I prepared for my first official fight. Every day, I was thrilled to train at Hyper. Bill was looking forward finding me an opponent in some amateur boxing event. Unfortunately, he couldn't find any. Led by the craze to fight, my nut sack sweated as I trained harder for the most essential amateur boxing tournament named Golden Gloves. Every amateur longed to earn the belt from Golden Gloves. Why? If you were an open fighter (which meant you had more than ten official bouts) and you won Golden Gloves, you would be automatically enrolled to participate in the U.S. nationals.

That most likely would enhance your chance to develop a professional career. In other words, Golden Gloves was your ticket to become a pro boxer. That was the reason why everyone longed to fight in this tournament. The most legendary boxing names in history, such as Mike Tyson, Floyd Mayweather, Muhammad Ali, etc., had won Golden Gloves. Many successful boxers were proud of their trophies and belts collected from Golden Gloves before they became KO makers.

The tournament was held at a basketball arena called Cicero Stadium. I signed up in the senior novice division, which meant all fighters had no more than nine bouts in the official boxing book. It wasn't the best decision to participate in Golden Gloves without any fights. I longed to prove how dangerous I was. I didn't care who would be at the other side of the corner or how big he was and how many bouts he had won.

A week before the fight, Mike and I had dinner at the apartment in Denley. Out of the blue, he talked about a friend named Jordan. He was recently deceased, hit by a giant hook of a railroad crane during the process of work. It was a sad tragedy.

Mike introduced me to Jordan a long time ago. He was around my age and was a thickset Bulgarian man. He never stopped smiling. Jordan knew how to enjoy his life. I had never heard Jordan complain about anything. We were hanging out in numerous music spectacles, and we had a ball. Jordan had a friendly behavior. Mike had a genius idea. He customized T-shirts that had Jordan's photo. His agenda was to wear Jordan's shirts at the fight night.

The day before Golden Gloves, I visited a Bulgarian Orthodox church named Saint Sofia. That church had bewitching architecture. There were fascinating icons painted inside. I slunk into the chapel, and prayed to the Lord. That place always had made me feel placid. The fight night took place in the first week of March 2017. Mike brought the shirts to the Cicero Stadium, and we paid tribute to Jordan by wearing those shirts and posting some pictures on social media. Mike made the presence of Jordan alive. It was a memorable moment that would always be in my mind. RIP, Jordan. You are not forgotten.

The tournament launched around the afternoon. Every fighter had to check in at the scale section. Then, we had to see a physician. Regularly, twenty bouts had been scheduled each day due to the finals. There were fifteen bouts ahead, which meant my fight should be after two and a half hours. Forty minutes before my fight, I made a dumb mistake. You will get the picture of what I am trying to say. I headed to the restroom to dress up. Bill was waiting for me to wrap up my hands. Closing the door of the male restroom, I pulled out a small baggie filled up with coco and nimbly did the pre-workout. Ah, what a feeling! My eyesight got sharp, and my body perceived almighty strength. I returned to the bench where Bill was waiting. The enthusiasm to fight jazzed me up. I was feeling like a cat on hot bricks. My bout was the next. The closer I strolled to the ring, the more nervous I was. A bunch of my friends came to watch the boxing event. All of them shouted and bellowed my last name. Glimpsing at them brought me a sip of confidence.

When I hopped in the ring, the adrenaline boiled my blood like water on the oven. The referee had to check the gloves, headgear, and mouth guard for safety purposes. I stepped close to the opponent. The rival was a white Wonder Bread and looked like he had just come back from a mission in Afghanistan. He was shorter than me and much heftier. Everybody was staring at the ring.

Let's get ready to rumble! That was it. The gong struck loudly. We both went bananas. I threw bombs like a minigun, but the power wasn't there. The rival looked like a dogface. He chased me like a raging bull. I could see his snake eyes through the boxing helmet. He tried to muscle me out. He was using his body to shove me into the ropes.

Going backward was my biggest mistake. At that time, I didn't have a clue how dynamic it would be to fight someone in the ring. After the end of the first round, during the break, I sat on the stool entirely knackered. While Bill was giving instructions, my eyes were slowly closing, and I passed out. Bill panicked. He slapped me a few times and shook my shoulders. He yelled,

"Hey, Dimitry, wake up. What the fuck! You are fighting!"

Momentarily, my eyes opened. Holy cow! Was I sleeping? There was no time for answers. The gong struck again. Round 2 was pretty much the same as the first one. The dogface was pursuing me, and I used my power to hold him in a clinch. The game plan was to save some time, which was another slipup. Why? Imagine what would happen if you would hold somebody stronger than you. The answer is simple: you would get tired twice as fast. It was pointless. It didn't make any sense. The second round ended as we were cuddling by the ropes.

In amateur boxing, the bouts proceeded up to three rounds, and for senior novice fighters, it took no longer than two minutes per round. In the third round, we both got bushed. The rhythm slowed down fundamentally. My sluggish pummels kept the dogface away. The rival acted like a bull. He bowed his head down and attacked straight ahead. He couldn't see what was in front of him, and I pressed his head beyond the ropes.

Luckily, that man had an awful defense, which gave me the chance to score more points. I tried to perform the best of myself. In the meantime, the crowd hollered thirstily and loudly. The Bulgarian folks were screaming my name as if I was a local champion. In the last thirty seconds, the fight streamed in slow motion.

The next moment, the gong shrieked. I took a deep breath. Bill took off my headgear. The referee gave me a sign to come nearby. The ref held both fighters' hands and whispered,

"The other contender had won the fight. You know that, right?" Peering at him, I merely shrugged like I was saying, "It is what it is. I've done whatever I could". The next second, the referee raised my hand as a winner. My thoughts were. You mother flower! The referee sniggered, radiating facetious visage. That was one of the most unforgettable moments in my life. I was the happiest man on earth. I thanked everybody, especially the coach. Bill was the man who had the most contribution to this bout. I won the fight in a split decision. The dogface was a tough boxer. He didn't quit, but I was the winner.

*****

A week ahead, there was another bout scheduled in the semifinal stage of Golden Gloves. I pulled my socks up and trained harder. The approaching bout would be more arduous against someone who had won his fight as well. My purpose was to wrap up that tournament as further as I could.

Golden Gloves had been an honorary tournament for decades. Hundreds of skilled boxers were ready to eviscerate others. A few hours before my fight, I wandered to Saint Sofia to express my grace to the Lord. Talking to God was vital to me. It was always good to visit a church. It built up a foundation in my subconscious. Also, it removed any negative thoughts.

The fight day came to pass. I did the same process, weight in and medical check, but also I made another mistake by snorting white chalk in the commode. The adrenaline was higher than Willis Tower. I was edgy like the last week, but this time, I had a scoop of confidence. Thrilled, I hopped on the ring.

My mind was steady and ready for battle. My agenda was to trigger sharp performance. The rival was a bald Russian dozer. He was taller than me, which meant he got longer arms. His long reach was an advantage. The Russian dozer came for a bloody war.

The gong rumbled, and both of us jumped fiercely to each other like two frenzied animals. His long arms were annoying. I was unable to cut the distance. Moving my head was an option but wasn't enough to win the fight. I was trying to figure out how to stop him. Turning on the beast mode wasn't successful as expected. I had been forced to protect and cover myself repeatedly. I heard Bill saying, "Move your head side to side!"

He constantly bawled at the corner. It was the last seconds of the first round, and I was still failing to score more points. It was a moment before the round completed, and…BOOM! It was like lightning struck in the stadium. Every noise at the sports center muted. Vertigo shook me deeply.

The referee loomed in front of me. My eyelids blinked like a light bulb just about to die. The Russian dozer caught me with his right looped hook. The gong had blasted and the round was over. I almost collapsed on the canvas.

My hazed vision got back to normal. The ref continued making the count even if the round was over. It was a confusing situation. The ref managed to stop the fight for safety purposes even when he saw a sign of my request to proceed. I respectfully disagreed with the ref's decision. But the resolution was made, and there was nothing I could do about it.

The Russian iceberg might be considered as the better boxer that night. However, the fight shouldn't have been stopped, especially when the first round was over. The boxing referees had great storage of experience. Some of them had made tremendous contributions in pro competitions. In pro fights, the referee could let the battle keep going on and on, depending on a fighter's condition. In amateur leagues, the referee would most likely stop the bout after a quick determination.

I returned home feeling as awful as some highbrow who'd failed an important exam in college. I sat on the couch at Denley Building with a painful headache, contemplating what had happened at Cicero Stadium. Thank God I have no major injuries. The voice in my head said. To participate in tournaments such as Golden Gloves was not a joke. Every year, a plethora of gifted boxers fought for glory, trophies, and belts. They might knock you down before you notice.

When you won a fight, you perceived yourself as a good, gifted boxer who might have a glamourous career in the future. I can be a great champion. That's my time. My steps will soon bring me over the top.

I just need to concentrate and keep moving on. If you lose, it will happen as precisely as the opposite reaction. I am the worst boxer in the world. What a shame. I can't believe what I've done. I've trained so hard for this fight, and I screwed up. I should have performed better, etc. The disappointment from that fight tore my inspiration apart. Then, I stood up on my feet and said, "You will keep training hard, and next time, you will come back stronger. That is not your last fight. You need more practice to create better performance."

The consequences threw fireworks of emotions, which made me love and adore boxing even more. It was remarkable how this sport affected people's minds. Boxing brought me an abundance of audacity and confidence. This sport became part of my life.

Chapter 12

It was the first week of May 2017, I cruised back from work. Mike sat on the couch wearing a deadpan face, like a murderer ready to commit a brutal confession. He spoke slowly,

"We have an offer for a two-bedroom apartment. Great price, within the same neighborhood. Are you interested?"

"Go ahead," I said.

Mike continued comfortably. "Two Bulgarian tenants are moving out of a furnished two-bedroom apartment. They suggest that we should look at the apartment. Do you want to check it?"

"Let's go," I said. That apartment was on the third floor in a town house a mile and a half away. That flat was huge compared to the tiny shithole in Denley Building. There were two large bedrooms, a kitchen, and an airy living room. The only issue was that place hadn't been taken care of over the years. Nevertheless, it was a good option, and the price was affordable. We accepted the offer, and the following week, we were dwelling in that furnished two-bedroom apartment. The previous tenants had called it Motel Zero because it was a thousand times worse than Motel X. We relocated from a tiny shithole to a huge hobo shack for a hundred dollars more per month. It wasn't a bad deal. Motel Zero was located on a street called Jill Lane. In that street were lined up around ten town houses of precisely the same size. The only difference was that the town house of Motel Zero was covered with ivy bushes. It looked creepy, especially at night. We didn't need any decorations for Halloween.

*****

As the days passed by, I couldn't accept the downfall of my last bout. The top priority on my agenda was to come back in the ring. My zeal was concentrated on stepping up my game and starting to perform better. When the boxing classes wound up, everybody nimbly left the gym (It was like they would miss watching the Game of Thrones). I did another boxing class. Pulling my socks in training was my primary intention. My time spent at Hyper got doubled, and often I drove back home entirely whacked out. That was how I liked it. The love in this sport became unconditional. That sport metamorphosed into bacteria that was lollygagging in my body for an unclassified amount of time.

*****

Coaches Bill and Joe had some altercations regarding the coaching method in boxing classes. They both were great leaders, but each of them had different structures of training. Bill concentrated more on dynamic practice. When he would pad with you, he literally would suck your energy. His idea was to push you over and help you develop a combination of incredible speed and technique. Bill always checked how we practiced and corrected us if it was necessary. His training style projected an astounding effect. Joe's methods were based on tuition lessons. He palavered about boxing history. Joe rendered an educational material focused on detailed boxing techniques. His theories mesmerized us. He successfully set up a social relationship among us. We all loved Joe's instructions. We did a bunch of variety exercises guided by him. Alas, it wasn't as intense as Bill requested. That was why Bill was getting frustrated. The beef between them came out in a particular training class. Bill, as an employer, gave friendly instructions to Joe to work on a more active training process. Joe was getting a bit overwhelmed. He disapproved Bill's tips and continued to run the show in his way, and that was driving Bill nuts. They remained chill and acted professionally. In some cases, I saw how they yearned to beat each other. The sparks among these guys continued for the next few months, then Joe mysteriously disappeared. He just stopped visiting Hyper as a coach. Bill was too busy managing the whole system of the gym. There were many different class programs, such as dumbbell strength and fitting training camp, in which he was in charge. He needed somebody to replace Joe. One day, I cruised over to Hyper and got ready to make my balls schweddy. On that day, we were ten guys taking boxing classes. It had been a few minutes already, and we still waited for our coach to kick off the class. Bill wasn't there, which was seldom. Fonfara was in California, preparing for his next fight. Then who was going to train us? At that moment, all of us looked at each other, trying to figure out what was going on. All of a sudden, a voice hollered loudly from elsewhere. "Pain is coming. I said pain is coming! Be aware!"

What the heck? Who is this guy? I thought.

A man in his early thirties rushed in Hyper radiating and imposing energy as if the boxing gym was his home. His name was Donovan George, most well-known as DON DA BOMB. Don was a boxing legend with a professional record of thirty-six bouts and twenty-five defeats with twenty-two by KO. Don had a prominent name in Chi-town. He was a three-time Golden Gloves champion and had an incredible performance in nationals. He turned a pro at the age of nineteen and conquered a lot of belts including the International Boxing Organization (IBO) World Super Middleweight title. The training sessions with him were fascinating. Don's methods helped us to explore boxing outstandingly. His contribution enhanced my obsession with this sport. Don's guidance gave us a deeper notion of the boxing world. His instructions allowed us to improve our ability to work out by expressing extraordinary energy. Don showed us how to practice by putting our hearts into boxing. Moreover, he taught boxing by using his own heart. That made him a successful leader. Many pro boxers who already started a pro career would beg Don to train them. It was because they knew that he would give them the right directions to accomplish significant results. Eventually, more and more students popped up into Don's training classes. The reason why was purely his method of training.

*****

Two weeks later, Bill announced that he would organize a Hyper Night at some school district nearby. He added, "I got opponent for you. Are you interested?"

"Hell yeah. I have been waiting for this opportunity since my last bout," I exclaimed. The official date of this event was scheduled a day before my birthday, which allowed me a great option to make myself the best present. Once again, I had to push the envelope of reaching out a remarkable performance.

Hyper had incredible benefits. Every member who frequently visited the gym got an alternative pass card providing them with twenty-four-hour access. A few buddies and I used this gym access to visit Hyper on the weekends, beating each other. There were situations when we had bleeding noses or when someone punched unexpectedly harder than usual, but that was the routine. We were boxers, not ballet dancers. An eventual victory would bring me back on track after the last disputed loss. The aftermath from my previous fight bothered me for the last couple of weeks but also had affected a stimulation to develop successful termination. It was incredible how the highlights from my recent bout would indicate my persistence in pursuing my target. Boxing had a structure that provided happiness.

The anticipated day came. It was time to take another journey in the boxing world. Once again, I stopped by the Saint Sofia church to make my appeal to the Master of the Universe.

The event had to kick off in the basketball arena of the school center. My applause to Bill; he made the event look legit. Bill hired a DJ to keep the crowd awake. There were a bunch of VIP tables spread around the ring. Plenty of food was served for every guest. Moreover, an enormous television platform would be streaming live the Fonfara's fight for the WBC title. The ring was in great condition. They even brought ring girls, which boosted the quality of the event. That spectacle was for amateurs. They made it look like a professional boxing event.

The school center got packed swiftly. There were around four hundred boxing fans. As Michael Buffer said, "Let's get ready for rumble!" The fight card had ten bouts scheduled for this competition. My exhibition bout was placed as the main event. It wasn't for any particular reason, just a spontaneous decision made by Bill.

That night, I switched the weight division from light heavyweight (178 pounds) to middleweight (165 pounds). When I was fighting in Golden Gloves, my weight was around 170, and I fought against opponents who were seven to eight pounds heavier than me. That was a tremendous difference in pound-for-pound battles.

The adrenaline flushed sparks in my mind. I felt excited and nervous. It was a repetitive psychological circle before any fight. At that moment, I was ready to hop at the ring and start throwing bombs. An hour before my bout, I headed to the restroom. I made another mistake. I freebased and snorted a few rails of the white lady. Straight away, my vision sharpened and my concentration enhanced drastically.

After winding up the dippy process, I quickly returned backstage to bundle up. Dozens of my buddies showed up in the school center to bolster my performance. They were ready to bawl my name at the top of their lungs. It is vital to hear your name yelled by your supporters. Bill gave us tickets to sell and make some money on the side. I gave all of my tickets to my friends for free. I didn't want to make a profit. To me, boxing wasn't a moneymaker dream.

It was a penchant that my heart had beaten for. The school center had become rowdy since the first bout commenced. The whole crowd was jonesing to watch the spectacular event. Finally, it was time for the main event. I boldly promenaded to the ring. It was hilarious how the boxing speakers wrongly announced my last name. I didn't give a damn what they were calling me. The most important thing was my performance. That was all I cared about.

That was one of the reasons why I loved boxing. When you jumped in the ring, the ball would be in your court. The sincerest place on the globe was the boxing ring (and I guess the UFC cage too). Once you jumped in, there wasn't time to talk trash, except on the cases when you were fighting a bum. You would enter the ring and show what you have got.

The referee made a routine check on both of us. My buddies screamed my name constantly. The other contender was a white cracker with the same height and age as me. He wasn't portraying acrimonious behavior. That didn't determine what he was capable of. Don't judge the book by its cover. You cannot underestimate your rivals. If you had made it, you would also have been in a state of shock as if your face would light up like you've been struck by lightning.

Here we go again. It's showtime! After the signal had been released, we both fluttered as bumblebees attempting to chase each other. Initially, the two of us bounced uncertainly. The first few punches from each side were awkward or, let's say, not related to boxing. The white American bird shit tried desperately to find a way of hurting me efficiently. There was no doubt about that.

Luckily, his jabs were harmless and even kind. That gave me a chance to perform better by putting in the extra effort. I took control of the fight by pushing him. That was how the first round ended. The second round broadcasted pretty much the same picture. With my basic straightforward technique, I muscled out the white cracker and pressed him to the ropes. Thereby, he was forced to move backward, which served as an opportunity to cut him off.

The chance for a knockout had been exposed. I used all of my power to put him comatose. Unfortunately, I didn't have enough acknowledgment to knock him out. In the meantime, the Bulgarian folks kept screaming my name, especially Mike. He had a profusion of experience yelling at soccer games back home. His voice echoed influentially around the whole center.

The third round wasn't different from the others. My strategy was to keep shoving the white cracker to the ropes. We both got tired. The American opponent endured against my frenzied raids. After all of my efforts, he successfully stood vertical and remained balanced. In the last seconds, the two of us turned on survival mode. A few punches were thrown around, and BOOM! That was it. The gong's sound blasted like a gunshot. Everybody at the center applauded us, especially my buddies. The American rival wasn't tough. It was just that my knowledge and power weren't enough to drop him.

No one pays tributes to a boxer with no power in his punches, but they would honor you if you could take hard blows.

After the final round, the two of us paid respect for each other by touching gloves. We both fought respectfully and clean. The decision had been taken rapidly. The ref raised my hand as a winner by split decision. It didn't happen the way I was expecting. Regardless, that victory was a gift, which couldn't make me irked.

After the fight, all of my folks came to Motel Zero to commemorate my recent success. June 3, 2017, had been stored in my mind as one of the most memorable birthdays that I ever had. I would always be grateful to God. He blessed me with such an incredible present.

Chapter 13

After the fight at the school center, I decided to hit the brake of the train. There weren't any scheduled fight events ahead. I decided to loosen up, just a smidgen. It was the summer season. I began to screw around with my buddies, although I hadn't stopped working out at the gym.

It was a scorcher Sunday. A friend of mine asked me to join his barbecue party in some public park district nearby Motel Zero. At the drop of a hat, I decided to accept his invitation. We were a few guys goofing around in that park. Chris was preparing arrachera on the grill. He was a nice guy with a curvy body, blond hair, and a twinkling smile.

Stan and his Mexican girlfriend waited for Chef Chris's food. Stan was a Bulgarian spring chicken. He always loved to dress like a stock market businessman. He was a short man, a peculiar yuppie who was as quiet as a tropical lizard. His job was associated with computer design.

Val and I had the responsibility to organize plates, drinks, forks, knives, etc. Val was a smart-ass motormouth. He loved to talk about every subject. Sometimes, he could be vexed by the way he was talking. Despite that, Val was an indulgent and friendly guy. He looked like the emoji portraying a smirking face. Fifteen minutes later, Val announced, "Listen up, guys. I have to get something. I'll be right back." We had no clue what he was talking about.

Chris and I had a good conversation. In the following seconds, Chris exclaimed, "Dimitry, look!" I turned around and goggled like a baffled owl. Holy cow! What a move! Is this for real, or do I have some hallucinations? What a body. What a hair. A drop-dead gorgeous chick as stunning as Ariana Grande swaggered along with Val. He held her hand as if he was going to propose. Her name was Klara. Her body was as fit as my favorite actress, Halle Berry. Her Hispanic skin drew my attention.

Staring at Klara, I stood immobile like a statue. Speechless, I couldn't resist her beauty. At that moment, somebody had to slap or punch me in the face to wake me up. Klara became my crush from the moment I saw her. Come on, dude! Don't show any weakness! Pretend that you are not interested! Portraying a poker face, I offered her to drink something. Initially, Klara acted like an abrasive person. Therefore, my behavior was a bit apathetic.

Klara revealed that her age was thirty-five, but she looked no more than twenty-five. Unbelievable! Val confirmed her age. They graduated high school together. That was how they had known each other. Klara had a natural beauty. She didn't need any makeup, and that was why my attraction rose significantly. The picture of how I met Klara would never be erased from my database. I could write about her for days, months, etc.

Let me ask you a question, have you met somebody who gives you the impression that you have known each other since you were born? That was how I felt when we started talking. Klara was the one who started chatting with me, and we had a decent conversation. Then, I changed into a more casual subject by asking ubiquitous questions. One of them was, "Klara, what do you do for a living?"

She replied, "I play violin."

"Wow, that's dope. You must be enjoying while you are playing," I continued, and she merely nodded. Klara was one of those kinds of art chicks who I was down for. That made me to crave her even more. At the next moment, Klara threw a glimpse at my T-shirt, which depicted the logo of two boxers peering at each other with the slogan of Golden Gloves.

"You do boxing?" she uttered, perplexed.

"Yeah," I shrugged, streaming cockiness. Then, Klara started talking about boxing. She expressed a basic knowledge of boxing history. Holy

Moses! She likes boxing! How cool is that? We discussed the upcoming boxing fight between the boxing legend, Floyd

Mayweather, and the beast of mixed martial arts, Conor McGregor. We ran into an argument, and both placed a bet in to determine the winner. Klara stacked fifty bucks for Connor, and I made a call for Mayweather.

We both leered at each other like those American western movies with Mexican standoff confrontations. The way she gazed at me was as if she was saying, "You will lose, dude!" And my face was expressing, "Girl, you don't know what the duck you are talking about!" There was some chemistry between us. I could tell that she was kind of interested as well. My heart was bouncing like a nipper for chocolate, but my mind sent notifications: Warning! Warning! Warning!

There was a significant reason why my common sense alerted me. Back home, when I was a nineteen-year-old spring chicken, foolish and unexperienced, I headed to some nightclub crammed with a bunch of ravers. I bumped into a girl accidentally. Her name was Sabina. We started chatting. We both were high on barbiturates. Then, straight away, she made a move and started kissing me. Unbelievable! I was puzzled. We started dating, and after two weeks, I was head over heels in love with her.

Sabina loved to talk. She knew how to put a man in a spot. But there was something that bothered me; her character was too vicious. No matter what had happened between us, I kept pursuing her. She was supposed to be a slamhole, but I wanted her to be my sugarboo. After two months of dating, we decided to spend a New Year's Eve together. A day before, Sabina texted me that she couldn't make it. On that day, my heart was brutally broken, and the pain was killing me. Sabina wanted to burn the bridges of our relationship. My head was up in the clouds. I chased her again and again. For some unexplainable reason, she always came back. We broke up and got back together four or five times.

I was fooling around, and wasting my time by chasing her for about two years. There wasn't any specific reason why she had left me. Sabina was a complete mess. She was promiscuous, switching men like I was changing my shirts. Sabina was the first person who broke my heart. It took a while before I returned to the mack.

In the end, I erased everything that connected me with her. That was the only cure that worked to bring me back on track. Since then, I have learned my lesson to protect myself from being blinded by love. There was an indescribable desire that I was perpetually infatuated with Sabina, and I felt the same way to this broad named Klara. That was why my mind alerted me with a warning.

Back to the barbecue scene, I was thinking of asking Klara for her phone number. What should I do? Listen to my heart or my mind? Maybe hundreds of men would try to get her contact information, but I decided not to take any action and let her go. After a few minutes, Klara walked away, leaving with a glamorous influence. Ah man! That girl is a crowd-pleaser. Thank God she is far away. Now, I am feeling better.

Thereby, I was lying to myself. On the next day, I cyberstalked Klara, and searched her on Google. Instantly, I found a few videos on YouTube of how Klara played violin. I had never listened to a violin performance before. It looked cool. Two weeks later, a few buddies and I cruised into the closest bar to watch the battle between Mayweather and McGregor. I wasn't eager to monitor this exhibition fight. Mayweather took control of the fight; and at round 10, the ref, Robert Byrd, had been forced to stop this bout.

Mayweather scored a plethora of clean shots. McGregor barely could defend himself. In my opinion, as an amateur, that fight was finished before it had even started. I wasn't too excited to watch it in the first place. Both fighters made tons of money that night, especially the winner. Also, many guys made tons of money, and one girl owed me fifty bucks, which I doubted if I would ever get.

*****

A few weeks later at the boxing gym, Bill approached me. He offered me to participate in an upcoming tournament called King of the Jungle, and I took the challenge. That tournament had to take action within the next couple of weeks. That was why I trained harder. King of the Jungle was organized by a sport district near Naperville. The athletic club had a comprehensive structure. That boxing event was spectacular. A plethora of boxers traveled from different states to fight at that tournament.

I was bouncing on the ring like a child on a trampoline. The fight was about to start, and my eyes were closing as if I was falling asleep like a baby leaning against his mother's bosom. The other contender was American Hispanic. I sized him up. He was much younger and stronger. His fuming face looked like he had just been robbed by some burglar.

Here we go again! The gong rumbled loudly. The rival hawked me like an insane crackhead. He turned for an onslaught, trying to knock me down literally in the first few seconds. My mistake was going backward that gave him the chance to push me to the ropes. The ability to defend myself was the key surviving in round 1.

The rival indisputably won the first round. When the second round growled, I was already worn out. The contender noticed the low percentage of my battery and incessantly swung punches that caused me to lean on the ropes. He looked like a wrathful bulldog hankering to tear off flesh.

In the third round, we were both moving around like grannies. Regardless, we tried to kill each other. The Hispanic bulldog got bushed by using most of his energy in the previous rounds, and I looked to put him to sleep and wrap up this bout as a winner. The first two rounds were given to the bulldog, which meant I desperately needed to knock him down to chalk up a successful performance. The gong blasted, and the two of us cuddled like best friends.

It was glorious when two bruisers were trying to beat each other and, after the final gong, they showed respect to each other. The ref lifted the hand of the American bulldog. I got frustrated. My performance wasn't good enough. I had never expressed my frustration in boxing events; I had always bottled it in my heart. The American bulldog deserved the victory. He was the better boxer that night. There was no excuse for being so sluggish, even if I had slogged hard at my job earlier the same day.

It bugged me the fact that I could win that fight. I could be the winner, and that drove me nuts. Pondering about my loss, I couldn't drift off to a complete sleep. My thoughts about the downfall had built anxiety and nagged me intermittently. Overwhelmed, I started to focus on boxing more intensely. There was only one way to make me feel better, and that was to triumph with another victory. Thus, I started training harder and kept looking for another chance to fight.

Chapter 14

It had been two years since I had been working with those Greek guys. Pete had always helped me. He knew that I was a person to be trusted. Sometimes, when my car broke down, Pete gave me a ride to work. He was like my grandpa.

Once in a while, he invited me to his house for the holidays. As days passed by, my knowledge in the electrical field had grown. It was a sophisticated job carrying a lot of stressful situations. However, that was how I liked it. Pete placed me to work with Jim. The reason why was that Jim was one of a kind, a walking disaster. One day, Jim picked me up from home because my car had gone kaput. We had to replace three light fixtures about fifteen feet high outside of the restaurant located an hour away driving southbound.

When we arrived, the owner, Keith, saluted us as if we were kings. He was an overweight Greek man, the savviest guy I have ever met. Keith knew how to manage the restaurant's business. He was a billionaire. Jim brought a double extension ladder and tilted it on the wall. I couldn't stand those ladders. They had never been safely secured unless we tighten them up. It was what it was. I had to bite the bullet and get used to it. The first two fixtures had been removed and replaced on my own. Jim held the ladder and observed how precisely and smoothly I worked.

Jim placed the ladder next to the third light fixture. I got a phone call from my mechanic.

"Jim, I have to pick up the phone."

"Yeah, that's fine. No worries. I will finish the last fixture."

I picked up the phone, and in the meantime, Jim climbed on the ladder. We both had no safety helmets. Using both of my hands, I grabbed the ladder. I leaned my head to cradle the phone by pressing my ear against my arm. Jim struggled. He failed to remove the glass lid of that old fixture. Pulling out those light fixtures wasn't easy because they were heavy and so cumbersome to work with.

Those objects had thick glass in the front, and if you would not know how properly to detach the glass lid, you would be screwed. Jim's method of work was offhand, the opposite of my pattern. When something went wrong, Jim was getting frustrated, and that forced him to swear in Greek language. Suddenly, Jim said, "Don't look up here!"

Talking on the phone, I obeyed his command without capturing what he meant. Then BOOM! Glass shreds had fallen on top of my head.

"Jim! What the duck are you doing? Are you nuts, crazy ass? Jesus!" I screamed at the top of my lungs. "Why did you have to break the entire glass?" The only rational explanation was that was how Jim worked. One piece of glass had hit my spine, causing me pain for a month. Thank God nothing major had happened. All of us knew how Jim operated, even Pete.

One day, Ventura, Jim, and I went for a lunch break in a Mexican restaurant. Ventura and I were starving. We had been working hard. We ordered big plates of meals. Jim was a stingy fartknocker. He ordered the cheapest soup on the menu.

As we were munching, Jim started gobbling from Ventura's plate. Ventura had a huge bountiful heart and shared his food with Jim. I wouldn't do it. Why? Jim was the foreman. He was making more money than all of us. I didn't know how much precisely, and it was none of my business. My point was that if you were making more money than others, why would you be so rude to eat others' food? When Jim ate, his mouth was always covered with food. It was so bad that he needed a bib. That was how Jim was. Despite his asinine deeds, I respected him. He had been working in

America for more than forty years. Jim was taking care of his family over the years. He was a good man.

*****

It was the last week of August 2017 when we finished the training classes. Don Da Bomb came to me and said, "Did you fight at the boxing event yesterday?" Baffled, I stared at him as if he asked, "Are you quitting boxing?"

"I don't know what are you talking about? What was this event?"

Don looked away and then gazed back at me. "I will find a fight for you."

"Whoa, are you serious! Thanks, Don. I appreciate the offer."

Don just nodded. His face animated as if he was saying, "No worries. I'll take care of you". He knew how desperately I was looking for another fight. For some weird reason, no one at Hyper had told me any information about the boxing event that transpired a day before.

For the following few days, Don and I started to hang out as buddies. He lived in a studio that wasn't far from Motel Zero. Donovan was a hilarious man. His stories always amused me. Two days later, he phoned a man named Sam Colonna. That man was responsible pretty much for the 95 percent of amateur fights organized in Illinois.

Don wanted to make sure that my name was on the list of boxing card. The fight was scheduled three weeks ahead. He trained me personally along with Dave Latoria. Dave was a professional boxer with an official record of fourteen wins and one loss. Dave was more than 260 pounds, built like a brick shithouse and as ripped as WWE wrestling star Batista. As an amateur, Dave became a two-time Golden Gloves champion. Dave had been quite successful in his boxing career. He had more than twenty years of boxing experience. He was a beast that you would not mess around with.

Da Bomb had shown me a completely different page in the boxing world. His knowledge portrayed a plethora of techniques that I had never known the existence of. The secret of his professional guidance could metamorphose you into a potential killing machine. Don taught me how to use my body, legs, and hands at the same time and also how to trigger the power of the right hand in an orthodox boxing stance.

He even added me as a member of his Team Boom. It was an honor to become part of his congregation. Several days later, Don called me for sparring. We went to a different boxing gym. The name of this gym was Final Round, positioned south of O'Hare, close to Interstate 290 in Hillside, Illinois. When we burst straight inside, I was stunned.

Final Round had top-notch equipment: a profusion of boxing bags, remodeled locker rooms, and two rings in pretty good condition. That gym had roomy space that you could train around a hundred guys at the same time. As we wandered inside, a bunch of guys was starting to stretch out and dawdled around, including Don's father, Peter George (Papa Bomb).

Peter George was inducted into the Boxing Hall of Fame as one of the most educated boxing coaches in Illinois and over the states. He was a well-known coach and had been in Don's corner for all of his fights. He had detailed knowledge of the entire history linked to this combat sport. His boxing data was based on a zillion hours of reading, watching, and practicing in that sport. He elaborated an honorable career for his son. Thus, many pro boxers were begging him to train them. Peter George had met dozens of popular boxing legends, promoters, coaches, boxing announcers, etc. He was the man who would transform you from an amateur into a professional fighter. Peter George could guide you in all the details, such as payment fees and medical examinations, to become a pro. Furthermore, he would provide you with a convenient rival to make a phenomenal debut as a pro. He had been doing that for numerous years.

Back at the Final Round, Papa Bomb and Don were in charge of setting up the sparring pairs. Don peered at me anxiously and cried out, "Dimitry! Get ready!"

The other boys kicked off a sparring practice. Not too long ago, I hopped in the ring. A young man jumped too. His name was Jimmy Quiter. He was an amateur with over seventy fights (a year later, he became a pro). His boxing stance was southpaw, which meant I had to switch to a different strategy. Jimmy knew how to take a punch.

Outside of the ring, he was an amiable person mirroring a friendly demeanor. The sparring among Don's guys enhanced my knowledge and brought me some extra confidence. I was lucky to meet Donovan. He had thrown me a bone, and I would never forget his induction.

*****

The forthcoming bout were scheduled on a Friday night in September 2017. The fight day cruised faster than a crocodile crawl. The Chicagoans said the summer was over, but the temperature was stuck in the mid-seventies. Thrilled and nervous, I drove by Don's crib to pick him up. Then we headed to the River Forest Country Club.

This country club had well-maintained golf courses surrounded by some entertaining facilities such as restaurants and alike. You couldn't just slink inside of that country club. You needed to be a member of that club (unless you were Mike Tyson).

When we got off the Geo, Don said, "Give me your bag. I will carry it for you. Look how they are going to stare at you when we burst in." Bamboozled, I handed him my bag, trying to figure out what he was talking about. We rambled to the locker rooms. When we came in, everyone goggled at me like I was Saul Alvarez. The coaches were shocked as if I pulled out a Glock 19, aiming through everyone. A word was fired from my mouth as if it came out of a gun. "Amazing!"

Don averted and said. "Told you." The ring was outdoor. Two bars were serving booze around the ring.

Jimmy had been on the same card. He arrived alongside Papa Bomb. The lavish event blasted out loud, and the first fight had commenced. Don sent me into the locker room. I went straight to the restroom and did the freebase. Whoop! Ah, what a feeling! Once again, that was my foolish slipup.

Instantaneously, my mind had gotten sharpened. I was thinking about who my opponent would be. Don was waiting outside. He was nervous as well. He puffed cigarettes one after another. Papa Bomb gave me the final instructions that brought me additional self-esteem. The crowd of royal swanks was hollering, and that boosted the adrenaline to the climax. I promenaded to the ring; my peripheral vision spotted how the crowd was shouting around.

When I hopped on the canvas, the rival was scowling at me. He was a Latin man ripped like Van Damme in the 1990s. He lurked at me, reflecting hostility. Relax, dude! Who cares how he looks? You have the best corner in Illinois. The faith slightly escalated the beats of my heart. A moment before the gong roared, Papa Bomb tapped my arms and exclaimed, "Where in the world you wish to be right now?"

"Right here," I spilled out. The first round rumbled, and we both turned on into the beast mode. The contender was faster, hovering around like an annoying mosquito. His countenance was like a pissed macho man who had just found out that I slept with his girlfriend. The macho man was bustling around, uncertain of what he was doing. His punches literally sucked.

However, he wasn't visiting us as a spectator. Since the gong had blasted, I had been using whatever Don taught me. I slammed the macho man to the ropes. The result was flabbergasting. Unbelievable! Team Boom strategy is working! There was no question who won the first round. In the break, Don and his father encouraged me and uttered guidance about stopping that macho man.

In the second round, the picture was pretty much the same as the first one. The macho man got worn down to a nub, perhaps because of my painful jabs. I longed to put him into a comatose. He switched to survival mode. My strategy was simple: to knock him out. That was the only way I would prove to myself how dangerous I could be.

At the second break, I drew a deep breath. My thoughts were. Dude! Your performance is doing fine! This is the last round. Show them what you've got. Team Boom kept backing me up by using helpful tips. The audience of royal swanks hollered, "Go, blue! Go, blue!" Blue was the color of my corner.

The gong for the third round blared. Standing up, I saw the macho man's face, then everything cleared out. He wants to quit! The way he looked at me was if he was saying, "I'm done. No more". The third round continued at the same pace. My inner voice yelled. Finish him!

I jumped on him like an insane inmate. I was throwing bombs confidently. When I punched, the whole crowd cried out in exclamation mark like a church choir.

The macho man yearned desperately to cover himself and prevent my fierce raid. His game plan failed. It must have been roughly a minute since the third round began, the macho man got wide open, and I blasted his nose badly. Blood ran from his nostrils. His muzzle reddened.

The ref cut us out, standing between us. He tossed me a sign to stay away while he was doing the count. My eyeballs stuck consistently in the referee. He made a sign that implied stopping the fight. That's it! It's over! At that moment, I felt like the happiest man on the globe. One of my dreams turned out to be true. The feeling of winning a fight via TKO had been welded into my heart as one of the most memorable moments. Like Mike Tyson said, "It was a love from a first fight." It was hard to compare. Perhaps, I would say that it was the feeling similar to when you become the most influential man on earth or just got promoted at the job where you had been enjoying working. Don bawled behind the ropes.

"I told you. You'll do it. I told you!" Thrilled by adrenaline, he hopped into the ring, grabbed my arm, and held my fist high as the winner. The crowd was howling rowdily, triggered by my performance. The ref handed me an eye-catching trophy. After I stepped out of the ring, a man tarted up as a flashy movie star, slunk out from the audience and handed me a twenty-dollar bill. Bemused, I glimpsed at Don as I expressed, "What the heck is that?"

Don said, "Don't worry about it. I told him to bet on you, and he won some extra cash." Jimmy lost his bout by points. Although, the whole team was happy with my performance. We discussed the highlights in the locker room. The next moment, an unknown guy was passing through the hallway. I asked that guy to snap a picture of us. Looking at that picture, my face had never been happier before.

Don and I hung out later the same night in some bar in the outskirts to commemorate my magnificent accomplishment. There was a plethora of booze and too much of the white rails, but I didn't care. It was my night, and I wanted to cut loose. The shindig continued all night long till dusk. By the end of the day, my throat got so hoarse that I could barely talk.

The next day, Don revealed information about another fight that had been arranged for three weeks later. Since then, my concentration multiplied.

Keeping my mind busy with boxing made me a joyful fool. Questions arose in abundance such as, "Is there any chance for me to develop a career in the professional boxing world despite my age of twenty-eight?" The answer was simple. It all depended on me.

Chapter 15

To be successful in some specific field, you need to sacrifice all of your time. Furthermore, you had to be devoted in following your dreams no matter what your friends and family had been saying to you. If I had listened to my buddies or family, you wouldn't read this book.

In the same way, I was dedicated to boxing. I was eating and breathing boxing. I pushed all my energy into developing a maximum speed, technique, and power in one function. After boxing classes, Don gave me some additional lessons. We became good buddies. Often, I hung out at his crib. We talked about boxing, chicks, and anything you could think of.

Don was a down-to-earth man. He had never bragged himself or gotten stuck up for what he was and what he did. He was above and beyond. That was why we hit it off. The fight night came to pass in the first week of October. Don and I headed up west from Chicago near Carol Stream. It was another country club but not as sumptuous as River Forest.

The ring was located in a huge barn encircled by a hundred seats. When we arrived, Don spotted Dereck Finley. He was a short black man exposing a heavyset body. He had a professional boxing record of fifty fights with almost equal wins and losses. Finley was a dangerous bruiser; no cap about that. He won by TKO against Da Bomb earlier the same year.

Don could beat Finley in a fight. Da Bomb struggled to lose thirty pounds by starving and staying in a sauna for two weeks. There were a bunch of fighters in that club ready to prove how tough and good they were. Restless as a cat on the hot bricks, I walked to the locker room. Once again, the same slipup of freebase occurred. I pulled out a baggie and snorted the coco. I almost vacuumed the entire ziplock, which was less than a gram. Ah!

A fussy sound echoed through my eardrums. My vision hazed for an instant. Dude, you shouldn't do that much of the white crap. So why did I do it? I wanted to make Don proud of me, and that was a wrong way to do it. The fight was about to start. I hopped in the ring, exuding equanimity. The adversary was a taller Cuban. He was around six feet three. That seemed to be an issue.

When Don came to some boxing events, the announcers dedicated a few seconds by honoring him officially. There we go again! The gong blared, and straight away, we both jumped fiercely on each other. Initially, the battle commenced at an extremely high pace. It was grueling to cut the distance beyond his long arms. My attempts to break through his barriers did not stop till the end of the round.

The Cuban giraffe had perpetually blocked my raided jabs. Thus, I became more restless. My strategy was to wallop his ass as soon as possible. That was why my fuel ran out too early. If I get him at the ropes, then I can develop a quick combination. I thought. The drawback of cutting the distance was making me agitated. The first round wound up equally. In the corner, Don spilled out sneaky tricks and motivated me. He knew how hyper I became, so his instructions were, "Protect yourself and catch your breath. Stay loose."

On the second round, I pushed the brake and slowed down a bit. The steering wheel of the fight had been taken by the Cuban giraffe. That man was tall enough to be a basketball or a volleyball player. In the last couple of seconds of the round, I lurked at him, looking for openings; and then WHOOP! The referee started counting on me. He asked me, "Do you want to continue?"

My answer was, "Yes, sir!" The Cuban version of Michael Jordan socked me on the left side of my chin with a clean looped right hook. He thumped me so powerfully that I almost wobbled. A few seconds after, the ref resumed the fight, and the gong blew loudly. That was the end of the second round. On the break, my head was woozy. Da Bomb encouraged me by saying, "You got to knock him down. I think he has the first two. Now is your time."

In the third round, both of us were exhausted. We were chasing each other like two hostile Rottweilers. His languid jabs helped me to cut off the distance. The Cuban giraffe was getting knackered. In the final seconds, he held me in a clinch for multiple times. I pulled off my right hand and dug a punch upon his ribs. After my body shot, I shoved him straight forward to the corner, and he collapsed on the canvas. It was a pure knockdown. While the referee started the count, I threw a glance at Don. He was yelling, "Jump on him straight away!"

After the count, I jumped at the Cuban like a frenzied father who had just seen his son shot by a sidearm. The fringing rival protected himself. He grabbed my arms and held them to save some time. The gong blared again. The fight was over. Everyone applauded us as we were both winners. The decision was up to the judges. Don had already prophesied who would be the winner. We both stepped over to the ref. He grabbed both hands and lifted the arm of the Cuban giraffe. I didn't agree with his decision, but there was nothing I could do about it.

The judges had tough decisions to make. That fight was tight. Nevertheless, I couldn't blame others for my failure. The disappointment fell on me as if a toolbox had been emptied upon my head. The feel of the loss made me nauseous. I was pissed that I screwed Don up. He attempted to make me feel better by sharing information about the fighter's background. He declared, "This Cuban Mowgli had won Golden Gloves earlier the same year, so you shouldn't blame yourself."

He wasn't wrong, but that didn't make me feel better. The frustration about my performance shook my self-regard. A question bobbed in my mind. What should I do? Either quit boxing and nurse my wounds by feeling self-pity and regret for the rest of my life or bury those pathetic emotions and step up my game. Which of those two options do you think a warrior should choose? The answer would not need to be specified.

The next few days, I bothered and begged Don to arrange another fight.

He recognized how overwhelmed I was. He managed to make a few phone calls, and not long after, he put my name in a boxing event scheduled after a few weeks. I was upbeat, like a child getting his favorite toy.

Unfortunately, Don couldn't be at the oncoming bout. He needed to take care of some family business. Instead, Don gave me instructions to contact Papa Bomb. He would be at my corner. Once again, I got butterflies in my stomach. Two weeks before the bout, I drove on Cicero Avenue to meet a Latino gang and grab some baggies filled with coco. Monday to Friday, I behaved myself.

On the weekends, I was hungry for a party. I snorted white rails with some folks all night long until I started feeling hoarse as if a construction brick was stuck in my throat. During the weekdays, I was a rock, hiding the dope from myself. The picture on weekends was in complete reverse. Vacuuming blow, I felt like a king, elusive. I didn't give a damn who I would be fighting. I was 100 percent confident that I would wallop his ass.

Da Bomb continued to train me personally whenever he had time. Otherwise, I worked out on my own to keep my body in fighting shape. The fight took place in the last week of October. The event would be streaming in a vast sports complex located in Libertyville, Illinois. That building was so immense. It took me a few minutes to figure out where the entrance was. When I pussyfooted inside, I was nonplussed. I had never seen such monumental sports hippodrome. The ring was placed on the second floor in a spacious compartment. Jimmy and Papa Bomb had been there already.

In those kinds of private events, the number of bouts had never been exceeded more than twelve. My exhibition bout had been lined up as third on the timeline. There was no time to fool around. I headed to the commode and did the usual freebase. Prepared for another bloody scene, I leaped on the ring.

Peter George encouraged me by using his inspirational speech. Then, I bowed my head, kneeling at the corner cushion and praying to Lord. The rival had a fuming face like a hateful naysayer. He was much shorter and younger than me. He was a muscular Irish American pit bull who was ready to disembowel humans.

Here we go again! The first round blared. We both jumped to each other as if we had beef for a long time. The rival was hostile, almost growling at me. He kept muscling me out over the ropes. He moved around, that forced me to switch on defensive mode and avoid his blows. I was looking for one uppercut that would conk him instantaneously.

That was a wasted opportunity in the amateur's division, and that was a big red flag for judges. It might work out in pro fights with more rounds. There was no time for that in the amateur's divisions. The first round was already given to the Yankee bulldog. I couldn't change anything at second and third, and the Yankee won that fight by unanimous decision. What nagged me was the simple fact that I could have beaten that bulldog; if I had taken that challenge more seriously. After wrapping up this exhibition fight, I remained speechless. The way Papa Bomb peered me was as if he was saying, "Boy, you need to work a lot".

Chapter 16

After the bout, I decided to slack off for a while and shifted to hedonism. I was raving the white crap and gulping bevy. Sometimes, I slipped against my rules, snorting coco during the week. Then in the morning, I dashed to work. No one had ever noticed anything. One particular day, I went to work after a long raving night. I had to bend a rigid pipe and install it underground where concrete would be poured. The job had to be done with precision. I did phenomenal work that even Jim was impressed. When I did coco, my mind was getting insightful. At that time, I liked it, but it was wrong.

As Halloween approached, a genius idea snapped into my mind. I did some cyber research and found a costume. I couldn't wait to have it, and the price was acceptable. It was Saturday night. On my agenda was the plan to hang out in the downtown area where a flock of gorgeous chicks was screwing around. I rang to most of my social pipeline to come along. They all refused, except Stan. He decided to be the chauffeur, which was fine with me. He picked me up around seven from Motel Zero, and we rolled over to River North. After making a few circles, we finally found a parking spot. As he parked his Honda, Stan looked at me wearing the costume and asked,

"Are you sure about that?"

"Hell yeah, Stan. Let's go." Stan had instructions to snap pictures whenever he got the chance. Both of us roamed over the streets at River North. Instantly, the cars passing by were honking at us. Everyone burst into laughter. As we passed Hooters, a hysterical squawk bellowed. A well-fitted black chick wearing a Hooters uniform ran out of the restaurant and cuddled me like I was her brother. She shot a load of selfies.

I couldn't refuse. That was the whole point whatsoever. After that, we continued wandering on our bizarre trip. A block away, we noticed a stalled police vehicle with flashing lights like a Christmas tree. Several police officers were leaning up against the car, and gibbering something. Cripes, man! I hope they won't bug me. One of them stepped over and asked,

"Hey, buddy, can I take a picture with you?" My smiling face was glowing like a lighthouse.

"Sure, boss!" Incredible! Even the cops are laughing. This costume is legit! As we rambled on the street, everyone passing cheered me as if I was a celebrity such as Brat Pitt, Kanye West, etc. So what did this costume look like? It was an outfit of huge flesh rocket colored in ivory. On top, I tucked newspapers to bloated the head (no pun intended), and the balls playfully jingled in front of my legs (they were filled with tons of newspapers as well). We aimed at the entrance of a club named Y bar. The security monitored me and burst into laughter.

"Hey, boss, what's the cover?" I asked kindly.

Cackling, the man said, "Just go!" The man folded his hands up to his abdomen and laughed out loud. He let us go in for free. The moment I burst inside, everyone looked at me like I came from a different planet. Then, the ice got broken, and they cherished me like they had known me since college.

That bar was packed. Around 85 percent of chicks took pictures and posted on social media with my costume. A bunch of guys was showing me thumbs-ups. My sidekick, Stan, had been snapping a plethora of photos. He caught images with me and five or six girls at the same time.

Bustling around, I noticed through the helter-skelter a VIP lounge filled with more than fifteen flight attendant broads. They jumped on me like a swarm of bumblebees on a flower. All they wanted was to shoot pictures.

When I tried to get the phone number of a particular feline, someone pulled me out and took another picture. It was getting freaky-deaky. A bunch of tipsy gals kicked, licked, and kissed the nut sack of the costume. A half an hour later, Stan suggested,

"I am going outside to get some fresh air. Do you want to come?"

"Sure. Good idea!" When we stepped outside, the exact scenario occurred. I was like the main attraction on the street. Some chicks were passing by, chuckling and taking pictures as if I was a movie star. All of those chicks whom I bumped into that night were fascinated by the costume, not the person inside of it.

The clock indicated around two in the morning; the Y Bar closed the doors. I asked my sidekick,

"Hey, Stan, are you hungry? Let's get something to eat." Stan just nodded. We jumped on I-90 westbound and took the exit on Harlem. We then rolled up to a joint named Taco Burrito King. That place was open 24-7. It was always crammed. I loved that place. Even writing about it makes me hungry and eager to stop by and grab something from there.

There was an eternal line of squiffed Halloween revelers, hungry to gobble anything. Once they peered at me, they started giggling. I didn't pay attention to anyone. All I wanted was to eat, go home, and doze off. I ordered a grande burrito with steak but no tomato. The food melted in my mouth in less than a minute. After we were done gobbling, both of us headed to the parking lot.

As I swaggered, something across the street drew my attention. Two girls struggled, trying to start the engine of their Acura. Those girls need some help. Let's see what we can do about it! Stepping closer, I questioned,

"Hey, ladies, what's going on? Do you need some help?" They looked at me, baffled. There was a pause, then they giggled at my distinguished costume.

"Well, it won't start," one of them uttered, flashing a jumpy face.

"Looks like the battery died. Don't worry, I am an electrician." I explained, exposing the composure of a plastered klutz.

"Hey, Stan, bring the Honda over here!" I bawled. Stan had listened to my command as if he was working for me. Stan parked his Honda across the Acura. I managed to open the hoods of both vehicles and got ready to operate. Stan assisted by providing jumper cables from the trunk of his Honda. Everything was set up, and the bond had been laid out. Then, I gave a sign to the girl (whose name still remained unknown at that moment) to flick the ignition. She attempted to fire up the engine, which initially choked.

After the third shot, the Acura's engine started working. Both girls were Mexican

American sisters. One of them was Claudia. She was married with two kids. She didn't portray any interest to date. The other girl was Joana. She was fascinated by my performance. She was a single twenty-four-year-old kiddo who had a chubby body. Her sweet muzzle looked like a candy.

A couple of minutes later, Joana gave me her phone number. In the final synopsis for the night, I had encountered around sixty felines (most of them were perfectly damn fine!), and none of them hadn't drawn any interest in me as a person. At the end of the night, I helped jump-starting a dead battery in a car of a Latino chick. The next day, we set up a date at Walgreens' parking lot on California and Diversey.

It was around nine in the evening, and we chitchatted in my car. Joana was an extremely humble person. I thought she might want to go somewhere, but she never brought up the subject. And so, our first date ended up kissing on the parking lot of Walgreens. Two weeks later, she yearned to make our relationship exclusive. She looked like a sweet, bountiful person. Joana didn't wear any masks or pretend to be someone else. That was why I decided to give her a shot.

*****

Living at Motel Zero had built up a level of comfortability. The landlord did not take care of the entire townhouse unless something irrevocable occurred. He was a Polish weirdo named Jacob. That man was a stingy retired school professor with a scrawny body and mustache like Tom Selleck. He acted like an obnoxious mother-in-law, always showing up when you didn't need him. We were trying to stay cool with Jacob.

In November 2017, Mike revealed his plans to move out and shack up with his girlfriend. He longed to get married. His intentions were to run on his own. Nothing wrong with that. I had always been encouraging him. We treated each other as brothers no matter what was happening. Mike wasn't the type of guy who wasted his time.

On the next month, he took his baggage to another unit located in the same hood. On Sunday, the second week of December, we managed moving all of his items for half a day. Considering those circumstances, I had to set up a strategy to bring another roommate.

*****

It had been a month since we started dating, and Joana already hankered to introduce me to her family on Christmas. I had never met a family of any chick before. Christmas Eve came through as fast as a bullet from an Uzi. Joana drove me to her parents' house. She was so thrilled to show up her new beau. In the meantime, I wasn't sure what I would do up there.

When we went through the house, a pleasant hospitable atmosphere was waiting for us. Her mom, dad, and three sisters plus brother expected the two of us. The whole household exuded a completely different culture. I enjoyed spending Christmas Eve with those people. They treated me as a member of their family. The food was extraordinarily delicious. I couldn't be more grateful. God bless these people. Four days prior to New Year's Eve, Joana had to fly to Mexico for vacation. She had booked the trip before we met.

After I escorted my girl to the airport, my phone rang. The screen displayed the name of Chris.

"Hey, Chris, how is it going, my man?" I kindly asked.

"Not much. We're going to celebrate New Year's Eve at home. Do you want to come over?"

"Sure, Chris. I will be there around nine."

"Cool. See ya soon."

Magnificent! I will spend a joyful time on New Year's. Those were my thoughts. New Year came unexpectedly fast. Tarted up nicely, I headed up to Cicero, where some beaners supplied me with yeyo. Then, I rolled back to Chris's condo. Everything went smooth with the Bulgarian fellas. I was drinking and dashing toward the commode. Snorting coco made me lose control that night. Regardless, none of the Bulgarians got the memo about what I was doing all night long. Right after midnight, Don called and invited me to his crib. I accepted his offer and requested an Uber, which was running significantly late. I had never judged any cab drivers. They were out to make some money to feed their families.

High to the hilt, I hopped in the car of the Uber driver. His South African accent was strong, which made it difficult to understand him. When we approached Don's building, I said,

"Hey, my man, you have to drop me here."

The Uber driver looked at me like I was throwing up at his car.

"No, sir! You had provided a different location, which is a half mile away." The Uber driver was trying to explain what it displayed on his Uber app.

"Naw, this is the right address! Stop the car here!" I almost bawled at him. I got out of the car and wobbled, trying to keep balance. The Uber driver swiftly disappeared. It was colder than a witch's tits in a brass bra at below 10 degrees Fahrenheit. I was so zonked that I didn't have any idea how bad the weather was that night. It was bone-chilling, one of those days in Chicago when you had to stay warm. Dude! Pull yourself together. You are almost there. There is no reason to be so anxious about it. There was another drawback. The battery of my phone had died.

Great! You frigging airhead. How can you let that happen? What I'm going to do now? You damn fool! I couldn't call anyone. My only choice was to look for Don's studio. It has to be this building right in this corner. Those were my grumpy thoughts. My body was freezing. My head felt numb as if it were a wrapped product that was ready to be shipped out of a Greek butcher. Even a polar bear would hide in a cave to survive.

It was around two in the morning. The night was dark. The streets were abandoned as if cars didn't exist. I was desperately looking for Don's place. 871. I need 871. Where is it? Dammit! My body was stiff. The alcohol didn't make me feel woozy anymore.

The cold weather transformed me into a sober teenybopper. It had been twenty minutes since I shuffled into the insane subzero weather. My bones felt a sharp stabbing pain. Number 871. I see it. Finally, there it is. Panicked, I knocked on the glass door. Don leaped off the couch and pulled off the drapes. Then he yanked off the sliding door. His expression depicted as if he saw a ghost.

"Champ, what the hell happened to you?" Don asked. We had started to call ourselves champ. The truth was, Don was the real champion. He reached out a plethora of achievements over the years. I couldn't name myself champ. Don merely called me back champ.

"Come on, get inside. Jesus!" he continued, bemused. Speechless, I burst inside his crib. Don turned on the stove.

I stepped closer to the oven to heat my fingers. Da Bomb rented a studio located in a town called Park Ridge. His place was cozy. His sanctuary looked like a room of Boxing Hall of Fame legends. A variety of framed pictures with legendary boxing names (including his) hung on the walls. Also, a few boxing belts (one of them from Golden Gloves) were neatly set up on the top of vintage-colored shelves. I couldn't stop gazing at his belts, dreaming that, one day, I might have one. Around ten minutes later, I sorted out that my hands didn't warm up as they normally would. They were so swollen, and looked bigger than the hands of the WWE superstar Big Show. The sharp stabbing ache didn't cast away either.

"Champ, this is very peculiar. Why are my hands not healing?" I blurted out in a state of confusion.

"Can't say what it is. Tomorrow, my mom will take a look. She is a nurse." Rolling to hospitals was the last thing in the world that I would do, especially without any health insurance. We discussed boxing for hours that inspired me to commit to another comeback. I must start over. I must show that I am a better boxer, capable of kicking someone's arse. While contemplating, it evoked the warrior spirit deep inside of me. Getting back on the ring was my top priority.

*****

The next day, Don and I sneaked to his parents' house. His mom, Rita

George, was a well-educated nurse. She peered at my hands, which hadn't changed since New Year's Eve.

"They will be fine. Give them a week," she announced. I felt a huge relief, listening to Don's mom. Two days later, Joana touched down from Mexico. She ran straight to Motel Zero. Joana wanted to bring me over to her house for dinner. When she spotted me, her face froze.

"Oh my God! What the hell happened to your fingers?" she grumbled, totally confused.

"Don't worry. I'll be fine," I stated, trying to soothe her even though I wasn't sure of my statement. A strong faith should bring the process of healing. Never project weakness. That was the top paragraph of my résumé. Also, it was a common way of thinking in the boxing field. The frowning face of Joana changed to a smile.

"We still have some time for…" she uttered.

After we bumped uglies, Joana drove us over to her parents' house to commemorate New Year's Day. We walked to the first floor, where the supper had been served. When we trudged in the living room, everyone goggled at me like I was a kamikaze armed with C-4, willing to blow up the entire neighborhood. Suddenly, one of her sisters broke the silence.

"Please take a seat. There is plenty of food that you ought to try." Obediently, I joined the decadent supper. As we finished the dinner, Joana grunted.

"You should go to the emergency room. Your fingers don't look good."

"Naw, I am not going to any hospital. Can't afford it. It will be fine. Trust me."

"You must seek some medical treatment, even if we have to drag you down through the health center. Don't worry about payment. We will cover the expenses. Please, I'll get you a ride. Besides, if you don't go, it could get worse."

Every one of her family peered at me dreadfully. My thoughts were. These people are really worried about my condition. Perhaps, this offer could be appropriate. Regardless of the dumb brick weather and without any further hesitations, Joana and her mom escorted me to Advocate Illinois Masonic Medical Center located somewhere in the Lakeview area. We spent two hours waiting to be admitted into the emergency room.

A precious blonde lady came through the unit. She was the attending ER physician. Her questions came through momentarily. My answer was short. I added,

"Since I had known how to walk, the blood circulation in my hands hasn't been good. Does that have anything to do with it?" My question came through like a student making conversation involving his teacher to confirm his knowledge.

"That might be the case. The injury of your hands is called frostbite. It's a condition in which skin and tissue look after being exposed in cold weather. Now listen carefully!" she announced. "I want you to grab a small baseball or a tennis ball and squeeze it ten to fifteen times daily. Your blood flow will return to normal."

"That's it? No lotions?" astonished, I asked.

"That's all you need to do. You're all set." With those words, she left the medical room.

Great. Now I will be back to the boxing ring. I thought.

The following week, I went to Pete's office. When he saw my hands, he almost had a heart attack. He didn't approve the idea of working with those injured fingers. Although, he gave me the option to do restricted labor, which brought even more pain.

The wisest option was to take a few sick days until my hands healed. That sounded like a proper method of bringing back the power of my hands. Being free from work gave me another chance to make a wrong move by calling my guy from Cicero and getting 8 ball of yeyo. A few hours later, half of that 8 ball was already gone. That caused me unpleasant nausea and made me throw up a nasty yellow liquid.

I looked at my pale face in the mirror, and attempted to clear my stuffy nose. My nostrils were filled with plenty of garbage. The following process was to pause the snorting of coco and switch to gulping booze. That was the cheapest way to knock myself out. The next day, absolutely the same story occurred. That was why I needed to work so badly. Otherwise, I would slip down to a long snowy way covered in coco.

Playing ups and downs became one of my preferred games. No matter how much I screwed up, I had always been covering my tracks. Pete or any other bosses had never become suspicious of what I was doing when I was off work. Besides, I was circumspect of my surreptitious deeds. That was my goofy way of having a ball. That was how stupid I was.

It was my method of getting relief after stressful workdays; toiling as a sparky boy and living on my own a thousand miles away from my family. I wasn't strung out on the white crap. I was doing it for fun. Snorting a load of coco made me feel glory. That was unwise, plus it cost me a lot of money. That didn't make me feel proud of doing it, nor did the fact that I had to reveal all of this classified information. Then why would I write something silly like that? That is my confession to God. This is how I clean my soul by admitting what mistakes I did.

Chapter 17

Two weeks after the medical authorities of the Advocate Illinois Masonic Medical Center released me, the condition in my hands significantly improved. That furnished an option to make a phone call to Mr. George (Peter George) and ask him for sparring at the gym where he coached.

The name of that gym was Oakley Fight Club located in West Town, Chicago. Oakley had two battle rings, a comprehensive weight lifting zone, and all types of punching bags. The moment I stepped in Oakley, I fell in love with that gym. Plenty of boxers and trainers came to spar from different gyms. Oakley was the type of boxing hub I always wanted to be involved with. In Oakley, I met a bunch of expert boxers, and at the drop of a hat, I created a membership.

Dozens of pro boxers were visiting Oakley. They taught me plenty of functional and practical tips. One of them was Dimar Ortiz. At that time, he had a professional career of twelve wins, one loss, and two draws. The way he boxed forced others to look awkward. Dimar could constantly switch boxing stances at any moment. His blows could swing from everywhere. He was a gifted and savvy fighter.

Another warrior who helped me a lot was Chris Chatman with a career (at that time) as a professional record of fifteen wins, eleven losses, and one draw. Chris had been competitive for multiple years in the boxing field. All of his losses were against undefeated fighters ranked in the top ten. Chris could fly like an annoying bee all around you. His battery never got low. Chatman could produce more than ten punches in combinations just within a few seconds.

Also, plenty of other pro fighters were swinging by Oakley: Jimmy Quitter, William Chouloute, Matt Cameron, Oscar Ortiz, etc. Baby Boom (that was how we called Oscar) and I had intensive sparring sessions. This transition made me look like an entirely different bruiser.

Mr. George was the man who contributed most to the process of boosting my skills as a fighter. I became a different boxer. Mr. George taught me how to trigger the power in my jab. I started blasting the noses of most of the bums at Oakley. Some of them were scared of sparring with me. A few weeks later, Mr. George set me up for a boxing event organized at the banquet hall of Drury Lane located in Oak Brook, Illinois. That was another chance to prove what I was capable of.

At work, we put in extra hours to raise a huge car wash building somewhere in the outskirts. There were sophisticated technologies, bonded sensors, and driers hanging at the very end of the structure. Also, the automatic cleaning process had equipment with umpteen electrical censors, which made the job more complex. We worked a gob of extra hours to wrap up that project and follow the deadlines.

After work, I drove to Oakley for sparring. Then, completely worn out, I had to roll back to Motel Zero. At home, I briskly munched some canned food. Then, I hopped in the shower, and after that, Joana demanded attention. We talked over the phone for more than an hour, which was meaningless. It made no sense to me, blabbering on the phone for such a long duration of time. There wasn't anything to talk about.

The daily report with Joana ended around one thirty in the morning. Then, I could hit the rack and drift off for several hours. The following morning, the same picture was broadcasting. By seven thirty, I needed to be at the car wash. The days were rolling in a similar sequence. When my stashed resources of coco got insufficient, I called my guy to get another package of 8 ball. Occasionally, when I roamed back from work, I took a few lines of the blow that fueled my tank with energy, then I rolled over at Oakley. Everything panned out into the right direction.

At Oakley, I was going the extra mile by investing all of my energy into sparring, which built up new methods on how to beat up the opponents more effectively. I started inflicting more power in my punches. Mr. George let me spar with heavyweights while I was fighting in the middleweight division. I broke dozens of noses at sparring. When I cruised at Oakley, a bunch of amateur boxers and their coaches were gazing at me, flashing fear. Many were terrified by my ferocious power. I had been given the moniker name "Bulgarian Bomber." That was how Mr. George called me. I wasn't joking around, and they knew it. In my mind, a giant billboard lit up saying, 2018 would be a productive year.

Contemplating about my future gave me goosebumps like a brand-new scarf hung around my neck. The forthcoming boxing event made me anxious and restless. What would happen next? The answer to that question will be exposed soon.

Chapter 18

Back in 2016, my phone rang perpetually. I had just finished my regular training. The screen displayed Pete's name. Dude, get on the horn! Pete voiced instructions related to the followed morning. Listening to my boss, all of a sudden, an ache in my wisdom tooth bothered me. It was like a nurse poked me with a big nasty needle, missing out the vein and hitting the bone.

My thoughts were. I need to work. Payments are chasing me like the hostile hound of Baskerville. The next day, I was driving to work and the pain was getting irrepressible. I must do something! I parked my Prizm at the side of the driveway of an opulent house in Skokie. When I stepped closer, Ventura and Jim were discussing the recently elected forty-fifth president of the U.S., Donald Trump. (They loved to talk about politics.)

"Ventura, how you doin', amigo?" I asked.

"Hey, I am okay. What about you, primako?" he responded, showing his cheerful grin.

"Amigo! My wisdom tooth is killing me. Do you know any dentist around?"

Ventura peered at me uncomfortably as if I had just called him a rat. Then he replied,

"Yes, I do, amigo. Actually, my neighbor is a dentist. He will take care of you. His name is Dr. Koita."

"Gracias, amigo!" My grin broadened. Straight away, I dialed the number and made an appointment on the nearest Saturday. I used painkillers to numb the pain. Otherwise, the pain was getting unbearable. The office of Dr. Koita was in West Chicago. His office occupied an aging house built in the middle of nowhere. The dental equipment he used wasn't the latest, but his dental services were very reasonable and affordable.

Dr. Koita was over seventy, and he tromped like a turtle. He came from India a long time ago. The face of Dr. Koita looked like a guppy fish: he had big protruding eyes and a facetious smirk. His accent was stronger than mine, and I could barely catch whatever he mumbled. Dr. Koita performed oral surgery. Then, he shot a dental x-ray to examine the status of my teeth.

"I spotted plenty of cavities in your teeth. You must take care of them. Are you aware of that?" He asked. His grin paled, and my head wagged negatively. Bewildered by his statement, I made another appointment scheduled for the next month. My thoughts snapped in. Hopefully, I won't have any other reason to cruise over his dental office. For the following nine months, I went eight more times to Dr. Koita's clinic. The reason I picked Dr. Koita was the fact that he provided cheap service. Nevertheless, it cost me $1,200 to keep my teeth in proper condition.

Chapter 19

The day I had been waiting for finally came. While I was looking for parking at Drury Lane, my mind flashed. Whoa, this place is dope! Hopefully, the GPS sent me to the right place. It's too good to be true! Drury Lane looked like the White House in Washington, DC. It was the most luxurious building I had ever been. The internal decor of Drury Lane, including the rooms and halls, looked glossy. Restrooms were glamorous with a romantic atmosphere. The chandeliers looked so outstanding that the price tag must be over a few grand each.

Long tables with a pricey white tablecloths and cozy chairs were neatly arranged all around. The ring was placed in the center of the convention hall. More than two hundred VIP tables were scattered around the ring. A swarm of butlers and employees was responsible for paying attention to the guests. Those guys were flittering around like annoying mosquitoes. They asking questions: "Do you need anything?"; "Would you like me to help you with something?"; "How can I help you?" etc.

For the next fifteen minutes, the whole banquet hall of Drury Lane became crammed with plenty of wealthy bigwigs, dignitaries, and nabobs thrilled to watch engrossing fights. One of the guests was Bobby Hitz, the man in charge of arranging official professional boxing events in Illinois. Peter George had umpteen fighters fighting in the card of Bobby Hitz's boxing events.

Mr. George and Bobby had known each other for many years. Don knew Bobby like they had been living on the same street for more than thirty years. They were working together in managing boxing fights for a long time. Everything at Drury Lane was gleaming. It was like a pro fight night. Drury Lane was the flashiest boxing event I ever fought. My mind sank into concentration. I was calm, listening to inspirational hip-hop music on my headphones. Suddenly, a hand tapped on my left arm. Who the heck is this? I turned stiffly.

"Jimmy! What up, bubby?" I cried out, streaming a broad grin.

"Doin' well. What a nice place, isn't it?"

"Yes, indeed. It's dope here! I'm thrilled to make a sharp performance." My words came like a reluctant speech of a retired champion. Jimmy giggled like a nipper waiting to have his favorite kid's menu at McDonald's.

"What's your weight, Jimmy?"

"Jesus, I must be around 170 pounds. You?"

"Man, 161 pounds. Light as hell. I overdid it. Mr. George will be pissed. He told me to be around 168."

"You'll be fine," Jimmy asserted. He made me feel better. In pound-for-pound amateurs, the difference in more than a few pounds was huge. Regardless, I didn't give a damn how many pounds I weighed. I was there to fight. I didn't care how heavy my rival would be. Whatever he was, he should be intimidated by my technique.

After a quick medical examination, the boxing event commenced. The crowd was thirsty for flawless victories such as a KO, a TKO, etc. A swarm of talented boxers (some were champions of previous years) were there to prove how good they were. Mr. George trundled around the banquet hall, exuding a serene calmness.

When he heard what the weight of both was, he had the expression of someone with an urgent case of diarrhea. My bout was approaching. Minutes before my fight was supposed to kick off, I saddled up and slightly scuttled to the loo for a routine freebase of coco. I swiftly tooted the blow and BOOM! My vision shook off.

I opened my eyes as fast as the doors of the malls on Black Friday. My eardrums hummed, and my whole body wobbled for a second. Whoa!

This crap is strong! That was just another reckless and useless slipup. A peculiar feeling thudded in my nape. It wasn't the smartest move that I ever made, especially in that particular event.

Let's get ready to rumble! Promenading through the rabble of dignitaries put me in a nervous state. I tried not to draw any attention to the overflowed banquet hall. The raucous crowd was screaming and shouting, which additionally tore my self-esteem apart. I hopped in the ring, looking to make eye contact with my opponent. Wondering what my performance would be, it made me nervous and blew my self-worth out. After I implored the Lord at the corner cushion, Mr. George grabbed my shoulders and said using an alluring voice identical to Al Pacino's,

"Where in the world would you like to be right now?"

"Here," I shrieked like a scraggy, peevish crow. The speech of Mr. George had always braced me. The rival was a short African American man. He was younger than me. He leered at me like he was a sulky looter busted in Walmart while trying to embezzle some gift cards. Don't let his mind games disrupt your self-confidence! The body of the black knight wasn't quite athletic (mine either).

In the boxing world, that didn't mean anything. Underrating challengers was one of the most common mistakes in this sport. The gong blared, and the fight began. Hails of punches poured on the ring. The black knight flipped in the onslaught, but he was uncertain. There was no power in his blows.

That's my time. More jabs work. Work, dammit! My punches and height successfully took advantage of the fight. The black knight was in a big trouble. I jabbed him repeatedly, shifting to different angles. The rival failed to hit back, and I made a triumphant performance. The end of round 1 wound up being dominated by me.

The time in the break flew away like an intimidated pigeon. As I stood up, my self-confidence rose as well. I peered at the black knight. His eyes told me everything. He is done. He wants to quit. Go ahead and beat him up. A downpour of jabs fell onto the rival's head. The crowd surprisingly echoed in exclamation as a result of my biffs.

The referee had no choice. He managed to disrupt the fight and began doing the count. The voice in my head cried out forcefully. He's done! After the count, jump on him. You hear me? Dammit! I rebuffed every other sound in the banquet hall. My eyes were pursuing the next gesture of the ref. Blood flowed down from the black knight's nose. He wasn't showing any interest in continuing the bout. The ref carefully stared at the black knight's muzzle. He looked frightened.

The ref was waving like he was a ramp agent landing planes in the airport. He ended that fight. That was it. The bout was over. I stopped him by TKO in the middle of the second round. I shellacked him magnificently. I was thrilled and exuberant. The crowd rowdily applauded like they witnessed an outstanding performance from America's Got Talent. The ref lifted my hand as the winner. Then, he awarded me with a glittering trophy.

This event was welded in my heart like one of the most memorable boxing events in my life. Right before I was about to leave the banquet hall, Mr. George said,

"Do you want to come over to my house for a drink?" It wasn't liberal and moral drinking in front of my coach. Nonetheless, I agreed to stop by.

Peter George's house was just a few miles away from Motel Zero. Gulping a Canadian club, Mr. George pointed out,

"This weekend, you can relax, but the following Monday, I need you back at Oakley. I had scheduled another fight within two weeks. Then you will be ready for Golden Gloves."

Listening to his speech, I confirmed by nodding. I slugged half a beer, then dashed to Motel Zero. While opening the door of my apartment, I stood mesmerized. Motel Zero was abandoned as if someone had been killed there a month ago. At the next moment, I was fumbling around in my closet and found what I was looking for. More dope. The yeyo had been hidden away for the last five days. I did four rail lines like a size of a pen on the aged oak table. BOOM!

My forehead recoiled as if somebody had punched me in the face. My eyes were glittering like pricey diamonds. My nose immediately got stuffed, which forced me to breathe through my mouth. Mr. George said that I could relax this weekend, not to snort coco, you frigging whack job!

An hour later, my smartphone rang. I peered through the broken screen, and Keen's name displayed. Ah man, not Keen. Should I pick or not? Naw, better not. Well, let's see what he wants. Keen was a good fella, but he was fooling around with many dipshits and hellions. They could put me into a lot of trouble. He could introduce me to guys who might get macho on me (It had happened before). The solution was to stay away from a chum like him. Otherwise, strife could be waiting around the corner.

"Hey, Keen, what up?" I asked reluctantly.

"I am at the front door. Come downstairs," he babbled like an enthusiastic name-dropper. Going down the staircase, my thoughts were. What the heck am I doing?

"Let's go for a drink. I heard you've won tonight." He said.

"Can't party tonight, Keen. I'm too tired. Need to rest."

"Come on, dude! Just a drink. It's only eleven."

"One drink. That's all," I snapped like an angry professor teaching math. An hour later, I found myself encircled by twenty ravers in a two-bedroom apartment somewhere in the northwest outskirts. The situation had been under control, and I was fucked up. There was so much dope that we could easily make a cream pie. When I gazed at my phone, the clock displayed half-past eight in the morning. A drink for nine hours. What a knucklehead, goofing off with some wasted crackheads.

I took an Uber in that foggy morning and crashed in Motel Zero till dusk. On Monday at Oakley, I saw an unknown bruiser. He was warming up. He was aloof, projecting an unfriendly expression. Who the duck is this guy! He was a white cracker. His peevish face could be noticed from a range of twenty feet. His body was ripped like Dolph Lundgren in his thirties. He and his coach came from Sam Colonna's gym to spar. Guess against who?

We both hopped in the ring. I had never known the name of the white cracker, and it didn't matter. I bowed my forehead in the corner to pray to the Lord. Oh Lord! Please give me strength 'cuz I don't know what the heck to do. This mother flower is so big!

The timer roared, and the hostile white cracker attacked me as if he wanted to kill me. That wasn't sparring. It was a pure fight. The white cracker was trying to knock me out cold, but his technique sucked. I stepped in, using my jab. His nose started bleeding badly, which made him pissed. I stepped on his toe, and bam! I threw another clobber right between his gloves.

I defeated and embarrassed that white cracker in front of his coach. Just another bum who thinks he is a good fighter. After the fray, I almost threw up my kidneys. Mr. George was let down. He declared,

"I know you've been drinking the past weekend. It reflects on your sparring performance. Don't drink. Otherwise, you're wasting the time of both." He paused for a few seconds, then continued. "Do you want to be a pro?"

His face said everything. One of the most anticipated moments was about to happen. For the past three years, my purpose was to jump into the world of professional boxing. Spending plenty of hours sweating at the gym and all of those bouts had given me the opportunity. My response slid out easily,

"Hell yeah!"

Mr. George didn't say anything. There wasn't anything to be said. He merely nodded. If I won Golden Gloves as an open fighter that would give me a ticket for the nationals and Papa Bomb was the man who could take me to the finals. Chewing over, I was cruising back to Motel Zero. That night was longer than usual. It took a couple of hours before I drifted off to sleep.

Chapter 20

I was thrilled about the recent news that Mr. George had revealed. In the meantime, the courtship with Joana didn't make any progress. Why? After a long day at work and sparring sessions, I came back to Motel Zero worn out as if I had been working on a farm the entire day. Then, Joana demanded to chat over the phone, which usually took an hour.

Conversations with her became tiresome, like a stressful job that you were chopping at the bit to resign. Furthermore, she gave me a bunch of drama queen crap. I couldn't comprehend why she was acting like that. For some unforeseen reason, my huggy bear started playing the role of a jealous wife. She had never spotted any proof that showed any contact of me and another gal. I didn't have time to cheat on her, and I had never thought about hooking up with different chicks.

Moreover, I am not the type of man seeking to do the boning at the first given opportunity. One particular evening, after we got off the phone with the huggy bear, Mom reached out to me through Viber. It was around half-past midnight, and I opted to accept an international call. When I hung up the phone, the peevish huggy bear ran out of hand on Messenger. She accused and complained. She typed, "Why are you still online, and with who you're playing around?"

"Had to speak with my mom for a few," I wrote back, stunned by Joana's reaction.

"Nah, you are lying. Tell me the truth!" she scrawled on Messenger.

I felt choked by the peculiar behavior of the huggy bear. Why is this broad busting my chops? Cripes, I can't even talk to my mother. What's wrong with this loco morrita? For a zillion times, I had been explaining to her that there weren't any other chicks. Despite my confessions, Joana kept flushing incredulous proclamations. The same picture had been rotating for the next couple of weeks. Thus, I was forced to reconsider if it would be better for us to scatter in separate pathways.

Joana was a terrific girl. She had helped me numerous times by cleaning, cooking, and buying me gifts. Also, she was attending to whatever I said when the lights were out. The huggy bear longed to get hitched, and if we hooked up as a married couple, that would be a beneficial point. Why? A wedding would sort out the predicament regarding my immigration status.

I am not a catty, malignant, and wicked monster consistently playing with someone's feelings (Sabina did it to me when I was a spring chicken at the age of nineteen). I couldn't be with someone chapping my ass at any time, being jealous without apparent reason. Wrapping my head around, I took a final solution to burn the bridges of that relationship. I tried to place her in the friend zone, and that caused Joana to hate my guts.

Most likely, she would dislike me for the rest of her life. I could sniff her bummed demeanor from a long range, like how a starving feline could scent a fresh lunch of gazelle from miles away. What she didn't comprehend was the fact that I did her a favor by saving her a bunch of headaches, stress, and a profusion of squabbles in a courtship with no future. We dated merely two or three months. What if we would sign divorce paperwork after being hitched for five years and then wasting money on lawyers? Later, I found out that Joana was shacking up with somebody. God bless her heart. She was a bountiful person and deserved to be loved.

Chapter 21

On February 28, 2018, my next fight was scheduled and promoted by the National Italian American Sports Hall of Fame located at Jerry Colangelo Center on West Taylor Street in Little Italy. Enthusiastic and nervous as usual, I roared the Geo Prizm on the eastbound 290 Eisenhower Expressway. I wanted to beat the traffic.

It took about twenty minutes of driving around to find a free parking spot. Entering through the doors of the Hall of Fame sports center, I was stunned. National Italian American Sports Hall of Fame was created by George Randazzo in 1977. Randazzo formed a fundraising dinner inviting an umpteen of boxing champions such as Rocky Graziano, Jake LaMotta, Sammy Angott, and Willie Pep. There was an abundance of framed pictures and glassed shelves of prominent Italian American athletes portraying boxers, tennis, baseball players being on top of the world over the years.

On the second floor, I bumped into a Formula 1 racing car used back in the 1970s. The Italian culture was sparkling at a much higher rate, which gave me the feeling that I was in Italy for a moment. The ring was placed in a separated ballroom on the second floor. A wine-colored rug was stretched out on the floor by the front gate, similar to the red carpet in Hollywood. I guessed they tossed it on purpose to make us feel like a local celebrity. The ballroom started bursting at the seams of upscale guests jerked to watch the amateur-boxing spectacle. Mr. George scuttled over an hour before the event initiated. His countenance was solemn and agitated. Sebastian, the hefty heavyweight of our team, was running late. Sam Colonna was getting out of hand.

"Where is he? Dammit!" Sam Colonna cried out. We all thought that Sebastian wouldn't make it, but then he showed up twenty minutes before the event started.

After passing the regular medical examination, I headed to the commode to make my accustomed slipup of the freebase. Fumbling in the side pocket of my jacket, I used half of the baggie. I winced my head back as if George Foreman had jabbed my snout. My pupils glittered like a full moon in midnight during summer. My fists jolted. My vision was shaking. My eyes broadened like those of a tiny tarsier.

I was trying to keep a low profile, slithering toward the backstage like a lethal Mamba, and pretending that nothing was happening. My heart pace was vibrating like a vintage alarm clock from the 1950s. Equipped with gloves and headgear, I warmed my body by throwing punches to the pads of the assistant coach. It is time! My subconscious voice whispered and cast out a state of heebie-jeebies. As a human being, I am an outgoing and amiable person. But when I hopped in the ring, I turned berserk. Empowered by the coco, I felt untouchable. Promenading to the ring, I scanned Andrew Golota. I wanted to talk with him, but his capernoited face was saying, "Don't bother me!"

Whatever, dude. Your bout is about to start. The voice in my head said.

Anxious, I sneaked through the ropes, pondering about my fighting strategy. The adversary was in his early twenties. He was a black man, taller than me. He looked like Evander Holyfield in his pro debut against Lionel Byarm back in 1984. There was something that fretted me. He was too calm.

The Black Panther emitted a severe tranquility. His chilling demeanor riled me up. Relax, he's goin' down. You have been prepared for a fight like this by sparring pros. The ref stepped closer to check my equipment. Ah, I know this guy. It's the same referee who had stopped the bout so unfairly at Golden Gloves. Well, who gives a duck! Focus on your technique.

Mr. George gave me his stimulating speech seconds before the fight.

The ref standing in the middle of the ring wagged his hand, sending a signal to commence the first round. Here we go again! Nervous, I throttled, tempting to hurt the Black Panther by tossing out endangering jabs. Rains of exchanging punches poured over the battle arena.

Initially, the battle was tight. I was impetuous, moving around and trying to hurt the Black Panther. Suddenly, gray-black lighting popped up. BOOM, vertigo! I wobbled for a second. As I got conscious, the ref was already counting. He wiggled his fingers in front of my face. What the hell? When did that happen? I didn't see that punch.

The audio sound of the crowd was restored like a supporting actor appearing after the shocking scene in some horror movie. Bamboozled like a white hamster, being lost in the middle of Madison Square Garden, I tried to close the distance and shoot more combination punches at his body. Jesus, I had never seen such fast hands like that before. Keep working at a close distance. Then whoop! A repeated unconsciousness occurred. What the heck? The ref cautiously set up the second counting.

"Don't stop the fight," I grumbled.

"Okay. Show me somethin'," he exclaimed, gazing at me prudently. Several seconds before the end of the first round, the Black Partner muscled me out into the corner's cushions. Many sharp blows swung from everywhere. Then all went blackout, like a cable company plugged off your source box and the only thing you could see was the dust on your TV screen.

While I was opening my eyes, the spinning world made it difficult to grasp the ropes. Regardless, I stood up at once. The referee had already halted the contest, waving like a patrol officer regulating overflowed traffic across the street of the vast musical venue. The Black Panther knocked me down by inflicting an unforeseen power as if he had struck me by using a thick heavy-duty shovel. Up until that moment, I had never been knocked down in my trifling boxing career, including sparring. At that moment, I felt like a bum, like a frigging mammalucco mortified at his coach's eyes. The ref raised the Black Panther's hand as the undisputed winner. That moment, I craved to pour out my bitterness. I thought the moment of my heyday had already come. Alas, it turned out that I had a gob to learn. Blushed, I couldn't peer at Mr. George. Then, Papa Bomb stepped closer and told me something that I would never forget. He said,

"Relax, kid! You can't beat a warrior who refuses to quit." I lost that night, no cap, but I didn't quit. I was ready to fight at any other second. I would fight with the Black Panther for twelve rounds. I would rather die in the ring than surrender.

Incensed and wretched, I walked out of the Jerry Colangelo Center. A horrendous feeling disturbed me. It was the same feeling when you had lost a few grand betting on your favorite football team. In the next few days, an unpleasant agony perpetually pinched my mind. Everything went in the wrong direction. Nevertheless, that fight had a trivial value. The most essential was the upcoming tournament, the Golden Gloves.

There was something else that nagged me, an obnoxious ache over my temples. It was like a noise throbbing consistently into my eardrums. On the first week of March 2018, I drifted at Oakley, I was bemused. In sparring sessions, I became sluggish and lethargic. What the hell is happening to me? Why am I having a lack of power? The thudding sound in my eardrums never stopped. This humming sound had interfered while I was sparring and gradually bugged me on and on. That became problematic. I had no choice but to reveal this disturbing information to Papa Bomb. He chattered,

"I think you have a concussion. This isn't cool. I am going to pull the plug. You are off from the Golden Gloves."

Mr. George was concerned about my medical report. He was worried about the health condition of all his fighters. That was why he revoked my participation in Golden Gloves; it was for safety purposes. Piqued by the updates, I approved Papa Bomb's decision. Cripes! I bust my ass sweating and going an extra mile of training, sparring to be prepared for the Gloves, and now I am out of the game. Mr. George was right. He made the right decision to secure my health condition.

Papa Bomb knew his business. He was doing it for a very long time. The following week, I kept visiting Oakley to stay in shape, but I was banned from sparring until the concussion vamoosed. Every night before I crashed, the annoying noise rumbled in my head. One particular night, I went to the restroom. Staring in the mirror, I was stunned. What the hell is that? The veins on my temple were vibrating, and it was too obvious. I had never experienced something like that before. The ache in my head was like an annoying thrum as if someone was clanging two kitchen pans one each other. Holy crap! What's happening to me? How long will this pain bother me? Should I go to a doctor? And if I go, how much will they charge? I don't have any health insurance. Those were my thoughts.

Chapter 22

It was Sunday morning around the middle of March. I woke up having a relentless headache as if Terence Crawford beat the hell out of me. My phone rang unexpectedly. Looking at my phone, the name George popped up. I bet he is calling to drink a cup of coffee.

"Hey, George, what up?"

"Let's go to get some coffee at Cafe Mirage. What you think?"

"Cool! I'll be there in half an hour," I replied.

George was a bald Bulgarian chum. He looked like he was a math professor from Harvard. He was a graceful and genteel guy. George loved to dress in flashy clothes as if he was a big show-off who owned a vast corporation that made tons of money. His descent was from a savage city in Bulgaria.

George was a dandy limo driver, a funny fella whom you could always mess around with. That was the reason we drank coffee together, but only once in a blue moon. An hour later, we headed back to the parking lot. When I placed the car key on the ignition, my Geo choked dreadfully. Oh duck! It must be the battery. I ought to purchase a new one! George gave me power using my jumper cables. It worked. The Geo's engine snarled like an angry dog. Although, the battery needed to be replaced.

The next day, I was rolling back from work. The traffic was unpleasant.

Waiting in rush hour, the Geo rolled slowly. At the next moment, I was baffled. Holy cow! The lights on the dashboard suddenly turned off. What the… No, you junky old clunker. Don't cha do it to me? Not right now, dammit! What am I going to do? The Prizm stalled and shut off.

I pressed the button for the hazard lights, wrapping my head around and searching for the phone number of some private tow truck. The worst nightmare for any driver is that his car breaks down while he is on the road. The same nightmare was happening to me. Panicked, I attempted to fire up the finicky vehicle. At the third shot, Geo's engine snarled again. The lights on the dashboard turned on. Oh Christ! What a relief. The Lord heard my prayers. The Geo started to roar over. I have to go as quick as possible to AutoZone and test this fussy battery. When I jerked to the auto store, a Mexican employee with a shaggy hair stepped over. He was holding a small computer to check the battery.

"It's fine. You can still drive with this battery," the shaggy man grunted.

"You sure?" I asked dubiously.

The shaggy man just nodded, showing his thumbs up. In the next few minutes at the same parking lot, I sagged in deep contemplation. It doesn't make any sense. What should I do? The AutoZone branch was merely located about two miles away from Motel Zero. The plan was to drive straight to my crib.

The Geo fired up. At the next traffic light, the Prizm was the first car waiting for the left turn lane on Grand and Mannheim, which might be considered as one of the busiest intersections in the area. My pupils peered anxiously into the traffic light, then switched over at the dashboard to confirm that the situation was still under control.

The signal for the left turn turned green, and my eyes broadened. The dashboard lights turned off for the second time in the past hour. My voice vehemently squawked like a man with a mental disorder. Ah man, don't give me this crap again! The Geo's engine suffocated. A vehicle's horns impatiently blared behind my back. Inadvertently, I occupied the left-turn lane.

I attempted waking up the suffocated Geo. A police vehicle was waiting at the light across the street. The trooper acknowledged my awful situation and abruptly ran the emergency lights of his police vehicle. Thank God he's going to help me. The deputy was an Irish American man exuding an extremely polite attitude.

"Go inside and hold the steering wheel. I'll push from the back," the trooper proclaimed. My face nodded obediently like a squaddie on his first day in the army. There was a gas station located on the northeast side of the intersection. We made a hard U-ey (U-turn) and turtled the deceased Geo to the gas station.

That's it. I have no choice. This car needs a new battery. My construction boots headed back to the auto parts store, which was approximately a two-minute walk. When I installed the new battery, the Geo's engine fired up and streaked to Motel Zero. The overwhelming thoughts in my head vanished. Now, I would be able to sleep without worrying about this rattletrap.

The next day, I was rolling to work and decided to veer off at Dunkin'. Holding a donut and cup of coffee, I sat in the aged Prizm and flicked the key. Then, my eyes goggled. The Geo died again. My shiny, sunny face metamorphosed to the morbid countenance of an angry urban camper. I closed my eyelids for a moment and envisioned how I smashed that Geo using an iron baseball bat as if I was a plastered hubby annihilating the Mini Cooper of his ex-wife who had been eating his dough for many years.

Ah shucks! Now what? I better call Ventura. Maybe he would be able to pick me up. The Mexican bull wasn't far away from the lot of Dunkin'. He agreed to give me a ride to the house where we were supposed to work. At lunch, I dialed Gill. He was an auto mechanic who had been repairing my car since 2016.

"Hello," Gill muttered stiffly.

"Hey, amigo. Como estas," I exclaimed.

"Nada trabajar. What's happening?" He sounded disturbed and uneasy.

"My Geo is driving me nuts. The engine has been turning on and off while the car was still rolling. I changed the battery, but it's still giving the same bullshit. What do you think?"

"Perhaps is the alternator. I got you, amigo." His statement brought me a slice of serenity. Later the same day, Gill roared over to the house where I was working. He needed to get the car key. Then, he headed to Dunkin's parking lot where the Geo lingered since that morning. Gill was a nonchalant Mexican in his late forties. He was around six feet tall, wearing crew cut like a cadet from Marine Corps.

His face looked apathetic and bitter although he was an upbeat and generous man. Gill had been going through a plethora of difficulties in his life. He was a man of integrity, which was why I gave him credit for working on my clunker. It was a hassle to find a good mechanic. Most of the grease monkeys would rip you off.

At the end of the working day, Gill phoned me back and reaffirmed that the alternator had been replaced. Everything went smoothly, just like I planned. While my butt sweated by laboring to make some dough, Gill was working on my car. Ventura dropped me at the Dunkin' where Gill had been waiting. Even though I knew it would cost me an arm and a leg, my face was exposing contentment.

"It's all set up, amigo," Gill announced, emitting a cheerful expression.

"Gracias, Gill."

The Geo's engine blared like an ole horse, exhausted from a running contest. On cloud nine, I was heading south to Motel Zero. After three blocks of driving, the lights on the dashboard turned off again. Luckily, there was a Chase Bank nearby. Somehow, I rolled the succumbing Geo into that parking lot. I had a bitter taste in my throat. Unpleasant nausea grew in my tummy, which made me feel like I was throwing up. You fuking shlock, a junky piece of metal. Why is this happening to me? Quickly call Gill before he is far away.

"Hey Gill, my car lost power again. I need your assistance, amigo!" My words sounded like a vexed customer grumbling about his messed-up order from a notorious fast-food store.

"Okay! I'm coming. Give me a minute!" Gill blurted. He sounded perplexed but not as much as I was. It wasn't any longer after we spoke over the phone and Gill came with his white Ford Transit minivan. His eyes streamed a state of confusion, portraying that he might have never seen something similar before.

"This alternator must be defective. Now, I'll give you power from my jumper cables. You'll drive to your house, and I'll be behind just in case something happens. Tomorrow, leave the Geo in front of your crib. I'll come later to replace the alternator. The labor is free. Plus, you have a warranty. So, it won't cost you anything," Gill stated while gazing beyond Geo's hood. He was wrapping his head around to sort out what was going on.

Gill made it up to me. He had a blissful soul as a man of integrity. We hit it off like cousins who had been helping each other since childhood. Later in the evening, I phoned Ventura and asked him to give me a ride the next day because Gill had to tinker into the ole Prizm. The following day after we finished work, Ventura dropped me in front of the lot where my vehicle waited. In a split second, I dialed Gill to acquire a report on the condition of my Geo. The Mexican mechanic explained that he had changed the alternators. Moreover, he notified me that the new alternator had a sticker that said Lifetime warranty. Relieved, I could draw a deep breath.

Streaming a broad grin, I uttered, "Gracias, amigo."

"De nada. You take care," Gill exclaimed. The following two days, the Geo had been well-behaved like an obedient dog after using the entire house as a doggy restroom. I had the same zest to drive this vehicle as the day I bought it. On Friday, I was rolling upbeat to work. We had to schlep in a butcher store located in downtown of Chicago. After the tiresome day at work, I attempted to fire up the Geo's engine. Without any issues, the Geo headed to the exit of Ogden on I-90 west outbound toward O'Hare.

The sun glittered incessantly. It was around half-past five when the rush hour hit its climax. The Geo smoothly merged into the five-lane each way turnpike overstuffed with vehicles that were bumper to bumper. The vehicles were pacing slower than a turtle. For a moment, I glanced to the dashboard to reassure that everything was fine. The state in my mind sprinkled an abundance of solace. Then in a split second, the engine stifled. It succumbed at the heavily loaded highway. Instantly, my vision turned purple-darkened. Stunned, I exclaimed,

"What the heck is happening here?" I didn't have any time to get pissed. Straight away, I honked in panic, peering at the driver on my right side. The driver was a Latin man in his middle thirties. His eyes widened as if he saw a genuine werewolf. I gestured that my car had broken down.

The Latin guy hopped out of his vehicle and pushed the Geo through the emergency lane. I don't know from where this primo came from, but I'll pray for him. God bless this man. His assistance won't be forgotten.

The Latin buddy scuttled back to his car. He just nodded after my appreciative waving. The next hour, I was waiting for the roadside assistance. A brief statement was spinning in my mind. This car is done. I want to grab an iron baseball bat and smash that junky, rusty, ugly, dirty, shitty piece of crap. The tow truck hooked up the deceased Prizm. We were roaring toward Motel Zero, my mind cried out repeatedly. You rusty, ugly, dirty, shitty, piece of crap. The following rational question was; what I am going to do now? Can't drive this rattling crap anymore. Need to buy a new ride, but how? I don't have any money.

For the next couple of weeks, Pete attempted to offer transportation to fetch my ass at work, which meant some of the electrical crew had been obligated to give me a ride. It would be awesome. Unfortunately, that couldn't happen daily. The Greeks could drive me two or three days a week. That wasn't enough to cover all of the expenses and monthly payments. My family couldn't afford to send me money. I relied solely on myself.

Without enough working hours, my financial profit would plummet fundamentally. Once in a blue moon, I worked with another electrician. He was an independent contractor like Pete. His name was Tom. He was from Bulgaria as well. He was a nice guy, radiating a sarcastic sense of humor, which was common among Bulgarians. Tom was a munchkin. His scrawny body was like a teenybopper from middle school.

Despite his physical structure, he was a vigorous and potent man. Tom resembled the prominent character Super Mario but without the mustache. It was fun working with Tom. He always forced me to work more for the same amount of money. That was his brainwash game, which didn't work on me. Unlike Pete, Tom didn't work on big projects. He couldn't assure transportation, which dragged me to the point that I needed to purchase another vehicle. Sitting on top of the fence, I thought what could be my options. I then dialed Gill to pick up his brain for any ideas. He might know someone who is selling his car.

While I explained how the end of Geo's era came, Gill announced,

"I've got a car for you. It's my wife's vehicle, a Nissan Sentra. Would you like to check it?"

"Bring it over, amigo." It was astonishing how, just when I desperately looked over for another ride and at that moment, Gill had a car for sale. Is that a freaking coincidence or is this normal? I'll leave the answer to you. They say everything happens for a reason.

Half an hour after our chin-wag over the phone, Gill skirted over. He operated a brown-colored 2006 Nissan Sentra. Observing through the window of Motel Zero, my grin broadened. That car had a convenient mileage of around eighty thousand. The condition of the body was decent. The internal side was acceptable. Also, the car was running fine. Staring at the Nissan, I was contemplating. This ride is what I am looking for. Besides, Gill wouldn't smuggle me another hooptie, would he? Naw, he wouldn't do that. Gill is a man of integrity. Since I had met Gill for the first time, my analysis of his personality was accurate. Furthermore, the Nissan looked a reasonable option, and I made a firm decision to take the shot.

"How much, amigo?" Thrilled, I asked while still peering at the Nissan. He merely gazed down, then rose his head and asserted,

"Twenty-five hundred bucks. This is my final price." Gill stared at me, expecting a straight answer.

"I like this car, amigo. Give me seven days, and I'll have the money." The haggle was being made. We shook hands, smirking like two owners of gigantic corporations conducting a bargain for millions of dollars. Everything was going smooth. The only rational question was; how the duck am I going to collect those twenty-five Benjamins? The answer was buried somewhere where I couldn't dig out. Once again, I was wrapping my head around, trying to sort out the conundrum.

The first name that popped up in my mind was Pete. Of course, he had been my employer for almost three years already. He knew that I was a man he could count on. We discussed the plight where I was stuck. Pete declared,

"I can give you a thousand bucks." That wasn't the same amount as what I expected. But it was a good start. They say, well begun is halfway done. I would always be grateful to Pete's financial bolster. Holding those thousand dollars in bankrolls, I had gotten the feeling that I would collect all of the money by the end of the week.

Super Mario was my next choice. His response cruised after a deep breath.

"Okay, I will give you a thousand dollars." Tom averred while continually peering at me and animating his grave countenance. A couple of seconds passed, and a dead silence evolved in which we both sat, in his GMC construction-work cargo van, as if we had just conducted an agreement by attempting to murder someone.

An hour later, Tom dropped me off at Mike's asylum. Mike tromped over and handed me three hundred dollars. On the next day, I called a junk-car company, and twenty minutes later, a wrecker swung by Motel Zero. It was time to drag out the pokerized (dead) Geo. A bony black man wearing a greased jumpsuit jotted a check of two hundred bucks. I had no clue how I collected $2,500 in three days. The master of the universe had led me down to the right path.

Gill pulled the Nissan into the front side of Motel Zero. The money and the key had been swapped. A minute later, I was driving my new ride called Nissan Sentra. Now the only thing I have to do is bust my arse working and paying back the debt I owe my friends.

Chapter 23

It was almost eight thirty in the evening when the Nissan Sentra parked in the lot at Oakley. I wandered to the gym, holding my training sack and chewing the cheapest gum I could find at the dollar store.

I headed to the locker room wearing my cheerful grin. The training commenced with a simple warm-up by using a jump rope. Three minutes later, my heels had a sharp and stabbing ache. For a second, my body lurched, and I almost stumbled on the floor. Holy crap, what was that? I used to easily do ten minutes of jump rope, and now I can't do three minutes. Is that the concussion? Where is this pain coming from?

Through the whole training, I was worn out before I started. Bummed of my hideous pain, I left Oakley. A throwback of jams was blasting out in the radio of the Nissan while roaring on the way back to Motel Zero. The music in my car was making me peaceful. The moment before I sat on the chair to eat dinner, my hands suddenly trembled. I felt woozy, and my skin had goosebumps. It must be a fever or the concussion. Quick! Do something before you get sick!

I made a chicken soup, then gulped Tylenol. The heat in Motel Zero wasn't working, and the temperature in the condo was in the mid-sixties, which was fine. However, my body had chills and shivered like a German warden patrolling around the base at midnight in January during World

War II. I decided to crawl next to the oven to get warm. I bundled up with a shirt, sweater, and blanket on top of it. Thirty minutes later, my forehead flooded with sweats. Then, I hopped in the shower, dressed up, and passed out.

A combination of weird images blinked in my mind. Monsters loomed such as those in the movie Thing—demons with brown horns. All those ugly faces kept floating over and over. What the hell! Cut this bullshit. Come on, you squarehead. Wake up! For some indescribable reason, I couldn't open my eyes. It was like some insurmountable power held me. Wake up! Flashing images of dickens and gargoyles were babbling something gibberish.

Come On. Wake up! The next moment, I opened my eyes. Cool sweat was dripping around my temples. Perplexed by the dreamscape, I was gazing around as if I was looking for someone. A daylight gleamed through the window already. Gasping, I needed a moment to draw a deep breath. Jesus, what the f—k. That was the weirdest nightmare I'd ever had since I'd learn how to talk. The monsters didn't bug me, but the unknown power that had forced me to stay still before I awoke threw me in a loop. Two days later, an uneasy fever anchored me on the bed. The temperature was high above 103 Fahrenheit.

An obnoxious headache emerged over my head as if Jake Arrieta had thrown a plethora of baseballs on me. My throat was irritated, causing me to lose appetite. While I was walking in the living room, the severe headache lurched me off-balance. I felt like a plastered man who had been drinking vodka all night long. Tylenol and Ibuprofen somehow put me back on track. This goddamn concussion is getting annoying.

It was Friday morning. I hurried the Nissan to an old house in Maywood. Tom was waiting for me. The Super Mario jibber-jabbered instructions about the job.

"I'll show you what has to be done. Need to leave you on your own. I'll be back," Tom exclaimed the well-known phrase spoken by Arnold Schwarzenegger in the blockbuster Terminator. He went on,

"Hopefully, by the time I get back, you will be done. If you have any questions, call me. But don't blow my phone." Tom proclaimed and left the remodeling house. He was smiling hellishly. That house was entirely desolate. I was the only one schlepping as a hardworking wetback.

Bending the EMC pipes was one of the most sophisticated parts of that job. If you messed up something, you needed to use another pipe. Every time you needed to use another pipe, the electricians got mad because those pipes were not cheap. Furthermore, you had to adhere to the rules of the National Electrical Code; otherwise, you would not pass the forthcoming inspection. The spooky house looked ramshackle, as if someone was smuggling kilos of smack before the police busted down the shenanigans.

An hour before lunch, the heavy fatigue crawled over my legs. Ah, duck! Need to pause for a second. Leaning against the wall, I had to draw a deep breath. Chewing over, I stared down at my Timberland boots. Jesus, this is so unusual! What's happening to me? Why am I so tired? These questions left me puzzled. By the end of the day, I completed half of the quest that Tom had demanded. Super Mario was grouchy and pissed. I did whatever I could.

Somnolent of the tiresome day, I headed back to Motel Zero. A mile away, I decided to sneak through the side streets to avoid the overflowing traffic. Dusk had already fallen. It was gloomy like the tuxedo worn by the actors in the movie Men in Black. Why am I feeling so exhausted? The next moment, the Nissan was zooming straight ahead to a parked vehicle on the driveway. What the f—? I hit the brake and rolled the steering wheel in a safe direction to a complete stop.

I fell asleep while driving half a mile away from my pad. This concussion is driving me nuts! Thank God nobody was on the driveway. The next day, I went to work with Jim. We worked at a bungalow somewhere in the Niles area. As we started toiling, I climbed on the ladder. Then, a moan echoed through the entire unit.

"What? What happened?" Jim grilled.

"My knee." Groaning, I grabbed my leg. For a minute, I felt anchored like a tree stump. At lunch, I was walking in the basement and fumbling through my electrician's pouch. Suddenly, a vigorous dizziness caused me to wobble. This Fucking concussion again! I can't take it anymore!

It was around five thirty that afternoon when I came back to my crib.

The fatigue made my vision dazed while entering into Motel Zero. Trudging through the hall, I fainted on the carpet. I woke up from an unexpected nap with a gape-mouthed expression. For God's sake, what's going on here? How long have I slept? The clock on my smartphone displayed that it was around midnight. Do I have narcolepsy? I gotta see a doctor. The problem is that I can't afford health insurance. I didn't come here to visit doctors, but what choice do I have?

*****

On Saturday, April 7, I was cruising back to Motel Zero from a tedious day at work. I need to loosen up. I'm parched! Gotta go to the liquor store. Naw, before that, oughtta ring to my guy. He can provide me with some goodies.

An hour later, I lay back on the couch, radiating a broad smile. A bottle of 100 Pipers (an imported whiskey from Bulgaria) and three baggies of yeyo were left on the table. Whoop! Whoop! A couple of hours later, on the same mocha-colored table, were overspilled white powder (as if I was cooking a cake) and a half-empty bottle of scotch. This isn't right! My legs are so numb. I can barely make it to the bathroom. Gotta stop this crap, at least for a while.

That was one of the wisest decisions that I had taken. The clock was ticking at three in the morning. The night was murky as the costume of Venom, the fictional character in Spider-Man. The yeyo made a fussing sound echoing in my eardrums. There was a dead silence in Motel Zero when the phone buzzed unexpectedly. Who the heck could bother at this moment? The screen was streaming an unknown number, which was kind of familiar. My face beamed viciously. There is only one man who would call in that particular time of the night. The voice in other line cried out happily.

"What's up, champ?" Don said. "My phone died. Can I come over? My friends will Uber me."

Thirty minutes passed, and Don rolled over. After a few glasses of scotch, Da Bomb hashed over something that made me stagger like a drop-dead gorgeous slamhole revealing that she had a baby and that I was the father three months after we were bumping uglies.

"I'm leaving the studio within the next fourteen days. Can I be your roommate? I'll pay you half of the rent. The other room is still available, right?" Don asked.

A clumsy silence occurred. It would be marvelous if someone will pay the half lease for this shithole. Besides, I need a roommate. I thought. Plus, Don is a cool guy. We get along. A terrifying silence, resembling Hitchcock's horror movie, burst in Motel Zero. Don gazed at me, waiting for an answer. It wasn't too long before I accept to his offer. He was like a big brother to me, a brother whom I never had. Da Bomb had taught me a lot, not only in the boxing field but also in general. We had a ball lingering around. Also, I wouldn't have to bust my ass working extra hours to cover the rent. Contemplating, I was elated to have him as a roommate.

"I'm down, champ." That was exciting news. Don and I hit it off quite well as roommates. We used to banter back and forth, goofing around like buddies. He treated me like a younger brother. In April 2018, we gallivanted to a bunch of joints, sports bars, etc. No matter where we shuffled, Don introduced me to everyone as his cousin.

For the first time in my life, I was being valued, and that feeling touched my heart. It rejoiced my mind. However, I was worried about the symptoms of an annoying concussion. Hanging out with Don was a delightful time. Unfortunately, it only lasted a couple of weeks before the concussion got worse.

*****

My energy was depleted from the exhausting job as an electrician. Later, the Nissan wheeled on I-90 toward Oakley. My body was extremely weary. I was tromping to the locker room, and my eyelids were closing like those of a hospital armed security guard dozing off while working.

The concussion distracted my concentration, and training became unpleasant. Some days, I trudged back from work, sprawled on the couch for a moment to take a deep breath, and stood idle for the next couple of hours. Cutting classes at Oakley occurred multiple times in the same week. Contemplating to postpone my training in Oakley worsened my headache to the point of infinity.

The worrisome thoughts about my future grew drastically. Those thoughts compelled me to take a firm decision. Need to slow down boxing sessions until the concussion flew away! I wasn't cheerful about making that conclusion. On the other hand, that was seemingly the most rational move.

*****

On May 5, 2018, Don and I headed up to Erik Sobczak's house. Erik had a birthday party, and he kindly invited us to his neat California ranch type of house. His patio had a set of a snazzy table and a couple of chairs. There was a bunch of food and booze. The weather was in the mid-seventies, which was pretty decent for the season. Only a few shy clouds were hovering around where human eyes could scan.

Pouring bevies, we were lost in long chin-wags, boisterous laughter had been roaring over and over. The blaring guffaws could be heard from a distance. Stories flowed from a few wild hogs drinking constantly and interrupting each other at every moment. Unexpectedly, a man in his mid-thirties, exuding a gleaming grin, appeared from the dooryard of the north side.

His name was Ray, Erik's friend. When Ray got hammered, his face was colored like a cherry, especially when he chuckled. Cherry Face was a greedy tax attorney, but he was also a nice guy, streaming a pleasant smile. Cherry Face was fun to goof around with.

Starring at all of those dudes, I was pondering. That is what I need, a drink and a delightful company that could pull me out from the stressful concussion that had been getting too annoying for the past couple of weeks. At half-past seven, Erik stated, "Guys, I've reserved a table at the Serbian place in Lincoln Park. There is live music. It will be quite entertaining, so finish your drinks and let's bounce."

An hour later, the Fantastic Four (us) rambled to this particular resto bar. The live music had blasted out from a female singer. She was one of those gorgeous chicks who you're down to have a few kiddos with already. Behind her, a few guys were playing on instruments in the northwest corner. There was a counter tab bar stuck at the end of the club. Tiny tables were spread out all over the joint. The space between those tables were too narrow.

Bulgaria and Serbia have a similar culture, especially in terms of celebrating. That made my time spent there fabulous. I briefly spoke to several Serbian lads. They were genuine people. The entire place made me feel like I was among my nation. The waitress was a sweet and polite gal. She fluttered as a sparrow through the overflowing restaurant. I was ordering a Serbian moonshine, Rakia. When the waitress fetched me the shot, I hollered, "Wait for a second, hon." I chugged the shot swiftly and grumbled to the Serbian waitress, "One more, please!"

My lips were numb as if some dentist had injected local anesthesia. The waitress gave me a look like I was a lunatic. That picture of chugging recurred eleven times. The frustrated waitress moved back and forth, making the same route as a carfare bus. That joint was bursting at the seams. There were so many Serbians out there who gave me the impression that we were in Serbia.

The waitress eclipsed beyond the wall of packed Serbians. She was broadcasting the look as if she was saying, "Would you stop drinking, please! I got other tables to cover". I didn't judge her. She was forced to stream an amiable smile as any employee working in this business. These people are trying to make some greenbacks like everyone else.

Gulping Rakia got me plastered. My vision got hazy, causing me to wobble. The birthday party in that club was running great. We were having a lot of fun, and fifteen minutes later, someone sneaked behind our table and accidentally pushed Erik. Distraught, Erik said something and pushed him back. At the next moment, everyone hawked on us by throwing punches, kicks, and bottles.

The picture of having a delightful time quickly changed into a massive fray. Serbians regrouped and attacked the Fantastic Four because we were the only ones who spoke English in the entire joint. In the middle of the crammed club, six or seven macho guys throttled me. To be honest, they patted me as if they were girls in a cheerleading team. My shirt was torn apart brutally. That was one of my favorite shirts.

Somehow, I managed to flee from the helter-skelter and rushed to the street. Then, my eyes widened. Da Bomb lay down unconsciously on the sidewalk, as if someone gunned him with a Desert Eagle. Ah, Jesus! I went to check Don. Kneeling next to him, I was screaming, "My brother! My brother!" A puddle of blood flowed in the back of his head. Jesus Christ, is he dead? The voice in my mind asked.

My forearms were covered in blood like I was a vascular surgeon doing an elaborate surgery.

"Call the ambulance!" I barked hysterically while staring at Don. An unfamiliar broad was standing three feet away. She was appalled.

"What happened to him?" my question sounded bitter while I was leering at the girl. She was luscious, reminding me of Keira Knightley.

"S...s...s...someone...s...s...s...smashed a bottle of booze from b...b...b...behind," the twin of Keira Knightley stammered. Oh Lord! I hope he will be fine. A loud siren blared. The ambulance scudded like a European flying hornet. A few minutes later, Cherry Face was rushing his Mercedes. He was following the paramedic's vehicle. Eric and I were dead serious, riding along in Cherry Face's Mercedes. The three of us burst inside the infirmary. A horrible feeling poked me. I hope he'll be okay!

"How is he? Is he going to be all right?" I asked a man wearing a white lab coat.

"Are you his relative?" the man in the white lab coat asked stiffly.

"Naw, just a friend. He is my roommate, but I know his parents." My response was honest, as if they interrogated me like I was witness in a courtroom, being convicted of first degree murder.

"If you are not a parent or sibling, we can't give you any further information. I am sorry." I stared at the doctor apathetically.

"Oh man, are you kidding me? Why? How come? Just tell me if he is going to be fine."

"It's classified. I am sorry."

"Come on, man! At least tell me that he will be fine." My tone echoed through the vestibule of the medical building. I know every hospital had a policy, and every first responder had to follow the rules strictly, frightened about losing their job.

"I am sorry." The man that looked like a doctor turned around and walked into the entrance that had a big sign saying EMERGENCY.

"Please, tell me what's going on," I crowed loudly like a bummed out wacko. My voice raised and created a ruckus that forced security to usher me to the exit. Obediently, we left the infirmary. I wouldn't start to fight the medical wardens. I had enough that night. Street fights were something that I purposely avoided. But if someone attacked my buddies, I couldn't stay apathetic. One of the most pleasant Saturday evenings had turned to one of the worst nights ever. Another hideous feature was the fact that I had to combat Serbs. They were hospitable people. I always got along with Serbians. They were like my brothers. The next day, at noon, I dialed Rita George to get more information regarding Don's medical condition. She averred, expressing a serene tone.

"Don left the hospital an hour ago. He got some stitches on the back of his head, although I'm pretty sure he'll be fine. How are you feeling?" she asked.

"I'm perfectly fine. Thank God."

"Yeah, I'll bring Don within the next few days. Stay healthy. Talk to you later. Bye," Rita asserted and hung up the phone. She was outgoing and amiable as always. I didn't tell her the truth. Why? Because I didn't want to cause any additional nuisance. It was just the way I was brought up.

The concussion was persistently thudding in my head, bringing headache and wooziness. Why am I feeling so tired and awful? I headed up to the bathroom where I stared in the mirror. There was a smidgen of a scratch over my nose. That's it? I was thankful that nobody whacked me with a bottle like they did to the champ.

On the weekend, Don flittered smoothly through Motel Zero's door, resembling how Kramer slid over the door of Jerry Seinfeld's apartment. He looked like he had just come back from a vacation in Hawaii. His rejoiced face had a wide grin like a man who had just won millions of dollars in the lottery. His usual line clicked like a flashlight from snapping a screenshot by using an iPhone.

"What's up, Champ?" He asked. It was astonishing how he looked like nothing had happened to him. Don had a tremendous pain tolerance acquired in boxing. He fought six rounds with a broken rib against Stevenson who held, at that time, the WBC belt in 2012. I could tell straight from the horse's mouth that the pain of a broken rib was unbearable.

Moreover, his potent right hand had been broken while fighting against Sean Monaghan. Don refused to quit and fought with his injured hand till the last round. The medical physician, the referee, and even his own father, Papa Bomb couldn't change his mind. Don had lost the fight versus Sean, but many people and magazines had spoken of him like a winner.

Don had won the hearts of the audience by showing the performance of a brave warrior that night. Everyone knew that he should be the winner that evening if his hand hadn't been broken as a result of surgery a year ago.

*****

Pete, the Greek employer, ran out of any immense construction undertakings. He had some inconsequential easy-peasy jobs. Thus, I was forced to seek more independent electrical contractors. Bobby, the Bulgarian groundhog (Mike's employer), was one of the shrewdest men I had ever met in Chicago. Bobby was a prosperous man. He had a particular standout to double his stacks. I had never comprehended how Bobby was doing it. His business was legal, and he wasn't playing in casinos either.

Bobby spent many hours in the construction world as a sole contractor providing plumbing service. He owned assets in real estate. One day, I was spontaneously in his house. Chatting about work, Bobby handed me a business card of a Serbian man called Urash. In the next couple of hours, I phoned him.

Urash spoke advanced English. The way he talked shot me a hint that his brain was snapping quickly. He was an ingenious man. He sent me over to a residential building located in Cicero. When I pulled the Nissan in the lot of that building, Urash had been waiting for me. He was six feet tall, had a volleyball-spiker type of body, and wore buzz cut like a member of the Marine Corps.

Urash had an electrical license for Chicago and the suburbs, which assured him an umpteen commercial and residential contracts. The Serbian man knew how to schmooze his clients. His mind was as sharp as a razor. He looked pretty much like a white version of the R&B singer Usher. Two Serb guys were standing alongside Urash, Goran and David. Goran was a short, and bony guy. David had an opposite proportion—stocky and towering. They both were jocund fellas.

For the following two weeks, we schlepped like oxen. In the mornings, I could barely open my eyelids while driving to work. My body was bushed. We had to carry tools and materials from ground level up to the sixth floor. The elevators didn't work. Respiratory issues forced me to stop and take a quick break.

Intermittently, I had to prop my arm on the wall to remain in balance. Lord Almighty, how long will this concussion torture me? I worked with sluggish movements. One particular day, at quarter to twelve, Goran and David called me for lunch. When they approached the apartment where I worked, they gazed at me, appalled. I was leaning against the wall, attempting to catch my breath.

"Are you okay?" Goran queried, bewildered.

"Yeah, I am fine." My words came while I was leering at the ground. At this moment, I couldn't eclipse my sullen face.

"Hey, man, if you are feeling sick, you can go home and rest. Urash wouldn't mind," Goran said. He was streaming a worrisome look.

"That would be nice, then who's gonna take care of my bills?" my voice yapped while I was grimacing. An awkward silence hovered over the three of us. Don't be a jerk. It's not his fault that you are being sick. Chill out.

My unpleasant behavior turned to a friendly grin, like a gray sky rapidly metamorphosing into a clear and sunny skyline. On the way back to Motel Zero, my Nissan sneaked through the crammed traffic. The count of the vehicles was equal to infinite. My eyelids were closing down gradually as if some Asian chick was rubbing my back. Mmm…knocked off! Doofus, don't fall asleep. Remember what you did a couple of weeks ago? Open your eyes, you dimwit.

Great consternation had bugged me while I was driving. I was exhausted from the outstretched working day. Around half-past six, the afterglow fell over as fast as a gluttonous hoodlum was carjacking a flashy Mercedes. The Nissan drove unhurriedly to Motel Zero. When I hopped out of the vehicle, Don yapped from the window above.

"What's up, champ? I am going to hang out with some buddies in Palatine. Are you in?"

"Naw, champ. Need to rest. Have fun." My only intention was to hit the rack. The concussion tormented me perpetually. Whoop! Whoop! The annoying beat in my head sounded like techno festival. My battery was low. I could barely crawl in the shower. Dude! You have to face the fact that you are sick, and you must take some precautions. Go and seek medical treatment. It's gonna be all right. The annoying concussion will end up soon. I was dragging my feet like a zombie. The light-headedness induced me to collapse onto the king-size bed. In a split second, I hit the rack for more than ten hours straight dormant.

Chapter 24

On Tuesday, May, 24, 2018, the brown Nissan pulled up at the nearest and cheapest bevy store I could found around. A few minutes later, I crept back in the Sentra holding a bottle of scotch and a twelve-pack of Modelo. I shoved the car key into the ignition switch, then my smartphone jingled unexpectedly. The name of Val had emerged onto the five-inch display. Oh man! What does he want? I haven't spoken to him for a while. I better take this call.

"Hey, Val. How you doin'?" I asked. Val was a man who could furnish any proportion of crap that you could imagine.

"Klara wants to give you something. She spoke vaguely about some bet which had been made between the two of you. We made plans for this Saturday. I will pick you up at seven." A pause occurred, then he continued like a first-grade student presenting his homework in the classroom. "Would you be able to come?" That question was equivalent to someone asking me, "Would you like to dine a free meal from your favorite Red Lobster?" after I had been starving all day long.

"Yeah, that's cool. I'm down. See ya on Saturday." Whoop! I hung up and grinned. Klara wants to see me nine months after we met. Is that for real? Or that's a foolish joke? Well, boy! Obviously, you have the chance to score a home run. Congratulations to the man who won a big reward for the weekend!

At Wrigley Field, the stadium speaker stately announced, "And the next hitter for Chicago Cubs with number nine is Dimitry! He struggled with plenty of injuries for the past two months. But he wouldn't miss the opportunity of notching the ultimate home run. The whole stadium remains quiet, wincing in anticipation of the performance of this astonishing player." This frigging squarehead.

A whim popped up in my mind. How come she wants to hang out after nine months of silence? We have met for no more than five to seven minutes. That's all.

Women are emotional. They act oddly, and most of the time, they can't even describe why. Many women follow their emotional brainwaves. That's natural. There is nothing wrong with that.

I didn't expect anything from her. Why? She might be one of those types of indecisive chicks who changed their minds incessantly. I thought we would never meet again, then out of the blue, she had told Val that we needed to goof around together. It didn't make any sense. It was a peculiar and unusual deed which made me plunge into a river of tentative thoughts. Wrapping my head around, I was thinking about the upcoming Saturday. I didn't know where we were going, which was ludicrous.

Saturday evening came across as rapidly as snapping a finger. At quarter to six, I hopped in the shower for twenty minutes. Bustling around in Motel Zero, I tried to bundle up as fast as I could. I had on black denim trousers and a white silk T-shirt. On that shirt, there were portrayed multiple mixtures in black shades of human figures projecting intercourse between a man and a girl. It was called Kama Sutra. That was my joyful method of saying Hello. On top of the shirt, I wore my black spring-season Emporio Armani coat. Not too long after I tarted up, Val called. His harsh voice notified me that he was already waiting downstairs. The perfume of Dolce & Gabbana was splashed all over my body. When I yanked the door and hopped inside, Val threw a glimpse on my shirt and began to chuckle. He pointed at the Kama Sutra.

"What's that shirt?" he quipped.

"Get outta here. Stop pulling my leg. I love this shirt." I exposed a tenacious, unbreakable equanimity and a scoop of self-perseverance. Every man must boost his masculine energy, especially when he interacts with hot chicks. The question I should have asked a long time ago shot faster than a round from an AK-47.

"Where are we going, Val?"

"To some live jazz club around the Buck town area," Val answered as if he had reported to his strict employer working in a high-paced computer corporation. Val made driving a pastime. He thought of himself as being a racer. The way he sped his vehicle reminded me to get an Uber on the way back into my asylum.

Sneaking in through the jazz club entry, we gazed around. That joint was bursting at the seams. There were a variety of yuppies and broads wearing vogue-style clothes. Val and I headed up to the countertop bar to get some drinks. The bartender was dressed like king killa kupo (drug dealer) who merely touched down from Columbia. I was chilling out at the countertop, and waiting for the headliner.

There she blows! Klara dashed as if she was running late for a date. Her black dress projected her astonishing figure, leaving my jaw hanging. She was sensuous and enthralling, just like Jessica Alba in the movie Sin City. Oh Lord, what a woman! Her glittered beam was similar to Jennifer Garner. Klara's face was aesthetic, a breathtaking mixture between Halle Berry and Salma Hayek. Her beauty was preternatural. Boy, don't get too excited! Keep it low profile.

Klara gave a friendly hug to Val. Then, she pivoted toward me. She embraced me warmly as if we were close friends who hadn't seen each other since grade school. We were entwined by the willingness to communicate.

"Hi, Klara. You look terrific. How you doin'?"

"Thanks. You as well. It's been a while since we've met." Klara declared while her grin twinkled as if she was posing for a commercial for the toothpaste Crest. I don't get it. Why is she acting like we have known each other for years? This is exclusively unusual. Chewing it over, I was thrown out into the gutter and put in a bewildering position.

"This is for you," Klara delved in her purse and handed me a crumpled envelope.

"What is it?" I asked. Klara answered my question without saying anything. She just pulled out an envelope. There were fifty bucks neatly hidden in that envelope. It looked like she was rewarding me.

"Naw, I can't have this money. Take your money back. Just buy me a drink." My statement came with a complacent smirk. She accepted my idea without any objections. While Klara walked toward the booze jockey (bartender), I couldn't stop peering at her. One of the most drop-dead gorgeous chicks in the club is buying me a drink. How about that? Damn, boy. She is smoking-hot Bella. When Klara fetched the drinks, I was looking in different direction (of course, on purpose).

"Come with me. I want to introduce you to somebody," Klara said, her eyelids emitted jollity. Oh, man. Just when I was enjoying at the moment and now I ought to say howdy to her boyfriend or fiancé. Bustling through the crowded joint, Klara introduced me to three of her besties; charming local broads whose names I momentarily forgot. The live music was playing in a laid-back rhythm. Carrying my ole chum Jameson, the night was going smoothly as expected.

I relished any moment spent with Klara. There was no secret that I was down for her, and she had already knew it. Val dragged his butt in front of the stage. He was hypnotized by the music. In the meantime, Klara was paying attention to me. We were dancing, stepping closer to each other over and over again. The gap between us was no more than six inches.

"What is this shirt?" she asked while patting my belly. Whoop! We have a winner!

"It's Kama Sutra." I said. My stony face didn't flinch. It was like a cover story filled with self-worth. She laughed, bowing her face to the floor and holding her hands to her stomach as if she was in pain. The way Klara looked at me could be described as if she was saying, "Boy, you rock!" There was some chemistry between the two of us.

Once in a while, she dashed to her friends, then she rolled back to me. Klara acted like a joyful offspring bouncing around with other tots in preschool. The music was so loud that we could hardly communicate. When I asked for her phone number, she ditched me out. Nevertheless, she gave me her Facebook.

"Let's have dinner. Do you like Greek food?" my question cruised by while I was wondering about her response.

"A dinner? Naw, that sounds like a date. We can go to the movies if you want." Her proclamation was austere.

"Movies. Well, yeah, why not?" Movies? Why she is acting so weird? Perhaps, she is looking for a friend! Ha-ha. Yeah, but I am not a nipper in the kindergarten making friends, and goofing off on the playground. Maybe you're thinking too much. Why don't you sip another Jameson and chill out, would ya? At the next moment, the concussion didn't miss a chance and made me feel sick.

"What is it?" Klara blurted. She projected a perplexed expression.

"Ah nothing. I'm just getting tipsy." I replied. Klara laughed at my crap.

I had decided to go cold turkey since I was getting sick. An hour later, Klara and I split.

How come she wouldn't agree for dinner, but she is down to watch a movie? Ah, don't stretch out. Your brain may explode, you damn fool. That was what I was thinking while Val drove me back to Motel Zero. On Monday, Klara and I chitchatted via Messenger. Klara consented to meet up on Wednesday at AMC Theater in Niles by half-past seven in the evening. We were going to watch a comedy titled Jumanji.

Klara voluntarily typed her phone number. Three days ago, she refused to give me her number, and now she is writing it on Messenger. How come? On Wednesday, the twilight had already hovered through the city of Chicago. At 7:25, I was chilling out at the lobby of the AMC, playing on my smartphone to kill some time. Where the heck is she?

Text message alert from Klara:

I will be there after 15 minutes, sorry!

We headed through the projecting room of the cinema and took the seats in the last row. We gazed at the boring commercials. My suggestion came out from nowhere.

"Hey, Klara, the idea to watch a movie isn't bad. But I would like to communicate more with you, to acknowledge you as a person. Let's go and grab a cup of coffee. What you think?" She gazed at me, puzzled as if I just said, "Let's just go and have sex."

"I'm jonesing to have a matcha latte. Let's take a hike."

The two of us left the cinema before even the movie commenced, as we had already seen that blockbuster. We rambled to Starbucks located in the same public square plaza. An hour and a half later, we kept chatting like two besties who hadn't seen each other for a long time. Wandering back to her car, Klara revealed,

"I really like you, but also, you must know I have a husband. We have been married for sixteen years, which means nothing can happen between us." BAM, BAM. I felt as if the Barney baby from the distinguished sitcom The Flintstone hit me with a skillet. What? She has a husby? What the heck? Then why has she been acting like a single person until now, rubbing my belly intimately, and boom! She is married. Well, dude! Looked at the bright side. At least, she has been honest with you. Since I had touched down in the USA, most of the chicks gave me the cold shoulder for whatever reason. That was just the way it was. I wouldn't mess around with a married broad.

"Sweet, where is your husband?" I asked. That was a dumb question. Why did I need to know where her husby was? It wasn't my business.

"His name is Jeff. He is a musician like me. He is performing tonight in San Jose, California."

"That's awesome." A few minutes passed. I almost stumbled on the floor. Shortness of breath forced me to lean against the concrete column in the garage to avoid falling. I wheezed for thirty seconds.

My face became pallid. The wooziness that roared in my eardrums caused me an unpleasant ache. A stabbing pain throbbed on the top of my head. Convulsive dizziness lurched me and caused an obnoxious weariness. I wanted to howl like an overwhelmed control freak after losing a potential client at work. I couldn't let myself grumble in front of a hot chick. Ah man! Not again. Not right now. This damn concussion is a frigging hassle. I'm sick of it! Get outta my head!

"What is it? What is happening to you?" Klara asked, frightened.

"I don't know. I feel under the weather. It may be a fever. Hurts by the skin of my teeth." My goal was to give her a runaway response; it didn't work out.

"No! It doesn't look fine. What's the matter? We are not moving elsewhere until you explain. What the heck is happening to you?" She insisted on a straight answer. I didn't have any choices left. I explained how the lousy concussion had been agitating me for the past couple of months.

Boxing is a tough sport. Sometimes, fighters get injured critically bad. Everyone who fought in martial arts knows the possibility of being harmed. I thought it was demeaning to whine about it. That was my chosen sport, and I didn't feel remorse regarding any circumstances. I wouldn't like people feeling pity for what had happened to me in boxing or in general.

Klara threw a repulsive look like I was talking trashy to her. Then, she cried out,

"You need to see a doctor. I know somebody. He'll check you up."

"Klara, I didn't ask for help. It's all good."

"You must check in to my family doctor. He is Bulgarian too. He is prominent here in Chicago. His name is Eugene, and he has been taking care of me for the past ten years. Here, take his business card," Klara declared. No matter what I said, she remained firm and tenacious. At the end of the night, we split like best friends. Klara was an intelligent and down-to-earth person. She spread a delightful sense of humor. Her black pupils were glittering like opulent pearls. Her bewitching grin lured people like a metal to a magnet. Her athletic figure was better than a highest-paid actress.

Klara was my crush. Nevertheless, I couldn't interact with a missus. My intentions to her were merely to remain just friends, which meant to stay away from her.

*****

On Thursday, May 31, I decided to take a day off. Usually, I was working during the week and chilling out over the weekends. However, that particular day was an exception. The influenza sucked all of my energy. My eyelids were constantly closing, and a horrible headache dragged me back to the bed.

I had no clue what time it was; and it didn't matter, not even what the weather outside was: sunny, cloudy, foggy, rainy, windy, etc. I didn't give a damn even if a destructive tornado was coming through. My agenda was to crash all day long and to avoid any phone calls. And guess what? Around forenoon, my phone jingled.

Oh man! You forgot to turn on the silent mode! I threw an apathetic glimpse over the screen; it was Klara. She was the last person in the world whom I would expect to reach out to me. I was still bummed out over the fact that she was married. Besides, I was reluctant to contact her under any circumstances, and there she blows! Why is she calling me? What does she want? Dude! Don't pick up the phone! Don't pick up the phone!

"Hey, Klara, how you doin'?" my voice roared unpleasantly. Pussy!

"I am doing okay. Listen up. There is a private clinic named Light Medical Imaging. That clinic is not far from Schiller Park, and if you are available, let's meet at this health center. They will check you out. Can you come?" A pause occurred for the next few seconds. Man, you shouldn't pick up the phone. For some inexplicable reason, I was infatuated with this broad.

"Yeah, cool. See you there." Thinking about her, I felt joyful.

The headache was making me drowsy. At half-past eleven A.M, the weather was lovely. Sun rays broke through puffy clouds. The brown Nissan rolled through the streets of Des Plaines. My somnolent eyelids could barely stand open while my hands steadily held the steering wheel as if someone had pranked me by giving Gorilla Glue onto my palms instead of hand sanitizer. Despite my sleepy face I was excited with collywobbles in my stomach.

I parked my ride in front of the health center ten minutes earlier, and she was already there. Klara was waiting in her purple-rain-colored 1997 Honda Accord. When Klara acknowledged my presence, she embraced me like we were siblings. Her eyes gleamed like those cutie, fluffy Pomeranian canines.

"You gonna be all right!" Klara asserted. Despite her attempt to cheer me up, a worried feeling pursued me as an obnoxious mosquito that was drouthy to suck blood. The private clinic had a modern and opulent design, which gave me the impression that the owner had splurged a bundle of greenbacks. Picturing what would be the bill after this medical examination was making the headache even worse.

Klara strutted over to the front desk and started gibbering something that I couldn't comprehend. In the blink of an eye, a blonde lady in her forties approached us. She explained what procedure they would be doing. A computed tomography (CT) scan was a technology system that allowed detailed imaging inside of the body. This technological component operated like a combination of x-ray and computer database of your bones and organs. Usually, it was a routine method that took from five to seven minutes. That was why you would not need to schedule appointments.

There was a mounted flatbed that slides your entire body to a huge circular main structure which snapped pictures via a spinning movement that splashed shafts all over the body (in my case, my head). CT scan system must take high-quality images, which required strict guidance. A single trembling might ruin the whole procedure.

"After completing the procedure. We'll send the result straight to Doctor Eugene's office, which may refer an appointment for the following week." The same blonde lady declared. The process was done briskly. When we wandered to the cashier, I was fumbling for my wallet, wondering. How much do they charge? Hundred fifty or maybe two hundred dollars?

Klara shot me with a frowning face like she had been insulted ruthlessly as if I offered her money after we had nooky. She pulled out her credit card from American Express and slid it faster than a cruel criminal could pull a firearm trying to rob 7-Eleven.

I peaked at the slip, which indicated a bill of almost four hundred bucks. The way Klara had paid was like she was the one having the CT scan. My face looked dumbfounded as if some street magician was presenting an unseen trick in Vegas. Then, I shook off from the shock and stated,

"Klara, are you aware that I wouldn't be able to pay you back?"

She mirrored a pouty glimpse while jotting her signature on the receipt.

"Don't worry about it," She said. How couldn't I be? Who the heck is paying a four-hundred-dollar bill, especially to someone you've just barely met? Nobody had ever done something like that in my whole life. It was too outlandish. I was grateful for her deeds, but I didn't know how to react. Thank you? I guess. Before we left the health center, the charming minstrel whispered,

"Keep me posted after your appointment with Doctor Eugene. I got to bail. See ya later."

Klara cuddled me tightly, which turned almost like a clutch. I peered at how she got in her purple-rain Honda. Klara roared off the parking lot like a lunatic NASCAR racer. My subconscious mind established a short report. What a chick! Heading back to Motel Zero, I couldn't stop pondering about her.

*****

On Saturday, just before the twilight slumped into the Windy City, my ride rolled to the townhouse of Motel Zero. After a few minutes, I left the Nissan into the reserved parking spot. Ah man, now I got stairs to climb.

The frustrating concussion was gradually throbbing in my head like a beat of an awful-sounding drum. My sluggish legs trudged to the staircase step by step as slowly as a snail would crawl over the ground by portraying no-rush behavior. While I was walking through the staircase on the second floor, sudden light-headedness overcame me.

What is happening to me? Why do I feel so knackered? I need a break. I have to sit on the stairs just for a minute. Imagine a twenty-nine-year-old man who was supposed to be a pro boxer sitting on the stairway between the second and third floor, and heavily panting caused by weariness. The only thing that kept him awake was the unpleasant shortness of breath.

While I tried to catch my breath, in my mind cropped up something that I had been thinking about for the last two weeks. Tom and Urash are not happy with my work. They keep carping about how slow I am. Pete doesn't have any jobs. The most rational decision is to switch to something that requires mild physical labor until I heal. But what options do I have?

Some minutes later, I made it to the door of Motel Zero. Unlocking the doorknob, I burst inside and heaved all of my working attire onto the huge pile that looked like a pyramid. Without even showering, I just sprawled in the king-size bed and swiftly nodded off for the next ten hours.

*****

It was half-past ten in the morning on Sunday when I woke up. I was grimacing. The pain in my head was throbbing like a dubstep party on Miami Beach. It was getting obnoxious. That didn't throw me into the state of being down in the mouth. The word surrender doesn't exist in my dictionary. Influenza made my body shiver. Cheese and rice, when will this fever go away! My mind hollered like a crow. Maybe when you go to the doctor's office, you will dig out the answers, you perplexed chuckle-head. The organic black tea and plenty of extra-strength Tylenol was my method to wrestle the nettle concussion. It worked. It put me back on the track like a wounded warrior ready to fight against a ruthless lion using his bare hands.

Leaning on the kitchenette sink like I was about to throw up, I antici-pated the water to get warm in the kettle. What should I do? Who could help me out finding another job? Snap! I got it! I grabbed my phone and dialed a Bulgarian fella named Simon. I had met him in the construction field a long time ago.

Simon had a shaggy blond hair and an unkempt sun-brown beard. He looked like a bear. Simon worked at a pizzeria named Sapino's. He texted me the phone number of the regional manager. His name was Dino. Dino sounded affable over the phone. He sent me to the nearest location in a town called Harwood Heights, which was a five-minute drive from Motel Zero.

On Monday morning, at half-past ten, I was hauling my butt to meet Dino at Sapino's. The pizzeria was located in the small plaza where a few different businesses were glued to each other. When I walked through the rear entryway, everyone gazed at me oddly like I was a plastered man seeking trouble. Dino was at the front, explaining something to one of the employees. He looked like a neat guy who splurged a lot of money for his floppy quiff. Dino looked like a classic European soccer player. His body was hefty like those guys spending a gob of time lifting weights and using steroids to look like Dwayne Johnson. He spoke a fluent Bulgarian, which left me staggered. Dino was yammering a bunch of instructions. He gave a quick lecture on how the business worked. Then, he dodged as fast as a teeny-weeny sparrow would fly away, intimidated by humans' reactions.

The employees at Sapino's were mostly Eastern Europeans. Some were

Bulgarians, Macedonians, Moldavians, Ukrainians, etc. Everyone had been involved in the process of making the pizza. When the order had been completed, the one next in the queue grabbed the items and hurried to deliver at the client's address. As long as you would not mess up something, everyone was happy. If you would deliver five large pizzas to someone who had ordered only one, then surely it would turn out to be an unpleasant problem.

All of the employees were amiable. The food was tasty. I didn't know which recipes they were using, but it was worth the money. The location was quite convenient. That was what kind of job I needed until my health condition recuperated. It was a less stressful job, and the gross wage was fine. Besides, it was fun to work with juvenile workmates. I was relieved that my plan worked well enough to continue making the dough to pay the bills. Those were my thoughts before my health condition deteriorated.

*****

On June 2, Saturday, I completed the night shift at Sapino's and returned to Motel Zero. I could barely handle climbing to the third floor. Gosh, I hate these stairs! Just before my chicken fingers reached the doorknob, blathering voices were roaring beyond the drywall. Pacing as fast as a snail, I entered through the living room where Don, two guys, and one chick (totally unknown) were fooling around.

"Hi, guys. Howzit goin'?" I asked. My wan face ejected a shiny diplomatic smile. I spoke English using a strong Bulgarian accent.

"What up, champ? Come on. Sit and drink with us," Don said, interrupting everyone by showing unbreakable self-esteem and great gratitude.

"Naw, champ. Keep the party goin'. I'll hit the rack. I'm feeling under the weather."

"Are you okay?" Don asked, concerned.

"I'm okay. Just knackered, you know." I wasn't okay. All of the guests, including Don, were puzzled. They peered at a haggard man trying not to collapse on the brown carpet. A severe headache accompanied by unpleasant fatigue forced me to crash onto my bed.

Around an hour later, footfalls rustling from the living room through the kitchen aroused me. Those guys must be really parched! They walk to the fridge any other minute. The clock displayed 5:00 a.m. Don and the other guys were shocked. They gazed at a man who plodded to the desolate kitchen and sat on the chair. He lay his head on the table and covered himself with a blanket. They all encircled me, coming from the other end of the condo. Don stepped closer and proclaimed,

"Hey, champ! You don't look well, man. What is it?" Everyone else started asking resembling questions.

"Hey, bud, you look horrible. You need to go to the hospital. Don't worry! We will take care of the bills!" Someone echoed beyond the small crowd.

"I will be all right, guys. No worries. Go to the living room. I need to stay alone, please." Everyone dashed to the den like an appalled deer. Cheese and rice! I'm so bushed. Can barely catch my breath, and now I can't even sleep. What an ironic disaster! Despite these circumstances, two hours later, my mind shut down to deep sleep.

The next day, around eleven in the forenoon, I woke up reluctantly. I had the same throbbing in the head. Thank God it's Sunday. Marching to the grunting fridge, I opened it and stared inside. There was only moldy food. What the heck? I need to get some groceries.

Don wasn't at Motel Zero. He was taking care of his kids and God knows what else. Along with my job and intricate health condition, I couldn't catch his pace. Sometimes, I spotted him once in a week. Nevertheless, whenever I needed him, he was always around. There was no question about that.

I put on some casual garments and sneaked into the Nissan for a four-minute drive to Jewel Osco. While parking my vehicle in the lot, I opened the door; and unexpectedly, my Nike sneakers could barely move. It was difficult to walk as if someone shackled me up using thick chains. What the heck?

The weariness made my body anchored to the seat like some hellion turd had poured the whole bottle of Loctite on the driver's seat like a payback prank. I bowed down to my knees. My body was immovable as a result of the difficult breathing. It was a grotesque picture. I looked like a junkie, overdosed by smack and lying on the bench of a public park. Keep it calm and steady, boy. You gonna be all right. Just keep it calm and stay positive.

The next moment, I opened my eyelids, dazzled. Gosh, how long have I been snoozing? Check your phone. Only ten minutes. That ain't so bad. At the store, customers passing around leered at me like I was a total weirdo panhandling for dough like an urban camper. That didn't concern me.

My purpose was to grab the most essential items and to get lost as soon as possible. I couldn't linger around at Jewel pursuing discounts or better deals. Ten minutes later, my sneakers successfully dragged me back to the Nissan. I was carrying two bags of commodities. My car roared back to Motel Zero. While I was trudging up through the staircase, my mind spoke. Lord almighty, I can't make it to the top. Time-out, time-out! I need a break. Those two bags are not heavy, but if I keep going, I will drop them. I used to tote much more bags without any pauses. Relax! The physical pain won't take it too long, as if you're passing through a short bridge. Those were my deep thoughts while my butt sat on the staircase. Thank God! Tomorrow I've got an appointment with Doctor Eugene.

Five minutes later, I invaded Motel Zero. I looked like Sylvester Stallone climbed through the seventy-two stairs leading to the entrance of Philadelphia Museum of Art, raising his hands in the first movie of the legendary franchise Rocky. The rest of the day, I was goofing around, eating chicken soup and watching the idiot box.

*****

On Monday morning at quarter to ten, I looked around while waiting on the white-leathered sofa at the lobby of Doctor Eugene's office. A few minutes passed, and a Mexican lady called out my name. I headed to the doctor's office where a gorgeous lady in her thirties sat on a chair behind her desk.

"Is that Doctor Eugene's office?" I asked her, perplexed.

"Yes, I am Katrine, his daughter. Dr. Eugene is busy today. Don't worry. I'm a physician too." Katrine chuckled, trying to make me feel better.

Then, she became dead serious. Katrine leered at me disdainfully and began to clarify the symptoms.

"Mr. Salchev, the results of the CT scan confirmed that you have a concussion. Thereby, all the headaches and light-headedness came through. Also, the influenza issues could be determined to be a consequence of fatigue, typically a result of numerous spars and recent fights in boxing," Katrine stated. Her deduced statement was a recommendation to rest for a couple of weeks which I couldn't afford. That was her brief lecture. She prescribed medications imported from Asia, which were way too pricey— over $260. At half-past noon, Klara called me. She demanded to know more information about the visit to Doctor Eugene's office.

After I reported the updates, she conjured,

"You must buy those medications." Klara surged, sounding like jazzed kiddo asking to eat ice cream at Dairy Queen.

"Nah, no way. I can't afford them. The price is too high." My declaration was firm and nonnegotiable. I was pretty sure that I would be fine without taking those medications. That was why I couldn't give credit for such high-priced medications, especially while I was busting my butt for a lower wage.

"Listen to me. You need those medications. Don't worry about the money. I will pay for it." She stood for her point. Her voice was imperative, and that was making me nervous.

"Klara, I won't be able to pay you back. You know that, right?" I said.

"I don't care. Just text me the names."

Her stubborn trait kicked in. I don't understand. Why does she want to help so much? We've just met, and all of sudden, she wants to take care of me. I don't mind, but it's so unusual. It doesn't make any sense! No one had ever treated me like that. Well, if she insists, I won't stop her.

"And by the way, what's your plans for your birthday?" Her question left me bewildered. How did she find out about my birthday? Ah yeah, presumably she cyberstalked me on Facebook.

"Since I have been feeling under the weather, I haven't planned anything yet. I guess I'll chill out."

"Well, I have an idea. There is a Bulgarian lady, a close friend of mine.

She does good body rubs. I will pay you for two sessions with her. Consider it a present." Whoop! That was a marvelous idea. There was something that wouldn't stop bouncing in my mind.

"Klara, why you're so nice to me?" There was a pause.

"Because I'd like to help people."

Come on, Klara, Cut the bullshit, would ya? Stop pulling my leg. Don't give me those runabout answers. Who am I? Shmuck on wheels, a scumbag. Those were the words spinning in my subconscious.

"Seriously, Klara, tell me. Why you are so nice to me?"

"I've told you already." Her sonorous tone sounded persuasive. A couple of minutes later, we ended the phone call. Despite her attempt to coax me, I wasn't certain why she had such a zest to help me out. It is what it is, dude! Who the heck gives a damn? Besides, you're getting a free massage. What's wrong with that?

*****

On Monday, June 4, Klara and I were supposed to meet in front of an enormous tenement building named Pavilion. Klara wanted to introduce me to her Bulgarian friend who would give me a body rub. Pavilion was just five minutes away from Motel Zero. Cruising to the huge tenement, I got lucky to snuggle the Nissan into the parking lot right next to the entrance. Just before I parked my vehicle, Klara had texted me that she was running late with five to ten minutes (Klara was always running late).

Waiting for her, my body leaned against the fender of the Nissan. The clock showed ten in the morning. The sun shafts scattered and portrayed the beginning of a picturesque morning. The blue sky was exquisite, like the eyes of Jennifer Aniston. Around five mutes later, Klara swaggered like a Victoria's Secret model promenading on a catwalk. I stood by my car like a hundred-year-old oak tree. I was stunned by her charisma. Gosh. She looks so damn hot! Her splendid dress accentuated her gymnastic figure. A delightful breeze of late spring and early summer joyfully played with her bewitching hair. The way she strutted toward me had been engraved in my mind for the rest of my life. I felt like I was a king calling out the most gorgeous woman in the kingdom to be his dame (my queen). Dude, you better stop dreaming before it gets worse. Jesus, she is so fascinating. This gal makes me feel like a powerful lord, even for ten seconds. I need to push this chick away. Klara flashed a smile as she sailed on a yacht to her favorite tropical island, celebrating the honeymoon along with her lover. I smiled back to her like a famished ape gazing at fruits. Klara gave me a hug like we were friends in grade school, then she handed me a plastic bag containing high-priced medications.

"Hello, Klara. You shouldn't buy those medications," I had attempted to sound as cool as I could.

"Don't start again. Let it go, please." Her announcement sounded like a rigorous judge giving me twenty years in a penitentiary for convicted murder without any chance of clemency. We were alone traveling in the elevator. I decided to elaborate a quick experiment. I stepped much closer to her. There was a two-inch gap between our lips. Her rejoicing countenance changed into a frown as if she saw someone crossing through an unauthorized line of a murder investigation.

"You are too close. You need to back off. Step back, please," she commanded, resembling a superior sergeant giving orders to a private. The elevator cruised somewhere between the sixth and seventh floor (I don't recall precisely).

When we burst in through the door, I felt like we were at a botanical garden. There were many plants, ferns, roses, begonias, etc. I felt like we bumped into a florist's shop. A cranky lady in her mid-fifties darted over. Her face had a bunch of wrinkles, and her grin was spreading around like a virus.

The lady brandished her hands and embraced Klara. They exchanged kind sentences, including comments about how they looked. Then, Klara introduced me to the lady. Her name was Gloria. She was a gasbag, flipping from subject to subject. Klara and I just listened to her. The next moment, Gloria peered at me and said,

"Take off your garments, young man, and leave them on the couch over here!" She pointed valiantly at the puffy couch that looked like a manky (dirty) sheep.

"I can't watch you getting naked," Klara whined while covering her eyes using her palms.

"Klara, I have my trunks on. I am not completely naked," I said joyfully. What the heck is wrong with this broad? Why is she feeling ashamed of me? I really gotta stop seeing this chick.

Thirty minutes later, while Gloria was gently rubbing my back, Klara jubilantly announced,

"Okay, guys, I got to take the hike. Tomorrow, I'll fly to California for a musical venue. I'll call when I get back."

"Sweet. Klara, have fun there. See ya later." Yeah, whatever, don't even bother. The simple fact that I couldn't make her my girl filled me with bitterness and made me feel estranged.

Gloria finished her creative work, then she curiously asked,

"You have one free session left. When would you like to come over?" Her question slid as if we must discuss the subject of ten-million-dollar transaction.

After a few seconds, I said, expressing a note of sarcasm, trying to mimic Al Capone,

"Let's make it at ten o'clock this Friday." The Al Capone character didn't work out, but Gloria approved the date by nodding. I boldly shook her hand like we were business partners and drifted away immediately.

Straight away, I dashed to the pizzeria. My shift was about to start in less than seven minutes. A few hours later, while I was fetching some lasagna, cheese bread, and a few cokes, my face grimaced as if someone was doing circumcision on me.

Leering at the Nissan, my mind was so baffled. I don't get it. I still have some respiratory issues, and it's too obvious. It is happening way too often. Why? I've changed the job. Driving pizza is less physical than working in construction. Why am I having a hard time breathing?

My perplexed mind stopped on the road that had a sign saying, No Outlet. The Bulgarian physician had described that there wasn't anything to worry about. However, the shortness of breath still fretted me consistently. Relax, the pain would fly away like a frightened pigeon. Heading back to the pizzeria, my ankles started to ache. It bothered me consistently, especially when I had to run somewhere. Every hour or so, I sat on the stool in the store to catch my breath. Most of my coworkers were peering at me, puzzled. The way they leered said, "What the heck is wrong with this guy? Why is he acting so weird?"

I couldn't judge them. Perhaps I looked quirky. They were watching a twenty-nine-year-old man sitting helplessly and trying to draw a deep breath as if he had just finished a thirteen-mile marathon. If it was a marathon, that would explain everything. But to be worn out when you had just delivered pizza? It wasn't making any sense.

That day occurred to be highly demanding, as if all residents from Harwood Height craved to nibble pizza from Sapino's. It was a magnificent opportunity to collect some greenbacks. Around midnight, I was rolling back to Motel Zero. The fatigue struck me so bad that I could barely move. My eyelids were gradually closing like how an automatic garage door usually closes. Dude, take a quick break, only for a few minutes. You've been working hard for the past nine hours. My body leaned back on the driver's seat, and I closed my eyelids.

For a moment, my mind envisioned how I lay on a deck chair at the beach island of Bora Bora. The sunbeams kept closing my eyelids. The environment was silent. Every once in a while, a sound of riffles was fizzing in my ears. After a long and tedious day, that was all I needed. The only thing I could hear was my breathing. The next moment, my phone rang and disturbed me from my two-minute nap. Who the heck is it? Ah, Don. I could barely pick up the phone.

"What up, champ?" my voice blared somnolently.

"Hey, champ, I'm looking at your car through the window. I saw you idled there for a while. What's the matter? Why are you not coming up?"

"Can't. Too tired. Give me a second."

"Hang on," Don cried out like a 911 dispatcher reacting to a call of a medical emergency.

"No worries, champ! I will come up in a minute." Don had hung up the phone already. Five seconds passed, and he burst through the entry faster than paramedics could. He opened the door and pulled me out from the Nissan. Don carried me up to the bedroom as if I was a homeless mutt shot by a firearm.

He reacted so fast as if my car had an installed C-4 and was about to blow up in a few seconds. I had no energy to hop in the shower. I dozed off faster than it took to snap a screenshot using the latest iPhone. I could walk up through the staircase on my own. Although, I would never forget how Don helped me out that night. God bless his heart.

*****

My birthday in 2018 wasn't anything special or something outstanding. The simple fact that my father had never acknowledged my birthdays since I had touched down in the USA created a frustration. It reminded me why I came to America in the first place.

Why would I keep wandering in the same tracks? Don't get me wrong; I don't hate my dad. He was my hero. The question arose, what kind of man would he be by not saying anything about his son's birthday when he was over eight thousand miles away? What do you think? How would his biological son interpret the misconnection with his father?

That was why I looked for some cheap booze to get stoned. What would be my thoughts after gulping a half bottle of scotch? Yeah, whatever, or it is what it is. What can I do about it?

The answer was simple—nothing. I could only swallow the bitterness and throw the chip on my shoulder out. Maybe, one day, I could be a father. Then, I would not repeat the same misdeed and would reassure that my child would be emboldened and exhibiting high self-esteem around his family. Furthermore, I would bolster his confidence from his entire childhood into adulthood. Unlike my dad, I wouldn't leave my child to be lost in his generation, struggling to find the right answers for the rest of his life. When people feel misplaced from their parents or a family member had mistreat them, they get cranky, growing with insecurities and having malicious thoughts that caused them to become ruthless and unjust. Those kids are more susceptible to initiate vast mistakes, such as drug addiction, suicide, assault, looting, etc.

*****

A day after my birthday, sunlight shone through the window in the bedroom and roused me up. The throbbing sound in my temple was persistently beating like a hip-hop song. I love listening to rap music, but that wasn't the rhythm I would like to hear. Wake up, you damn ballsack! It's time to dash munchies for bank-rolls. I kneeled at the edge of the bed and looked down at the brown carpet, then my pupils widened. I was horrified as if the creature from the movie Lights Out loomed in front of me. Holy cow! Dude! Look at your feet!

My toes were bigger than Arnold Schwarzenegger's legs. They were so swollen like the size of clay bricks. I had never seen anything like that, not even on the TV. There must be some proper explanation! I don't know how the Nike sneakers will fit on those feet. That's why I had such a terrible ache while I was working yesterday.

Well, Mr. Dimwit didn't give up. It was a simple mentality of a boxer. I never quit. The show must go on! Pacing like a granny turtle, I bundled up my employee garments and cruised to the bathroom to rinse my mouth. Looking at the mirror, I was stunned. The veins in my temples were thumping again. The concussion kept jiggling like a church bell. What else did I need? A couple of minutes later, an awful pain in my back bugged me. Sleeping on my lovely mattress caused an unpleasant ache right in the spine. Not cool!

Vexed by the morning surprises, I traipsed to the storage room and grabbed my Nike sneakers. I bought them for eight bucks from Goodwill four years ago. That was the only pair of shoes that could fit on my ogre's feet. If not, there were no options. I had to search for medical assistance, which I desperately avoided on purpose.

In the next five seconds, I was bemused for the second time that morning. God knew how, but my feet snuggled well into the sneakers. Unbelievable! The Nike sneakers were absurdly wide. I wouldn't believe it if someone told me that story. How could that be possible? It appeared to be true. God was my witness.

It looks like another fun day is waiting for me! The voice in my head whispered. Every step had bothered me. Since I had learned to take care of myself, I became stoic. A particular phrase popped up in my mind as a slogan that cried out. Dude, suck it up! That attribute underlines a significant part of my portfolio. The brown Nissan roared to the pizzeria, and once again, I was running late. It was eleven in the morning. Everyone at Sapino's had a bleary look. They prepared pizza using mild speed.

I sauntered to the cash register to speak with the manager. He had a charming smile and a chubby Eastern European face. After he had checked my foot, the manager goggled as if his regional manager had told him that he had been laid off. He didn't croak a single word regarding my legs. I merely intended to inform him; that was all.

No one could stop me if I longed to embark on a cruise to the infirmity. As soon as the clock hit three in the afternoon, the orders started coming in quickly. Everyone in the unit was moving around and schlepping as hard as a Mexican wetback. I decided to bottle up the ache of my ogre's feet. When I came back to Motel Zero, the concussion brought a heavy light-headedness. Relax, kid. Don't get subdued. You're just crossing through a bridge of hardship. All the pain you're feeling now will subside, and you are going to be back to normal. The language of fortitude had spoken in my head. That voice always encouraged and cheered me up, especially when the situation got eerie.

*****

It had been a month since I paused boxing sessions, but I felt that had passed a year already and I couldn't shim my obsession to box again. I missed that sport. The compulsion through this particular martial art was ramping up.

Dreams occurred how I was making KOs, TKOs, or merely win by unanimous decision, or to spar and dig into the heavy bags. I missed everything related to boxing. I had to prevail over the unsurmountable passion through this sport and brazen it out.

I had a lot of stress that piled up from the annoying pain in my feet. The ache was causing a serious conundrum. Regardless, I wore an emotional mask of a nice guy pretending that nothing was going on. My coworkers at Sapino's had noticed that something unusual was happening to me.

Although, I am not those peevish guys who would carp and grumble about his problems.

*****

On Thursday, June 7, the tiresome picture of my daily base was indistinguishable. I could barely get out of my bedroom. I struggled to put my swollen feet in my morbid Nike sneakers. Then, I screeched the tires of the Nissan heading to the pizzeria.

Just another day in paradise! That was the holy truth. I was jonesing to dash some munch for dough. Delivering food became a cushy and delightful job. I hadn't had any mental lacerations since the tragic smashup had occurred with the groggy truck driver from Iran.

There were multiple reasons why I kept working so consistently despite the drowsiness. First and foremost, I had payments that needed to be covered. Borrowing money was not a proper solution. Besides, I had already owed money to my friends for the Nissan. And the latter was the craze to complete deliveries. It was fun rolling to residential addresses and handing orders to people. The job at Sapino's was less stressful compared to the sophisticated, hard work in construction. Nonetheless, I planned to get back into the electrical field once I improve my health condition. At the end of the schlepping day, I got that feeling of a deadbeat man as if Jarrell Miller whooped my butt in round 1 of intensive sparring.

When my chicken fingers reached the doorknob to open the townhouse's main door, suddenly, heavy dizziness struck me as if I was some stoned wino wobbled while scrambling up on the stairs and tried to hug the guardrail for support.

Those high-priced medications don't work. I don't have any idea what to do. I guess I need a consultation with another expert, a second opinion. In the blink of an eye, my body sprawled in the bedroom, and I dozed off. On Friday morning, I woke up barraged by severe light-headedness. My feet looked swollen, as if a bunch of angry bumblebees had stung me badly. I rolled the Nissan to Pavilion. I was driving slowly like a ninety-year-old fart. I tried to catch up on the following appointment with Gloria. She did a decent job a couple of days ago. Thus, I attempted to visit her despite my drowsiness. The feeling that the world was spinning had never ended, like I had been plastered 24-7. Trudging to her flat, my dubstep jukebox (head) was playing repulsive sounds. There it is—614. I think that's her door. After a quick rhythmic knocking, the door opened. Gloria slurred "hi" with her wrinkled smile.

"Come in. How are you?" her voice kindly mumbled.

"Hello there. I'm cool. How's it goin'?" I couldn't start grumbling about the ache, especially to a lady whom I had just met a few days ago.

"Okay. Go over there and start undressing." She pointed to the massage table like a female commander of the United States Air Force. The way she emphasized undress sounded like we were going to have sexual intercourse.

While I was in the process of peeling off my garments, Gloria asked,

"How is Klara?" KABOOM! Her question struck me like someone had pinched me using a zap stick. How am I supposed to know? I don't talk to her. I guess she is trying to make a simple conversation.

"Honestly, I don't have any idea." My swift response changed her happy countenance to a frown expression. Perhaps, she expected a different answer. I wouldn't dig more about what was going on with Klara. It wasn't my business whatsoever. My motto is, "Stay away from the chick's drama"

"What's the matter with your feet?" Gloria had an appalled face. Her question left me baffled.

"It's been like that for a week." I wasn't sure precisely how long.

"You need to go to the emergency room! I've been massaging people for more than thirty years, and I've never seen something like that before. This session is revoked. Please go to the emergency and find out what's wrong with your feet."

She didn't suggest. She begged me like she was saying, "Please save my life," after being raped and thrown on the streets like an empty can of diet coke. Gloria's eyes were filled with consternation. Her frustration made me ponder more deeply about going to the infirmary. Maybe she is right. I should go to the hospital. By the time I bundled up my sports garments, Gloria grabbed her phone and started blabbering to someone.

She is talking on the phone. With who? Nooo, I hope that's not Klara. When I walked to the living room. Gloria hung up.

"Gloria, did you talk with Klara?" I asked.

"You need to understand I'm doing it for your good." Her subdued voice made me even upset.

Don't involve Klara. She is in California. I don't want other people to feel blue because of me. Whatever, dude! It is what it is. She called her already, and there's nothing I could do about it. In the next minute, Val phoned me. Guess who forced him to call me. I will leave the mystery to you.

"Hey, Val, what's going on?"

"Not much. I've just finished work. I'm on my way to pick you up. I've heard that you feel under the weather."

"Don't bother, Val. I'll be fine."

"I live two blocks away from Gloria, dude! Let me pick you up." "Hey, Val…Val…" the signal broke.

"Go ahead and take care of yourself." Gloria said. She kicked me out kindly.

"I will. Thanks. Bye." I creeped out of her botanic garden flat, which had a pleasant aroma of lilacs, and walked out to the elevator. Holy crap, what is going on with me? It was quarter to three in the afternoon when Val wheeled over with his red Honda Civic.

"Hey, Val," I waved at him like a man requiring a cab in the downtown area.

"What are we going to do? How you feeling?" Val looked concerned. It took me more than thirty seconds, before I could answer. Val didn't wait for any response. His words were spat out as fast as I could wink.

"Let's go to my apartment. I'll make you some soup. It will make you feel better. Then, we'll go from there. Come on."

"The Nissan…"

"You can leave your ride here. No worries. They won't tow your vehicle. Let's go."

At that moment, I was so bewildered. I couldn't make any straightforward decisions. I guess he is right! While Val was driving his red-dragon Honda, I got dehydrated like I hadn't drunk anything for days. My mouth was as dry as a bone.

There we go again! I can't catch my breath! Val lived on the second floor in a residential building that was no more than three minutes drive from Pavilion. Val was waiting for me at his door on the second floor. It took me around thirty seconds of crawling to the second floor, as if I was an eighty-seven-year-old man. Gosh, those stairs.

The apartment where Val lived was spotless and neat. I passed through the main entry, and the kitchen was straight ahead. There was a moderate size of table slammed right next to the wall on the east side. Momentarily, I trudged over and nailed my butt on the wooden chair. In the meantime, Val ran here and there through the whole apartment. He was walking so fast that my eyeballs got exhausted chasing him. Do I have to mention that Val was seven years older? He poured the chicken soup into a bowl and served it on the table. Great service, no cap. Then, Val asked,

"So tell me, how are you feeling? Do we need to call 911?"

"I can't catch my breath." Panting, I could barely express myself.

Val didn't have a clue what was my medical report, neither did I. While I was telling my story, a stabbing pain struck my throat. It was a similar feeling when you swallow a huge ice cube. It took me a lot of energy to have a brief chin-wag. I tried to catch my breath, pretty much like Stevie Kenarban (a fictional character in Malcolm in the Middle) would speak.

Wheezing heavily, I was pondering what would be my next step. Roughly ten seconds later, I grabbed my smartphone and dialed 911. Forty seconds passed, and a siren of an ambulance was rumbling out from the window. Val stared at me. He was terrified. His body almost shivered.

"Come on. They are here!" For a moment, I thought the paramedics were at the door already. Val attempted to help me out. He wanted to make sure I would not tumble on the floor.

"Val, I can make it. No worries." When I was competing in boxing divisions, I encountered many skilled boxers. They could hit like a hammer and inflict severe pain. I am a warrior who accepts the pain as something normal. That is part of my life. I was handling the pain, but having difficulties breathing was a different page in the book of my life. Val couldn't comprehend what it was to be a warrior that never quit.

"Hey, man, I am just trying to help. That's all."

"I appreciate it, but I don't need your help! Thanks! Cool your jets, Val. I'm not dying." My tone became condescending, arrogant, and unpleasant.

At that moment, I felt distressed, as if I was locked in a basement, realizing that an endangered tornado was approaching. We trundled down the stairs. There was dead silence between the two of us. At the parking lot, the paramedics were already fluttering around like flies over a carcass. They peered at me with trepidation. One of them was a man in his forties who had bushy hair and a body like Captain America. He approached us.

"Guys, are you ready?" the bushy man asked.

"Can we just follow the ambulance?" Val quizzed unconfidently.

"Sure, you can. In that case, the hospital won't charge you for transportation fee. We are heading to Presence Resurrection on Talcott Road. Follow us. Let's go."

That was a brilliant idea. Val saved me a lot of money that day. God bless his heart.

As silent as a corpse, I mulled over the forthcoming visit to the infirmary. Those respiratory issues brought me awful fatigue. Gosh, I gotta notify the supervisor of the pizzeria. He must know where I am going. Most likely, I won't make it to work. At quarter to four in the afternoon, we reached a vast building with a big sign that said Presence Resurrection.

The paramedics showed us the emergency entry. We pussyfooted through the entrance. The guy with bushy hair reported my condition to the lady at the front desk. Momentarily, I was urged to sit on the nearest bench. My legs were fragile like a flat tire.

It took me an hour and a half to be admitted to the ER. If I had decided to take a ride with the paramedics, they would put me straight into the emergency department. I did not mind waiting longer. Besides, I was knackered enough. A short break would be fine.

Val tapped my arm and pronounced,

"Stay here. I am going to park the car, and I will be right back with ya, okay?" I just nodded. There was an ole lady around ten feet away from the bench where all walk-in patients waited to be seated. She disturbingly moaned while holding her abdomen. Oh Lord, I hope that lady will be all right. Her groaning sounds awful like she is about to die.

Hospitals are sanctuaries where God and death are working. There, you can witness diverse emotions such as relish, surprise, anticipation, pain, sadness, happiness, anxiety, suffering, praise, love, bitterness, compassion, etc. Six minutes later, Val scurried back. He trotted fast like a horse, as if he was about to miss a free ticket for Super Bowl.

"Hey, Val. I acted kind of arrogant earlier, and I shouldn't. I apologize for being such a jerk."

"It's fine, dude. No worries." Val grinned like a kid who just saw a naked woman for the first time in his life. Then, a silence fell between the two of us. A thought spun in my head and I couldn't take it anymore. I deeply sighed and spilled the bean.

"Val, if you have to do something, just go. Don't feel obliged to stay along. I'll be fine here. Soon, they shall call my name. Perhaps the physicians will give me a diagnosis then they will prescribe me some medication, and they will send me home. Besides, Mike will be here soon. You know that."

"Nah, I'll stay with ya." Val was short and adamant. It was a tremendous privilege to have someone that I could rely on, especially while being over eight thousand miles away from my country.

A young Asian girl in her late twenties stepped over. Her grin was radiating like an expensive jewelry. She uttered, "Follow me, please." While the Asian nurse walked, I trudged like the walking dead, trying to catch her pace.

She guided me to the emergency where I sprawled on the stretcher. I was panting like an exhausted German shepherd who had just finished running a couple of laps in Soldier Field. I was impatient to speak with a physician. After the next couple of minutes, someone pulled out the drapes. An attending ER doctor wearing a pricey haircut and specs kindly introduced himself and began to ask all of the routine questions such as, "When is your birthday," "Where is your residence," "What kind of job do you do," "Why are you in the hospital?", and so on.

I tried to explain my story using broken English. Another brunette nurse slightly crept in and poked me to attach an IV in my forearm. Ah Lord, I hate needles, especially when they are too thick. She held seven or eight test tubes for blood analysis. The clock struck a quarter to seven when Mike showed up. His eyes were baffled. I had never seen him like that since I had known him.

A minute later, the same Asian lady came over. Her face was bewitching like the prominent actress Lucy Liu. Her words sounded uneasy.

"Transportation will take you to the inpatient health care department on the third floor, okay?"

"So, am I going to spend the night here?" I asked, and she just nodded. Her grin faded. Her demeanor made me wonder why. Perhaps a night in the hospital won't kill me. An hour later, transportation escorted me to the single room of the ICU. Mike and Val followed us, discussing in Bulgarian the subject of how pretty the chicks in hospitals were—the most trending topic among Bulgarian guys. The inpatient care room had a comfy and snappy sofa, two armchairs, and a decent TV. The room looked perfectly fine. The inpatient room at the Bulgarian infirmary where I was taken, after the car accident with the Iranian truck, looked like a fleabag hotel.

At a quarter to ten, Val was snoozing, anchored on an armchair. He was waking up every five minutes or so. He looked like a man who didn't sleep for the past seventy-two hours.

"Guys, I'll see you tomorrow. Dimitry, take it easy," Val said blearily and left the room.

Mike and I had a detailed discussion of what could cause the oversimplification of my health condition. We both failed to attain any statement. The window in the medical room portrayed a morbid night as black as the legendary character Darth Vader. Peering through the window, I said,

"Mike, go home, dude. It's half-past ten already. You don't need to stay here."

Mike just shook his head, showing disagreement. He wasn't buying any of my words like I was talking to a deaf man. A few minutes later, Mike passed out lying on the sofa. He didn't feel quite comfy sleeping on it. His body flipped side to side pretty much throughout the entire night. I tipped my hat on that, Mike supported me like he was my biological brother. It helped when I was bemused on my first night in the infirmary. The consternation couldn't let me fall asleep till dawn.

What's next? How long will they keep me here? Those questions kept floating in my mind over and over again. A nurse woke me up at quarter to twelve and handed me lunch. Oh my God! They give you food here. That's lit! My face was filled with joy when they fetched me a tray of tasty flapjacks. At that moment, I felt like a rejoicing nipper eating his kids' meal from McDonald's.

In my country, the infirmaries would not serve you food. You eat whatever your relatives bring. An angelic view of sunup emerged in the sky and mesmerized me while I gazed through the window. Mike and I had a deep conversation and suddenly, the sound of knocking on the door interrupted us.

"Come in," I hollered, wondering who it could be.

Val and the cutie-pie (Klara) burst straight in through the door. Mike, Val, and Klara were staring at me. They had rejoicing smiles. Klara was one of those people who always made me happy. We talked lively, jumping from topic to topic as if we were employees working in a big corporation discussing a new project.

A few minutes later, an unknown voice interrupted us.

"Excuse me, fellas." We all stared at a young man. That man was exuding benevolence. He was a boy in his early twenties. He worked in the transportation department. The man declared,

"Mr. Salchev, I have instructions to take you into the radiology department for a CT scan."

"Okay. We'll wait here," Mike jubilantly replied." Around twenty minutes later, Mike, Val, and Klara were chitchatting when, through the door, another transportation employee rolled over a twenty-nine-year-old man consistently writhing and wriggling on the hospital stretcher. The Bulgarian folks were transfixed. They had a nonplussed countenances. My friends watched how I was suffocating and struggling to catch my breath. The attending nurse put an oxygen mask connected to an aluminum cylinder with a pressure regulator. My body kept bouncing intensively as if the hefty Braun Strowman assaulted me by holding my neck using both of his hands till complete death.

I glimpsed at Klara's weeping eyes. Her spirit reflected hope. I had the motivation to continue fighting by catching a deep breath. The nurse increased the pressure regulator to a maximum rate, and the oxygen began flowing much faster than before. Oh my God! What a relief. Now I can inhale and exhale as a normal human being. I thought. What the nurse did fulfilled me with absolute joy. At that moment, I comprehended how priceless it was to have the ability to breathe. Mike, Val, and Klara persistently stood tongue-tied, like mannequins in front of some sportswear store.

"Guys, please go. He needs to rest. Come tomorrow!" The nurse kindly walked out my friends. I could only wave at them. The whole process of choking generated heavy fatigue. My body remained idle after a few nurses checked me out. My eyelids shut down, and I dozed off like an infant after a long squall.

On Sunday, somewhere in the afternoon, Mike stopped by the hospital. He was carrying plastic bags filled with bananas, oranges, and some almonds. His eyes gazed at me disquietingly. Then three attending physicians stepped through the door. One of them was cuddling a clipboard. He looked terrified.

"Mr. Salchev, the diagnoses of influenza, headache, and swollen feet are symptoms of an infection. I'm afraid that we had found a bacterial infection in your blood vessels that lingered too long in your organs, which caused endocarditis and affected your aortic valve. The only solution is to do an urgent open-heart surgery. Unfortunately, we cannot perform those types of procedures in this hospital. So you'll be transported to Loyola in Maywood where an impending surgery will be performed. I'm sorry for this unpleasant news."

A few minutes later, the physicians walked out of the medical room like a few intimidated cats. Bingo! Congratulations, you've just won the reward of the decade, and that is open-heart surgery! Wait, what? What is open-heart surgery? What a mess. How can you screw up like that, you dimwit dork? Goofball! Open-heart surgery? I don't even know what it means. Dammit!

The bad news always comes first.

My face was dead serious. My eyes struck at Mike. I looked for his encouragement. We both remained speechless. A spooky silence came upon the medical unit. I decided to tear up that silence by saying,

"This is just the way it is. I haven't any options left, right?" I wasn't even sure what I alleged. Mike merely nodded, skipping his comments.

A plethora of scattered stars glittered like diamonds in the murky sky, resembling a magnificent painting of a prominent draftsman. The door had opened again. It was the puppy with the gleaming eyes, Klara. Her breathtaking beauty impelled me envisioning how we would hold hands and mutually peer at each other while walking in a slow-motion video on the beach bay of Santa Monica. Stop dreaming, you damn butthead! Klara stepped close to the bed and patted my shoulder. She then grabbed my hand and held it tightly. A commiseration feeling was compelling in her eagerness to talk.

"I am sorry." She said quietly.

"You've known already?" My question came as if a kid would ask his teacher in school.

"Val told me!" Klara sniggered like an offspring in fifth grade wandering along with her classmates on the way home somewhere in the outskirts on July afternoon.

"Okay, but how did Val know? Ooh, I got it—Mike."

Klara burst into laughter. Her jollity broadcasted a smile of a happy gal having fun with her best friend. My first impression was wrong about her. She merely wants to be platonic friends, and as a matter of fact, I'm down to have a hottie friend. The door swung again. The puppy with the gleaming eyes twitched for a second. Don and Mr. George came through the door.

"What's up, champ? Oh, hello. My name is Don. Nice to meet ya," Don greeted, projecting his broad grin of a glorious and friendly warrior.

"Hi!" Klara timidly squeaked while she jerked to the window at the end of the room. She practiced a long physical distance. For some unspecified reason, she depicted a severe disrespect addressing Don. She didn't accept the fact that he was portraying courtesy.

"How you doin', kid?" Mr. George grilled like a leader of a SWAT team. A few seconds of awkward silence passed, and I replied like a man who didn't comprehend the question in the first place.

"Hopefully, everything will be smooth with the following surgery." My cloudy thoughts were congested. I didn't know what words were coming from my mouth. I was lying on the medical stretcher like a frightened calf.

Mr. George stared at me. He declared,

"You will be fine, kid. You will see. You are more than welcome at Oakley."

"I am not sure if I will be able to fight again." A wind of anxiety slumped over my shoulder. My eyes stuck at the cabinets above the sink as if I was an immature lad who could not grasp what his parents were teaching him.

"You can be a coach!" Mr. George asserted like a supervisor of immense cooperation as he expressed his suggestion of marketing a new product in a business meeting.

We discussed boxing while Klara leaned against the window. She was as quiet as a mute. Her presence faded as if she wasn't there. It was quarter to ten when Don and his father left the inpatient care room. Klara had querulous behavior. Her expression described an indignant opinion about Don and Mr. George.

"I don't like these guys. They weren't nice to you." The puppy with gleaming eyes grunted. Well, these guys had already done a lot for me, more than most people I ever met in my life. The fact that they visited me at the infirmary like everyone else (including you, Klara) expressed how they perceived me as a person.

The puppy with the gleaming eyes couldn't comprehend this statement of rationalization. She would not listen to what I had been trying to explain. My purpose was to change her grimace by jumping into some positive topics. She left the inpatient care radiating a glittering grin. At midnight, the spooky silence filled the medical ward, and I closed my eyelids. Deep thoughts disturbed me. What's gonna happen after the surgery? No one could say. Maybe I won't wake up. How am I gonna tell my parents? My mom will get a heart attack, and Koko would be pissed. An hour passed before I dozed off.

*****

It was a quarter past six in the morning when the paramedics woke me up by jerking inside of the inpatient care unit. I slightly lounged on the gurney as they briskly pulled it up. They quickly put me in the ambulance.

The trip took about twenty minutes. One of the paramedics was an attractive African American woman with an incredible dreadlock. She was a charming chick. Her behavior was chill as if she smoked blunt. Her body was as acrobatic as a running champion. She was driving the ambulance, an awful chauffeur. I got the feeling that we could be involved in an accident during the trip. Multiple times, the ambulance cruised over the curb while turning on the roads. The ambulance parked by the ER at Loyola, the attendants escorted me to the intensive care. The nurses and medical assistants began to poke me left and right on my forehand. They noticed that I didn't make any frowning faces or become whiny while they were poking me. That was why they sent a student chick of Latin origin to practice on me. When she poked me, the needle struck the bone. It hurt as bad as a dentist pulling out a tooth without local anesthesia. I barely managed not to squeak like a little girl. Around noon, Klara came over. She stepped closer to me and whispered,

"I've got something for you." She giggled joyfully. I looked at her like a baffled monkey watching some humans making wacky and odd movements, trying to impress the animals.

"Just watch!" Klara said while hanging images of legendary boxers such as; George Foreman, Sugar Leonard, Tommy Morrison, Julian Jackson, etc. I don't get it. Why is she being so nice to me? We barely know each other. Maybe she's just expressing her friendly behavior. Klara hugged me and went to use the restroom. A few minutes later, a young girl, probably my age, approached the ICU. She was a medical assistant cuddling a black clipboard.

"What is this?" I asked, puzzled.

"Your friend Klara wants your medical records, and I need you to sign right here if you agree." My face scowled like the forty-fifth president of the USA, Donald J. Trump, after an inept question from a reporter at a press conference formed at the White House.

"Naw, I won't grant authorization for these medical records. Thank you." I tried to obscure my peevish visage. Then, I crowed,

"Klara!" The puppy with the gleaming eyes scuttled to the medical cot like a lovely pug responding to the command of his master.

"Why have you asked about the medical records without my permission? How can you do this to me? Don't ya think I should be informed before you had claimed any sort of papers?" I asked. My face didn't look happy.

"I just wanted to share them with Dr. Eugene to ask for a second opinion. I thought this would be very helpful."

"I disagree with you, and I would appreciate it if you notified me of any of your suggestions before you take any further steps, okay?"

Klara nodded and merely bowed like a butler who messed up managing his employer's birthday cake. She trundled to the entry. Just before her fingers reached the doorknob, she turned to me. She displayed her intentions to talk. Her voice sounded jumpy.

"Fine! You're right. I'm sorry. Listen up, I'm running late. See you later." Klara walked away, spraying a silence as if she was visiting the queen of England, remaining quiet because she could insult the queen. Then she was out of sight. A foolish feeling made me think about her. Klara doesn't deserve any of my raging anger. I thought. I wanted to embrace her like a close friend. My reproachful monologue was sort of brusque and catty over the Bulgarian minstrel. I didn't want to sound like an asshole. That wasn't my purpose because I adored her for everything she did for me, but I couldn't let her be in charge of my medical reports without my knowledge. I hoped she had understood my standpoint.

Whether she drags her arse back or not, I have the right to decide what the best thing for me is. Besides, the most important now is to focus on the upcoming surgery.

At eleven in the evening, the ICU in Loyola (which was pretty tiny, smaller than a master bathroom) was desolate. It took me a few hours of thinking before I dozed off. My second night at Loyola passed faster than the jab of Gervonta Davis.

"Good morning, Mr. Salchev. How you doin' today?" A male voice interrupted my delightful sleep. My eyes surveyed the medical unit. There were a bunch of doctors in the ICU. They stared at me uneasily.

"I am fine. What's going on?" My words sounded hazy. I was still in the process of wakening.

"The results of your blood test imply traces of a bacteria named Streptococcus, which has caused you to struggle for the past three months. This germ can be a deadly infection which appears very rarely. So far, we had determined the Streptococcus came through one of your teeth, then crept into the gum, clung in your blood vessels, flushed in the muscular-walled tubes forming part of the circulation system called artery, and went to your aortic valve. We can schedule open-heart surgery on the fourteenth of June, which is this Thursday. What do you think, Mr. Salchev?"

What? This is a nightmare, and I am sleeping right now. At the next moment, I will close my eyelids and clench for several seconds. When I open my eyes, the unit will be empty. Okay, here we go! Open sesame! Whoop!

The doctors were staring at me. One of them grilled,

"Mr. Salchev, do you understand what I'm saying?" Mesmerized, I replied,

"Yes, sir, I do. I mean, what choices do I have?" What could you possibly reply to this type of question?

"No, I'm afraid you don't have any. One more question, Mr. Salchev. Have you ever used any drugs or any opiates?"

"No, sir," I lied.

"All righty then. We will be checking with you later."

"Thank you. Bye," I said and the doctors left the unit so swiftly as if they entered through the wrong patient's room.

Did he say that the bacteria came from my teeth? Boom! You've just hit another windfall, Mr. Ballsack! I spent around twelve hundred dollars on dental visiting Dr. Koita last year. He was taking meticulous care of my choppers, and now I have bacterial infections coming from my teeth? Great, just great! Filled with bitterness, I tried to crash. Alas, I couldn't.

*****

The reason why I didn't divulge the truth about using dope was that I wasn't feeling comfortable admitting it. I don't feel proud scrawling it in this book either. Also, the doctors might jot in the diagnosis that Mr. Salchev was a drug addict. That was absolutely wrong. Why? Since I had touched down in America, my status was financially independent. I was not chilling at my apartment and spending money on drugs like some junkie. I was working my ass off to make money. I had been making wire transactions from my banking account into Bulgarian banks to finance my family, and that process had occurred continually. Multiple times, I had shimmed those baggies containing white chalks in my closet for weeks, even months. Plus, I had rarely dashed to work drunk or under the influence of any narcotics. Who am I, a cretin? They would kick me out right away. The premieres with coco ran mostly on weekends to amplify an extra gratification. That was all. Just because I made a single slip up; it didn't make me obsessed with that crap. I wasn't a strung-out hophead. I did it for fun. Furthermore, I could go cold turkey whenever I decided. Boxing and cigarettes were fields where my addiction had established a fetus. But all of those intelligent physicians would never fathom the philosophy of the white lady. They would deduce that I was a freak who had collected this data from reading some articles on the internet or listening to a pricey shrink.

It is everything in your head. Your mind must command your prejudices and vices where the most crucial point is to never cross the boundaries of preconception. How you can do it? You have to adjust your mind-set to stay above and beyond any addiction. Then, you have to discover something that swerves your mind-set from addiction.

It could be a person. He/ she can take you to delightful places where your mind flows in the lake of love; or you can find a pastime that keeps your mind diverted away from drugs, gambling, drinking, etc. And if you learn how to follow the commands set by your subconscious, then you will be set free from any addiction. The word I need here is discipline. It is easy to say it but is much harder to practice it.

An hour later, a canny black lady fetched a tray of scrambled eggs, pork sausage, and orange for dessert.

"Thank you. God bless you," I uttered. The lady responded by exuding an amiable grin. All medical employees had a unique contribution for the extra mile they took working in the hospitals. Therefore, we need to respect them.

After two minutes of munching, the entire plate looked empty, as if there hadn't been any food on it. Klara rushed through the entry. Her fast-paced gait made her look like she was a New Yorker. I stared at her with a friendly smile.

"Hey, listen. I am sorry. You were right. I shouldn't piggyback without revealing my recommendation to you."

"It's all good," my words burst out, spraying the same smile.

"When are you going to tell your parents?" her urgent question metamorphosed my glamorous expression into a disturbed frown.

"After I'm done with Loyola. There is no need to give them extra anxiety. They will freak out." The Bulgarian minstrel surveyed me wordlessly. Her eyes manifested compassion. Her pupils articulated the sympathy of a sister who fretted for her brother. She cuddled me like I was her best friend. Then, Klara went out of sight.

Not too long after Klara left, a crew of sawbones jerked into the medical ward. One of them introduced himself as Dr. Edwin McGee. He was the surgeon who would perform the open-heart surgery. He was a professor, medical director, heart transplant specialist, and operator in the ventricular assist device program. His professional characteristics spread out in many fields, including aortic surgery, heart valve replacement, valve repair, etc.

Dr. Edwin McGee looked as if he was a son of Jesus. He was an erudite person who gained experience for many years in cardiac surgery. Edwin McGee confirmed that the impending surgery was scheduled for Thursday morning, and he forbid consuming any type of food and liquids twenty-four hours before the operation. Also, he asserted that an antibiotic would be flushed daily through the IV to prevent the Streptococcus from growing. The medical experts sneaked out through the door. A spiritual thoughts crawled over my mind. I had never been so rattled and anxious since my name had been printed on my birth certificate.

*****

God almighty, please show mercy to your child. Let your encompassing power show forgiveness to a hellion like me. Your kingdom will exist for eternity. Express your justice and leniency to a sinner who has always adored and loved you. Let your empire project a predominant strength over the earth and the universe. Please make the heart of the young man beat in a regular pace. Because your love is my salvation, my words will glorify you. Oh Lord, please forgive me. Amen!

That was a brief, sincere message to the master of the universe. At that moment, I hoped that he heard my prayers, and if his willpower was to leave this world, so be it. I cannot judge God's decisions.

It was Thursday, around five in the morning. The hunger irritated my mind. I impatiently anticipated the upcoming surgery. The thoughts about the forthcoming open-heart surgery kept me awake throughout the entire night, and I looked like an intimidated bat.

The sunrise bobbed beyond the horizon. A couple of shy clouds hovered around like a bunch of spectators gazing through the window. At the next moment, Laura darted over at the intensive care. She was the nurse who took care of me for the last two days. Laura was one of those lovely people with whom you could disclose all of your stories. She was a brunette in her early thirties, with enthralling long hair and twinkly dark eyes. Her figure was in great shape, except for the five-month baby she carried. Oh Lord, please give your blessing to this woman. She is one of your angels doing her divine mission to help others.

"The surgery is postponed for tomorrow morning. They won't allow you to eat any food or drink any liquids for another twenty-four hours. I am sorry." Laura's statement threw me in a loop, but I couldn't be mad at her. She was there to help like everybody else who had worked at Loyola. My haggard countenance divulged a flame of grievance. Drawing a deep breath, I stared at the snow-white ceiling. Marvelous, this is what I need! What can you do about it? The stress filled my thoughts with deep consternation that gradually nagged me for the rest of the day. I hoped that the following morning, they would not say something like, "I am sorry, Mr. Salchev. The surgery is postponed for Monday." Hours and hours passed. I peered at the idiot box, flicking through the channels. I tried to think about something else, but the starvation was disturbing my common sense.

*****

Delightful jazz music was playing over a high-class restaurant filled with many clients. The milieu of boisterous people were enjoying the pleasant atmosphere. Waiters rushed back and forth like NASCAR vehicles. A grinning bald man came over. He wore a black and white waiter's tuxedo with a peak lapel glued around his neck.

"Mr. Salchev, would you like some Château Lafite Rothschild, the crop from 1996?"

"Excuse me, Rene, would you be so kind as to repeat the question please? It's too loud over here."

"We apologize for the inconvenience. Here at restaurant Chi-Bistro, we rely on high-quality service. Did you make any decisions from the menu? Or should I come back in a few?"

"I would like a well-done braised lamb shank with a baked potato, black truffle and butter, and a bottle of French Chateau Canon 2014. That will be all. Thank you."

"Great choice. I will be right back with you, sir! May I have the menu, please?"

*****

As the hours went by, the ghostly silence kept my eyelids open. I couldn't fall asleep, not at this moment. The morass raised a list of issues which I was worried about. What's coming next? This thought bothered me as if a chigger scurried over my body. It would be terrific if someone would splash his experience of vascular surgeries and give me some hope.

I sat back on the medical stretcher like a couch potato for the past forty-five hours. There were no urgent calls for a bowel movement or wee-wee. My mouth was dry like I had just finished munching a whole jar of peanut butter.

Every five to ten minutes, an eagerness compelled me to check the clock on my phone. The inner voice in my head talked to me as if Grandpa sat next to me and braced me using his wisdom. Guys, please, I can't take it anymore. Let's wrap up the process. Those were the words that I wished to exclaim. What time is it? Almost six. The transportation employee should be here any minute.

Thirty minutes later, someone flicked the switch, and the fluorescent light fixture flashed so brightly that it made me blind for a moment. I couldn't observe the person staying by the entry as if he was a vague figure resembling a ghost. After a few seconds, my vision cleared out.

"Hey, good morning, my man. How you doin'?" I asked. My bleary face changed into a terrified kid who was waiting at a dentist's office.

"Doing just fine. I'm from the transportation, and I have orders to escort you to the operating room in the lower level," a corn-fed black man in his forties uttered politely.

Here I am, Lord. Bless me with your delightful power. Let's get over it. The corn-fed black employee rolled me through the corridors. He paced like a frightened turtle. The closer we shuffled, the faster my heartbeat pounded. The trip from the ICU to the surgical room took more or less five minutes, but I felt it had been hours.

The corn-fed black man parked the stretcher at the waiting area. Three minutes later, someone pulled the drapes. Two male physicians stepped closer. The older man was talking,

"Mr. Salchev, we will start preparing you for the surgery. Initially, my colleague will poke you on both of your arms for the IV, okay?"

"How long will I be sleeping?"

"For a couple of days, but you will feel it like a short nap."

A short nap? Yeah right. Stop pulling my leg. How is that possible? The older man grinned mirthlessly. His younger assistant had poked me four times already. His work was an epic failure that caused the older man to poke me twice more. Luckily, he was precise. They rolled me into an airy surgical room filled with whizzy technology. I hadn't been so antsy in my entire life. The thought that I might never awake after this surgery made me very nervous.

"Guys, are you sure I will fall asleep before you—"

The Bulgarian man trailed off and passed out at once.

Koko (Dad) and Mom before they
made me.

In this picture, I was 1 year old.

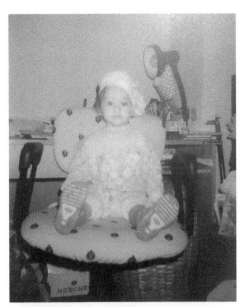

My sister (Sunny). She was 1 year old.

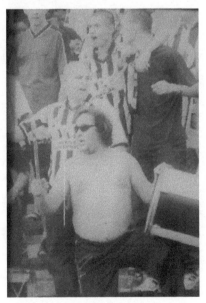

Koko (the shirtless man). He was
well known at the ballpark, supporting our local soccer team called
Lokomotiv Plovdiv.

My sister at 21.

This was my Mazda after the car accident in July 2011.

The Moldovians and I had fun on the beach in Pentwater. From left to right: Mihai, Sergio, Michael, me, and Victor.

209

Me, after a bad hangover.

On a break, while I was working on
the farm.

I was pissed after a bad day working as
an electrician.

My first victory at Golden Gloves.

At my first fight.

Boohba.

The cops wanted a picture with me
wearing this funky costume on
Halloween.

My first victory by TKO. From left to right: Peter George, Donovan George, me, Salomon (our padman), and Jimmy Quiter.

My victory by TKO in Drury Lane with Peter George and Jimmy Quiter.

My trophies and Don's belts at
Motel Zero.

Mike and I. I was 27, in this picture.

This is Gill (Gildardo). The auto mechanic
who backed me up so many times.

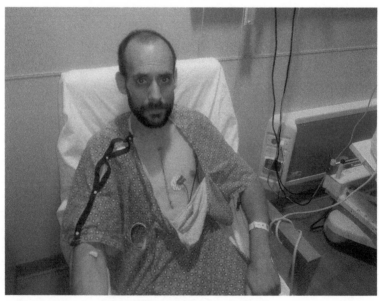

Me, after surgery in June 2018.

That picture was taken in 2020.

Chapter 25

The moment I opened my eyelids was the moment of pure resurrection. A righteous feeling fell over my shoulders and brought me a mouth-wide smile. The simple fact of returning to life is the most beautiful emotion that a human can feel.

Initially, I wasn't sure whether I was alive or tripping in a dream. A few seconds in advance helped me realize that I was awake. Gosh! Lord, it's good to be back. I am pretty sure the process of bringing back people's lives is one of the reasons why many doctors are spending years of learning and wads of money to acquire such an extraordinary career. My eyes rolled over, and surveyed the scene in the medical room. Laura sat like a nun on the armchair. She bowed her head and seemed focus on her lap. Suddenly questions arose in my mind. My words spread out with glee and gratitude.

"Hey, Laura, how you doin'?"

"Oh, hello! I'm so glad to see you awake. How do you feel?"

"I feel like a reborn child at age of twenty nine. How long have I been sleeping?"

"They gave you anesthesia, and you were unconscious. It is a required procedure due the surgical process. That forced you to crash for two days. You acted like a hectic monkey who had escaped from the zoo. Then, you tend to pull the tube out. The doctors had no choice but to inject you with extra anesthesia for another two days. Overall, you slept about four days." Laura divulged her detailed report of what had transpired while I was sleeping.

Holy cow! I don't recall being awake with a tube in my throat. The surgeon was right. I slept about four days, and it feels like it's been a short nap. That's insane! The only factor that matters is that I am alive. At the next moment, I sat up and tended to wiggle just a tad. An obnoxious twinge stabbed me, and I almost screamed. I felt pain in my torso area.

My eyes curiously sneaked through the gown. Holy mother of God! What the heck is that? An eight-inch incision had been slashed vertically right in the middle of my chest. Beneath the chest, three plastic tubes were pinned close to the midriff area. Those tubes resembled the plugs pinned to the babies born with those plugs and ready to be transferred into the data program in the first of the notorious Matrix franchise where Morpheus explained to Neo what the Matrix was.

There was another tube hooked to my flesh rocket to extricate urine into a gallon. Then I longed to move just a smidgen. Holy cow! What happened to my legs? I thought. My feet were anchored as if I had a limb infarction.

"Laura, what happened to my legs?"

"After the surgery, you will have to learn how to walk again. It may take a couple of weeks," she elucidated.

Yeah? No one had told me anything about that before the procedure. It is what it is, dude. Be grateful to God. He brought you back on earth. Those words had flopped back and forth like mega-million balls with numbers bouncing erratically in the lottery box. The rest of the day, I walked through a bridge of emotions and thoughts about my future till the clock's hand hit midnight.

*****

After a couple of days, the transportation employee rolled me into a room on the fifth floor of the wing called Five Tower. That room was airy, the same size as a one-bedroom apartment, and only one patient could use it. There was a broad window spanning the width to the whole room, with a view of the east side of downtown Chicago. The sight presented marvelous scenery. The Windy City had always been one of the most exquisite cities on the entire globe.

I shall say, Chi-town is as beautiful as my mother and as loud as a steam locomotive.

At quarter to eight in the morning, the crew of sawbones followed by Dr. Edwin McGee came over. Dr. McGee was the man who had God's power to save human's lives.

"Good morning, Mr. Salchev. How are you feeling?" Dr. McGee stated contentedly. His eyes radiated jollity.

"I feel like the happiest man alive. Thank you."

Dr. McGee smiled. His face transformed to a blushing infant who had been told a kind compliment by a stranger. A second of silence had passed before Dr. McGee continued,

"We didn't implant a mechanical valve. Thus, we used a tissue valve. Also, the Mitral valve has been repaired. A piece of homograft has been cut and replaced from the aorta. The function is to dispatch oxygen and blood from your heart to the rest of the body. The surgical procedure lasted for six hours, and my assessment can be classified as a successful open-heart surgery. You won't be able to walk right away. A physical therapist will take care of your healing and walking process. An appointment in my office will be made in advance. Any questions?" Dr. McGee peered at me using his owlish face.

"I would like to know the function of those plastic tubes stabbed into my chest and how long will they be attached on me?"

Dr. Edwin McGee replied without any hesitation. His glassy eyes surveyed me as if he had installed an artificial intelligence that analyzed any information of my reactions.

"Tube thoracotomy or intercostal drain is a flexible plastic tube that had been inserted through the chest wall and into the pleural space. It is used to remove air pneumothorax fluid (pleural effusion blood) or pus from the intrathoracic space. Each of those three plastic chest tubes has bonded to a chest-wall drainage system, typically considered collecting blood, drainage, and air. Those medical chest tubes will be attached to your chest for a week and a half."

His scholarly answer had brought me a headache. Nonetheless, I comprehended the core of Dr. McGee's detailed lecture.

"Now you need to rest, young man. Hopefully, you will get discharged from the hospital as quickly as possible."

The crew of sawbones left the room faster than a man's fart. The sky was painted in blue with a few chubby clouds. The odor of summer could be smelled even beyond the window. I could barely wiggle my legs. I had to call the nurses for assistance. It was quarter to two in the afternoon when they served me lunch. I could barely ingest half a taco with steak, no tomato, a gob of sour cream, and some lettuce. After the surgery, my appetite was lost. Some hours later, a knocking sound came from the door.

"Yeah, come in." George (the dandy limo driver), Mike, Val, and Klara sneaked in through the entryway. Before anyone could say anything, Klara jerked to the medical stretcher. She cuddled me with her exotic body and kissed me on my forehead and almost everywhere except the lips. She hugged me like I was her favorite puppy. Klara's seductive lips were so warm and delightful that my skin had goosebumps. Why is she kissing me so much like I am her husband, and should I mention the fact that I didn't shower for the past two-and-a-half weeks? Perhaps I smell like a raccoon.

The cutie-pie leaned closer to my eardrum and slowly whispered,

"I got something for you. Just wait until the others left." What the heck is she talking about? What's in her mind? Her animated demeanor left me bewildered. She hugged me as if I was her fluffy bear.

All of my folks kept rolling their eyes at each other. They were puzzled as much as I was. We chattered for half an hour. My buddies were exhilarated to see me, and I was elated to communicate with all of them. It was like I had a reunion with my classmates from high school.

After my folks left the unit, Klara stood in the room. She was exhilarated. She fumbled into her purse and pulled a tiny gray jewelry box.

Then, she came closer and handed it to me. Her gleaming eyes were spellbinding.

"This is for you. Please, open it," she said and stared at me with anticipation. Wordless, I opened the box. The inscription on the cover said,

I love you
Be strong and get well soon
Klara.

She loves me? How come she could love me? We have barely known each other for a month. We were hanging out as platonic friends, and now she loves me?

No one had ever treated me like that, not as a friend. Her gift made me dumbfounded. Her emotions puzzled me as if a professional pitcher had thrown a curveball at me.

"Klara, how come you love me? We've known each other for only two months?" I exclaimed.

"I love you like a friend. Doncha ever had a girl being only your friend?"

I stared at her, flummoxed. What do you mean, Klara? What friends, Facebook buddies? As much as I liked her, as much as perplexed I was. Her comportment made me confused as you are while reading this paragraph.

"Come on, remove the paper. Look what's hidden beyond the cover," she suggested. I shot a glimpse, trying to sort out what she was up to. Beyond the lace was an obscured chromium necklace with a square tile which had been engraved, 06.15.2018.

That was the date of the open-heart surgery. Sweet. This gift is legit!

"Awesome! Klara, I don't know what to say. I'm touched. This is a mind-blowing present, a priceless item. Thank you so much, Klara."

While I uttered those words, my mind cried out. Klara, you are an extraordinary, breathtaking human, one of the most gorgeous people I had ever met. From the bottom of my heart, I shall say how grateful I am. Our pathways had been crossed irrevocably. I couldn't say this confession out loud. The reason why was the fact that I was so scared to expose my heart to her. Why? Because I was aware of how bad it is when someone you love leaves and stabs a wooden stake in your heart. A gob of people know the taste of bitterness when they have been dumped by their lovely partner whom they adore. Some people can't bear it and tend to commit suicide or can't engage in a commitment to others for a very long time.

Klara smiled. She continually cuddled me. Her mesmerizing eyes reflected benevolence. Her blissful words sounded as if an angel were speaking.

"I'm so glad you like it. I know you will get well soon." Her hand tapped on my shoulder. I looked at her glittering eyes. Then, I stared at her lips. Holy moly, I'm so jonesing to taste those. Nah, you ballsack. Frigging scumbag. Don't you dare to attempt such a foolish sin. She is a married person. Besides, you don't know what her reaction will be. Plus, you are at the damn infirmary, fused to the medical stretcher.

"I got to bail, but I'll come mañana. Do you need anything?" Klara asked.

"Naw, my appetite is still on vacation somewhere in Costa Rica," I replied. The cutie-pie giggled at my joke. The only thing I need is you, Klara. I thought. The way she disappeared was like she had never been at this unit before.

A brunette nurse came after Klara left. She was a Filipino lady in her mid-thirties. After a quick chat, the lady flushed the remedy through the IV to deal with the lousy bacteria. While she handled the process, a question slid from her lips.

"You need to start eating, Mr. Salchev. You don't feel hungry at all?"

"Not at all. You're right, though. I need to eat. For the past three weeks, I have lost forty pounds. That's insane!"

"I do agree with you, Mr. Salchev. Just try to eat. Tomorrow, you will start the physical therapy," the Filipino cried out.

"Wonderful! Let's do it." An exciting thought crossed my mind. The main target that I aimed was to get discharged from Loyola as soon as possible. Later, the evening became inscrutable and creepy as if we were filming a movie with vampires. The TV in the room echoed quietly. It made me to close my eyelids, but I couldn't fall asleep. My mind was looking for answers.

How am I gonna reveal this situation to my parents? Everything is so messed up. How should I start? One thing is for sure. They will go nuts. An hour later, I drifted off. A fussing sound of a machine broke down the silence. The fluorescent light slashed the darkness. At first, I couldn't open my eyes. Two medical employees operated a high-tech machine to the medical stretcher. The purpose of this technology was to obtain an x-ray imaging of my chest. This process recurred every single day at four AM. After that, I couldn't fall asleep for the rest of the day.

*****

It was Tuesday, June 19. The sunlight spread from the east side, and the humidity disseminate around like a destructive plague. The air became heavy, and it was not easy to breathe.

A young feline pussyfooted through the entry. Her lab coat was as white as a snowflake, and her fetching blonde hair was curly. She was about my height, with a gymnastic body and a face that resembled an adorable German shepherd. The feline revealed that her name was Kaetlyn. She was the physical therapist. Her focus was on tutoring and providing information on the ability to walk. Kaetlyn taught me how I should stand up, sit down, and do every other activity. My feet were idle like an infant who had just had his first lesson of walking. It was like I had never walked before in my life. Kaetlyn held my hips (like we were going to have sexual intercourse) to secure my balance. Otherwise, I would stagger and most likely collapse on the floor, like how Lennox Lewis knocked down Mike Acey.

Kaetlyn was an affable person, and she was always smiling at me. While we strolled, the German shepherd therapist questioned me literally about everything. Is she hitting on me? Nah, you damn ballsack, why would she do that? You just woke up after open-heart surgery, and you think you're Mr. Special!

It was close to ten o'clock in the forenoon. Kaitlyn swung by for another physical procedure.

"Are you ready to walk?" she asked me. Her grin glittered like luxurious rims of a snazzy Cadillac.

"Can't wait. Let's go." I responded I was anxious to walk. It had already been a week since the physical treatment had started, and my legs slowly scurried to convenient speed. Come on, you ole man, move those legs. Show them what kind of warrior you are. Kaitlyn was flabbergasted. When she initiated the first day of the therapy, she saw a man who could barely drag his feet along with required assistance. Four days later, the same man projected unbelievable improvement in his ability to walk.

"Dimitry, I'm so proud of you! The way you walk tells me that you don't need me anymore," she said. We wandered through the corridor on the fifth floor. As we were strolling, I peeked over the other medical wards. There weren't any young patients, not as young as me.

"Do you want to get back to your room?" Kaitlyn asked despite the fact she had already known the answer. I merely nodded. The German shepherd therapist was holding me slightly over the hips. When we stepped into my room, we were walking cheek by jowl. We looked like a loving couple entering through Woodfield Mall in Schaumburg on Sunday. At the next moment, my eyes broadened.

"Hello. Am I interrupting something? No worries, I will leave," Klara said. Her face was frowning.

"You're totally fine! You don't have to. We've just finished the therapy. I'll leave you alone. See ya later." Kaitlyn asserted while staring at me.

"Hello, Klara. It's nice to see you again." The puppy with gleaming eyes had always made me joyful, no matter how many issues were hovering over my head. Klara had that frowny face. She attempted to conceal it, but her effort reached an epic failure.

"What is it, Klara? Are you okay?" Why is she so bummed? What's happening to this broad? The answers to those questions remained unanswered. Initially, we started chatting about diverse subjects. We talked about dancing. Klara was a musician. She loved tripping over a variety of styles in music. Her elated vibe was back. Her pupils were twinkling so brightly like a marble countertop of a sumptuous kitchen in a house worth millions of dollars. At the next click, she had noticed my subdued silence.

"What's wrong? Tell me," Klara urged to know the reason. She wouldn't stop bugging me until the answers bounced on the surface.

"I don't know what to do. I got no money for rent and food. My parents don't acquire anything on stack, which means they can't send me money. It's like I'm stuck in a street that has a sign saying No Outlet. You follow?" What a cretin. Why you act like a dummy whimper? Why do you talk to her like a timid adolescent would? Her eyes rolled up and down like a robot with artificial intelligence seeking an appropriate answer.

She sat next to me on the medical stretcher and announced exultantly,

"Cheer up. I've got an idea. We will set up a donation account on GoFundMe platform via Facebook. That's how we can bring you back on your feet, financially. I am going to snap a picture of you right here on the medical cot. Just unbutton your gown so the incision can be visible. Everything will be just fine. Trust me." Despite her words, I wasn't sure that her proposal would work out. Who was I to get money from other people? It sounded unrealistic to me, and it would no work out! Dude, give her credit. You never know from which top hat the rabbit could hop out. Plus, you haven't any choice left.

"I just don't like the idea—people who don't know me collecting money on my behalf. The whole concept makes me feel so uneasy." Stop being whiny, you damn wanker! What's the matter with you? The voice in my head exclaimed.

"Everything will be all right. Soon, you will get discharged from Loyola," Klara stated. I would pass her the buck about her encouragement.

Klara made a good point, no cap! God, I am jonesing to kiss this broad. This ain't right. She is married. Besides, I am not sure that she has the same feelings. So you better keep your pie hole shut and stop thinking about it. Just forget it! Klara, the twin of Jessica Alba, ambled to the door. Watching how she was shuffling through the entry, my mind cried out. Holy shmoly, look at her patootie.

*****

During the last week of June, I made a splendid improvement in walking. I was rejoiced in being able to trudge to the commode on my own. A physician lady wearing a short pixie cut and white robe came over.

It was the same physician who pulled out the chest tubes pinned in my abdomen two weeks ago.

It wasn't the greatest feeling in the world, but surely, it improved my physical condition. The blonde lady with the short pixie cut gave me a red-wine-colored pillow in the shape of a human's heart. That was a precious gift given by Loyola. It was a memorable moment in my life that energized my self-esteem and brought me a cheerful smile.

Around forenoon, Kaitlyn, the German shepherd therapist, darted over at the medical room for the last session of the physical therapy. We wandered close to each other, chatting about many subjects. Kaitlyn didn't need to hold me anymore, but she did it for safety purposes.

"You are doing well!" The therapist politely exclaimed. She was smiling at me perpetually. We drifted back to my inpatient unit.

"There we are. I guess you don't need me anymore. Oh! What do we have here? Is that pillow yours?" Kaitlyn asked while gawking at me.

"Yeah! They say it's from Loyola," I enunciated.

"May I?" She asked, and my hand gave her permission. She grabbed the permanent marker and jotted the following:

Keep up the great walk. I am so proud of how far you have come in physical therapy and this surgery!

Kaitlyn

Her short verse made me feel touched. I had met a very few generous people in my life, and Kaitlyn was one of them. Dude, ask for her phone number, dadgummit! I looked straight at her green eyes and announced,

"Kaitlyn, I am so glad you helped me. You are a magnificent therapist."

"Thank you. You are so sweet. Take care of yourself."

Pussy! The consternation of being rejected put you in an uncomfortable position. What the heck is wrong with you? All you had to do was to ask. The worst thing she could do is to rebuff you. Who cares! The voice in my head lampooned me. I stared at Kaitlyn like a goofy nerd. I rubbernecked at how she was walking out of the unit. I looked like a geek, blinking foolishly, after losing a hand for twenty grand on poker. You numb sack! You had a chance, and you've blown it already. There is nothing else you can do about it.

You can't pursue girls. Otherwise, they will consider you as a needy man seeking a regular hookup.

*****

Wednesday, June 27, was just another balmy day. A clear, bright sky shone over the White City. The skyscrapers were aesthetically breathtaking. Those buildings erected from the window of the Five Tower compartment at Loyola. They looked just the way I saw them when the Greyhound bus dropped me off my first time in Chi-town.

My appetite was back in business. Before the vascular surgery, my weight was a hundred and forty pounds, around thirty pounds less of the weight when I used to fight. The process of emaciation had been changed. I ordered a tasty flapjack with blueberry syrup, a pad of butter a side of two infinitesimal pork sausages, and a small cup of orange juice.

The late brunch had been gobbled for several minutes. When the nurse dashed over to pick up the empty tray, a quiet knock on the door drew my attention. Klara paced happily through the room. Her grin was wide, as usual. The cutie-pie with the gleaming eyes was bouncing around joyfully like a seven-year-old who was going on a trip to Disney World. Why is she so upbeat? What is going on with this broad?

Before I managed to ask, she had cut me off.

"Look! Here is the amount of money collected from GoFundMe." I looked like a goofball who accidently dashed into medical lecture at Northwestern University.

"Wait a minute. Is that for real?" My mind was crowded with thoughts like a traffic jam in rush hour at Canal and Jackson Street in the loop of downtown Chicago. The puppy with the gleaming eyes just nodded. She exuded a twinkling smile.

"Hang on. Let me get this straight. Are you telling me that these generous people had donated two grand from social media?" I asked. Klara nodded but this time was less elated. Her countenance could be described as, "Yeah, dude. That money is yours."

That was the first time in my existence when someone whom I had never met make such a marvelous gesture. Klara melted my heart and turned me into a jackass. Ever since she appeared in my life, her presence felt like an angel hovering down to the Earth to help me out at such a crucial point in my life. The puppy with the gleaming eyes was the only one who visited me the most at the hospital. She merely missed one day throughout the entire hospitalization. Unbelievable! She doesn't even know me.

It was like that was part of her job, and I was paying for it. Hypothetically, my sister wouldn't be able to hop into the infirmary as often as Klara did. Why is she coming to Loyola every single day? She is bumping too close to my heart. That's ain't safe. Maybe I should tell her that she has to take the train and stay away from me.

"Klara, there is something that you should know." The Bulgarian minstrel eyed me like she was watching a movie in a cinema. I was trying to say it out loud. My speech flowed like that of a nervous comedian.

"I'm gonna be discharged from Loyola after two days," I said.

She almost hollered with jubilant emotion and cut me off again.

"That's great news! I was about to jump on the same subject because you look much better. Besides, your appetite is almost back to normal. You're walking and moving around like a healthy man."

Her joyous speech boosted my self-assurance. It was something that I truly needed at that particular moment. I couldn't destroy our relationship. She was there for me. How could I say, "Klara you need to go and never come back!"

The Bulgarian bombshell glanced at the heart-shaped pillow. She grabbed the permanent marker, and wrote:

Don't miss the moment when you will get back stronger than before. The bright side of your life is coming soon. Don't be insecure about embracing it. Keep thinking "I can."

Klara

While I was perusing her poetry, thoughts snapped in my subconscious. It was the same feeling when you read a phenomenal article written about you in your favorite journal or social media platform. God Almighty, I am blessed and grateful to meet one of your kids (Klara), who has been sent down on earth to help me cope with this morass. The Lord Almighty brought back my self-esteem. I needed my strong character to clear up the fog in my mind, and Klara was the source of communication with God. That was why I praised her as a compassionate person who had reserved a VIP spot in a theater performed at only one place, and that place was called my heart.

The puppy with the gleaming eyes had on-fleek outfit. It underlined her athletic figure. Her fluffy brunette hair was so mellow, like the hair of an infant. Klara left the medical room. She was running late to get ready for a musical event. I didn't want her to leave, but I knew she would be back soon.

A few minutes elapsed, I envisioned how Klara was standing by the medical stretcher, and her gorgeous eyes were peering at me with the silence of hope. The rest of the night, I couldn't drift off easily, but then I did. I slept peacefully. Before I passed out, my mind was filled with questions such as; "What is coming up next?" "What will God have engraved on the page that has the title, Tomorrow"?

I'll get back to work at Sapino's. Yeah, Dino should let me in. He already knows I'm a hard worker. Until I heal, the strategy is to take it easy at work. The most important is to go cold turkey and forget about binge drinking. From now on, I'll live a healthy life. That's the only way I could come back in the boxing ring. The Lord showed me how to prevail and diminish the morbid storm in my head. The same storm that could put my mind to destructive consequences. All of these thoughts kept my eyelids open. I was staring at the ceiling for a while. Many tasks had to be completed. Since I had been living on my own, no one else could sort out the chaos that fell over my head. Thoughts about payments, bills, bank accounts, rent, and work spun in my head. I had the faith that, somehow, I would find the right answers to clear the mess. That was what I thought before I slumbered.

*****

It was Friday, June 29, 2018. The glowing sky was clear as the surface of glassy water in the Maldives. I was so cheerful, observing the sunup. That was the day when I was discharged from Loyola.

Thrilled, I telephoned the kitchen department and ordered my last brunch.

An African American man with bristled long hair kindly fetched an apple juice and tray of scrambled eggs covered with cheese. The munchies had been nibbled for less than two minutes. Even a starving pit bull would take longer to finish a well-done ribeye steak. The next hour, an attending male physician with big green eyes and a swimmer's figure came over with an urgent pace. His grin resembled the Oscar winner Joaquin Phoenix, acting as the protagonist from the movie Joker.

"Hello, I am Kevin. How you doin' today? I believe you must be pretty anxious to get discharged from Loyola. The only reason I am here is to give you some helpful tips about what precautions you need to follow for the first few months. You cannot drive for about four weeks. Also, you cannot lift any heavy items. The restriction is a gallon of milk or six to seven pounds. A home nurse will be visiting you at your apartment once a week to check and clean your IV, the one you ought to flush antibiotics to deal with the bacteria infection. In a few minutes, a nurse will give you instructions on how to wash your surgical incision and what medications you need to take in advance. She will give you a list of treatments that you need to follow. Is there anything I can be helpful with, Mr. Salchev?" Kevin meowed. He stared at me with anticipation.

"Actually, yes. How long does it take to heal completely from this type of surgery?"

Kevin replied hurriedly like a parrot who had been questioned about Oreo chocolate cookies.

"From six months up to one year. From now on, you ought to be extremely cautious, Mr. Salchev."

The physician with the athletic swimming figure vaporized momentarily like the genie did after he popped out from Aladdin's magic lamp. For the following minutes, I pondered deeply. Who could come to pick me up from here? I got it! My eyes glittered like an emerald.

It was about four in the afternoon when an amiable nurse escorted me in a wheelchair through the main entrance of Loyola. George, the dandy limo driver, had parked his black 2017 SUV Lincoln Navigator. That was a very comfy and flashy vehicle. The interior had an abundance of space.

I hobbled to the sumptuous vehicle. Gasping, I crept into the passenger' seat. George observed the entire process. He was worried. Well, Mr. Lucky Pants, at least, you will be escorted as a pimp from Loyola. Yeah, no cap! The feeling of being discharged from the infirmary, especially within a sophisticated surgery, resembled celebrating a promotion while working for Google. Regardless of what would happen for the rest of the day, I would persistently emit a gleeful expression.

George peered at me with trepidation. The way he looked at me was as if he was saying, "I hope he would not pass away in my car." His question came up both with severe alert and chill countenance.

"You look kinda haggard. Are we heading to Motel Zero?"

"Nah. First, we're going to get a decent meal. Take me to Café Mirage." My pronunciation sounded like Donald J. Trump giving stern commands to his employees. After we chowed down a double plate of well-cooked pork chops with rice and broccoli, George escorted me to the ivy dwelling of Motel Zero. I couldn't conceal my grin. The immature joyfulness pinched me like an electric shot. When I opened the door, Motel Zero was godforsaken, it looked precisely the same as before I cruised to Presence Resurrection. Gosh, I am so happy to be home!

I trundled to my bedroom, sprawled on my king-size bed, and closed my eyes. Gosh, I am so happy to be home! That was my last thought before I fall asleep like a dead raccoon that was sprawled in a desolate countryside.

An hour later, a harsh sound of door swinging disturbed the silence. A merry voice of giggling rumbled from to the entry.

"Come on, Axel. Athena, watch your steps. Grab the guardrails," Don uttered to his kiddos. I stirred up from my king-size bed to say hi.

"What's up, champ? I've been missing you, buddy. So glad to see you. Look! We bring Boohba!" Don said. He stretched out his broad arms to give me a brother hug. His grin cheered me up.

"We have been taking care of Boohba since you've been in the hospital," Don said.

*****

Boohba was my female lizard, a leopard gecko that had a yellow white skin and scattered dots all over her seven-inch body. The lady from the reptile store told me that this lizard was a female. Thus, I named her Boohba.

She was the loveliest pet I ever had. Boohba just sprinkled love to everyone. For whatever reason, she got along with people. Therefore, I became codependent with her. Boohba was the ultimate pet for my lifestyle. If you gave her water and fed her, she would give you all of the love you could ask for. Her eyes were always reflecting relief.

Boohba had been my funky pet since I came to Chicago. She could stay still on my shoulder for a long time.

Back In 2016, I had been wandering on Streeterville close to the Navy Pier with Boohba on my arm. Most of the pedestrians stared at me and saluted me with phrases such as, "Man, this is so cool" or "OMG, is that thing alive?" It was risky to ramble in the street of Chicago with Boohba on my shoulder. Why? She wasn't completely tamed. Also walking through the helter-skelter in downtown Windy City in the middle of July with a lizard standing on your arm was sort of insane. One balmy Sunday, the weather was as hot as the feeling you had if you were a pork sausage on the Weber grill. The humidity embraced me as if a boxing contender were grabbing my arms in a clutch at a difficult bout.

I had that flaky idea to cruise with Boohba over downtown in White City. I parked my Geo clunker (at that time, the engine was still running) close to the CTA Blue Line station near Rosemont. The subway made hoarse sounds that resembled a horror movie based on a novel written by Stephen King. I kept Boohba in a smartphone box bought from T-Mobile. A few holes were pinched on that box so she could breathe.

The trip took no more than half an hour. I took the stop on Grand Avenue and headed to the Navy Pier. Should be a lot of tourists around there! As I strolled over along with Boohba, the pedestrians on Grand Avenue tipped traditionally, exuding greetings. After ten minutes of strolling, I was at the Navy Pier. My body froze for a second.

Hallelujah, I was right. This place is crammed! There are a bunch of tourists enjoying the scorcher day. Let's go, my worm queen. We have some work to do! I trundled among the maw of crowded sightseers. All of a sudden, a pleasant female voice echoed behind my eardrums.

"Hey! This is not real, right?" a blonde girl asked. She had a gymnastic type of body. Her vogue outfit looked expensive. Her Russian type of skin shone through the sunrays. Her brown eyes gawked fondly at Boohba.

"Well, you tell me? What do you think?" My voice sounded like a frisky lad playing his favorite game.

"Martha, come! Look at this dude's pet." A brunette hottie stepped over. I was mesmerized by her figure.

"This is Martha, and I am Geri." After a quick introduction, we exchanged numbers. On the next day, the three of us went to Starbucks for a cup of coffee. It turned out that these broads were visiting Chicago from Las Vegas. Geri spilled out a wishy-washy answer that she worked at a hotel without classifying any specific position. I figured out that was a subtle way of saying, "I am a prostitute."

Martha revealed her career as a stripper. This lizard is remarkable! After a few minutes of strolling, and I got a date with a drop-dead gorgeous stripper and foxy hooker. We had an animated chatter, jumping on different subjects. We hit it off as best buddies. The girls burst into laughter at my jokes, even if they knew those jokes weren't that funny. What do you know Mr. Lucky Pants? You are getting laid with a threesome. Thrilled about my new friends, I envisioned nooky plans for the next possible opportunity. At Starbucks, both started to grope me, using their playful legs under the table. The temperature over my crotch area increased. In the following six minutes, Martha obliquely exposed a sign indicating that she was allowed to be kissed.

Geri looked at me repulsively like a frenzied housewife who had just ascertained that her husband had cheated on her. I'm sure my wife will kick me in the nuts reading that classified story. I will take the chance. The joyful Geri flipped her character into a vagrant housekeeper. She started talking rapidly like an auctioneer competing in an international championship.

"We had an amazing conversation. It was fun chatting with you. Unfortunately, we need to go, but don't hesitate to call us if you stuck in Las Vegas," Geri pointed out.

"Why you leaving? The fun is just about to start," I replied. Damn, holy shmoly, I don't get it! First, they sent me carnal signs, and now, they are leaving like that? Geri looked at me with the corner of her eye. An awkward silence occurred. A few seconds later, she started talking. Her expression mirrored fulfilling compassion. Her answer slid fast like a Lambo would whoosh on the Turnpike 294 north to Wisconsin.

"We have to go. We made a promise to my cousin. We are staying at his bungalow in Arlington Heights. We have to be there at ten o'clock." Geri said. I stood in front of Starbucks on 25 East Washington Street like a perplexed twelve-year-old boy who was lost in Manhattan. What the heck is happening here? Why did she act like that? Martha was mute as if she had never been able to talk since her mother gave birth to her.

Dude! Nothing you can do about it! As we split in different directions, I had already known that would be the last time we would see each other. A week later, Martha contacted me. She suggested meeting in Las Vegas. Unfortunately, I couldn't travel outside Illinois, and she comprehended the reason. The immigration status. I missed the fun that night, but it was a delightful experience. That wouldn't occur without Boohba. Since then, my gecko lizard has been an essential chapter in the book of my life.

Chapter 26

Back in 2018. It was Saturday the last day of June and the first day after I had been discharged from Loyola. My only goal was to dawdle around and act indolently to accelerate the process of healing. Dude, check the mail? When was the last time you looked in the letterbox? The answer could not be answered. I tramped down the staircase, carrying heavy circumspection. There we go! Let see what we got here.

There were a bunch of envelopes. A red-light and speed ticket. Sweet. Welcome back to the real world, knucklehead. What else? All of a sudden, my eyes widened. What is that? A letter from Jacob, the landlord! I better check this out.

From: Jacob Pedzinski

Dear tenants,

I wrote this letter to declare that the building had been sold to a businessman. Officially, since first of July, this building is no longer my property. Kevin Miller is the new building manager. He will contact each of you to give you more information. If you have any questions, the phone number of the Building Manager is 312-XXX-XXXX.

Best regards: 06.10.2018

What? Great. This guy just made my day. I've just got back from the hospital, and Jacob decide to make the sale of the decade! What a coincidence.

Dimitry, you are a lucky boy! They say curiosity kills the cat. Well, that cat hopped on my cabeza. I decided to suss out what was going on and dialed the number mentioned in the letter.

"Hello, Kevin speaking," a squeaky voice echoed on the speaker.

"Hey there. My name is Dimitry. I am the resident on the third floor of Jill Lane, east side. Would you give me more information about the building and the new management?" 'Cuz I don't know what the heck is happening! My thoughts had grown from a flame into a conflagration.

"Hi. Yeah sure! We have been thinking to raise the rent up to $950. Anyway, we haven't determined when this change will be functional." He meowed in a squawking girly manner as fast as a Mexican commentator would yammer in a soccer game.

"Ugh... Do you have any intentions to remodel the units?" I asked. My mind cried out. Cuz I am not paying $950 for this hoboshack.

"Yes, we are looking forward to renovate only the bathrooms of each apartment." His vocabulary was as squeaky as a boy introducing himself on the first day in preschool. His proposal didn't sound acceptable. I had to discuss that with Don, even if I knew his answer already. On the way up through the stairs, I dragged my feet slower than a grandma. Just picture how wrathful the feeling would be of a twenty-nine-year-old athlete who shuffled slower than a ninety-year old man. My subconscious got exasperated when I thought about my medical report. Two hours later, Da Bomb showed up. He rushed through the door like Chris Tucker did in the movie Rush Hour.

"What's up, champ?" Don stated. He emitted his cheerful smile. Even if I had a brother, he wouldn't have treated me as compassionate as Don did.

After my detailed narration about Jacob's letter and the recent conversation with the squeaky Kevin, Don uttered, using his masculine voice,

"No way, champ! We can't pay that money for this frigging shithole. Listen up. Mom will look around for a better offer on a two-bedroom apartment. She has a natural flair for finding good deals. I'll take care of it." He shot me a smirk, like Don Rickles did on David Letterman's show. Da Bomb cheered me up as if he was my compadre. That was so helpful at that particular moment in my life.

The dusk changed the sky from ocean blue to a dark-colored raven. That was my first night at Motel Zero since I was released from Loyola. I wanted to sleep, but my mind refused to shut down. The sojourn from Loyola had reflected morbid dreamscapes. My mind was filled with an unpleasant flashback of images from the recent hospital visit.

This collection of hellish images kept changing like how you would persistently flip pages of a scrapbook. God Almighty, please help me to prevail those circumstances. Dude! Take a deep breath and pull yourself together. Whatever is coming next, you have to find the way to float onto the surface of the ocean called anxiety. You will overcome that nightmarish spree. You need to be stronger. Don't allow your anger to overcome your sanity. Oh Lord, give me the power to conquer the state of this predicament. Those thoughts kept whirling in my mind like garments rotating in a washing machine. Naw, I can't fall asleep. Jesus, what the heck should I do now? What time is it? Ah, damn it. Four o'clock. The weariness kept my eyelids halfway closed (or halfway open, whichever you prefer). I took some sleeping pills, but the medication caused me a headache. I thought it would help me pass out. Alas, it turned out to be a bad idea. The question was, "How can I fall asleep?"

After a few minutes of contemplation, the LED light bulb in my head turned on. Let's take Boohba out of her tank until I get bored. This method sometimes sorted out the sleeping puzzle. I grabbed my gecko queen and dropped her on my cheap computer desk. She commenced scurrying slowly, just before she shifted the gear into a nutjob fast-paced reptile.

What the heck am I doing with my lizard at four in the morning? God, I just want to sleep. An hour later, I was gradually falling asleep. I returned Boohba to her tiny artificial cave, and I crashed on my bed. The next day, the hunger woke me up. The clock was ticking around two in the afternoon. Holy cow, I need to gobble something. My stomach was making weird noises. A little later, I brushed my teeth and scrambled several eggs on the skillet. Around twenty minutes later, Don rushed through the door like Wile E. Coyote from the Looney Tunes.

"What's up, Champ?" He stated, exposing his broad grin, as usual. "Look! I brought some grasshoppers for Boohba." He went on.

"A grasshopper! What's that?" I looked at him, perplexed.

"That's cricket, Champ, ha-ha, you Bulglish." (Don used to call me "Bulglish" because when I got zonked, I spoke an undefined language between Bulgarian and English). Don and I had long conversations where we misunderstood each other. We asked questions like "What are you saying, Champ?" or "Champ, I don't understand a word of what you just said."

"Come on, let's feed Boohba," he said. I followed him like a dog tracking his master. Don grabbed the lid of the tank and lifted the artificial cave.

"Ah, where is Boohba?" Don cried out. I stared at Don as if I had seen him for the first time in my life.

"Holy-shmoly, I must have fallen asleep in the morning while she was still out!" Cheese and rice! I thought I put her back in the aquarium. Oh f—k! NO, NO, NO, NO! What have I done? You frigging loony ballsack.

"Come on, let's find her. She's gotta be somewhere here," Don said, and we both initiated a deep search all over Motel Zero. Both of us fumbled and left no stone unturned in every single spot of Motel Zero. It was like we had lost a gemstone worth six figures. Both of us piled a pyramid shape of garments and items. Motel Zero resembled the result of a ruthless earthquake or as if a Russian missile struck the apartment and made it look like a dilapidated building.

The following hours, we didn't stop searching through the entire apartment. Phrases such as; "Where is she?" Or "Where can she be?" kept recurring until eight in the evening. Then we both got worn out. The weariness induced me to lay on the sofa. I crawled over the couch as Charlie Sheen did in the movie Platoon. Terrific. What a lucky man you are. The second day after you got discharged from the hospital, and you've just lost your adorable pet. Good job, Dimitry! I had umpteen precious memories spent with that reptile, and now, she was gone as a result of my half-witted behavior. Don peered at me, exhibiting empathy. He adored Boohba.

The two of us felt blue, staring quietly at the idiot box. It was the same feeling you get when you lose somebody close to you.

*****

239

Two weeks after they released me at Loyola, I had to return for the follow-up appointment. I couldn't drive yet, and because I was too cheap, my plan was to schmooze someone escorting me to Loyola. George, the graceful limo driver, agreed to give me a lift to the infirmary only because he wanted to scope out the hot chicks working at Loyola.

As I headed to the hospital, a chubby Mexican nurse checked my vitals. Then, she sent me to the pocket-size medical room where I anticipated an attending physician. An Asian lady wearing a white robe scuttled through the entry and slammed the door as quickly as if the whole infirmary had been ambushed by hundreds of hoodlums. "Hello. How you doin' today? I'm Dr. Clay." Her grin exposed a friendly attitude.

"Doing well. Thank you. Trying to heal faster. Do you have any good news for me?" my question came like an awkward sneeze.

"Well, let me look at the inventory of medications that you are taking. Hmm…furosemide is the medication that makes you urinate the fluid inside of your body. The water pill…you don't need this medication anymore so you have to stop taking this remedy, okay?" Her instruction sounded like an order from a vice admiral of the Navy. I looked at her like an obedient pug, complying with the command of his master. Dr. Clay left the medical unit, and George drove me back to Motel Zero. The scorcher day was too dangerous for me to dawdle outside. The heat literally could cause you to faint on the ground, especially a man who had recently been released from the infirmary. The sawbones from Loyola had forbidden me to be outside. That meant in the hours between forenoon and afterglow, I had to avoid being exposed to the sun. I felt like a woodchuck hiding in his burrow.

Two hours later, Klara called me. Whoop! Whoop! You better pick up the damn phone, you dimwit scalawag!

"Hey, Klara, how you doin'?" I asked. I was exhilarated, as a boxer who made a KO on his debut as a professional.

"I have good news! I'll come and pick you up after an hour. Does that sound good to you?"

"Hell ya." It was like someone had asked me, "Do you want a mansion priced for a million dollars as heritage? No obligations or commitment to the government and IRS whatsoever."

A few hours later, Klara texted that she was at the building of Motel Zero. Happy as a clam, I walked down the staircase. I paced as briskly as I could. Klara was waiting at her purple Honda.

As she saw me, she jumped out of the car with a speed of an African jaguar. Daaamn! She is so dishy! Her hair was dangling naturally like Catherine Zeta-Jones from The Mask of Zorro. Klara jumped on me like a daughter to her father. We were thrilled to meet up as if it had been several years since we saw each other. Klara cuddled me a few seconds longer.

"I am so glad that you are finally out from Loyola. There is something that you need to…check this out." I stepped closer and looked at her smartphone. The information on the screen made my eyes widen like a sifaka's.

"Is this for real?" I asked. Klara nodded. Her phone projected the number of five thousand dollars collected via GoFundMe. A mixture of emotions between confusion and happiness flashed in my mind. The feeling that a contingent of people whom you never met collected money for your recovery was priceless. I am grateful to all of those God's children who decided to contribute to that charity platform. God heard my prayers and showed mercy just before I was about to slid into a deep precipice of dejection. Everything transpired thankfully to Klara, a divine angel mailed by the master of the universe.

"Klara, where do you wanna go? Do you want to eat somewhere?"

"Naw, I am not hungry. Let's go for a walk," Klara proclaimed. She loved strolling. Also she loved being entwined spiritually among nature. We rambled at the Forest Preserve area located a mile away from Motel Zero. As we padded on the cement sidewalk, both of us were sharing a mutual happiness. Then Klara asked directly like a journalist following a celebrity,

"Do you prefer to cash out all of the money?" That was an essential question, and I felt pleased that she broached the subject.

"I don't think it is smart to withdraw all of them at once. Just give me five hundred. The rest I'd like to stay stashed in this account. Of course, if you don't mind?" I stated. Great strategy, boy! Now you have an excuse to stay in touch with her.

"Naw, I don't mind at all. That's your money," Klara responded compassionately. All of a sudden, I stopped walking and grabbed my chest where the stabbing ache had been bugging me since I left Loyola.

"What is it? How bad is the pain? Would you like me to drive you to the hospital?" Klara asked. She was appalled. She didn't know what to do. The fear on her face could be read as easily as the headline of a poster. Yeah right! I've just got back from there! Cannot afford to visit the infirmary every single wince of discomfort.

"I'll be fine, Klara. I'm just tired. Can you give me a ride back home?" I looked at the puppy with the gleaming eyes, and tried to snap a smile despite the torment I felt.

"Yeah sure! I shouldn't force you to walk that long. I'm sorry!" Klara gazed at me with sympathy. Her eyes were oozing, almost weeping. There was a silence while Klara drove to Motel Zero. She checked me out by throwing a glance to make sure I would not start braying like a dying donkey. Klara parked the purple Honda, she averted and said,

"Are you sure you gonna be okay? I just feel that was my fault and…" she paused and leaned closer to me. There were no more than four inches between our lips. What the heck is happening to this chick? She never acted like that. Gosh, I'm starving. Ought to eat something!

"I will be fine, Klara. No worries. Talk to ya later."

I hopped out of the purple Honda and entered through the ivy townhouse. I traipsed warily on the staircase. I grabbed the protecting handrail just to make sure I would not collapse on the stairs. Then, something in my head clicked as quickly as flipping a light switch. Why did I have such an unpleasant ache half an hour ago? I guess that was a part of the healing process. Relax, boy. It will be fine. It takes time. Your heart is too weak. Sooner or later, you will feel better.

The rest of the evening, I was in deep ponder. I had too many questions which no one could answer. The following morning, I decided to walk around the building. Remember, boy. The doctors advised you to stay away from noon hours, so get your buttocks moving and go downstairs before the weather knocks you out, would ya? Don't screw up. The last thing you want is to go back at Loyola. Those were my thoughts while dragging my feet like a zombie from Resident Evil. I sneaked out through the entry of the ivy townhouse like a looter in destructive apocalypses. I was panting uneasily. It was so bad that I almost tumbled on the ground. Cheese and rice! What the heck is happening! Can't walk like that! Maybe it's because I've rushed the walking procedure. I should take it easy. Had to share that with Don in the evening.

I waddled like a penguin up to the stairway of Motel Zero. It was around ten in the same evening when Don sneaked through the door. We had casually discussed my unsuccessful stroll. Don couldn't make any additional comments.

"Need to sleep, champ. I'm tired," I said in a brief sentence while heading up to the bedroom. Don just nodded.

An hour later, croaky noises rumbled from my bedroom. Don sped urgently through the doorway. His eyes looked terrified. His countenance was appalled as if he had just seen a creepy ghost. What could intimidate a valiant super middleweight champion who is ready to risk everything he got in the ring? Don showed composure, but he remained wordless. He couldn't grasp what he saw at that moment.

The picture in my bedroom was as familiar as a horror movie. What had transpired could not be described as normal. My body was constantly squirming and writhing on the bed as if I was being possessed by demons and needed an exorcist. I couldn't breathe. My body was convulsing. It looked like I was having a clonic seizure. Just envision someone strangling you, pressing his hands on your throat and trying to kill you. Then you became panicked while you were striving to catch your breath. In the meantime, your body was shaking. That was how I felt. Don looked at me in deaf-mute appeal. He sat at the corner wordless and bemused.

At the next moment, he uttered, "Champ, let me know if you need to go to the hospital."

"Naw," I tried to say. A rasping sound rumbled over the gloomy room. I could barely stutter something. Don deciphered my signal by nodding and staying immobile. Nah, I am not going to the hospital. Not again. I will be all right. Dammit! The voice in my head cried out. That was the truth. When I said I'm not going back to the hospital, I meant it—period.

I would rather pass away on my last breath, but I wouldn't go back to the hospital. That was the kind of person I was, a pigheaded man of his word. That was how I tolerate my behavior. I wanted to be heard and understood. That was one of the reasons why I wrote this book.

After thirty minutes of physical and mental torment, I could take a deep breath as a normal person. Just like that, without any physical interference, I commenced a normal breathing. Unbelievable! That was a priceless moment, a moment when God heard my prayers and decided to save my life. He touched my throat and handled the respiratory issue. That was the second time when I realized what a treasure it was to be able to breathe regularly as a normal human being. The rest of the night, I dozed off faster than the snap of a finger.

*****

The next day, the sunlight broke through the window of my bedroom, like how a gunshot could break through an old television. A squeaky sound had rattled from a squirrel who was crawling up to the roots of the ivy dwelling at Motel Zero. Gosh, this annoying squirrel is busting my nut sack! Well, whatever. I might as well get up.

After I ate chicken soup, my plan was to give it a whack and walk around the area. Ten minutes later, with a sluggish pace, I came to the main entry of the building. I had to go on a walk twice a day. That was what the doctors had instructed me to do, and I followed those instructions like an obedient canine. After forty feet of limping over the pavement's footpath, my heartbeat became abnormal. A process of heavily gasping occurred like how a man would breathe after participating in a race for ten thousand meters at the Olympics.

Oh Lord! What should I do? If I stay on my feet, soon, I'll topple into a coma. Hurry up! Sit on the curb! It took a minute of heavily panting before I could get up on my toes again. Holy shmoly! I had only gotten around sixty feet from Motel Zero, and I was already wheezing like an exhausted dog who just had finished running two miles. At the time I was out from

Loyola, I could walk twice as far without gasping. This ain't right. Maybe I need to return to the infirmary. What should I do?

Those thoughts came faster than sunlight. My ankles hobbled in slow motion to Motel Zero. When I ascended the stairway to the third floor, I started panting heavily. Gosh, I hate these stairs. They are making me so sick! This ain't right. My health condition is similar to when I went to Present Resurrection a month ago. Dude, you gotta go back to the infirmary! You can't mess around with your heart. Something is wrong, and you need to sort out what it is. How? Go back to the hospital, you frigging goofball.

The worst nightmare became true no matter what I believed. I wobbled to Motel Zero like a sluggish person who had just ingested a bucket filled with ice cream. What the heck are you waiting for, Christmas? You ain't have many choices left. Call the ambulance, dammit! How long have you planned to stay like that? Or maybe you're willing to make it worse. What's the matter with you? You ain't gonna get better by idling on the couch, you damn feeb. You hear me? The voice in my head cried out.

Twilight had fallen over Chi-town. I rubbernecked at the gloomy screen of the TV. Do it! Okay, fine, I'll do it! For Christ's sake! Reluctantly, I grabbed my smartphone and called 911. Around sixty seconds later, the sirens of an ambulance blared from Motel Zero's window. The paramedics barged through the doorway and walked me out through the staircase.

The emergency medical technicians gently placed me into the ambulance like how a mother would place her baby into the crib. Here we are again! Back to the infirmary, Mr. Half-wit! The sirens blasted out in my eardrums as if a minor apprentice practiced playing on a saxophone next to my earhole.

The paramedics explained that they could only escort me to the closest medical institution. That was why they drove to Loyola in Melrose Park. Two hours later, another ambulance drove me to Loyola in Maywood where I should have been taken in the first place. I must emphasize; all the emergency medical technicians were very well trained and had the agility to react to urgent medical demands.

It was close to ten in the evening when the paramedics dropped me off at the ER, where a fetchingly redheaded Irish nurse with cute freckles checked my vitals. Around midnight, an African American personnel from the transport department rolled me into the inpatient care. I was in a separated room along with an old Polish outpatient, who expressed a harsh grimace when I said Hi to him.

The rest of the night, my brooding face couldn't let me pass out. Aggravated questions kept popping in my subconscious over and over again. Why am I back here? What is going on with me? Oh Lord, please show mercy! The next morning, another medical assistant cruised me in the cardiac department for an echocardiogram. The medical employee who managed the examination procedure was a Korean guy in his thirties. His haircut looked the same as a bird's nest. He had an obese body resembling Bud Spencer. He was a kind man. We chatted throughout the entire procedure.

"My name is John," he said. After the process had been completed, John declared,

"Well, that's it. I will send the results to the cardiologist. By the way, I am going to drop you at your room, personally." Nonplussed, my mind got tangled like a printer jammed with a lot of paper.

"John, my man, that's not your job!"

"I know, dude. But I don't want you to wait for another transporter. It may take more than half an hour."

The Korean man was very generous. When he dropped me at the inpatient room, I said,

"John, it was nice chatting with you. Thanks for the ride."

"You're welcome! God bless you, brother." John responded, and swiftly vanished out of sight. Around forenoon on the same day, I closed my eyes to sleep, and all became black like how my smartphone got blacked out when it was out of service as a result of dropping it in the toilet. All of a sudden, someone knocked on the door like the sardonic—perhaps I also could say, inscrutable—and an iconic clown Pennywise, the villain from the bestseller IT, written by Stephen King.

Mike, Stan, and George burst straight in. All of them gaped at me with compassion.

George said, "What the heck is going on with you, dude? Why are you back at Loyola?"

I responded, "Shortness of breath. I am expecting the doctors to give more details. I've just got the echocardiogram exam."

Stan said, "Bud! If I was in your shoes, I would take the hike and get back to Bulgaria." Listening to Stan's proclamation, my countenance changed from a polite guy into a catty hillbilly who had just lost five hundred bucks on a live poker table. Stan's announcement was way too far from my inclinations.

Mike said, "I am pretty sure the physicians will sort out this misunderstanding. With God's power, everything will be back to normal. There is somethin' else you need to know. Bobby the Groundhog and his wife had designed two donation boxes with your image attached. One of them had been placed at the deli market named Malincho—a notorious store among the Bulgarian community. The other box had been set at the Bulgarian church, Saint Sophia." I was astounded. Holy shmoly! Bobby did something divine. God bless him and his family.

Mike spoke the language of sanity. His statement was godly and righteous. What Mike had stated helped me to have a more positive outlook in the future. After a few minutes of intensive giggling, George announced,

"I got some errands to run. Come on, guys. Let's bounce! Dimitry, see ya later."

He drove the other two boys. Mike and Stan followed him like apprentices pursuing Yoda. Before he vanished, Mike mimicked a phone handle, which meant, "Call me if you need anything". His tacit mimicry didn't need to be declared. We had known each other long enough to comprehend what we talked about by using any kind of sign language.

It wasn't too long after my folks departed and the crew of doctors came over. One of them, a male with a disdainful face, leaned close to me and uttered,

"Hello, Mr. Salchev. I am Dr. Green. It's nice to meet you. How are you doing today?"

"Hello, Dr. Green. I am fine… I guess. My question is; why do I have to come back here? What is going on with my heart?" I stared at him, dismayed. I was anxious to hear his answer.

"Mr. Salchev, why have you stopped taking furosemide? It's the medication that causes you to discard fluid retention via urinating." I goggled like a monkey who gawked at a human trying to mimic a baboon. Is he for real? Did he say furosemide? The remedy, which I had been urged to stop, ordered by the Asian doctor that I had visited two weeks ago!

"Well, Dr. Green, as you might know, two weeks ago, I had a scheduled appointment here at Loyola. Dr. Clay whom I saw for the first time had ordered to stop the furosemide without any specified reason. Do you think this might be the reason why I'm here?" My tone was humble and friendly. Seemingly distraught, Dr. Green remained silent. We both knew what the answer was. Come on, doc! Spill the beans!

"I guess that might be the case. From now on, you must continue taking furosemide twice a day. We need to observe your health condition for one more day. Then, you will be dismissed from the infirmary. Have a—"

At that moment, Klara intercepted our chin-wag. She scuttled over through the entry like a malicious hoodrat.

"Oh, I'm sorry for interrupting you, guys. I will wait outside," Klara said while she was turning her fabulous tooshie toward the entry.

"That's fine. We've just finished. Thank you, Mr. Salchev. Take care of yourself," Dr. Green said. He then passed Klara by giving her a smirk. Klara rolled over her eyeballs and briskly gave me a hug.

"Hey, tell me what's going on. Why are you here? Do you like loitering in hospitals?" she asked and cackled goofily. Looking at her, I burst into laughter. Her jollity cheered me up. After I explained the story, she blurted out. "Don't worry. You're gonna be just fine. Trust me." As she finished her speech, Klara slightly grabbed my hands and started to move rhythmically.

I grabbed her left hip and slightly put my right hand around her waist. We began to dance in a slow-motion quickstep. The old but gold song 'You're the One That I Want," from the movie Grease blasted out in our minds. Several seconds later, Klara suggested,

"Move your right hand into the upper side of my back." I slid my right hand down, close to her buttocks.

"I said up!" Klara croaked. We both looked at each other and instantly burst into laughter. I was laughing so hard that the pain in my chest struck badly as if I ate moldy food. I sprawled on the medical stretcher as if somebody shot me with an AK-47.

"Are you okay?" She asked. Klara expressed her commiseration. We stared each other. Klara looked at my lips. Dude! She is ready to be kissed. Take your chance, chumpy boy. As I was listening to my bossy subconscious voice, I leaned closer to her. There you go, Ballsack! Whoop! The next moment, Klara moved away, and I missed the target. An embarrassing jiff occurred. Her pupils looked agitated as if she was saying, "What was that! What's wrong with this guy?" Klara was surprised. A ghostly silence fell in the medical room.

"I got to bail. See ya later," Klara blurted out. What an epic fail, you Mr. Damfool. Did she get upset? Maybe or maybe not? I was still chewing it over and questioning myself for the past half an hour before I hit the rack. On the same day at three in the afternoon, my smartphone rang. It interrupted me from my serene nap. Ah man. I forgot to turn on the silent mode. Who will it be? I stared at the screen. Oh, it's Don!

"What's up, champ? Are you okay? What did the doctors say?" Don cried out. He was exhilarated, as usual.

"I will be fine, champ." Am I? "What is goin' on?" I responded. I felt tired and my eyes were closing. Do you really think you will be fine? This vital question kept stabbing me for the past two months.

"Yo, champ, my mom found a great deal for a two-bedroom apartment located in Albany Park. The rent is $1,200 per month. As you're aware, my credit score is screwed up, and I know your credit has plummeted since you got sick. That means my mom will run her credit to get this apartment. We can't afford to wait any longer. This offer may fly away at any minute. You understand what I'm saying?"

"I guess so." I could barely keep my eyes open. Why do I feel so woozy? It was like I am in a broken-down chopper, falling into a ravine and spinning like a casino roulette. It was the same sleepy feeling when you were so bushed that your eyelids were constantly closing at every other instant.

"Champ! I'm sending you pictures of the apartment. Take a look at this apartment and tell me what you think. Don't rush, but we need to make a firm decision today. Are you picking up what I am printing down? Champ"—no answer. "Champ…champ!"

"Yeah, sure. I got it." Suddenly, I opened my eyes. Dude, look at the images. Hmm…it seems like this apartment looks perfectly fine for this price. There isn't any Photoshop. Don is a good friend. It's always fun around him. Yeah, let's give it a shot! Besides, I don't see a reason what can possibly turn it down. Jesus, Lord. Why am I feeling so drowsy? Hurry up, man! Tell him your answer. He is waiting.

"Okay, champ! I'm in. Let's do it," I murmured while my bleary eyes kept closing.

"Great, champ. Did they tell you when you're gonna leave the hospital?" Don asked. His words came with the speed of a shark's bite.

"They are kicking me out tomorrow, champ."

"Sweet. See you at home then." That's exciting news. Finally, I've got a decent apartment where I can live peacefully.

An uproar of a girlish talk had interjected my thoughts. A nurse standing on the threshold was saying something to her colleague. Then, one of them averted and swiftly approached the bed where I was lying.

"Hello, Mr. Salchev. How are you feeling? I'm Jazmine. Nice to meet you." A young brunette Latina who had a fetching front cover swaggered across the room. Her curvy figure had the color of the seed of an avocado. Jazmine's tooshie was oversized, although, it still drew my attention.

"Hello there. I'm fine. Are you going to torture me?" I said with a smirk on my face.

Jazmine didn't accept my joke. She leered at me like a street cat with an apathetic glimpse.

"That's the antibiotic which you've been taking against the bacteria."

"Shoot, what was the medication that you gave me an hour ago?" Utterly baffled, I remained quiet.

"Oh, that was Tramadol, a sedative remedy for your chest pain." Wait, what? A painkiller. Hold on. Dammit, that's why I was feeling so drowsy. You need to be alert of what you are takin'!

Jazmine left the medical ward. She snubbed me without saying anything. It was like I had just told her, "Jazmine, you are a cutie, but your fanny is the size of King Kong. It won't work out between us, hon." She was peevish for some untold reason. I disregard her like how you would ignore the page of this book. Once again, the doorway of my room became a traffic jam of people. They were coming in and out like vehicles going through an automatic car wash.

It was quarter to four in the afternoon when Emily burst straight to the entry. Her trepidation was making me feel uneasy.

"Hi, Dimitry. What happened? Why are you here?" She didn't know anything about the heart surgery until I had called her. After I narrated the tale of my heart and respiratory issues, she got goosebumps. She then interrupted me disdainfully.

"Why didn't you call? I'm so sorry to hear that bad news. I think you should go back to Bulgaria."

Holy crap! Initially, Stan had told me to go home, then Val, and now Emily. I don't want to go back there, not right now. Why should I abandon my dreams? Albert Einstein said, "Never give up on what you want to."

I rebuffed Emily's cursory declaration. Why? Should I listen to someone who didn't have a clue what was happening in my life? Emily was an indulgent person. I loved and praised her. The last time we spoke was two years ago. Her philosophy was way too far from mine. As we ended up our dialogue, Emily disappeared.

An afterglow had already fallen over the sky as if an outage had halted the electricity of the entire city of Maywood. The darkness outside became as black as the color of my Nissan's tires. My worried face turned to a pallid expression as if the fictional character Billy the Puppet loomed at the medical ward. Oh Jesus Lord! Help me to doze off, please.

The nights lasted longer than the days. It had turned out to be a difficult to nod off. Truculent insomnia had pursued me, and when I got lucky to snooze, horrendous nightmares of something indescribable, images of multiple faces, were flashing in my subconscious. Guises of unknown malignant monsters exposing sharp teeth bigger than a shark's bothered me. Hideous creatures, which shouldn't be named kept cropping up like the changing images of slot machines.

Those demons were grinning sardonically at me. Get the duck away from me, you frigging surreal ugly mother flowers! It was around five in the morning when I drifted off. An hour later, a cutie Mexican nurse disturbed me and handed me the antibiotic that had been wrestling against the gruesome Streptococcal.

*****

The next morning, I nibbled two slapjacks with crockpot blueberry syrup. Then, I drained a small size of apple juice to rinse my mouth. A brunette nurse handed the discharge papers, and I was saddling up to leave Loyola. While taking my clothes, I was thinking. How can I get a ride to home? The more I stay in the hospital, the more anxious and impatient I become.

Most people who had been floundering with acute maladies in infirmaries had already known how anxious a man could be while staying in long term. I couldn't find anybody available to give me a lift. Thus, I was forced to Uber myself to Motel Zero.

Two hours later, I was chilling on my couch in my sanctuary. I had been thinking how dumb I could be to lose my little girl. Feeling blue, I cruised to my bedroom. Boohba, where the heck can you be? Perhaps she has kicked the bucket as a result of my reckless stupidity. That was your fault, you doofus! What have I done? Pondering about my foolish mistake, I found myself standing next to the computer desk. Then, all of a sudden, I looked at my feet and BOOM! I looked stunned as if my mom would tell me that I was an orphan and that they adopted me twenty-eight years ago. Boohba was standing on the brown carpet.

"Boohba! Where have you been?" I bawled, flabbergasted. The worm-loving reptile didn't even look at me as if I didn't exist. Look at her! She is so emaciated. No wonder! She's been lost for two weeks without any food! Okay! Slowly reach her and try to grab her. That's your chance. Be very cautious! Ah, dammit! Did she run away? Where the heck did she go?

When I kneeled, Boohba was in a tiny mouse-hole under the out-of-service radiator. It was impossible to put my hands there; it was too narrow. Great! Now what am I gonna do? Yeah, that may work! Some seconds later, I came back carrying stainless steel barbecue's tongs. I placed a small piece of cheese. Boohba charged to grab it, and I plucked her using those tongs. The next moment, Boohba was back in her aquarium. Bingo! I couldn't comprehend how I brought her back. I thought I would never find Boohba, and she came from nowhere. An hour later, Don burst straight through the doorway.

"What's up, champ? How are you feeling?" Don gave me a brotherly hug as if we were fraternity members.

After a short chin-wag, I uttered, "Don, I want to show ya something."

Da Bomb just nodded. "You found Boohba! No way! Good job, champ! She must be starving. Let's get her some grasshoppers. Now you've learned something from me, my Bulglish brother." Don chuckled. He then proceeded, "What you're up to, champ?"

"I have no idea. Probably will goof around, watching TV and gaining some extra pounds by eating McDonald's Big Macs. Why?" I asked like a salty farmer grouching about his vehicle that had been mysteriously stolen.

"I'm going to a place located three miles away from here. You comin'?" He asked.

"I don't know, champ. Can't drink. What am I gonna do up there?"

"Come on. Let's hang out, brother. What are you gonna do up here? We don't have Netflix, HBO, or Hulu. You've already canceled the Xfinity service. The only source we have is a cheap antenna from Walmart for the boob tube."

"Boob…what?" I stared at the Da Bomb, utterly perplexed.

"Hang loose, bud. Boob tube is a slang for TV, my Bulglish brother. Come on, let's roll. Champ, there is a place I want to show you."

"What place? What are you talking about, champ?" Bewildered, I peered at him. He glimpsed at me and said, "You'll see." Don tried to cheer me up, but I didn't feel comfortable. The formal IBO champion operated the Nissan. We headed east on Belmont Street, somewhere before it crossed Harlem.

Where the heck are we going? I knew that Don wouldn't set me up in any unpleasant situation. A few minutes later, Don parked the car on a side street next to a ubiquitously-styled, low-profile building. When we sneaked inside, I looked around like an intimidated squirrel. My eyes kept blinking like a broken-down traffic light.

There was a private club inside of that building. That club had a small chamber with some neatly positioned furniture as if they were going to shoot a scene for a movie. A countertop bar was placed at the corner where a big Italian man who looked like Clem Caserta had been serving drinks. Everyone there was playing cards, eating pizzas, and smoking cigars.

A few broads were sitting on the couch, but mostly, there were guys. Those fellas looked like they just got out from the cooler. In the west side of that club, was a garden patio where you could lounge and chill in. Those joints weren't accessible just for anybody. You needed to be a member, or someone had to sneak you in. I looked around and realized that everyone there was puffing cigars.

"Hey, guys, that's my cousin Dimitry." Don started to introduce me to others. Everyone out there was greeting me as if I was a member of that club. It felt like I was at The Chez Bippy, Sonny's bar from Bronx Tale.

"What is this place, Don?"

"This one? It's a herf place, a cigar place. Everybody here is BOTL."

"Champ, what's BOTL?"

"It means brother of the leaf. A polite way to call someone cigar smoker." That's cool, but I can't stay here! I had open-heart surgery two months ago for Christ's sake! The voice in my head protested. Don stared at me tacitly. He comprehended my trepidation.

"We are leaving in five minutes, champ. I know you can't stay here any longer, as your health condition may get worse." Don was a sharp-witted fella. He was persistently aware of what was going on.

Awareness is one of the strongest abilities of humans, one that can push them to the summit of success.

Just before we left the smoky place, my smartphone rang. Hmm… that's a text message! It might be some offers or discounts from my mobile service provider. Once in a while, they send me some flyers— Klara! My grumpy face transformed into that of a happy boy. I ogled at the screen where the message displayed:

Klara: Hey, how you doing? Hopefully, you feel much better now.

She is thinking about me! How cool is that? Hurry up, Mr. Squarehead. Do something, but what should I reply? "Good, cool, nice"? Naw! Sounds like I'm a virgin nerd. Don looked at me. He saw a man who walked side to side, acting like an uncertain student in first grade.

"Hey, champ, what's eating you? You looked kind iffy. Are you okay?"

"Yeah, this gal just texted me. I don't know how to respond." I looked at Don with a flaky smile as if I was saying, "Please help me".

"Champ, just tell her that you are busy at the moment and you gonna call or text mañana. In this case, she will be thinking about you," Da Bomb blurted with his emblematic equanimity. Jesus Christ! That's it. He is absolutely right. This is a helluva good hint.

"Dimitry! You wanna play darts?"

"Don't bet any money 'cuz I'm gonna kick your ass," I declared.

Don cracked up. He added, "Stop pulling my leg. Champ, let's go. I'll drive."

We headed up to a few honky-tonk bars somewhere in Elmwood Park. One of them had some ubiquitous name as G Bar grounded on the Grand Avenue. Both of us hung out and spent some quality time as best buddies. At most of the barrelhouses where we shuttled, the folks we bumped into had always cheered and greeted Don.

As we started the challenge of playing darts, Don made me look like a loser. He had beaten me so bad as if I was a twelve-year-old tenderfoot who had played for the first time. While we disputed our darts contest, Klara had replied with a single "K," which told me that she ignored my text.

Don and I palled around back and forth pretty much for the rest of the night. There was no need to sink my muzzle into hard liquor. It was a blast from the past. We both cracked up to each other. At quarter to nine in the evening, I peeked facetiously at Don and stated,

"Gotta tell ya, champ. I can't wait to move out from Motel Zero into Albany Park." I opened the subject, even if I knew it was pointless.

"Hell yeah, champ! I'm sick and tired of this hoboshack. We'll be cool outta there," Don said. He was shoving balls in the holes and bobbing around the pool table. Gosh, he keeps beating me so bad. I can't play anymore! Ah, you nitwit. Who cares! Stop whining like a wimp. Just have fun, would ya? All of a sudden, I felt a tremendous pain in the stomach. I almost tumbled into comatose. I bowed forward, holding my stomach.

"What's the matter, champ? Are you okay?" Don asked.

"Yeah, I'm fine. Perhaps the pain comes from the ribs where the incision is." A ferocious giddiness had shaken my vision off. I could hardly proclaim.

"Champ, better drop me at the Motel Zero," I declared.

"Yeah, I think that is a good idea." Don and I vanished from the dive bar like how a silhouette of a phantom would mysteriously disappear. The clock on my phone showed half-past midnight. Once again, I failed to drift off. It was just another long evening of watching shows on TV.

*****

The next morning, my hungry stomach woke me up. I stared at the clock. It was half-past nine. Hold on for a minute, dude! What time did I pass out last night? Five. That is four hours and a half of sleep. That's all. After ingesting three chubby eggs and a toast smeared with honey, I decided to go outside for a short walk. My phone jingled just before I closed the main door of the townhouse. Who the heck could it be? Whoop! Whoop! It's Klara. Better take this phone call, Mr. Shabby Pants!

"Hey, Klara, how you doin'?" I asked, maintaining composure while my entire body bounced convulsively with excitement.

"I'm fine. The most important is, how are you feeling?" The question, "How are you feeling?" had been reiterated as many times as Donald J. Trump had been mentioned as the president of the USA.

"I'm going for a walk. As you know, the doctors have advised me to walk daily." I proclaimed.

"Honestly, I need to walk too. Listen, I'll come to pick you up, and we will go together. How about three?" Klara exclaimed. Jeez, dude, it's so easy to meet up with this broad. How come?

"Cool, I will see you at three o'clock," I said triumphantly like a child replying yes on an offer to have his favorite Breyer's chocolate ice cream. Once again, butterflies fluttered in my stomach. I ambled back to Motel Zero and waited for my VIP escort.

Around three, I got the phone call.

"I'm here!" she reported. When I walked through the entryway, the puppy with the gleaming eyes was waiting for me at her Honda. She peered at me, emitting a fetching grin. Klara cuddled me. She leaned her ear on my chest and started listening to my heartbeat. Then, she averred,

"I'm so glad that you are here next to me. I was worried about you. I prayed to God for you." Her speech threw my in a state of bewilderment. I thought we were only friends. Why does she talk like that? Shall I say something or better to keep my mouth shut? There is something else. Why does she keep hugging me longer? By the time I was stuck in traffic of thoughts, Klara asked,

"Where do you want to go for a walk?" She grinned delightfully. Her question was clear, but my mind had ambiguous thoughts.

"It's July, and the weather is torrid. Let's go for a walk to the River North area. There, we can stroll by Lake Michigan," Klara suggested. She was still leaning her head on my chest.

"That's a great idea. Let's rock downtown," I mumbled while struggling to get into the purple Honda.

When we rolled over inbound to the city, Klara let the cat out of the bag.

"Dimitry, I want to ask you something, but you have to promise me to be honest, okay?" I was stunned by her question. What the heck is she talking about? My expression remained calm, and my emotional mask had been taken off.

"Yeah, sure. You can ask me anything you want. I won't keep secrets from you."

"Did you get any phone numbers from female nurses at Loyola? You know, for a date?"

Wait, what? Why is she so concerned about that? Well, whatever. Who cares? We are having a simple conversation. Let me think…

"There was one broad…"

Klara cut me off like a rumble blast from a firecracker.

"Naw, don't tell me. I don't wanna hear any more of it." Wow! This is odd. Is she jealous, or am I just getting too excited? Her tone changed like a frustrated celebrity when they are forced to answer a dumb question.

"Listen, I can't keep the money from GoFundMe any longer. My suggestion is to make three separate withdraws, and today it will be the first cash-out. What do you think?"

"Hell yeah. That's fine with me. No worries. Mike will help me out. He is reliable."

"Can you give a credit to this guy? That's a lot of greenbacks," Klara queried like the homicide detective of CSI Miami Horatio Caine interrogating some Mexican by asking questions related to a murder.

"If there is someone in this world whom I could trust, that will be Mike," I said.

We spent over three hours wandering in downtown, but I felt it lasted for only thirty minutes. The two of us discussed a plethora of different topics. Also, I teased her pretty much all the time as if she was my younger sister. Her smile was glittering. Her enticing pupils peered at me fondly. The time spent with Klara was always a divine gift from Lord. As we headed back outbound to Motel Zero, Klara made a stop at the bank. She crept out of her eggplant-colored Honda and walked to the ATM of JP Morgan.

After she handed me the money, Klara mumbled so quietly like she didn't want to be heard.

"Here, take the money and count it. Please make sure that's the correct amount." Her compassioned eyes gazed at me incessantly. She remained quiet, but somehow, her face looked like she was saying something essential. A minute later, I broke the silence.

"Can you drop me at Motel Zero?" my question poured out almost as if I was pleading.

"Sure, of course," she said automatically as if the first female robot Sofia was talking. The growing dusk had painted the sky with shades that looked like an orange peach. After five minutes of driving, Klara parked her eggplant-colored Honda in front of the ivy townhouse. She turned off the engine and looked at me. Her silence looked like she was trying to say something, but her common sense pulled her back into wordless statement. For the following couple of seconds, we didn't utter any words. It wasn't even necessary.

Something is going on between the two of us. I couldn't resist any longer. My body leaned forward, and the distance between our lips became intimately shorter. Klara didn't jerk at all. She became inert, stationary like a monument. The gap between us shrank too much, and we were about to cross the line. An inch had separated both of our lips. Now is your time, dude. Make your frigging move or forget about it!

At the next moment, Klara moved her head, and I missed my target again. A chaste kiss on her cheek had occurred like I was a five-year old offspring kissing his girl classmate from preschool. Why is she so surreptitious? What am I doin'? Freaking bonehead. We were supposed to be just friends. A clumsy moment occurred inside of the eggplant-colored Honda. My epic-fail movement embodied an awkward situation, which no one would like to be facing. The embarrassment had made us idle and wordless. Come on, knucklehead! What the heck are you waiting for? Say something. Be sorry and apologize. Klara disrupted my congested mind.

"I got to bail. See you later." Her expression had labeled the phrase, "I don't know what are you trying to do, but I don't like it". Klara was nonplussed; but she wasn't warlike, grouchy, or merely mad at me. Before she roared back to the city, Klara cuddled me tightly. As I watched how she departed from Jill Lane, my mind was trapped at an impasse.

Thoughts of what had just happened bummed me out, as if an annoying spider was crawling over the back of my neck. I don't get it! The way she looked at me describes how eagerly she wanted to be kissed, but if this theory is true, then why did she moved into the opposite direction. And why didn't she grumble? Perhaps she isn't ready or maybe I have misinterpreted the whole scenario. Later the same night, Don came to Motel Zero. He rushed through the entry like a bull chasing a red flag.

"What's up, champ? Did you have fun with Bulgarian fiddle chick?" Don uttered. He brought up the subject that I had been jonesing to chew over. Elated, I narrated my peculiar experience.

"Can't sort out what we are, Facebook friends, platonic friends, not friends at all. What the heck should I do, champ?"

"Well, champ, the word you are looking for is situationship, but I don't know what she is up to. Could be everything. Women are unpredictable," Don attempted to help as much as he could.

"What is situationship, champ?" I stared at him, boggled. As he heard my question, Don was deadpan, then he started laughing.

"That's a relationship with no label on it, champ. It's tough to be defined. It something resembling your story."

"Yeah, why does it have to be so complicated? I don't get it." Don had noticed my subdued countenance and announced,

"Whatever is, you must clear out what kind of show you both are going to play on the stage. Otherwise, you might get twisted. You know what I am saying?" He asked and I nodded uncertainly.

"There is something else we need to talk about, champ." Metaphorically, Don had stretched the gum, talking lengthily and gaggling like a flock of geese.

"On August 1, the lease for Albany Park will take place. Can you call someone to help us with moving? I know you can't lift any heavy items. You'll only show the directions like a traffic control officer." He asserted and I cackled so bad that the pain in my torso made me grimace.

"What's wrong, champ? Pain in the incision?" Don looked worried.

"Hard to tell, champ. I assume it's the chest." The pain forced me to bow my head down like a butler would to his royal employer in a castle worth millions of dollars.

Don prudently gazed at me and uttered, "I'm going to the dive bar on Grand. Call me if you need anything, okay?" I just nodded, showing thumbs-up. As the years passed, I have learned to be a true warrior who brazens the pain out and sucks it up. You don't know how strong you are until you have to fight for your life. One of the greatest preachers and authors, Joel Osteen, wrote, "The pain is a sign of new birth."

The temperature that night was over seventy, but it felt like ninety. The humidity made me feel dehydrated. The cheap TCL AC unit was sewed by the window was blowing hard at full speed to cool the room down. It was just another evening filled with foggy thoughts. I need...need to see Klara! I drifted off around the first morning hours.

*****

It was Monday, July 16. Around forenoon, I woke up with a severe headache. In my mind, there wasn't any storage space left for grievance.

God had saved me and rendered me a second chance. Live, laugh, and enjoy the value of your life. I was so grateful to be alive because my time could be shorter than the shortest lie expressed ever. An hour later, I gobbled a bowl of milk and Corn Flakes cereal. After I finish the breakfast, I will call Klara…or shall I text instead? It had been ten minutes of thinking, and at the end of my epic hesitation, I decided to dial her. Initially, Klara didn't answer. She called back around twenty minutes later.

"Hey, Dimitry, how you doin'? I was busy at home. That's why I couldn't pick up the phone. So what's up?" Her joyful voice sounded disrupted, like she was anticipating an important call. My question burst out like a bowling ball blasting down through the alley at full speed.

"With God's will, I'm doing fine. Klara, I'm thinking of goin' for a walk. You wanna come over?" That was my way of saying that I needed to see her. She got the memo already. Klara was one of those chicks called a "study whore." She narrated multiple tales related to her timeline involving the university where she graduated. Also Klara talked as if she was Google itself. She always had an opinion on everything.

"I can't make it today. I have to play in a huge private event. Need to concentrate on rehearsal. How about Wednesday at three in the afternoon?" Her pronunciation became mellow and serene as the song "Hello" by the enthralling singer, Adele.

"Terrific. Sounds great! See ya on Wednesday." While I was pondering, my grin widened like Jim Carrey playing in the movie Liar, Liar. I don't care what she thinks about me and what relationship we have. The only thing that matters is to see her. Klara did a plethora of favors for me, more than I could ask for. Her actions of care caused me to become very fond of her.

The rest of the day, I spent lying on the sofa, and staring goofily at some sitcoms on Laff. The hunger scratched my tummy. I dragged my ass to McDonald's and ordered a Big Mac meal and a coke with easy ice. During the time spent at home, I started to count my blessings and focused my thoughts on getting back at Sapino's.

Dude, what was the name of the supervisor at Sapino's? Oh yeah, Dino.

He is a cool guy. He knows that I'm a beaver. That night, same as others, was longer. My eyes were still open, as if someone had taped my eyelids using industrial tape. I heard a symphony orchestra of crickets performing a delightful outdoor venue of Beethoven's Ninth. Listening to the music, I drifted off around five in the morning.

*****

Wednesday, July 18, came by quickly like a Ducati Panigale V2 was zipping on the turnpike. The sun rose without clouds. At ten, the weather outside was as hot as hell. Klara picked me up, and we went for a walk at Forest Park. While we strolled, I revealed my plans for moving out to Albany Park. She goggled like a nonplussed gal who met her celebrity crush at Golden Globe Awards.

"Wait a second. Did you just say Albany Park?" Klara asked and I nodded.

"That's where I live. Are you kidding me? We will be neighbors!" Klara cried out. She wasn't happy about my divulgence. Her eyes looked sullen.

I decided to cheer her up by grabbing her arm, saying, "Let's snap a selfie together." Klara stepped back and shook her head for disapproval. What in the name of…! Why is she acting like that? Who am I, a pus bag klutz? Why is she refusing to have a simple selfie with me? I am not a selfie-taking guy at all. Klara is the first person whom I have ever asked to snap a selfie. Her behavior made me feel bummed out.

The stronghold built up in my mind had cracked up. I couldn't be quiet like a mannequin, not anymore. I needed to know what the whole burden was that she secretly carried.

"What's wrong, Klara? Why don't you want to have a picture with me?" I wrapped my head around trying to sort out her peculiar attitude. My mind was confused like a terrified rodent stuck in a vast maze.

"I don't know. My hair looks awful. I just don't want to take a picture." Her reaction sounded like a final verdict from the Supreme Court. What the duck? This is a wishy-washy answer. Why is she acting so stealthfully? Dude, don't bother. You have a big fish to fry like, for instance, to bear with your health condition.

After ten minutes of walking, Klara witnessed how I excruciatingly wobbled as if I was about to faint on the floor. The reason was the deficiency of oxygen in my blood. She was dismayed, shooting her owlish pupils at me. Her Bulgarian accent sounded frightened,

"What's happening? Tell me, how are you feeling?"

"I guess… I'm tired… Need to sit somewhere," I could barely talk.

"Look! There is a bench over there by the grassy knoll." Klara was pointing to a wooden bench and table all painted in crocodile color and was located twenty feet away from us. As we trundled to the table, Klara was holding me closely to make sure I would not tumble. Struck by drowsiness, I sat on the bench.

Klara sat too close to me. Her pupils flicked from my lips to my eyes and vice versa. She kept looking at my lips and then back to my eyes. Klara tousled her gorgeous hair and acted like she was mesmerized. Both of us were wordless, but we communicated by using our minds. Holy smokes, what are we doing? That's insane! This broad is married! Well yeah, but in the meantime, she didn't resist at all. Many times, she had sent me a subtle proposal for a canoodling. Even a blind man would see the picture.

A connection between our lips had been made. We kissed genially, way more intimately than Leonardo DiCaprio and Kate Winslet did in the movie Titanic. What have you done! You frigging dinkle ball! The two of us comprehended what kind of mess we had been embroiled in. However, both couldn't stop kissing. Snogging Klara was the most impassioned feeling I had experienced along with broads since I remembered my name.

We stopped kissing, as we pulled away from each other, we grinned contentedly. After a few wordless minutes, I decided to break the silence.

"There is a European café called IL Cortile a mile away. Let's have a drink. What do you think?"

"I might come, but I can't stay too long," Klara asserted.

"Well, I didn't mean to spend the night there," I said in an attempt to tease her.

"Stop it!" Klara nudged me with her elbow while giggling like a breathtaking meteorologist would after making a blooper during broadcasting live on TV. IL Cortile was a delightful café. Many European residents were visiting that joint. The marble countertop bar was on the west side of the corner. There were no more than ten tables spread over the masonic floor. A bunch of track lights was attached to the ceiling. They were hung in different directions like observation cameras in a penitentiary. We sat at the west side of this joint. A luscious chick as enthralling as Emma Watson approached the table that we had occupied.

"Hello, Nelly. How you doin'?" I saluted the waitress. Nelly was a Bulgarian chick reflecting a magnanimous personality. She was voluptuous. Her dull hair and glittering brown eyes were entrancing. I had known Nelly since I started visiting this joint a few years ago. Nelly and I chatted for less than two minutes; but it was enough for Klara to become, peevish, and jealous. Nelly blushed. She walked away after she saw Klara's visage. Klara waited for Nelly to whiz off. Then, her voice was mellow but bossy.

"Dimitry, I have been married for sixteen years. There were a bunch of guys who had offered tons of money, jewelry, cars, even a career to be with me. And I pulled out the plug on all of them. You are the only one that I… I cannot be…" She couldn't finish. My eyelids were gradually closing, like an exhausted kiddo listening to his mom's lullaby. I almost drifted off, attempting desperately to stay awake.

"I'm talking to you for God's sake!" Klara cried out. She hardly screamed. Her expression looked insulted. She thought that I perceived her story as dry as a dust. That was what she thought despite how I had been sharing with her my problems about the annoying insomnia.

"Klara, I am trying to explain to you how difficult it is for me to fall asleep and has been happening over and over since I've gotten sick." Despite my disclosure, the twin of Jessica Alba remained pouting and speechless.

Klara had an orange juice. I decided to play like a humble chap and ordered a bottle of water. After we had finished our drinks, we cruised back to my dwelling. The silence between us continued even when Klara parked her eggplant-colored Honda in front of Motel Zero. She gaped at me, speechless. Dude, she is waiting for your apology. No frigging way. I don't owe her any apologies. I had an idea.

"Ciao, Klara. Talk to you later." That time, there were no pecks or cuddles. I just waved at her remotely like an odd neighbor who always says hi and nothing more, pretending he was busy doing something urgent such as cleaning his cat's bed. I pulled out the door handle and hopped out of the vehicle. I closed the Honda's door and pivoted toward the townhouse's entry. Then out of the blue, the voice of Klara croaked behind my shoulder,

"Wait!" she bellowed like a timid goose. When I turned back, Klara stepped closer. Her forearms embraced me tightly, and we started smooching vehemently as if we both had been off the market for ten years.

"I can't stay too long, not more than twenty minutes," Klara uttered. She stared at me, wheezing from the kissing workout.

"Cool. Stay as long as you wish," I responded.

"I'm serious. I have to bail soon, and don't give me that crabby look when I leave. Don't even think about it."

Peering at her, I just shrugged playfully, razzing her stern persona.

"As you wish. You can leave right now if that is what you want," I quipped. We kissed and cuddled at the parking lot for more than three hours. We just couldn't stop kissing.

The night was aesthetic and serene. The locust band played mollifying songs. A pleasant whiff like those in California's dry weather hovered around. That hour had passed momentarily but had been welded in my mind for the rest of my life. Geez, I don't want to move from here. All I want is to stay with her till my last breath.

Klara was everything that I needed. Her spirit filled me with happiness and jollity. No one ever made me feel rejoiced in this way. I had been down for her since the first moment I met her, and now we were kissing. This is so cool. Relax, you inept dipstick! Hold your horses and freeze your meals. Don't forget she is married. Let's put it that way. Even if she is married, it doesn't necessarily mean that she is happy with her husband. Maybe she wants to break up with him, and perhaps she is thinking of filing for divorce. This is wrong! I must clarify what's goin' on in her mind.

It was half-past eleven. The night became dark, as if I scuba-dived the bottom of a deep cave. I could barely recognize a man with a white shirt. We were kissing and cuddling, then switched to heavy petting. All of a sudden, a smartphone rang.

"Hold on. It's mine!" Klara murmured. She glanced at her iPhone.

"That's Jake, my husband! I got to bail. I'll give you the money next time. See ya." The cutie-pie hopped in her Honda. The engine hollered like an annoying lion and noisily darted away. Klara left the parking lot of romance, and I couldn't sleep for the next five hours. My restless mind drifted over and over into streams of contemplation. The next morning, I felt gleeful despite the annoying insomnia which had repeatedly tortured me for the past two months.

*****

Thursday, July 26, was a dangerously torrid day. NBC had alerted all of the residents living in the Chicago area to avoid walks or running errands between ten in the morning and four in the afternoon. The high tempera-ture exceeded ninety degrees. A healthy man could have a stroke loitering around for umpteen hours under the surveillance of the sun. Geez, I need to start working. The bills cannot wait. Can't just idle like a couch potato and blow up the money from GoFundMe. What time is it? Ten! Dino will be at work. Go ahead, feeb. Call him.

"Hello!" Dino grunted. His accent sounded disturbed and bewildered.

"Hey, Dino! It's Dimitry, the man with the recent heart surgery. We spoke a month ago, and you've told me to call you when I'm ready to work."

"Oh yeah. How are you feeling? Do you feel ready to drive?"

"Absolutely. I'm good to go." Am I?

"Okay. Come tomorrow to the Harwood Heights location. I'll be there at half-past ten. We are going to sit, munch some pizza, and we will go from there. Does that sound good to you?" Dino finished his pep talk. At the drop of a hat, I agreed. Ha. I knew it! Dino is cool. He is a man of his word.

Thrilled, I spent the day staring yawningly at the picture box, and hiding from the world like a lizard under the dirt. The night became mundane, and it seemed to last forever. The insomnia didn't have a day off.

The next day, I hopped off my king-size bed, brushed my teeth, and put on the shirt with Sapino's logo. I tromped down the staircase and stepped toward the brown Nissan. I drove the Nissan into Sapino's parking lot.

Dino dawdled on the stool at the cash register. His attire looked like he was a yuppie traveling for work. He was decked out in a snazzy white Dolce & Gabbana shirt and flashy blue trousers. He was mesmerized at his iPhone.

"Hey, Dino, it's good to see ya!"

"Hey, how are you feeling? Thank God you are out of the hospital. Can't imagine what you've been goin' through," Dino said. His broad grin was cryptic, resembling Bruce Willis playing Butch in

Pulp Fiction. Wonder why this chap has an oddly upper-crust expression reflected on his face? I thought.

"Oh man! You don't know how grateful I am to see ya." My words sounded with equanimity. Dino gazed at me mirthlessly. His speech burst out like an ultra-intelligent techie.

"Dimitry, let me put it in this way. I spoke with the owner of Sapino's. We cannot allow you to work. The reason why is because you don't have any health insurance. God forbid if you got involved in a car accident. It will be bad for all parties. Do you follow what I'm saying?"

Dino was dead serious. His visage uttered something like, "Can't help you, dude! You are screwed, so why doncha make me a favor and buzz off?" The letdown made my throat rusty as an electrical metallic tube. I felt like I would throw up at any other second. I stated uneasily,

"Yeah, I get it. So, there is no other way you'll let me drive on my own responsibly?"

"I'm afraid that won't work too. I'm sorry." Dino tried to give me a compassionate look. In the blink of an eye, I headed back to Motel Zero. While driving, I pondered. Stupid. You damn feeb. You counted on someone who barely knows your name to save your ass! Duck! Now what am I going to do? Isn't insurance the reason why they dismissed me? I guess they want to cover their tushies.

Regardless of Dino's denial, Sapino's was a great entity and a prominent food chain. Hopefully, they will retain a high rank in the future. Dino had overridden my ability to work because of my health report, and that was a tremendous breaking point in my life. It made me feel sick, bitter, and ready to puke at any moment.

I realized how the society of disabled people bears with their own rough life. That morbid world presented a sphere of features such as aggravation, depression, and resentment. Those emotions could easily crack up my cemented mind.

At that particular moment, all I could was to appeal to the Lord for salvation. Only the most high God would bring healing and bright days into the darkness where I was trapped. Walking through the stairway of Motel Zero, the shadow behind my back stalked me like a hitman. My despondent face struck on the floor as if I was looking for a lost item.

Shall I call Pete and ask to work for him, even though I've already known his response? Probably I should. It's been a long time since I spoke with him. Stop being a whimper! Make that frigging call! The conversation with Pete was brief and unenthusiastic. Pete was candid, just exactly what I had thought. He disapproved the idea of giving me any authority to work, not considering the years of my devotion. He was afraid of my health report, and I applauded his resolution. We remained close friends. He had helped me a bunch, and I would always be grateful for his collaboration. God bless his heart. He was taking care of me as if I was his nephew.

I spent the rest of the night rubbernecking at the pallid ceiling. I was looking for the right answers. I didn't know what was right or wrong at that particular moment. Whatever it was, I would not surrender.

*****

Two days later, around four in the afternoon, the sunlight was so warm that it could scald the skin of an old person. Klara had cuddled me as if I was her favorite pet. We canoodled as if we were doing it for the first time. We sat on a random bench in a public district area somewhere in Franklin Park. The way we cuddled was resembling two UFC fighters who locked themselves in the bloody cage. At one point, our tummies started chatting to each other by making bizarre creaks.

After a while, I broke the silence.

"Are you hungry, Klara?"

"Not really. You?"

"Yeah, I'm starving. The appetite has been scratching my stomach for a few hours. Come on, let's eat somethin'. I know a place that has decent food, and it's located a few blocks away from here." My words came out enthusiastically, then I paused to hear her response.

"I guess… I can have a salad," Klara talked quietly, like an uncertain child who had been asked to try an unknown type of seafood. After several minutes of rolling, Klara plugged her eggplant-colored Honda at the parking lot of a European joint named Café Mirage placed on the Twenty-Fifth and Lawrence Avenue. Café Mirage had an expanded and neat eye-popping patio. Inside had a swanky design, a snappy bar, and flashy furniture. As we strutted snobbishly to the entrance, we were suddenly both transfixed as landmarks.

"This place is packed!" Klara cried out.

"There is an empty table up there. Hurry up!" We occupied an abandoned table at the corner of the east side. Fifteen minutes later, the food had been already served. Klara had a Caesar salad, and I demolished a side dish of yellowish mashed potatoes and a few pork chops that later made me squeak like an ill hog. Out of the blue, Klara said something that put me in a restless spot.

"You have to give somethin' to Dr. McGee as a gift. You need to show your appreciation for his contribution in performing that complex surgery."

There was a pause. My mind was flooded by a lake of confusion.

"Klara, I need to concentrate on the healing process. I'll take care of that later."

"No!" Klara snapped. "You must buy him something when you have a chance to see him." Klara radiated her wrath.

"Klara, listen."

"No, I don't want to listen anymore," Klara cut me off curtly.

"Klara, what do you want from me—to kiss his butt!" I raised my voice, evoked by her reaction. Her countenance became repulsive, like a judge in a courtroom having a hard time understanding the broken English of a Mexican wetback. Bitterness reflected in her pupils as if, at any moment, smoldering steam would billow out of her ears. "Do you see this table? As we stay here, I am gonna flip over the whole stand." Klara threatened me using a serene tone. Her rage was overt. What the heck is wrong with this broad? Why is she acting like that? Shall I just stand up and walk away indifferently? We waved at the waitress and covered the tab. There weren't any words spoken after our altercation. As we trundled to her car, Klara mouthed, expressing her jumpy voice,

"I'll drive to JP Morgan and then will drop you at your place." Her tone became subdued, as if she had just admitted her mistake. I just nodded, attempting to avoid eye contact.

As she stopped her vehicle next to the ATM, I blurted remorsefully,

"Klara, I overreacted about the subject of Dr. McGee. I didn't want to sound like a total douchebag. I'm sorry."

Klara peered at me peevishly as if I had depicted her as a vicious trollop. Her expression was dark and sullen. She articulated her contempt.

"Listen up. There is one more bank transaction left. In the future, I think we should consider not seeing each other." What is that supposed to mean? Why the heck does she talk like that?

"What do you mean, Klara? After all of what we have been goin' through, I can't just forget you by a snap of fingers." The resentful feeling metamorphosed my tongue into a bucket of sand, dry and heavy.

Klara sat next to me, but I sensed her soul thousands of miles away. She remained wordless, although her face looked like she had something to say. Klara left the parking lot of romance muttering only ciao without giving any kisses or cuddles. Staring how her vehicle disappeared in the darkness, I mulled over. What a nutjob! Why would she talk like that? I guess that might be our last date. I tried to spend the night in a serene slumber, but I couldn't.

*****

On the next day, I hotfooted to the dwelling where Mike lived. Mike welcomed me with his delightful hospitality. Lounged on his tomato-red couch, I spoke clearly,

"Mike, I need to ask you for a favor!" Mike lifted his eyebrows and merely nodded.

"I need you to hide these greenbacks. You are the only one I can trust."

Mike deliberately peered as if I had asked him to murder someone for me. Then I handed him a bulging envelope. Mike grunted like the bell of an elementary school.

"You are moving out from Motel Zero on Sunday, right?"

"You've just hit the nail on the head. You comin'?" I asked

"Are you kidding? I won't miss the fun." Mike cracked me up. I tapped his arm like an old chum. A few minutes later, I drove back to Motel Zero where I idled like a quarantined triggerman.

*****

Sunday, July 29, was the day of the moving fiesta. Repositioning from one place to another was one of the most obnoxious processes. Carrying personal items, clothes, furniture, etc., made me nauseous. The bizarre era of Motel Zero ended.

A spotless and neat apartment was ready to be occupied. Another page had been riffled in the book of my life. The delightful August's whiff encouraged us to start the moving process. It was nearly past ten in the morning when Don came along with a big and stocky Italian guy who had a wolf-like face, named Anthony.

A few minutes later, Mike cruised over. He was holding an extra-large brewed coffee from Starbucks. Two Bulgarian chums were following him. One of them was a butterball man named Jeremy resembling Fester from The Addams Family. The other guy was a lanky man who looked like Lurch, also from The Addams Family. His name was Alex.

Mike, Fester, and Lurch worked hard as if they had been paid five grand already. Those fellas were sweating as if they were at a Jacuzzi in XSport Fitness. Don arranged and nestled every single item on the U-Haul truck that he had rented earlier. Since the physicians had advised me to not lift more than eight pounds, my contribution was to observe the entire moving process. The best job ever, isn't it?

After two hours of schlepping, we rolled to Albany Park. The townhouse was located on a side street called North Kruger Avenue. At the townhouse, Papa Bomb waited. He was puffing cigarettes purchased from

DuPage County, where the taxes were cheaper. Next to Papa Bomb was the potent thickset heavyweight Dave Latoria. He was blabbering something to Papa Bomb.

The flat was immaculate. The entire apartment had a hardwood floor. The kitchen had neat and clean cabinets, garbage disposal, dishware, etc. The bathroom had glistening white tiles and a stylish shower. A roomy dooryard had been neatly mowed, waiting for us to set up a barbecue party. The bedroom where I would be sleeping was much smaller compared to the chamber at Motel Zero. Regardless, the whole flat looked snazzy and squeaky-clean. The whole nine yards were settled for less than an hour. The moving squad did a tremendously good job.

"Is that all?" Papa Bomb queried.

"Yeah. Well, there are a few items left at Motel Zero. I'll take care of it," I declared. Mike, Fester, and Lurch vanished after we finished the moving fiesta. I gave a lift to Mr. George and Dave Latoria. Don needed to spend some quality time with his kiddos. Later that night, I had to meet the road-men to take some Xanax, then straight away I dragged my tooshie back to Kruger Avenue. The pill kicked in and knocked me out at once. I crashed like a corpse lying in a puddle of blood somewhere on the South Side.

*****

The next day, an annoying sound echoed and woke me up like someone had just blasted an air horn above my noggin. It was some of those Mexican amigos who were doing landscaping. The agony of getting a new job got worse. Question such as, "What am I going to do?" had been reiterated thousands of times. A lousy voice blew inside of my head like a psychotic monkey shrieked panicky in front of me. Stop it! Get lost, you fringing pus bag!

It was around forenoon when my phone rattled. It was Klara. Wait, what? Klara! What does she want?

"Hey, how are you feeling? Listen, I have some time to kill. Do you want to go for a walk?" she chirped so rapidly that I hardly comprehended her words. Her call threw me on a cloud nine. Go and have some fun! You half-wit knucklehead! Accept her offer. She just wants to rub the elbows. Stop sitting on the fence, would ya!

"Yeah, cool. When will you be here?"

"I believe after thirty minutes," Klara said, and of course, she came an hour later. I was elated to hang out with her. Klara stopped her vehicle on Kruger Avenue. She had an ivory sleeveless shirt that reflected her athletic body. The lines of her waist looked equal to Victoria Beckham's. Ten minutes later, the eggplant-colored Honda didn't move because we were busy with smooching. Then, we cruised to the closest park district. While we walked on the trail, Klara announced as if she was blowing the gaffe publicly of being pregnant.

"There is something I need to tell you!" Oh Christ, what now!

"This Tuesday, I'll fly to Bulgaria. Do you need anything from there?"

"Naw, I'm cool. How long will you be goofing around there?" My expression looked like an owlish professor. Klara began to titter like Jimmy Fallon at The Tonight Show.

"I'll touch down in Chicago after a week and a half," Klara blurted out, then she grabbed my hand.

"I gotta bail. I'll see you when I come back." We huddled like volleyball players after scoring a flawless spike. Pocahontas dropped me off on Kruger Avenue. She cuddled me longer, as if that would be our last time spending together. As I hopped out of the eggplant-colored Honda, she peered at me as if she wanted to say something else. Holy crap, will I see this broad again? I guess only the master of universe can tell.

As I trundled through the door, Don was waiting for me. He cried out.

"Champ! Go to your room. The landlord is coming. She isn't supposed to see you, remember?" Startled, I puttered to my room like an obedient canine. I was lying on the king-size bed and staring at the ceiling. After an hour, I got anxious. Suddenly, a hurricane of murky thoughts burst in my mind. Holy crap, this isn't right. I can't be cooped up in my room like an inmate. I don't approve of being hidden like that. Hidden from the landlord and, at the same time, paying an equal amount of the rent. I felt like I was hidden as a terrorist like Osama bin Laden.

At that moment, my common sense was suppressed. My mind was filled with tornado of thoughts. Perhaps everyone who has told me to get back to my country wasn't that wrong. Can't follow my dream anymore. My health condition hasn't allowed me to fight for my goals. Maybe it's time to leave and go back to my family. I suppose that will be a rational idea. A wrathful emotion crawled onto my forehead like a large tarantula. It was almost the same feeling when some entity or government had compelled you to do something against your will.

This storm of murky thoughts kept rotating in my noggin throughout the entire day. On the next day, in the forenoon, Don, his mom, and the kids scuttled to the spotless flat. I showed my friendly request to speak with Don. He refused to talk about something that linked the subject for this apartment. Instead, his mom was pleased to interpret that unintentional misunderstanding. "We've been telling you that the landlord wasn't supposed to see you since we found this apartment. This is provisional and might take up to a couple of months." Regardless of her persuasive speech, my face had gradually been reflecting a sign of disagreement. My words were spoken in a peaceful but solemn tone.

"Yeah, but nobody said anything about hiding. I don't like to play hide-and-seek." I choose my vocabulary respectfully.

"Well, in many ways, yes. But I don't want you to feel bent out of shape. As I said before, this will be only for the first several months. Later, it will be just fine. There is nothing that you need to worry about," she uttered so amiably, just like how my biological mother would say.

Staring at Rita George, I nodded. My squinted eyes resembled Clint Eastwood at the image cover of For a Few Dollars More. The storm of murky thoughts blasted in my head and metamorphosed into an obnoxious typhoon. The wind of resentful thoughts became a baleful gust.

Reflecting my disapproval, I went to my room. I was looking at the light-gray painted wall. I'm sick and tired of everything. Naw, I do not agree. It doesn't work the way I wanted. I've been going through a lot lately, and I don't deserve to be hidden like that. I guess it's time to get back to Bulgaria. Those thoughts created an outrage of wrath. The next morning, I had an unflinching solution. The inner voice in my head echoed like a strict employer of a global corporation. Ha! I got it. I know exactly what to do!

*****

On Sunday, August 5, just a week after we had moved from Motel Zero to Kruger Avenue, was the day when I moved out from Kruger Avenue. What foolishness, isn't it? Mike came to help me out. By "help," I meant he literally carried most of the heavy items. We were dragging the furniture and household items outside when a white Chevy van slowly rolled close to the curb and parked on the side street. A man resembling Johnny Depp got out from that van.

"Hey, qué pasa, amigo!" the man cried out. He was grinning broadly like a city-folk vaxhole was smiling and bragging about being fully vaccinated against Covid-19.

"Hey, Jonathan, you are late!" That was my way to say, "How you doing?"

"Where is the coffee?" Jonathan exclaimed. That was his way of saying, "Shut up, Jag off!"

"Come over here, mother flower!" I shouted. Jonathan was a shrewd chap who had migrated from Argentina. He was a frenzied soccer follower. He had a stodgy body, but his height was shorter than Kevin Hart's. Jonathan had lived for fifteen years in the USA, but his strong Spanish accent could be noticed from Florida. Jonathan was a wit and was a very successful construction contractor. I had met Jonathan at Hyper where we sparred regularly. He was off his rocker. It was always fun to screw around with that fella. An hour later, the hard workers, Jonathan and Mike nested all of my junks into the snow-white Chevy.

"Where are we rolling, amigo?" Jonathan asked.

"We are heading up to Schiller Park at Public Storage. Just follow me," I said, overjoyed like some twenty-four-year-old techie who had just announced the official date of his wedding. Twenty minutes later, with Timberland boots, green camouflage pants, and cloud-colored sleeveless shirt, the Argentinian version of Johnny Depp had tidied most of my items at the ten-by-ten size of Public Storage.

Jonathan worked so hard that his sleeveless shirt was soaked with sweat as if he had stayed in the sauna for hours. As we trundled through the antechamber of the Public Storage, I stated like a young man making a speech at his commencement from some community college.

"Jonathan, you don't know how grateful I am for your help. I owe you a huge favor." My eyes were tired but not as much as the Argentinian Johnny Depp. Jonathan was bushed. His eyelids blinked faintly.

"You owe me nothing, amigo. Nada. Gotta hit the road! You take care of yourself," Jonathan said and hastily dissipated as if I had just called him a gluttonous pig. Mike left two minutes later, and my gloomy Nike sneakers headed back to Motel Zero. At that time, I still held a key for Motel Zero. I dozed off at the early hours of the following morning on the frowsy brown couch that we had decided to leave when we were moving out.

*****

The day before I moved out from the apartment on Kruger, I decided to go back to Motel Zero. I didn't ask anybody, not even the building manager, Kevin. I didn't even know if Motel Zero was empty. I didn't have anywhere else to go. I had to take the risk and suss out what I would have to do with my future.

Don didn't show any zeal to speak with me. His mom picked up the phone. We had dissensions about my residence on Kruger. I had explained my intentions, and she accepted my decision. We didn't have any arguments or clashes. The following weeks turned out to be a quicksand where I had to make one of the toughest decisions in my life. It was like when you were stuck at dead-end street, but no matter what, you needed to keep going forward. At that moment, I have learned something vital.

When you have to take the most difficult decisions in your life, listen to what your mind says, but don't forget the opinion of your heart and don't rush with the final decision.

*****

On Monday, August 6. The weather was gorgeous, but it didn't matter because my half-wit brain had been occupied with difficult ponders throughout the whole day. What shall I do? If I hop on the plane to Bulgaria, I may never come back to America. I don't want to leave. Besides, I ought to obtain some job to bulge my budget. Otherwise, I wouldn't be able to stay here in the U.S. What kind of job position could I have? I don't have work authorization permit to work in the U.S. Can't work in the construction industry anymore…or maybe I could? What about Klara? I don't want to demolish my relationship with her… I… I like her… I guess!

People say life is good. I absolutely do agree. But sometimes, life can be a malicious, ferocious tramp, and it can easily harm your sanity. Humans aren't prepared for the factors coming through their lives. I will refine my theory. A man woke up in the morning, started up his Maserati, and drove to his multimillion job. Suddenly, the Maserati got involved in a lethal car accident that took the life of that man. How would his family feel about this unfair death? They weren't prepared for this volatile end.

Let's say another man got up early in the morning (as usual) and went to work in a metal factory. During his duty, he had lost his eye or leg. How would this man feel till his last breath? He wasn't prepared for that type of ending. Presumably, financial compensation would come around, but any subsidized check would not make him the same as when his mother gave birth to him. Also, how many people did predict the destructive Covid-19 virus?

The people say, live and learn. What I have learned is, we need to praise God as our savior. I believe there is a power on earth that cannot be described by expensive technology and science. The superintendent of the universe has that power. He will protect you or render support and unlock the portal that leads to a plethora of doors containing opportunities. Joel Osteen wrote, "God can make a way where you don't see a way." Straight from the horse's mouth, I believe that is true.

Later the same day, the sun eclipsed beyond the lodges. It could be noticed from the sliding window of Motel Zero. The humidity could be traced from miles, like the reek of a decayed body of a chubby raccoon.

I was bored. I scrolled up and down on the screen of my smartphone. Then out of the blue, the Messenger clanked disturbingly. It was Klara.

She sent a video of her goofing around on the beach somewhere in the

Black Sea. Pocahontas drew a huge heart on the sand. Beneath, she had written my name with capital letters. Oh man, for real? That's lit. Nobody has ever done something like that in my frigging life. Does she really care about me? Only God knows. Whatever it is, I don't care. I want her, and I am staying here in America. I will keep fighting for my goals. I won't surrender or betray my heart's feelings. I am not a quitter.

It must have been a hundred times that I had replayed the video. She encouraged me to follow my dreams. Her video reconstructed the foundation in my mind and brought back the zeal to live like a healthy man. It became dead quiet in the hobo shack of Motel Zero. I hit the sack on the brown couch like a bushed warden who had a long day at work. A few hours later, the sound of the bell annihilated the dead silence.

"Ah man! What time is it?" The clock on my phone displayed quarter to four in the morning. What? Who would bother me at that time? No one knows that I am here! Dude, don't make a move. He would stop in the next jiff. I was wrong. The bell perpetually rang as if there was a sign of an emergency. Okay, screw it! I have to find out who the heck is bothering me at this time in the evening. Without turning the switch for the lights, I peeked through the window. On the parking lot, there was a white Ford Edge parked next to my Nissan. Ah, dammit, I know the owner of this vehicle.

Hurriedly, I snugged some clothes and trundled down the staircase. A blonde chick in her late twenties was at the door. Her name was Kimberly. She was desperately head over heels in love with Don. The IBO champion had ditched her because she was a mess and a freaking retard on top of that. She had three little kids and a husband. But her marriage didn't stop her from pursuing Don wherever he went. Miss Piggy—that was how we called Kimberly—was buying him booze, cigarettes, and whatever Don demanded just to be with him; and in the meantime, she was giving hoochie woochie to different guys for dough.

"Jesus, Kimberly, what are you doing here?" I blurted out, giving her a friendly hug.

"Where is Don?" Miss Piggy grunted, sobbing.

"I have no idea," I lied.

"That's malarkey. Where is Don?" Miss Piggy was diligent. She put effort using her theatric skills of a weeping and devastated chick. She bumped into the wrong guy. I am not a rat. I loved Don as if he was my biological brother, and I would not grass him up to anyone, especially to a harlot.

"Don't stay here at the door. Let's go upstairs," I offered, and Miss Piggy nodded. We chitchatted in Motel Zero for a bit. Miss Piggy subtly told me that she was down to do a mouth solo if I told her where Don was. I was down for a wild mambo as well. Regardless, I wouldn't share any information about Don, and Kimberly realized that. She left the townhouse, and I hadn't seen her since. I drifted off after watching a few porn videos.

*****

The next day, the hunger in my tummy stirred me up. I trundled sluggishly through the hallway that linked the living room and the kitchen. There was an empty bag of Cheetos Puffs left on the top of the cabinets. The fridge was entirely void except for the smell of the food that was there.

There is nothing in the fridge! You nitwit, dumbass! I need to buy some groceries. I hopped in my ride and rolled to the nearest deli market. I was waiting at the red light on River Road and Lawrence. I glared goofily at the traffic light. Suddenly, I turned right, and my eyes widened. Bobby the Groundhog (I used to call him Groundhog because he moved like a groundhog when he worked) also waited at the light. His white Mercedes transit, resembled a baby version of Moby Dick. Bobby made a sign that projected a phone handset. Then, in the blink of an eye, my dummy smartphone rang.

"Hey, Dimitry, how you doing, bud?" Bobby asked.

"Bobby! What up? I'm doing fine. Running into some errands," I said happily like a buzzed honky at a sports bar watching Dallas Cowboys winning the Super Bowl. After a second, I grilled,

"Bobby, do you know someone who needs a driver?" My question echoed as if I was begging.

"Ya, there is an Italian fella. His name is Ennio. He owns a pizzeria in Norridge. I will text you the address, but don't wait till tomorrow, though.

Go there as soon as possible!" What Bobby uttered had me in absolute awe. He gave me hope when I was hopeless, just like Klara did.

Without wasting a second, I plowed the Nissan up to Norridge. The business sign of the pizzeria was placed in the parking lot on Cumberland Road. In that lot, there was a shopping center encircled by multiple small retails. Annetis looked like we were still living in the 1980s. Inside the pizzeria, there was a tiny dine-in area (only four round tables). An Irish girl was stretching her forearms on the cash register. I stepped closer and asked,

"Hello there. I am looking for Ennio. Is he around?"

"Yeah, he is in the back. Wait here! I will be right back," the girl said politely. She had a curvy body, crab-colored hair, and glasses like Harry Potter. In a split second, an Italian man in his early sixties, with sky-colored blue eyes and short unkempt hair, popped up.

"Yellow, I am Ennio," the man with unkempt hair uttered in a mellow and amiable voice.

"Hi, I am Dimitry. Bobby sent me to speak with you about a job as a delivery driver." My voice sounded like a twitchy kiddo asking to have his first job.

"Oh yeah, Bobby, the Bulgarian plumber. Nice guy! Come, have a seat." Ennio pointed to the chair, and we both glued our buttocks on the chairs. Speaking to Ennio, my words came out as if a wretched cunt would talk on the stand in a court for her trial.

"My last question is, can you lift three or four cardboard boxes at the same time with your heart condition?" Ennio glared at me straight into my eyes. He emitted a solemn expression, like how the chief criminal investigator might have asked O. J. Simpson the question, "Did you kill your wife and her friend?"

"Sure, yeah, I can." Can I? "That wouldn't be a problem. Matter of fact, I've recently needed to move some items to my storage and feel perfectly fine." My heartbeat raced.

"When will you be able to start?" The face of Ennio amended into a facetious hoot resembling the improv comedian Pat McGann.

"I would be able to kick off mañana," I cried out with exultation. Ennio shook my hand, happily.

Then I steered the Nissan back to Motel Zero, where I wasted my time anchored on my couch for the entire day. The next day, at ten in the morning, my Nissan was parked in front of Annetis. I was ready to stockpile some greenbacks. A quick induction in the policy of functional mechanism that Annetis had been following prompted for the first few hours. Then, we commenced playing the game named, cross my palms with silver. The functional process of Annetis was very similar to Sapino's. If you would not mess up the order, everyone would be cheerful. The distance of deliveries was short and could be easily dashed, no muss no fuss. Usually, the clients tipped the drivers well despite other drivers grumbling and exuding a gluttonous grievance for more cash.

A few Mexican fellas were responsible for the cooking process in the kitchen, but Ennio was in charge of every function manned at Annetis. He was a hard worker. The Italian boss observed the employees for ten to twelve hours a day. He was always there, even if there were no orders at all. His only days off were Christmas and Thanksgiving. Every other day, he hovered and scanned around Annetis like a wild eagle. I had never seen a hard worker like him before.

*****

Thursday, August 9, slid off faster than hip-hop rapper Twista yattering on "Runnin' Off at da Mouth." I woke up with an exulted feeling. Why? It was Klara! Pocahontas will have touched down today, and later, we will get together.

That day the work at Annetis went smoothly. The grin on my visage was flashing throughout the rest of my shift. At that day, I worked merely for three hours. Then, I plowed the brown Nissan back to Motel Zero. At six in the afternoon, a pleasant whiff of rainy August crept around. It was one of those days when you look at the sky and you surmised that it would start to rain at any second, but actually would not. From the sliding window at Motel Zero, I monitored how the eggplant-colored Honda drove in the parking spot. There she blows! My subconscious voice exclaimed. Come on, Mr. Lucky Pants, get down there! She is waiting for you! My feet tramped down to the front entry.

"Dimitry!" Pocahontas chanted while puttering like a gleeful puppy welcoming his master. Damn! She is so perfectly fine! We cuddled longer. Klara tilted her head on the left side of my chest. She said,

"I've just remembered this June that little heart…how? How much you struggled, and now you're here showing great energy. You look much more dynamic since you've been in the hospital. That makes me so happy."

No words were coming out of my mouth. I stared at Klara, grinning. Her glinted pupils were expressive as if she was saying, "I miss you so much!" Her question floated like a flamed fireball thrown from a mangonel.

"Where we are goin'?" Her enthralling expression mesmerized me.

"I'll show you. Let's roll." Pocahontas followed my directions. After ten minutes of spinning the wheels, she parked in front of a hotel named Aloft. We headed inside, where a lavish bar was placed next to the check-in lobby. As we rambled toward the bar, a dozen of people glared at us as if we were some prominent bigwigs such as Brad Pitt and Angelina Jolie.

Pocahontas had cosmopolitan vodka, cranberry lime juice mixed with orange liquor. I rinsed my saliva with Ginger Ale. After two hours of tittering and cackling, Klara drove her Honda back to the parking lot of romance. Lying against the Honda, we had pecked and cuddled for a while like eighteen-year old teens. My pupils were mesmerized by Klara as if I was watching the pageant of Miss Georgia, Betty Cantrell. Whoa, mamma mia! Damn, she is over the bridge! My mind whispered like how Haley Joel Osment had said to Bruce Willis, "I see dead people," in the movie The Sixth Sense.

"Klara, come upstairs. I need to show you something."

"Ah, nah… I would prefer to stay here!" Her sentence lifted my eyebrows in a state of misunderstanding.

"No, Klara! I didn't mean that. Jeez, there is something upstairs, a gift for your birthday."

I barely finished my sentence, and Pocahontas exclaimed fervently, bouncing like a baby doe.

"You haven't forgotten my birthday! Actually, its tomorrow, but we can't hang out. You know why. I am so happy. What is it?" her voice squawked like a squeaky toy for dogs.

"I'll show you. Follow me." We cruised through the staircase. Klara chased me, holding my hand as tightly as if there was a Wellbond glue between our palms. Opening the door, I told Klara to close her eyes until I said otherwise.

"No peeking, no peeking." Grinning, I trundled to the empty bedroom. I delved beyond the heavy-duty bags in the closet. Come out. Come out, wherever you are. Ha, got ya!

"May I look?" Klara mumbled from the family room.

"Hang on just a second!" Gosh! Klara, wait for a moment. Klara was as impatient as if she had been holding on to a bowel movement for hours. She barely could stay still. Her mouth didn't zip. Pocahontas was nailed to the floor as if she was waiting in front of the restroom which had been occupied by someone else. I ran my flip-flops across the living room where Klara stood. Her head was pointed down to her feet like a nun making ceremony vows. That was part of my plan. I wanted to keep her in suspense for as long as I could. That was my cheerful way to tease her.

"Now you can open your eyes." Klara gazed at the present and shrieked like a high-maintenance gal, freaking out about getting a brand-new Rolls Royce as a gift from Hugh Hefner or as if her hubby had handed a title deed for a sumptuous 150-foot yacht.

"Oh my God! This is so cool. I really need that," Pocahontas cried out fervently.

"Well, this is just a gift. Nothing too crazy. Anyway, I hope you'll like it." What I handed her were two bookend supports with the shape of a lion, Klara's favorite animal. There was a Happy Birthday wishing card with a cute Rottweiler sticking out its tongue amusingly, taped on the butt of one of the lions. She pulled out the card, opened it, and started perusing.

Klara, I'm writing this note to pay a tribute to the girl that makes me smile for twenty-four seven. The one that bolstered me in the toughest moments of my life. Klara, you are a friend whose forename is engraved in my heart. Happy Birthday Klara, this is your day. Make sure you enjoy it, unprecedentedly. I hope you will remember me the same way I do. God bless you.

From: 08.09.2018

"Oh my God! I love wish cards! How did you know that?" Her glinted eyes flashed like a high beams of a Volvo truck. Tears almost dropped from her eyes. Klara was hellishly happy. Till that moment, I had never seen her grinning like that. Klara's hands crawled down close to my tummy, then her hand crept down further to my dark-blue-colored trunks.

"Your shorts are too tight," Klara mumbled as if we were filming a scene in a romantic drama. Pocahontas looked at me as if she was expecting permission to proceed. There wasn't any authorization given.

"Let's go. I'll walk you down to your car. You need to get back to your home." KABOOM! My proclamation cut her romantic intention off. I rebuffed a manifest chance for cleaning the pecker. Who would do that? Who would cancel this type of opportunity? The silence of Pocahontas showed a sign that she was agreeing with my statement.

We wandered down to the eggplant-colored Honda. The sky was dark already. My dummy smartphone showed it was half-past nine. Klara leaned against her vehicle and kissed me. There weren't any speculations to declare. Then, she unzipped my trunks, kneeled, and started playing on the saxophone. Judging by her mouth rendition, Klara was a hell of a good musician. At that moment, I didn't care if cops could bust us or even if an earthquake had occurred; I wouldn't revoke the musical spectacle. Swoosh! Swoosh!

Klara made me feel like a sane human being. She just reminded me what an ultimate gratification was the process of the mouth solo. Around ten, Klara took the hike, and I spent a peaceful night even though I couldn't nod off until the early hours.

*****

"Someone is knocking on the door. It's…ten already. Milena, go check who could be at this time," Koko said, puzzled. Mom went to the entryway. When she swung the door, she almost got herself a seizure. She goggled like a monument such as the Statue of Liberty.

284

"Dimitry! My son, I can't believe in my eyes!" Mom howled. She was sobbing. Koko heard some noises. He rose from his armchair and stepped closer. He saw how Milena held her son who came back from the USA.

"When did you touch down?" Koko asked, bewildered. His question put me in a confusing deliberation. Cheese and rice! Now I can't go back to the States. What am I going to do, Lord? NO!

I aroused. I sat up uneasily, pondering, Holy cats! What a dreamscape. I took a deep breath as if I stood at a flying chopper prepared to skydive amid a range of thirty thousand feet. A few minutes later, I dozed off.

*****

On Monday, August 13, I awoke around ten in the forenoon. I hastily bundled up, ate a smoked turkey sandwich with jack cheese from 7-Eleven, and limped toward the Nissan. I was trying to overspeed the clock, driving to Annetis.

At eleven, Mark and I were the two drivers dashing for dosh. Mark was a tall American guy with snow-colored mustache. His farm-wrinkled face looked like he grew up far away from the city. Mark was a sodbuster or, maybe I should say, a peasant. He was a man of integrity. His presentation about the job was helpful. I was heading inside the pizzeria to log in the computer system. I saw an unfamiliar man. He was a hipster standing on the cash register. His pupils monitored me carefully with shrewdness.

"Hi, I am Dimitry. How are ya?" I grinned falsely like a politician meeting an alderman member in the local council.

"Hey. James. Nice to meet ya."

I thought this guy must be a hundred percent thoroughbred Italian. But it turned out that he was half Italian and half Mexican.

James was the same age as I was. He had black eyes like a crow and curly hair resembling the rapper Lil Dicky.

His body was moderate, similar to the shape of a bottle of wine. As I stared at him, suddenly, a sound as comparable as when you received a new text on Messenger clinked up in my mind. There is something about this chum, but I can't figure out what.

James and I labored astonishingly well like Will Smith and Martin Lawrence in Bad Boys. Why do I have the feeling that I know this guy from elsewhere? It was a remarkably productive day at work. In the evening, I headed back to Motel Zero. My mind was mulling over. Now it's time to count my blessing. I need to find another place to live. Kevin, the building manager, had granted me to stay for two weeks at Motel Zero; however, I couldn't live there any longer.

The question was. Who can possibly throw me a bone? Hm…yeah. There is one nutty man who most likely would help me out. It was remarkable what I needed to face two months after the open-heart surgery. I was the only one whom I had to trust and the only one who had to take care of the whole nine yards. Dude! You have to bite the bullet. Just be patient. Bright days will come around.

Then, I recalled when I watched Joel Osteen on his YouTube channel saying, "If you can see the invisible, God will do the impossible." That was my last thought before I drifted off on the frowsy couch, which happened to be the only furniture in the abandoned apartment.

*****

Wednesday, August 15, was my first day off from Annetis. I used the time given by Ennio to run a vital errand. Around half-past ten, I sped the brown Nissan through the Turnpike of I 90 westbound hitting the northwest side in the outskirts. I had to visit a friend. My ride ended up at a reconstructed European duplex located in Palatine. A snappy pool popped up from the north side. Paved trails surrounded by mowed lawns made the duplex look flashy. Cool. Nice and quiet. This dwelling is dope! A few seconds later, I pressed the button of the intercom.

"Hey, come on in. I'll buzz you in," a harsh noise blared from the intercom. I opened the door like a pissed man who had just found out that his untamed girlfriend had cheated on him. Going to the second floor, I tromped to a door at the end of the corridor. The latch clattered, and a male face showed up beyond the door.

"Dimitry! Where have you been, ole hoss!" the man yapped.

"Victor, you crazy nutty bastard. How you doin', bud?" Victor was the Moldavian krunk who labored with me at Tod Greiner Farm in Michigan. At that moment, he was living in Windy City. We used to keep in touch by being rummies consuming a plethora of booze multiple times. The moment he saw me, Victor cackled. He gave me a rapper type of hug.

"I have lots to tell you, Victor," I said. He glared at me foolishly, trying to analyze what I had meant.

"Spill the tea, ole hoss!" Victor said. We sat on the cloud-colored sofa that used to be white back in the day. Victor had lived on his own at a squeaky-clean two-bedroom apartment with a roomy balcony. After ten minutes of the concise version of the heart surgery story, Victor was nonplussed and appalled. There was a pause of a few seconds, then he cried out.

"Holy Moses, Dimitry. What the heck is this crap?" His question sounded more as an exclamation mark.

"Victor, I need to ask you for a favor," I observed him gravely.

"Sure, ole hoss. What can I do for you?"

"Well, I would like to live here, just provisionally, until I find a place for me. I can't promise how long it will take. What I can assure, is that the half of the rent will be covered."

Victor nodded agreeably. He tapped my arm and said,

"Sure, amigo! You are welcome here, my brotha. You know that, ole hoss."

My solemn face transformed into a cheerful expression that mimicked J. K. Simmons in the commercial of Farmers Insurance. A massive burden was lifted from my shoulders I was cheerful like a happy chimp having a fiesta of bananas.

"When you gonna move your stuff, ole hoss?" Victor broached the subject while draining his sixth beer. His eyes squinted owlishly like Master Yoda.

"Soon, amigo. Really soon. I'll let you know. I won't carry any heavy furniture or domestic appliance. I'll bring attires, bathroom accessories, and some silverware. That's all." At half-past eleven, we finished chatting, and I drove the Nissan toward Schiller Park. While my ride was rolling on the turnpike, a sound of a text message rang on the dummy smartphone. When I glimpsed, my eyes widened. Klara! Speaking of the devil, there she blows.

Hey, what you're up to? I got some time to kill before a gig at a wedding venue. Let's have lunch. Meet me at Blossom Cafe at 12:30. Text me if you can make it.

"Hell yeah, you bet!" I hollered gleefully while holding the steering wheel. Happy as a kid, I drove toward Blossom Café. It was around quarter to one when Pocahontas parked her eggplant-colored Honda. She's always late!

Klara swaggered, wearing a remarkably groovy black strapless dress. She was flaunting her luscious figure similar to Kerry Washington. ARW-WOW! What a sex pot! My mind howled. I stared at her like a hungry werewolf drooling saliva.

Blossom Café had a swanky design. The restaurant was spacious, exuding fashionable lighting. The menu at this joint was phenomenal. The prices were reasonable. It also had a convincing location, just a mile away from Motel Zero. A gracious hostess escorted us to a table with booth seats. We sat face to face. After the food had been served, Klara galvanized me,

"You know that we won't talk to each other after I handed you the last transaction from GoFundMe, right?"

Wait, What? What the hell is she talking about? Who talks like that? Why she brings all of this crap, just like that, without reason? What is this? I don't deserve this type of crappy behavior. At that moment, the bitterness made me to stand up and leave that place without getting into any arguments. Why? Because I was sick and tired listening to her sketchy crap all over again.

There wasn't any response from me. It was like my tongue had been tangled into a knot. What kind of answer could be uttered? Puzzled by her statement, I shrugged my arms apathetically. Klara proceeded stretching the gum.

"I can't live like that. I don't like it. Let me ask you a question. What are you gonna do if we haven't known each other anymore?"

KABOOM! What a strike! Ladies and gentlemen, I present you Klara, the Bulgarian violinist reaching the top rank in the division of providing a Dear John letter! I was jocund to reply to her bizarre quiz. The response had a demolition feature.

"Well, I'm gonna do exactly what I've been doing before I met you."

How do you like me now, Klara? It's so simple! My answer zipped her mouth up, but her face looked like she wanted to say something. For some reason, Klara had a mission to get us into a squabble. Her mission became impossible because my vibe was sublime, and I craved to remain happy for the rest of the day. Briskly and kindly, I called the waitress for the check.

After the tab was covered, we left the Blossom Café quickly. Pacing in front of me, Klara muttered over her shoulder,

"Ciao!" She talked to me without even looking at me.

Yeah bye, Felicia! What the heck am I doing with you in the first place? Klara, why do you have to be so cantankerous? Maybe I should talk to her. Ah, what's the use! You cretin scumbag! Klara whooshed her Honda like a police vehicle rushing after an urgent 911 call. Dude! You should stop fooling around and destroy any contact with this broad. Someone who doesn't let you close to their heart doesn't deserve your attention.

Up until that moment, Klara was the one who had helped me the most ever since I had known my name. Just because someone was kind to you doesn't mean he cares about you. That will be my last time seeing this chick! That was my thought while rolling the Nissan to Motel Zero.

*****

Monday, August 20, 2018, was just another occasional day at work. A huge array of clouds billowed in the sky. The sunbeams could barely break through the wall of those clouds. The wind was sweeping the streets of Chicago. It made you think about how clean that gorgeous city was.

Walking with a transplanted aortic valve got improved drastically, not well enough to jog or run but perfectly fine to complete pizza deliveries. The brown Nissan stampeded through the streets of Norridge, Harwood Heights, and the Chicago area as an Amazon Prime vehicle.

Ennio had checked my heart rate habitually. His empathy was quite noticeable regarding my health condition. He alleged that my heartbeat was pumping at the range somewhere around eighty. The most essential part of working at Annetis was when the cash register employee checked me out of the computer system. The bankrolls of singles bugled my packs. It wasn't much but certainly sufficient to pop them up at a hip-hop music video.

Worn out after a long day at Annetis, I parked the brown Nissan and headed to my asylum. At quarter-past eight, the dummy smartphone hacked me off. Let's take a look who it can be…Klara? Dude, you ought to delete her number. Do it, dammit. Stop wasting your time!

"Hey, Klara." (Dammit.) "How are ya?"

"Listen up. The following week, an international violin contest will take place in Indianapolis. Do you wanna come with me?" My pupils glinted as if I had just tooted a twelve-inch rail of white chalk.

"That's such a great idea, Klara. Let me look at the room prices for two at the local hotels nearby," I said. A gawky pause occurred.

"A room for two?" Klara repeated as if she didn't hear me at first. Her tone changed fundamentally.

"If we go, I guess we would stay in two separate rooms?" another gawky pause appeared ironically.

"I guess that's fine too. Let me talk with my boss, and I'll call you back mañana."

"Fine! Ciao!" she grumbled and hung up before I attempted to utter something. I haven't finished, Klara! I won't call you again. Jeez, what the heck is wrong with this broad? Dude, what have I told you? Delete her number! The voice in my head exclaimed.

My legs shuffled uneasily through the hallway of Motel Zero while I was thinking. Why did she become so shrewish? Her demeanor is so cruel. Can't comprehend why she is treating me like that, as if I called her a wretched cunt. Shall I speak with Ennio for a day off, or would it be better to keep my mouth shut? On the other hand, that will be my first vacation since I have touched down in the Land of Liberty. Also, I don't give a damn if we sleep in two separate rooms. It wouldn't make any difference, 'cuz I don't want to get involved in any argument linked to this drama queen.

It was two in the morning when I hit the sack in deep dormancy. On that night, Motel Zero was entirely mute as if I was the only human on the entire globe who survived after a catastrophic nuclear weapon bigger than Hiroshima and Nagasaki had annihilated and brought the end of mankind.

Chapter 27

On Wednesday, August 22, at the end of my shift at Annetis, I scuttled to Motel Zero. I tossed all my work clothes into heavy-duty construction bags purchased from Home Depot. All of my tatters had fitted precisely in five bags, just enough cargo for a one-way trip. It was an afterglow, around half-past eight, when I approached Palatine.

Mike had agreed to disassemble the bed frame of my king-size bed and shove it in his Ford Transit van. He had a spare key for the unit of the Public Storage. Mike refused any of my assistance during the process of piling up all the pieces of my bed frame. The game plan was to meet Mike at Palatine. When I pulled my vehicle in front of the lavish dwelling in Palatine, the screen of my dummy smartphone lit up with an incoming call from Mike. Wonder why he is ringing.

"What up, Mike?" I asked.

"Yo, my van broke down on 294. I'm waiting for the wrecker to drag the frigging van. I can't make it today. I am sorry."

"Forget about the bed frame. No worries. Do you need anything?"

"Nah, it's all good. Somebody is calling me. Talk with ya later." Mike hung up the phone. At that moment, my jammed thoughts projected. Just great. What a lucky man I am. Now I will sleep on the cloud-colored sofa. I erased all of those pathetic thoughts and started retelling myself how blessed I was to have a place to sleep. The master of the universe had showed me mercy by giving me a second chance to live.

The following morning, I aroused, lying on the sofa like a junkie who tripped the night before. Holy smokes, this couch is comfy! Even better than my mattress. It was quarter to ten when I donned work clothes, getting ready to haul my ass on the turnpike and start working. Shall I call Klara? Ennio had given me a green light for off days. Besides, she waits for my response. Yeah, let's give it a shot. Who cares if she doesn't pick up the phone? Leave a voicemail. Klara took the phone call at the first ringing. Is that coincidence? Considering that she was always busy with something.

"Hello, Klara, how are ya?" After her quick response, I blurted rapidly, almost as how Eminem spilled a traffic of words in the song "Rap God." "My boss gave me a thumbs-up for Indianapolis, so I guess I will book a hotel with two separate rooms."

"I'm so happy to hear from you. Please don't bother booking anything. I'd reserved one room for us at Hyatt Regency," she meowed like a little kitten.

"Terrific. Sign me in." What did she say? Did she book one room for us?

"Can't wait to spend some time with ya. I'm running late. Talk to you later." Those were my last words before I hung up. Klara craved to speak longer, but I cut her off by leaving the chat unpredictably. I don't get it. Initially, she has rejected the idea to stay in one room, and now she even booked one. How come? Whatever, dude. Look at the bright side. We may watch Netflix and chill.

Pocahontas was a loose cannon. She changed her mind like how I changed my socks. Her reactions and proclamations had always stunned me. In spite of her weird reactions, I was exhilarated about the imminent vacation. What would happen when we are out of town? Is she ready for the wild mambo, or is that just a hallucination? Well, I guess there is only one way to find out. Pondering, I crashed on the cloud-colored sofa in the early hours of the next day.

Chapter 28

At half-past two in the afternoon on Monday, September 3, I stood like a confused tourist on Clark and Adams Avenue. My knapsack was glued to my back. I was wearing a baseball cap of Chi-town, kinky trunks, and a black shirt of Emporio Armani. Wandering back and forth, I was nervous as if I had a date with Selena Gomez. Klara had to pick me up from there, and then we had to roll to Indianapolis. She was adamant about the idea to operate her vehicle to the Hoosier State. I wouldn't mind having a driver escorting me to Indianapolis. Klara was late for about fifteen minutes. She is always late!

Pocahontas parked her Honda close to the curb. She hopped out from her car as briskly as if she was going to wallop my ass. I was astounded by her modish dress. She was as stunning as a top Italian model working for Miu Miu. We had brief strife about the precise point where she was supposed to pick me up. Regardless, it was fine. Her phenomenal figure forced me to cuddle her longer than I had ever held anybody else.

"Let's roll," she chirped, grinning. As I was staring at her, my inner voice cried out. I'm having a private vacation with my crush. How cool is that? We traveled through the southbound tollway, blasting a variety of hip-hop, R&B, and jazz music. After four hours of driving, Klara left her Honda in a prepaid underground parking garage in Indianapolis. She dialed her hubby to inform him where she was. Her husband knows that I'm chilling with her? When she hung up the phone, I started interrogating her.

"Klara, does your husband know that we both are here?" I was perplexed as if I was been pranked by the hidden camera show known as The Carbonaro Effect.

"Yeah, I've told him that we are staying at the same hotel, but in different rooms. He trusts me. No worries." My thoughts were. Jeez, Klara, what kind of breed are you? There is something lecherous in this woman, and I don't approve it.

We shuffled to the lobby to check in. An African American male pushing his thirties was chilling by the lobby. The bored face of the black homie perked up when he saw the beauty of Klara. He couldn't take his eyes off her. The homie tried to seduce and coquet Klara by speaking freely of jive talking, which ramped up my value as a man. Klara turned straight to me and grunted like a sulky marmot,

"Dimitry, we are taking a room with two separate beds. You know that, right?"

"Sure!" I shrugged. The clock showed quarter-past ten when we burst into room 1136. The room was stylish, located on the thirty-fifth floor. The bathroom had a marvelous design, and the interior looked contemporary.

"I'm gonna draw a shower, Klara. You wanna join?" I asked, showing my shark grin.

"Hell nah!" Pocahontas cried out. She bellowed like a pissed traffic guard working at the airport having a bad day hollering, "Move out dat vehicle!"

After the shower, I lay on the bed, and pretended to sleep. Klara also hopped in the shower. She attempted to get ready for bed. The lights were out. Her words floated through the whole room,

"Good night, Dimitry!"

The next moment, I jumped off my bed and hastily snuggled into hers. I longed to peck Klara for a good night. The kissing panned out to heavy petting. Oh Lord! Klara has a body better than a forty-eight million women!

Our bodies entwined as if we were sketched into a framed picture. We were swimming into a river of love. Nothing else mattered, even the fact that I was digging a hole. Voices of a carnal act sounded from our room.

What a night. It was a night of supercalifragilisticexpialidocious love. I couldn't sleep. In the meantime, Klara fell asleep at once.

The next day, at half-past ten, we went to a brunch place called Smilin–Bakin. The name gravitated us to burst in and spend some greenbacks, but the sign had bizarre shapes of eggs and spatulas looking like the whole kitchen threw up. In other words, it was too much.

The food was so tasty, I could eat there every single day. At eleven, we entered into moderate-sized theater called Frank and Katrina Basile located on 450 Ohio Street, Indianapolis, Indiana. Walking inside the theater, we realized that the preliminaries of the international violin tournament had already started. The theater had a stage on which a pianist performed a melody on the noteworthy piano. Next to the piano was the violinist.

Most of the participants were of Asian descent. Everyone from the audience must adhere silence during each performance. Any noise could easily distract the contestants. Klara had described earlier that the winner would receive a reward of one million dollars and a contract for multiple tremendous concerts.

Klara shook her head joyfully while listening to the performance of the minstrels as if she was coaching them. I didn't have a clue how fascinating that music could be. Listening to each contestant was ineffable. In the break, I mumbled, "Klara, why you're not participating in that contest?"

"Because I am too old. Every contender must have been under twenty-five." I merely nodded. As the tournament continued playing, I was so relieved. Listening to the renditions urged me to close my eyelids into a peaceful snooze. Pocahontas nudged me conceitedly. At the next break, she shrilled,

"You can't fall asleep here. You're showing disrespect." Her visage remained frowning.

"Klara, I really enjoyed the music. I'm feeling sleepy because last night, I couldn't—"

"Get back to our room and take a nap then!" she cut me off. Her ruthless grumble sounded more like an order.

"Klara, I love this spectacle. It's delightful, and I'd love to hear the other musicians."

"Nah, Dimitry, why doncha do me a favor. Go to our hotel room and take a nap." Klara was quite stubborn and adamant.

After two minutes of disputing, I uttered,

"Fine! I'll go." Klara kicked me out of the theater as if I was some petulant dipshit causing a lot of trouble. Expressing a grouchy countenance, I cruised back to Hyatt, which was no more than a five-minute snail-pace walk. It was like you made two round trips in Jewel Osco.

Heading to room 1136, I hopped on one of the beds and immediately passed out. A clattered noise of someone moving caused me to hatch out. Instantaneously, my eyelids had opened, and I goggled like a puzzled pug. What the heck is that! Am I dreaming? Naw, it's real. Gotta be. Should be, right?

Klara leaned against the wall and gazed at me like a porn actress. She was hungry for lust. She faced me, wearing a risqué net dress disclosing her naked body. Yeah, that's what I am talking about! I felt like John Holmes sprawled like a king on the bed in a luxurious penthouse, initiating the first couple of seconds in a type of movie granted only to adults.

Pocahontas jumped on me like a puppy on his master. After we finished the intercourse, we both drew a bath, together. In the evening, we rambled to explore the city. Indianapolis was an amazing town. It was neat, clean, surrounded by a plethora of restaurants, landmarks, houses of worship, and lots of fountains.

Klara loved to stroll. It outlined her as a person. With my heart condition, I couldn't catch her pace. It was like a snail striving to reach the pace of a cat. How could that be possible? My hunger compelled me to stop somewhere to eat. Klara had a pouty face because I cut her stroll so early. We choose a random place to munch. Ten minutes later, she bemused me again by saying,

"Dimitry, you are not hanging out with me because of my money, right? You need to know that I don't have any savings. I spent all of my money." Sheesh, Klara! How have you come up with such astonishing and funky statements?

"Klara, I don't care about your money. All I care about is you as a person." Is that answering your peculiar question, Klara? Klara thought that I was freeloader. No one had ever asked me those types of questions because I had never mirrored any signs to take advantage of anybody financially. Klara had many sensors of misguidance. She was delusional. What she believed was way far from the truth. That was a trademark of her personality and could not be erased. She thought that her analysis was correct, and you could not change her mind no matter what you would do.

After my response, she had a wordless expression, leaving the subject without further comments. But her zeal to talk over the same topic didn't vanish, and that was fine with me. I had never pushed her out of her zone. Why would I? After we ate the food, both of us headed to the Hyatt. While we wandered on sidewalk, Klara stretched out the gum in a long monologue like a politician could talk. She depicted how her husband was loyal and how she loved when he cuddled her and yada yada. Perplexed by her yackety-yak, my broody thoughts hollered. Dang! Then, why are we rubbing elbows, Klara?

"Klara, if you are still head over heels with your husband, why we are together and—"

"Yeah, I heard ya," Klara cut me off. She was fired up with a grouchy expression. Pocahontas continued stretching the gum by speaking a surreal philosophy and floating in her delusional universe.

Oh gosh! This broad is a nutcracker! I have a headache already! Need to take an Advil. We stopped at the front side of the Hyatt. Pocahontas craved to go up to our room, and I walked to the front porch of the Regency. I sat on the stone ledge wall built with a small lawn and rubbernecked at a random tree like a crazy person.

I longed to cool my jets and hang loose. Jeez, I need a drink! Gotta go to 1136 and grab more dough! Quietly, like a burglar, I opened the door of the luxury room. The room was empty. Where did she go? Whatever, dude. Snatch the clams and go to some dive bar. Hastily, I took what I was looking for. When I opened the door, and suddenly, my eyes were shocked. Klara was standing right on the other side of the threshold. She tried to say something, but the awkward moment made her speechless.

"I am going for a walk," I barked like a morose lad and sneaked through her as if we were two strangers trying to pass each other in a crammed subway train. An hour later, Klara was perusing some novel while she was lying on the bed. Then, the latch of the door clattered.

Pocahontas looked frantically at the dull silhouette that stood by the entrance. Her mouth was wide open like a nonplussed gal watching the movie Grotesque. When Klara saw the plastered Dimitry wobbling into the room like a walking dead, she almost puked, disgusted by the odor of a mix of brandy and pint.

Dragging my feet like a zombie, I tumbled headlong on the bed. Two hours later, Klara awoke me and handed me a glass of water. She urged me to talk.

"Klara, I don't want to have any arguments with ya. I'm here to share and enjoy the opportunity to have a decent vacation." A tear fell from her eyelashes. A pause in which we were peering one to each other occurred. Then I asked,

"Klara, are you gonna break my heart?" There was a pause.

"Naw, I won't," she quietly said as if she didn't want to be heard. The following morning, Pocahontas declined to have any nooky. Her demeanor was too cranky, and the reason why remained undefined. She was always unrestful God knows why. When we were leaving the Hyatt Regency, Klara pushed me as if we were running late for dinner with the Duke of Sussex, Prince Harry, and Duchess Meghan Markle.

Klara failed to recall that I had a vascular surgery, but I had never broached the subject. Why? Because she was too crappy anyway. Besides, I had started believing that healthy people could not understand the pain of being crippled. However, I have always respected the strangers who did comprehend what it was like to live and cope with such a hardship tattooed in my brain till my time would pass.

*****

It was Thursday, September 6, when we rolled back to Chicago. We had spent three days in Indianapolis. It wasn't sufficient but enough to take a deep breath after the plethora of stressful moments that had been pursuing me since January.

Indianapolis was a gorgeous city. The memories collected from that city had been welded into my mind as the happiest journey since I had immigrated to the USA. Lord, I am blessed. Thank you for your divine kindness that allowed me to explore this incredible city. Those were my thoughts while I tromped on the paved trail in Palatine like a happy adolescent who had just purchased his favorite PlayStation.

*****

Sunday, the same week after we rolled back from Indianapolis, was my first off day. The weather was remarkably fine. The sun had been left alone without any clouds. Considering the break from work, I decided to spend my day chilling at the palatial apartment in Palatine. It wasn't too long before I phoned Klara. Her hello sounded clumsy.

"Hey, cutie-pie, how you doin'?" I inquired, overjoyed to hear her voice.

"How many times have I told you to not call me like that?" Whoop! There it is. Klara is making a storm in a teacup. As a matter of fact, that was the first and last time I called her cutie-pie. After a few minutes of exchanging confusing lines, Pocahontas finally answered my question.

"I'm walking at the World Music Festival of Chicago with my bestie."

"That's cool! I'm thinking of joining as well. Do you mind if I come over? I'm bored being on the couch all day long."

"Actually, yes! I won't let you see me today!" she exclaimed like a grouchy little girl losing her favorite shoes.

KABOOM! Why has she made me think of myself as a despicable and erroneous person? Everything that I say seems to be wrong. I don't get it. Our conversation ended embarrassingly. When I took a deep breath, the affliction in my heart was making me frail. Gosh, I need an Advil. The chat with this gal has given me a severe headache.

I had never felt a headache after chatting with chicks, not until I met Klara. For the next couple of days, I longed to keep doing my job and remaining polite. I maintained my professional behavior among all clients from Annetis. Most of the time, James and I bantered back and forth as if we had known each other since we grew up in the same kinship. He always helped me around. If there were any issues regarding work, he covered my back.

*****

On Thursday, the next week, the business at Annetis was running slowly. We all sank in deep boredom. I sat on one of the chairs, playing some foolish game on my dummy smartphone. Then an incoming call from Klara popped up on the screen. I slid the green image showing a handset and said,

"Hey, Klara."

"Do you like me?" she asked as quickly as a bullet out of a gun. Is she for real? Who could ask this type of question? My response came after a short pause.

"Of course, I like you, Klara. Why do you think I'm hanging out with you?"

"Well, you've never called me beautiful. I feel so awful. My stomach has a lot of pain. The anxiety is killing me. I have a huge headache." She didn't stop complaining over the phone. Her monologue knocked me down. James interrupted me by sketching a short comedy scene projecting that it was my turn to drive. I was thrilled to have the reason to cut her off.

"Klara, I need to hit the road for another delivery. I'll call you back later, okay?"

"Fine!" she cried out and hung up using a jumpy tone like a sedated psychopathic gork tangled up on the stretcher at a hospital for mental illness. At nine in the evening, the cashier checked me out of the system, and I drove on 90 West toward Palatine. Victor was making a chopped salad when I burst in.

"Hey, ole hoss, how was your day? Did you make any decent money?" He asked while giving me a fist bump.

"Yeah, it was fine. Everything went smoothly. Gotta make a phone call. See you in a minute."

I rang Klara as fast as how I dialed 911 a month ago. After a minute, I asked Pocahontas, "Klara! Please tell me why you acted so waspish this morning? What's wrong?"

"Well, when we were in Indianapolis, you said that I've always complained and talked with a grievance. That is not true. You've hurt me a lot, and I'm so…so"—a sound of weeping occurred—"embarrassed. Why did you call me like that?" The Bulgarian minstrel paused. She expected an immediate response, like how a state police officer would wait for an answer after finding a big bag of a blow in someone's car.

"I'm sorry, Klara. I didn't mean to hurt you." Despite my apology, she was joyless.

Her voice was mollified, but after a minute she said "Dimitry, you are selfish!" WHOMP! Klara had just cast sulky accusations and rebuked me cynically without any reason. No one had ever called me selfish. Her words pissed me off. Alas, her prosecution did not affect me. The fondness I had for Pocahontas had compelled me to forgive her. Normally, if somebody want to scold me like that, I would reject them, but not her. At that moment, my head was flying somewhere in the clouds. I didn't pay attention to my self-preservation. I was blinded by her magnificent influence. From the bottom of my heart, I deeply loved her.

The strongest addiction for one human is another human. Everyone has been smitten with a crush at least once in their life. That chemistry doesn't fade easily.

"Klara, I've just wanted to see you. Let's get together?" I sounded corny.

"I can this Thursday," she meowed apathetically.

"Great. I'll see you on Thursday!" We ended up the phone call spontaneously. Hanging up, I cheerfully bounced up and down like a donkey. Oh Lord. I need a drink! Consuming any type of alcohol three months after heart surgery wasn't the wisest and healthiest move I made. The anxiety of what had occurred was bumping on me like a plethora of locusts.

Victor and I glugged a bunch of Stella Artois. I needed alcohol to engulf the suppressed feeling. A few minutes later, something nagged my mind. Staring at the label on the bottle, I contemplated my next step. I have to find a place to live closer to the pizzeria. Can't drive back and forth every day to Palatine. I've already piled up a lot of miles in the Nissan. If I keep making miles, that vehicle will cost me an arm and a leg for maintenance. I know someone who might be helpful. I oughtta make a phone call mañana. Those were my last thoughts before I started snoring, smashed by the Stella Artois.

Chapter 29

It was half-past ten when I hatched out with hangover. The brown bottle flu thudded in my head like a boy learning how to play on his drums and trying to figure out what he was doing. The taste of my mouth was so gross that I needed to brush my teeth for couple of minutes. Dude! Make that phone call, dadgummit! What are you waiting for? The santa's beard would not grow black again. My inner voice cried out. I had obeyed the command and grabbed the dummy smartphone.

"Hello," a hoarse woman's voice croaked.

"Hi, Natasha! It's Dimitry, the guy who had lived at Denley. Do you remember me?"

"Yes, of course, Dimitry. How can I help you?" her husky tone echoed like a manatee.

"I am looking for a one-bedroom apartment. Do you have anything available?"

"Frankly, I don't have anything related to one bedroom, but I do have one studio whatsoever. Are you interested?"

A studio wasn't what I was looking for. There was a pause.

"Yeah, I would like to check that studio. Is that studio located at Denley's dwelling?"

"Naw, it's on Wehrman Avenue, which is the building right next to Denley. I'll be there in an hour. You wanna check it today?" Natasha had rumbled like a worn-out horse. I'll be dipped! I've just had a spare time precisely for the next hour and a half. Is that coincidence?

"Yah, I'll come. See you at Wehrman," I muttered and bundled up. The brown Nissan rushed through the turnpike like a contender in NASCAR. Natasha was waiting in her murky Audi Q5. Her haircut looked like a nest of storks. It had enough space to hide a few kilos of cocaine up there.

Natasha saw me shuffling my sneakers toward her car. She jumped out of her snappy vehicle as if she was my mistress. That would be the case if her face didn't look like she was the wife of Count Dracula. We chitchatted for a while. She heard my tale about how I got sick and yada yada. Natasha had kidney surgery. She felt a commiseration of my unpleasant medical experience.

"Come on. Follow me," Natasha kindly grumbled as if she had intentions to handcuff me on the main gas pipe in the boiler room and rape me. We stopped at the front door of unit 104. The studio was on the basement level. On the floor were mounted light-gray-colored tiles. The size of the room was an identical archetype to my bedroom at Motel Zero. The bathroom was tiny, like it had been created for elves. A small kitchen was installed by the entry that linked the bedroom and bathroom.

There was a small window installed in the middle of the sleeping room. It pointed out to the woody fence where some sunbeams could hardly break through. It is dark here! The cabinets seemingly looked older than me. In those dwellings, the apartments had ears; you could literally hear what the neighbors were grumbling while you were taking a bowel movement in the bathroom.

"What's the rent?" I asked her uneasily.

"Seven hundred. All appliances included. You need to pay only for the electric," her mellow tone echoed. A deadly silence sealed the studio. Geez! Can't take a firm decision right now! This clean shed isn't looking like my best choice. On the other hand, Natasha hasn't required any credit score. The price is affordable, and it's right next to Annetis. Also, my social pipeline—Mike, George, and Evan—are living at the next block. I don't frigging know. Natasha stood at the entry and eyed me wordlessly. Come on, half-wit, say somethin'!

"Can I give you a straight answer later?" I committed to rumble something.

"Sure! Take your time, but be advised that others are asking for the same unit." That was a typically pragmatic, sharp answer of a realtor agent. The following hours, a clumsy nuisance disturb me. I tried to pursue the voice of my heart.

That studio is really itty-bitty, like a tiny box, but who cares? I don't need to live in an airy apartment. It will be just me. Besides, that will be a provisional option. Hell yeah. I'm taking it. I'll call it the office digpot! Why? Because it looked like an average size to an office, and the space was a dinky equivalent to a digital memory potentiometer (digiPOT). I texted Natasha and initiated the deposit for the studio. It was a prosperous day.

While folding my attires, my thoughts struck me like an electric shock. I am so excited. Tomorrow, I will hang out with Klara. This is so cool, isn't it? After midnight, I lay prone on the sofa, like a deceased gunner sprawled on the meadow somewhere in Stalingrad during World War II.

*****

Thursday, September 27, was a cloudy day. The broadcast predict a severe downpour. Klara and I had to meet in front of the Wehrman dwelling. She would be the first person to have an idea where the tiny box of office digpot was. I wheeled on the Turnpike I-90 toward east faster than Sonic the Hedgehog would. Klara roared ten minutes later. She was always late.

She drove so fast that she almost crashed her eggplant-colored Honda at the parking lot. Thank God there was a bump stopper. Her shirt was torn up; she looked like a lecherous hoe. You could see her black bra from fifteen feet. I hadn't seen her dressed up like that, as if she was my biatch making cash for a living like a prostitute.

"Hi, Klara. I'm happy to see you. I believe you need new brakes, 'cuz you almost—"

"I know!" she cut me off. On that day, I saw her for the first time since we had driven back from Indianapolis. When we burst into the office digpot, her countenance goggled like a bewildered raccoon.

"Is that the place you've been talking about?" she groaned by showing strong disapproval.

"Yeah, it's a small studio, but I'll make it cozy."

"Look at the window. You can't see anything from outside, just an aged fence." Klara kept cutting me off as if she was disdainful royalty.

"Dimitry, you can't live in this... This is a shelter for Lord's sake. Are you nuts?" Klara criticized me as if I did an absurd slipup. "Klara, this place is provisional until I fix my credit score." Pocahontas glared at me, mirroring a grouchy face. "Dimitry, this place has no space. Where are you gonna put your bed?" Her revulsion indicated vexed disapproval. The minstrel kept grumbling about the office digpot until my mouth opened.

"Klara, if you have a better idea for any apartment, say it right now! Plus, I don't understand why you are criticizing me so much. You won't live here!" I yearned to avoid my comment, but she taunted me so bad that I couldn't take it anymore. Then, she stopped talking as if she had no opinion about my place.

Pocahontas zipped her mouth. She tried to help me out, but her method wasn't helpful. What I would need was someone to advocate and support me, not criticize me. At the next moment, we finally switched into more jubilant subjects. We both chuckled back and forth. Klara sniggered out loud as if she had several shots of vodka already. Our conversation turned out from irksome bicker into a casual chat between two bawdy lovers. We started the heavy petting. Klara pulled out my shaft and started playing. Cripes! I hate the way she talks to me. Regardless, she is pitching my tent, and I frigging love it!

"Listen up. There is no time for that. I gotta bail. Need to do some errands," Klara whispered. She stretched out the gum about how busy she was and yada yada.

"Yeah, I have to start working soon," I said, realizing what the time was. The lust for having intercourse was intercepted by the clock.

"Let's go. I'll walk you to your ride," I offered as any pushover would. Wandering through the parking lot, I said,

"I am not the guy for you, Klara." What a frigging numb sack! What the heck is wrong with you, dammit! You sounded so depressed and suppressed. Geez, you better step up in your game, you stupid sod.

"Naw, actually, I believe you are the right guy for me." What? Then why you've acted so standoffish, for Christ's sake! I couldn't state those words out loud. Why? My infatuation toward her had reached the highest point, and that was mostly because I didn't want to get involved in another argument. There were a bunch of bigger fishes waiting to be fried in a pan of setbacks.

As we strolled over to her vehicle, my eyelids boggled, and I proclaimed,

"Klara, look at your front tires. You have no tread left in. They are completely out of whack! That's why you can't stop the wheels properly. You have to get new tires. There is a tire shop at Walmart located in Nails with great deals. Please, do me a favor and come with me to this tire shop. I am concerned about your safety, Klara. What do you think?"

There was a pause before the fiddle gal responded,

"Yeah, I can go on Monday in the forenoon, I guess. Does that work for you?" she said quietly.

"Yeah, absolutely. See ya on Monday." I was happy to hear her answer. Klara left Wehrman's parking lot as if she was offended, and I started to work at the pizzeria. Later I was pondering about our situationship. What will happen next? Where will this relationship go? Will our courtship flourish, or may we take into separate directions? Those thoughts nagged me over and over again. Washed out, I roared the Nissan to Palatine. I had to hit the sack early because I needed extra energy for the following day.

*****

The following morning, I awoke uneasily regardless of my eight hours of undisturbed dormant. There wasn't any time to fool around. Shoo! Gotta drive to Wehrman. Hurry up, you aged oaf! Fifteen minutes later, the brown Nissan sped on I-90. At Wehrman, Val was leaning on the hood of his dragon-red colored Honda as if he was going to pose for an auto commercial and hung up with two dummy chicks.

"Hey, it's nice to see ya, bud. How are you feeling?" Val barked.

"Doing just fine. Thanks for backing me up. I don't know what I would do without you."

Val just agreeably nodded while he was glugging his extra-large coffee from Dunkin'.

"Where is the storage?" he asked, spilling out a smidgen of the brewed coffee on his piebald flannel shirt.

"Follow me. It's not even a mile from here!" For the next two hours, we made three round trips from Public Storage to Wehrman.

As we burst through the office digpot, Val curiously asked, like a kid interrogating his mom about how the babies were being made.

"Dimitry, I don't see a space for your bed. Where are you going to sleep?"

"Well, I don't need a bed anymore. I'll sleep on a couch." I got used sleeping on the sofa in Palatine, and that was bearable. Mike had tossed my bed frame in one of Bobby's houses. Val and I emptied the ten-by-ten storage unit. For less than three hours, all of my household junks had been transported. We worked like wetbacks who were patching and sanding drywall in a sumptuous house. No more Public Storage charges! It was half-past three when we finished fetching my household items.

"Thanks, Val. I owe you a bunch of Coronas. Gotta bounce. See ya later."

At four in the afternoon, I commenced dashing to Annetis. Before I started working, I was already bushed. The exuberance on my face didn't fly away. Why? It was just that everything that I had planned worked out. After work, I headed to Palatine. Just before I reached Palatine, I stopped at some unknown packy, and bought a six-pack of Smirnoff Ice. I gave the bevy to Victor as a sign of my appreciation. Victor was rejoiced. As usual, we sat for a drink; and the next hour, I hit the curb, dozing off at the sofa.

*****

Saturday was one of the last days in September 2018. I was off from work. Although, it wasn't a day for screwing around. At a quarter past eleven, I steered to Wehrman dwelling where George, the dandy limo driver, waited in his Lincoln Navigator.

"Are you ready, Dimitry?" George asked. His Bulgarian accent echoed like a frightened turkey.

"Ya, let's roll," I blurted out. The Navigator rolled to Baxton Studio furniture outlet located in Bensenville. It was a spacious retail store that exhibited umpteen furniture and household accessories. We were in a rush. I had no time, willing to linger out and to capture the best deal.

Fifteen minutes later, my attention stopped at one opulent black-leathered couch. The price was reasonable, and without any uncertain thoughts, I purchased the item. The couch had two parts. One of the parts was snuggled into the Navigator. Thank God the vehicle was big enough. The other piece had to be left at the store for a later pick-up. As we headed to Wehrman, George grumbled like a whinnying horse.

"Dimitry, I will be able to help you with one of those items.

After we unload one of them, I gotta hit the road."

"Sure, dude. I am grateful that you came."

"Yo, who's going to pick up the other part?" George glanced at me.

"Don't worry about it. I will come up with something." We had a rough time manhandling the couch into the studio. It was like we were hauling a big mare. To move furniture with open-heart surgery was a tough assignment.

Sometimes, life could be very unfair to you, regardless, you needed to remain strong and suck it up. Four hours later, Mike rolled over to pick me up. We headed up to grab the last piece. His Ford Transit van was quite beneficial, and the other part was ready to be carried. Perhaps Dwayne Jonson could tote the couch by himself, but I almost keeled over.

After we placed the second part, the voice of my common sense bellowed. That's it. Consider it done! No more moving furniture. Both couch pieces were placed at the corner of the studio like the letter L.

A decent assembling TV stand was facing against the couch, and a small coffee table was adjacent to that couch. A gray rug was lying on the floor close to the TV stand and, on top of that TV stand, was hanging a vintage sign that said 'Blessed'.

Hallelujah! The studio was all set. At the end of the day, I felt proud of myself. I successfully coped with the quicksand that had been harassing me for the past few months. I wouldn't be able to do it without my buddies. Four weeks ago, I thought that my time in the land of Stars and Stripes had already been over. Now I have my shed a mile away from my job. Thank God, I am blessed. That was my thoughtful synopsis before I dozed off.

Chapter 30

Monday came quickly like a commercial for a bra. It looked like the weather was in a bad mood. Despite that, I was joyful. This was because I had a rendezvous with Klara. Enthusiastically, I tucked the brown Nissan into a parking spot of a Walmart tire shop, where we were supposed to meet. I was scrolling through social media when Pocahontas hastily popped up like a renowned rock star.

"What's happening here? Where are the employees?" The minstrel eagerly jibber-jabbered without saying hello. Hold your horses, dammit! The voice in my head cried out.

"How you doin', Klara?" I asked, wrapping my arms around her. Klara looked agitated. She wasn't drawing any attention to me. We burst into the tire shop where a Mexican guy pushing his mid-fifties was blabbering on the phone. His tattered garments looked filthy, as if he hadn't washed them for a month.

He greeted us politely. As soon as the Mexican guy spotted Klara, he struggled no to drool saliva on the cash register. Ya, amigo. She is an eye-popping helluva chick, and also, she is mine! Am I getting jealous, or is this just a misled feeling? Nah, she wouldn't pounce on this Mexican guy. No way. Is she? We finished the transaction, and the Mexican proclaimed,

"Great, I will call you when the tires are ready."

To demonstrate that Klara was my girl, I leaned close and tried to kiss her. Klara turned her head in a different direction. She whispered tersely, "Dimitry, I can't do it anymore!" Wham! That was the moment when Klara broke my heart. An outrage blasted in my mind. I thought she would be my future. It panned out that she was my failure. Klara was the one, the true love. Yeah, cut the crap, would ya? What a bonehead, a frigging retard! You are such a delusional knobhead.

How the heck did you let that happen to you, scumbag, a nutcase, a vacuous airhead? I looked unflappable, but my self-preservation was getting furious, ready to explode at any second like a volcano just about to erupt.

After everything we had been going through, she ditched me so disrespectfully in front of a Mexican employee at Walmart. How demeaning was that? And the most stunning fact was that I knew it would happen. The inner voice in my head tried to admonish and thwart that menace. Alas, I had rejected that voice. A deep faith rooted in my soul and made me believe that we could be happy together. What a mess! Just imagine. Four months after I had open heart surgery, and someone broke my heart. Yep, that's me. I am the winner. Wowsers.

As we had been planning, both hopped into my ride and went to the botanic garden for a walk. Holding the steering wheel, I thought. Gosh, what are you doing with this gal? She has just thrown you into the friend zone. Stop wasting your time! Regardless of the commands mailed by my subconscious, we wandered at the botanic garden.

Klara portrayed the role of a gleeful schoolgirl. She was so happy. She didn't stopped talking, and I was mute as if I had never been able to speak. Klara, would you shut your pie hole? I had a headache. I felt that at any following instant, I would throw up and keel over on the trail road. Pocahontas kept stretching the gum in pointless stories. Listening to her, my mind cried out. I had enough!

"Klara, I need to go right now!" I muttered swiftly, like a Chinese professor.

"We've done only ten minutes of the walk. What's the matter? What's going on? Why has your face changed since we have left the tire shop?" Ha-Ha-Ha. Yeah, Klara, I can't sort out why I am acting like that. Maybe because you've just dumped me! Does that making sense to you? I couldn't stand any second with her. I cannot tell why we went there since she had ended up our whatevership. I guess I was still transfixed by her crushing announcement. I had to split immediately.

We were strolling back to the brown Nissan as fast as we could. On the way back, we barely said something. It was one of those clumsy moments when you broke up with your ex and you both remained speechless. The brown Nissan was back in the parking lot of Walmart. I shot her with a glimpse, saying, "Would you just buzz off, please?"

She mumbled something vaguely that supposed to mean, "Ciao, Dimitry!" Then, a rumbling sound of slamming the door occurred. At the next hour, I started working at Annetis, wearing my emotional mask of the nice guy. I pretended that nothing happened. When I finished work, I ran by the packy store and grabbed a six-pack of Smirnoff Ice. Then, I drove to Palatine.

By the time I arrived in Palatine, the bottles had already been emptied. Intoxicated, I lurched like a Russian alky. Hammered, I wobbled to the second floor, bumping into a few walls and trying not to collapse on the carpet. Somehow, I remained vertical. When I opened the door, Victor was chilling out on the sofa and glugging Grey Goose.

"Yoooh, ole hoss, come here. The party is about to start." Victor had bellowed like a wounded barbarian. Obedient like a German shepherd, I sprawled on the sofa and swigged vodka. Gulping the booze, I was swimming in the sea of thoughts. The pain became bitter. I was getting drunk enough, urinating in the wrong side of the toilet. I didn't care about anything or what could happen next.

Klara made me feel blue. Every single beat of my heart thudded for her. She tried to put me in the friend zone. Who am I? A benchwarmer, a call guy on standby? Uh-uh, not me. I am not wasting my time playing foolish games. I am not a nerd that thinks or hopes he will get his ex back. There is no turning back, period.

When you put yourself in a vulnerable statement, you declare weakness. Great disappointment is hidden behind great expectations.

At the next hour, I hit the rack, completely hammered. Right before I passed out, a voice in my mind hollered. I am gonna destroy this heart! Damn, you half-wit, frigging head case. I don't want to live anymore. In the morning, I aroused unpleasantly. I mirrored a disgusted grimace. The hangover was unpleasant, as if I fought Dmitry Bivol last night.

In the process of waking, I bumped into a knife-edge situation. What time is it? Gee, it's almost ten. I have to work, don't I? I don't want to see anyone's face. The only thing I wanted was to get bongoed. That was all. At the same time, I needed greenbacks to buy alcohol.

Dude! Go to work. Ennio is an outgoing person. He has been loyal to you since you burst into the pizzeria. Don't screw him up. At work, my visage looked joyful, but my soul reproduced a mournful and emotional disaster. After work, I cruised to office digpot. The only thought in my sick head was to open the fridge, grab a bottle of Smirnoff Ice, and start drinking. Twenty minutes later, a black Range Rover stopped in front of Wherman. A swift swap among human palms occurred. I staggered back into office digpot and opened the baggies that contained white chalk. I made one of the most heartless blunders in my life. Four inches of rail had been tooted for less than two seconds. The man with open-heart surgery does rails of dope. Hip hip, hooray! What a smart-ass. Chump! An hour later, the baggie had been thrown into the dustbin. A scrunching sound of opening another baggie initiated. After snorting a few more rails, I dove into a lake of booze till the early hours.

A stabbing pain coming from my heart valve stirred me up. Holy chiz, I don't want to wake up. Crap, I am off today. What am I gonna do now? Yeah, there is only one thing that I want to do. I am getting tipsy. Without any compunction, I rolled the Nissan to the Shell gas station and bought alcohol while others were working. I grabbed more Smirnoff Ice.

It was around eleven in the forenoon when I started drinking. By one o'clock, I got hammered and passed out. Everything went black like the screen of a broken-down computer. The same story repeated when I woke up at six in the evening. Nothing else mattered: drinking, snorting some dope, and playing nerd games on my smartphone.

I was wasting my time by harming my aortic heart valve. No matter how much I drank, the affliction didn't vanish. The chip on my shoulder was giving me bad ideas. I was feeling wallow because my life was turning screws. The wrath got me bent out of shape. The depression wrapped around me like an octopus clutching his victims. The despondency had punctured my heart like a wooden stake used to kill vampires.

It gets pretty ugly when someone loses the faith to live. I couldn't afford to visit a psychiatrist. My buddies were too busy with their own lives. They could not fathom how the gloomy hurricane of depression had affected my mind. I felt like a wounded fighter exiled into the darkness. It was just me. I was the only one who could pluck himself out of this morass.

The foggy storm in my head didn't hand me any enthusiasm to keep fighting, pursuing dreams, and smiling. The depression swerved me into the dark thoughts where I pictured being dead in a coffin. My common sense was torn apart like newspaper. My loyalty to the master of the universe disappeared partly. One tiresome day somewhere by the end of September, I headed to Burlington and brought the dullest drapes. They were as black as a winter evening in the land of Lincoln.

I cruised back to office digpot. I mounted the high-quality drapes right above the inconsequential window. There was no sunlight. The office digpot metamorphosed into a dungeon. I called it, the room of depression. During work at Annetis, flashbacks of Klara's guise pursued me over and over again. When I saw or heard something related to a violin, my mind linked to Klara. It was getting quite annoying. It made me nauseous, willing to throw up.

The reflections of Klara were ceaselessly pursuing me. The gate of behaving myself couldn't withstand it anymore. I had enough. Need to swing over to HB (Heavenly Bodies gentlemen's club). It was Friday night. James and I happened to finish work at the same time.

"Yo, c'mon, James. Let's cruise to HB," I sputtered, standing with him in the alley of the pizzeria. James looked at me, streaming his shark smile like a honky man winning a hand with large stacks of chips at a gaming table broadcasting live on WSOP.

At midnight, James roared his black 2015 Cadillac CTS on Irving Park Road westbound. Sprawled on the passenger seat, I was thinking. Holy smokes, this ride is Gucci! When we burst in, the burlesque was overcrammed. A bunch of strippers were twerking on the dancing poles, and a plethora of wanks gaped at them.

The George Washington bills were raining on the dancing stages. A couple of fog machines produced a vapor as if we were filming a movie scene from Batman. Once in a while, the DJ dropped the beat to announce promotions and the fake names of the strippers. There were tequila shots and bottles of beer lining up on our table.

The dancing girls had been buzzing over the guests like wasps billowing on honey. Usually, I kept my singles for the hungriest strippers. But when I hit the curb, I became unpredictable. Around forty minutes later, I got plastered. Out of the blue, a sexy stripper approached me. She was an erotic showstopper similar to Kaia Berger, one of the sexiest top-notch models in the Land of Liberty.

Don't get me wrong; Kaia Berger is not a stripper. The stripper sat on my lap as if I was her biological father. The gal rubbed her humps at me, trying to grab my wallet. Nice try, bimbo! That cunt was trying to play ugly games, but I had been in bordellos before she even graduated grade school. Then the stripper started rubbing my groin. "What's your name?" I quipped by showing cocky behavior.

"I'm Summer. And you?" she queried me automatically.

"My name is Winter. Nice to meet ya," I flung my answer with a condescending grin. Summer giggled, pretending that my response was being funny.

"Come on. Let's have a lap dance, sweetheart." Summer said. She was hungry to collect cash. She got to feed those kiddos. She revealed that some hoodrat got knocked her up, and she gave birth to a boy and a girl. Of course, maybe that was why she became a stripper. Whatever. Who cares? You must keep your back clean because those people are heartless and ruthless.

As we padded to the purple cubicle concealed with darkpink drapes, Summer looked at me and tried to allure me by dancing playfully. Her figure was heart-stopping, resembling the fascinating figure of the American actress Beth Behrs. So frigging hot! Summer was an awful dancer. Regardless, I enjoyed the way she twirled her patootie.

In the second song, I couldn't believe what popped up in front of my eyes. This is not possible. My mind hollered like a frenzied NFL player. Summer's face, the dancing star, had morphed to Klara. This is so gross! Klara, get the duck out of my mind. Dude, you are so messed up in the head. It will take time to recover from this quicksand. The most important is that you will be fine. Be patient. That was what I thought while Summer was ushering me to our table, where James was right about to drowse.

"Goodbye, hon. Hope to see you soon," Summer said, flossing her unreal grin. Ya, whatever. The next moment, I fumbled into my pocket to check how many bills were left. It turned out most that of my money flew away. Then, I said to James,

"Let's hit the road, bozo!" He agreed.

James denied requesting an Uber. He insisted on driving plastered. After five minutes of debating, we toppled outside of the parking lot and hopped into his Cadillac. James not only craved to drive hammered, but he enjoyed operating a vehicle while under the influence of alcohol. James urged to give me a lift to my sanctuary, and I gave him a thumbs-up. Why? James was stubborn. He had refused to listen to my opinion, and I was sick and tired arguing in the middle of the parking lot at HB's.

Around four in the morning, the Cadillac rushed to the east side. The music blasted out the track of Drake's "0 to 100." James drove completely reckless, speeding up unnecessarily. I was visualizing how we would bump into some tree or streetlight and smashed like a swamp rat demolished by an immense Peterbilt Model 579. I didn't give a fuck. I wanted to die, to close my eyelids and never wake up again. All of a sudden, I heard the Cadillac screeching the tires and then completely stopped. My squinted eyes scanned a sign that indicated Wherman. "Later, dawg!" James said, and I just nodded. My legs dragged to office digpot. Crawling inside, I grab a bottle of Smirnoff to knock myself out. I guzzled the booze, picturing how I pulled up a sidearm and hit the trigger. Bam! I wanted to paint the walls red. Believe it or not, if I really had a gun at that time, you would not read this book. One more Smirnoff, and I will step out of the stage. My mind said. I crashed after draining five more bottles of Smirnoff. In the morning, I was soaked with some rancid liquid splattered all over the couch. The picture on the couch looked nasty, resembling pizza that I ate for free at HB the night before.

*****

November 2018 darted faster than a cheetah chaseing a gazelle. The weather got colder than a witch's titties in a brass bra in the middle of winter. At that time, I wandered outside, wearing a warm piebald coat. On the top of my messed-up head, I put on a black do-rag, and on top, I had a Chi-town baseball cap which I wore backward.

I looked like a newcomer rapper attempting to release his first album. Every single day was similar. After work, I drove to the packy store then immediately hauled my butt to office digpot. I didn't want to go anywhere or to hung around with anybody. I spent dough mostly on booze and bills. Coco cost me an arm and a leg. Every once in a while, some of my workmates would ask me,

"Why does your face look so serious?"

"Well, your guess is good as mine, and I wonder why too."

The collection of pain spasms in my heart were popping up sporadically, especially when I was carrying out large pizzas. Intermittently, I had to sit on the chair to catch my breath. My heart bounced as a ping-pong ball. Ennio was forced to check the rhythm of my heartbeat a few times per day. Regardless of my medical condition, I was still working.

My English level ramped up radically. There was a coworker named John, a Mexican American who had hair that resembled a horse grease tail. John was a butterball. He loved to eat any food, especially pan and stuffed pizza. It was not a big surprise. John was responsible for accepting phone calls and orders. Once, John declared,

"Dimitry, you talk like Stitch."

"What do you mean Stitch?" I asked, baffled.

"Lilo & Stitch, the animation movie, you know. Stitch was the alien who tried to speak English."

Whoa, this isn't very nice! The morbid storm of depression arose in my mind with bitterness and antagonism. The butterball Mexican had mocked me sardonically. It's funny as a crutch. I can drop this chubby douchebag like a bag of dirt. It would take less than a second. But I only nodded, mirroring a facetious visage. Why? Because I appreciated the favor that Ennio gave me while I was uncertain about my future in the USA. It would be nonsense to blow up the credit that the Italian boss had rendered.

*****

Thursday, November 8, was just another humdrum day at Annetis. While I was reading a bestseller written by Stephen King titled Doctor Sleep, my phone disturbed me with a clattering sound. Who is it? Klara! I had a text message saying,

Dimitry, I hope you are doing fine. I miss you so much.

What the heck is that? A few weeks after, she decided to burn the bridges, and now she misses me! Naw. I've lived and learned my lesson. I don't play those games anymore. I don't have any spare time to waste on situationships. I loved Klara deep down in my heart. Unfortunately, no matter what I did, she would not be my girl and she had never been my girl. I had tasted something that I could never have. I didn't mind her, and at the same time, I didn't want to see her.

Ending our relationship was the most rational decision that she had taken. I focused to put extra effort into erasing her from my memory. Otherwise, my feelings would be engaged in an unconditional state of unhappiness. In the evening of the same day, James and I headed to Hooters to screw around by ingesting some boneless chicken wings and drinking draft beer.

James whooshed his Cadillac and, at the same time, gulping Hennessy from a small bottle. I was watching him from the passenger seat, pondering. Oh Lord, I feel like a baby in the woods. What the duck am I doing in this vehicle? James drove plastered. He was a reckless, dangerous, and disrespectful driver. While he waited at the traffic lights, he pulled a finger at the other drivers who were stopped right next to us.

James was a trouble seeker. He sped up and blew the horn on purpose without any reason. It became quite annoying and risky. He had the same proportions as Doctor Jekyll and Mr. Hyde. When James was sober, he mirrored a friendly demeanor and integrity as a son of a righteous chaplain. When he got hammered, he metamorphosed to a pure scumbag, mischief, or a frigging brat. At ten in the evening, James sped his Cadillac somewhere around Portage Park. His careless driving had urged me to think. Can't stay in this wheel anymore. The petulant behavior of James is making me nauseous.

"James, you must drop me at home. I feel under the weather," I grumbled, staring blatantly at the glove box.

"Come on, dawg. Stop lying. You were fine a minute ago," he grunted and whined like an unfriendly crackhead. No matter how much James protested, he agreed to drop me at Wehrman. At the parking lot, James became aggressive. His anger was exposed like a tipsy peckerhead longing to fight everyone in the streets. He hollered by talking meaningless crap on my behalf. He bellowed something like,

"You ain't sh—t! Mother flower. You think I'm scared of you?"

James thought that I was powerless carrying a damaged aortic valve. At one point, I couldn't spar or fight with other boxers in great shape. But that didn't mean I was not dangerous, especially to plastered street fighters. Usually, guys who hit the curb by slurping a lot of booze thought they were macho and could beat anybody. Thus, they antagonized others to bump in a battle.

"James, I don't wanna fight with you, for Christ's sake. I don't need any troubles, man." My statement fired up James, and he became a hostile rioter. He didn't let me go through Wehrman's entry, and I had no choice. Locking my elbow and using an open palm of my hand, I triggered all of my body weight and jabbed the chest of James. I dropping him down easily. Sprawled on the cement, James goggled at me as if he saw the undisputed heavyweight champion Tyson Fury. He then left the parking lot grinning like the Marvel character from Spider-Man, the Green Goblin. The fisticuffs ended before it started. I didn't use my knuckles on purpose. My intentions weren't to hurt him, but he felt the power of my body. Thank

God nobody called the police. The last thing I wanted was to interact with constables and explain the entire scenario of how we ended up into a worthless confrontation.

Panting, I burst into office digpot and started swigging more Smirnoff Ice until I blacked out. The agony disturbed my subconscious. A fore-warning signal loomed in my nightmares. The affliction imposed by the heart failure caused me to wake up after a few hours. The pain of the aortic valve and the shortness of breath were getting worse. Something is about to happen, but what? Only God had the answers.

*****

Days in November had rotated monotonously: work, home, over and over. The affection for Klara didn't leave. I knew it would take me more time to forget her. Drinking alcohol after work turned to my routine like a ceremonial and religious denomination, just as how you would go to church every Sunday.

The dispiritedness was getting worse. It was so bad that I blocked the phone numbers of all of my friends, including my parents. I didn't want to talk to anyone. All I craved was to stay alone in the dungeon named office digpot. My family didn't have a clue what was hovering in my mind.

James and I remained friends, even though we stopped palling around. He saw me only at work. I didn't need some name-dropper embroiling me in midnight trips, cruising through the city while he was hammered.

My health at work was getting problematic. Multiple times, I almost dropped a single square cardboard box that a nine-year-old kid could hold easily. Sporadically, I had to stop working. I needed to draw a deep breath while walking with those cardboard boxes.

Ennio was forced to send me to my crib over and over again. He wit-nessed how I limped through the pizzeria. Often, he urged other drivers to complete orders that I was supposed to take.

*****

On Monday, November 12, just another tiresome day at Annetis, I sat on one of the chairs to catch my breath. "Who's next?" Ennio hollered from the kitchen. Usually, that phrase was used to emphasize that an order had been ready to be delivered and the driver who was next in the queue could do the takeout. At that particular moment, it was my turn to run the order. Holy smokes! I am so worn out, I can barely move from the table.

"Can't make it. Marcin, do you mind taking this order?" Marcin was a colleague from Poland. He had a face resembling a penguin. Marcin was a funny fella and, at the same time, an annoying chatterbox. He never stopped blabbering. His mouth had never zipped up. Everyone was frustrated when he was talking. Marcin was so annoying that all of the employees from Annetis were forced to keep social distancing from him. Marcin wasn't a backslapper or a terrible person. He just chatted perpetually. He agreed to supersede and took my order.

Ennio caught the spontaneous swap and darted over. His face looked panicked.

"What is it, Dimitry? How are you feeling?" He asked. His pupils mirrored anxiety and trepidation.

"Bushed!" I could barely talk. Everyone at the pizzeria had observed me like a bunch of famished vultures glaring at the entrails of a carcass that resembled a zebra. Ennio goggled as if he saw a corpse.

The Italian capo grabbed my hand to check the pulse.

"Can you drive to your home?" Ennio grilled.

"Yeah, I will be all right." My scowling face projected an expression like, "Hell yeah, man. Are you kidding me?"

"Great! Now listen to me carefully! Why don't cha grab your favorite chicken soup, get home, and rest? I'll see you mañana at eleven. Okay?"

I wasn't joyful to hear that, but I couldn't argue with my boss. I had light-headedness and almost stumbled on the floor. It took less than five minutes driving back to the Wehrman building. Panting, I burst straight into office digpot and fell asleep on the couch without showering.

Chapter 31

On the next day, the alarm on my phone woke me up. The headache was still tumbling in my head. Feeling as crooked as Rookwood (very sick) and sluggish like a snail, I could barely shuffle to the john to rinse my mouth.

After brushing my teeth and a long wee-wee, I tromped slower than an eighty-year-old man and hardly made it to the couch. Gosh, I've never been so tired! I was resting on the couch for the next thirty minutes. Then, I checked the clock. Ten thirty—duck! I won't make it to work. I could barely stand up on my feet. Better call Ennio. That was one of the very few times when I called for a sick day. It wasn't something that made me feel proud.

"Take care, kiddo! Talk with ya soon." Ennio hung up. He didn't have any time to talk. There were some big orders that needed concentration. Great! Now, what the duck am I going to do for the rest of the day? Around a minute or two, after I spoke with Ennio, James rang. He sounded worried. I had never heard him talking like that.

"What up, dawg? How are you feeling? Ennio told me that you are sick."

"Dude, I am so bushed and—"

"Hang on, dawg. I am coming," James cut me off before I could finish my sentence. He was a stubborn Italian. Once he had something in his mind, you couldn't change it. I knew what was about to happen.

In the next few minutes, the doorknob twirled and James scuttled through the entry. Is the door open? I don't know how. I must have been so weary that I left the door unlocked the night before. Is that a coincidence? James stepped to the couch and carried me out of the building as if I had been shot by a firearm. It was like God had sent him to take me out of the office digpot just before the situation got critical. If James hadn't come at that moment, I would have been lifeless and died in the office digpot.

My arms were motionless as if someone tied me up with a straitjacket. The weariness had transfixed my entire body. The only thing that I wanted was to drift off. The most unbelievable fact was that there was no pain. I could barely feel my body. I became 80 percent disabled. James pulled up the door of his Cadillac and gently placed me onto the passenger seat.

"Which hospital?" James asked, staring at me worriedly. His face looked so scared as if I was about to pass away at any second.

"Drive...to...," I stuttered. The deficiency of energy had blocked my ability to speak. James didn't wait for any directions. He plowed the Cadillac somewhere east on Irving Park Road. A few minutes later, he shoved his luxury auto in the parking lot of the immediate care unit that was a block away from Annetis. A cute Asian nurse sat me down in a wheelchair. She didn't have much choices as I had no balance.

"I'll touch base with you tomorrow. See you later, dawg," James barked and swiftly disappeared like a thug who had just successfully emptied an ATM. The Asian cutie dragged me through a spacious and unused room. It was so spooky and silent that, for a moment, I thought that a bunch of nurses holding chainsaws would burst through the entry and slash my entire body, painting the room in gore.

Those were just my thoughts. I wasn't afraid of leaving this world. I had pictured this moment many times before, especially when I was drunk. Another female nurse with a turkey neck stepped over and asked me questions, like where I lived and why I was there. I could sputter only. Her countenance mirrored that she couldn't comprehend what I had mumbled. After she asked her questions, my eyelids closed, and I slumbered instantaneously.

Then, an odd feeling occurred. Another blonde nurse who had a heavyweight type of body and a farm-country face was slapping me and hollering,

"Hey, wake up! Are you listening to me? Wake up!" It was very peculiar when she slapped me. I felt comfortable.

To slap a boxer is the same thing as to pet a lion.

A rumbling sound of sirens was blaring. The ambulance dropped me to Presence Resurrection, the same infirmary where they had found the bacterial infection in my blood. The paramedics left me in the ER where a breathtaking Irish nurse had taken care of me. She persistently observed the monitor displaying the vitals. She was phenomenal as the gorgeous actress Bella Throne.

Cheese and rice! What a schlepper! You're tripping in a critical condition, and now you've smitten with this redheaded gal. What's wrong with you? Concentrate, dammit! Thirty minutes later, I waved at the enthralling nurse, projecting a desire to vomit. The hottie nurse handed me a green basin, and I threw up a few times.

The severe heart blockage didn't allow me to ask for her name. A few minutes later, my eyelids became heavy and slowly closed. So worn out! I just want to sleep for a minute! My entire body was stationary like a tombstone. My eyelids were shut, resembling the rolled down drapes of a theater.

The audience (nurses and physicians) were expecting the spectacle to recommence, but those drapes didn't roll up. An hour later, a female sound blared. The Irish nurse bumped in awe. The drapes of the theater rolled up, and I witnessed how that nurse was bouncing and spraying emotional sparks of exuberance. I didn't know what they did, but the heartbeat pumped regularly and I felt better. Several hours later, they transferred me into the intensive care unit.

*****

The next day, I forced myself to unblock all of my contact numbers. Around ten in the morning, Mike rang. His dismayed accent could be easily identified. Two hours later, he burst in at the unit. His eyes were frightened.

Mike brought a Bulgarian preacher named Billy, who worked as a pastor at a Greek monastery located somewhere in Wisconsin.

Billy was a witty bloke, cheerful and gracious. He was bald, wearing a trimmed beard called balbo. His bored eyes were as big as the size of a ping-pong ball. But when he smiled, he reflected a charming charisma. I tipped my hat on Mike. It was a noble gesture to usher a minister at the infirmary. That was why I honored him as a good cobber (friend).

"What did the doctors say?" Mike asked, confused.

"They want to implant a pacemaker, which will control the heartbeat and prevent from an eventual heart attack."

"When?" Mike was impatient like Gordon Ramsay waiting for a rapid response from one of his chefs.

"I don't have any idea. The physicians ought to discuss the impending procedure. Regardless, it has to be done soon, 'cuz I can't afford to warm the stretcher at the hospital for a long time."

Billy commenced reading a few paragraphs of the Orthodox Study Bible. It fulfilled my self-contemplation. Despite the prayers, when Mike and Billy walked out of the medical ward, my faith faded. The next few days were identical. The sawbones kept telling me that I needed a pacemaker, but no one implied any particular day for an eventual procedure. At the same time, I strove to explain how difficult it had gotten for me to stay at the infirmary. There weren't any benefits given by the government or Social Security to bear me up financially. My family could not be able to send any money. All the utility bills, including the rent, were eating my savings; and I was afraid to plunge into swamps of debt. Spending savings without work would bring me to a calamitous end. But those intelligent surgeons didn't get the memo how bad my situation was. For the past couple of days, they didn't arrange any other processes. I digested three meals per day and sat back idling at the medical stretcher. That was all. I felt like I was living in the hospital. What a bummer! I was getting frustrated and aggravated. It made me feel uncomfortable, like an urban camper begging to stay in a shelter.

Friday, November 16, was my fifth day at Presence Resurrection, and there wasn't anything happening. A Filipino nurse had been taking care of me during that day. She was in her mid-twenties with a thin body and hair as long as a horse's tail. She nimbly walked through the medical unit. The Filipino portrayed an antagonizing behavior. Her countenance looked as if she got pissed for doing something wrong.

"Excuse me, miss. Would you tell me if the doctors will come to talk with me?" I asked politely like a greaseball traveler asking for directions on his first day visiting Manhattan.

"I don't have any idea," she grumbled.

"Listen, I need to know 'cuz I can't stay too long—"

"You will stay here as much as you have to," the Filipino interrupted. Her pouty face didn't look friendly. At that moment, the murky thunderstorm in my head culminated into a gust of blasting thoughts. My subconscious had a mental breakdown. You can't command me!

"Gimme the discharge papers. I am leaving the hospital!" my tone was serene and, at the same time, about to explode like a man having a chaotic discontentment.

"Mr. Salchev, you can't just leave. You are very sick." The nurse proclaimed.

"I said gimme the papers, or I will just walk away," I repeated to the nurse who was in shock.

The thunderstorm in my head caused trepidation. Ten minutes later, George, the dandy limo driver, picked me up from the main entrance of the infirmary. Presence Resurrection had saved my life twice. This medical entity was a great hospital, and I couldn't claim any bad feedback. Nevertheless, the way that particular Filipino nurse had treated me was wrong. That was why I decided to walk away from there.

James should drive me to Loyola. Alas, my medical condition didn't allow me to provide him any guidance. So what shall I do next? That was a vital question that kept nagging me until I hit the sack in the cozy couch in office digpot.

*****

On Saturday, the next day, I headed to Annetis to speak with Ennio. His standpoint was essential, and I knew he would rather talk in person. When

I went to the pizzeria, Ennio was at the counter organizing the store. He was jubilant to see me. After he heard about my visit at the infirmary, his grin flew away. He started talking like a pastor at a Catholic church.

"Dimitry, go to Loyola. You need to have this procedure done! Listen to me please. This isn't a joke, and you know that better than me. Do not postpone this process 'cuz you might haven't any chance later. You might succumb, for Christ's sake! Please, do yourself a favor and go to the hospital," Ennio protested.

He brandished his hands up and down, side to side. He was very expressive and animated, an archetype to his Italian heritage. His enthusiastic lecture made him persuasive. He wasn't hollering or chanting like a haughty jailer bellowing at a J Cat inmate. While Ennio was blabbering, I kept nodding.

"You are completely right, and I promise I will go to Loyola. Please let me work for the weekend." Ennio was the salt of the earth. He sighed by inhaling and exhaling heavily, like a husband hearing a ludicrous idea from his wife to spend a couple of G's for swimming courses of their six-year-old son and saying, "He is too young to swim. He hasn't even known what the word swimming pool means."

Ennio mirrored an agreeable signal. He tapped my arm tacitly. His grin revived like all of the deceased fictional characters from the prominent blockbuster Avengers: Endgame. For the rest of the day, I worked for a couple of hours and made sixty bucks from tips. On Sunday, I worked at Annetis for less than three hours. I almost stumbled on the floor while carrying a few orders. Ennio had no choice. He sent me back to office digpot.

Chapter 32

Monday, November 19, was a bone-chilling day. I stared at the streets and roads, passing nimbly through as they fell out of sight. The Lincoln Navigator streaked to Loyola. George, the dandy limo driver, was holding the steering wheel. He was mesmerized at the traffic light. He was silent as if he was a mute person.

While I was glaring at the streets, my thoughts got jammed. The kismet blew the whistle. It was time to pussyfoot into the hospital. What will happen there? Will I live, or will I perish out there like a juvenile squirrel trying to cross Michigan Avenue in downtown Chicago? Only the master of the universe would answer to all of those questions.

The pain was not problematic. I was whacked out as if I had been working for several months straight on a farm. The lack of energy almost put me in sleep. The afterglow had already fallen upon the sky. It was getting dark like the color of Batman's snazzy vehicle. The Navigator stopped right at the entry of the emergency.

"See you later, George. Thanks for the ride," I could barely mutter. George merely nodded. He was worn out but not as much as I was. It was half-past six when I hobbled into the ER. I shuffled in slow motion to the admission register. A cutie African American Nutella had asked me for general information.

To make the long story short and to not push you into the sphere of sweet dreams, twenty minutes later, I was escorted to the Five Tower, where I didn't need extra medical care. They poked me so many times that my forearms looked like I was inserting needles of smack for pleasure. They sent me there because the vital records had displayed regular results. A Filipino nurse named Gina (or just G) took care of me. She had a phenomenal figure, the greatest tooshie I had ever seen in the medical field. Looking at her, my mind said. Gosh, she is a showstopper sexpot. G had taken care of me since June after the open-heart surgery.

"Hello, D! What brings you back here?" G quizzed while mirroring a glistening grin.

"Well, I miss you, G. What's new?" She was laughing even if she knew it wasn't funny. Or maybe she was just admiring my optimistic demeanor. Who knows? Whatever the type of quicksand occurred, I had always tried to bite the bullet and brace it out. I had never complained or expressed any grievance or whinnying like a boo-hooing wimp. G double-checked my IV. She wanted to make sure that everything was kosher. Around midnight, I drifted off to a serene sleep.

*****

"Wake up, Dimitry! Are you okay? Tell me how you are feeling!" a familiar female voice shrieked and thumbed in my eardrums. Argh, man! What the heck is going on? How am I feeling? Sleepy, for Christ's sake. I've just been sleeping until you woke me up! Why is this girl bothering me! My somnolent eyes were merely blinking. A female silhouette stood in front of my eyes, but it was too vague to be identified.

"G, is that you?" I slurred, feeling drowsy from the spontaneous wakening.

"No! This is Aubree. I am helping Gina. She will be here shortly. I came because your heart isn't monitoring normal rates." What the duck is she talking about? Aubree goggled like an appalled zebra rubbernecking a ferocious lion.

The consternation in her pupils could be easily deciphered. A few

331

minutes later, a bunch of nurses and a few attending doctors filled the medical ward like a swarm of bees. I didn't count them, but they were at least fifteen. They all peered at me, intimidated and dismayed. One of the physicians looked perturbed. She grumbled something indistinct, and one of the nurses rushed from the ward. My body became immobile. Why am I so washed out!

"Mr. Salchev, your heart rate has been dropping between twenty-eight and thirty-five. It is too low. The nurse will give you a medicine, which should increase your heart rhythm." The female physician had stately announced as if she was saying, "I'm getting married." I merely nodded.

The nurse came back, holding two pills in her palm. She handed me a cup of water, and I swallowed the remedy. Then, all of the medical employees had waited thoughtfully for the result. For the next few minutes, there weren't any changes. Ha! You have to gimme something stronger. My thoughts cried out while I showed a smirk.

Another nurse brought an electrical defibrillator. She placed the medical appliance right next to the stretcher. Holy smokes! Is that for real? Am I messed up? This crap ain't a joke. I don't like that thing. This is one of those machines from the movies that gives electric shock to patients with critical conditions. The only difference is, we are not filming! Gosh, I am so knackered. My eyelids were slowly closing. All of the nurses and doctors were peering at me as if I were some alien who had just arrived from elsewhere in the galaxy. At the next moment, severe drowsiness knocked me out.

*****

The weird feeling of someone pushing the stretcher aroused me. Where the heck am I? Square light fixtures mounted on the ceiling were passing upon my eyes over and over again. Where are they taking me? A sweet lady in her mid-thirties resembled Amy Schumer pushed the gurney, where I was sprawled like a dead horse. That lady leaned close to me as if she had an intention to kiss me.

"Hey, my name is Chloe. I am a surgical assistant, and we are taking you to the surgical room. We will implant a temporary pacemaker. Don't worry, it's a short procedure, which will take around twenty minutes. You will be all right. I promise."

I had lost the ability to talk; I could merely make a humming sound. What Chloe had said emboldened me at some point. It was vital and beneficial to hear someone saying those words at that critical moment. The pain didn't disturb me; I was just falling asleep.

My chances to perish from suffocating were pretty high. The dual door swung, and the gurney burst into a room where an electrophysiology procedure was about to be initiated. All of the physicians moved urgently. That moment resembled an episode of the TV show ER. A man equipped with a mask and surgical gown approached me.

"Hi, Mr. Salchev. I am Doctor Smit Vasaiwala. We will implant a temporary pacemaker. It's a ten-minute procedure, and you will be awake during the entire procedure. You shouldn't feel any pain. Okay?" I was lifeless; I couldn't even say, thank you.

They tied up my legs and arms. Holy crack! What the heck will these people do to me! Ah, duck! That hurts! A sharp, stabbing ache shot through me momentarily. Breathless, I wasn't able to see clearly. A bunch of human hands were jerking in front of my eyes. At the next moment, what happened was quite intricate to be described. That was a moment of benevolence, a moment when you got the feeling that God had intervened and made righteousness by sparing your life.

While I was feeling that I'm going to die, suddenly, I could take a deep breath. The master of the universe handed me another opportunity to breathe again like a normal human being. That was angelical, the beauty of a medical profession, a moment of salvation when the magic touch of surgeons saved a human's life.

The Lord showed mercy. He had given me another chance to live, despite how I had tried to harm myself. What I had done to my body was unacceptable. Regardless, God had condoned my sin, which shouldn't be forgiven. Hold on. Who am I to judge? The Lord knows his business. He sent doctors and nurses to rescue my soul, and they had done a fascinating job.

Since then, I pray to God for all of them to be healthy. The surgery was successful. Half an hour later, a bald African American man transported me to the intensive care unit where they monitored me. I drifted off at once. It was around three in the afternoon when I woke up. My squinting eyeballs were rolling around. I wiggled side to side and peeked through the gown. What the heck is this?

Two colorful tiny wires slunk beyond my skin at the left side of my chest. The wires were connected to my heart. Those wires were powered by a voltage controller like the size of a lunch box. A knock on the door interrupted the creepy silence.

"Hello, Mr. Salchev. I am Josh. We are the cardiology team. How are you feeling?" a Latin man wearing glasses resembling those of Peter Parker asked.

"I am fine, I guess!"

"Great. Here is what we've planned. Tomorrow, early in the morning, another procedure is waiting for you. A permanent pacemaker will be implanted in your body, and if everything looks good, you should be able to go home on Thursday for Thanksgiving. Oh, I almost forgot. Your aortic valve is narrowing, and it fails to open and close regularly. After Thanksgiving, you will have to come back here. We need to do a minor procedure called transcatheter aortic valve replacement (TAVR), which will replace your damaged aortic valve with another biological valve. The purpose of this procedure is to avoid another open-heart surgery. We need an EKG to observe the function of your heart. Any questions?" Josh crooned by ending his medical lecture.

"When will this EKG be?"

"Uh… I believe later today. You take care," Josh blurted, and the doctors left. I wasn't shocked. I knew the valve was damaged. I was dumb enough not to pay attention to this fundamental consideration regarding my heart condition. The EKG had been done as quickly as the duration in one round in boxing.

At seven in the evening, James invaded the ICU like a minder of congressmen. His exuberance flashed a ghostly grin.

"What up, dawg? How you doing? Here, I brought you some chicken soup."

"Thanks, James. The surgery went smoothly. I'm fine. Actually, I might be outta here on Thursday."

"For real! That's cool, dawg. Have you met any nurses with big boobies?" James asked.

"Naw, but I saw lots of tiny titties with huge patooties." Ha-Ha-Ha. We both tittered like some illiterate punks sniggering while watching 'The Roast of Charlie Sheen'.

"Nah, man! What the duck are you doing? Knock it off. James, did you hear me? Dammit!" James stared at me facetiously. He scrunched a baggie containing white chalk and snorted it using his car keys. Then he pulled out a small bottle of rotgut and drank deeply. James thought it was fun, but I completely deplored his attitude.

"Not here, duke! Go to the frigging john, man!" No matter how much I grumbled, this squirt never listened.

"It's all good, dawg! Don't act like a fucking nimrod. I'll see you at the pizzeria." James left the medical ward, and I could take a deep breath. On the next day, the procedure of inserting the permanent pacemaker model of Medtronic had been performed successfully. The device was inserted right above my heart.

Glaring at the three inches of the surgical incision, my haggard face was bothered by traffic of thoughts. What the heck am I going to do now with those two heart surgeries? Yeah, I know the answer. I am going to make a seismic come back at the ring. I will fight again. I don't give a damn if it's amateur or pro. I will restore my training shape and kick someone's arse. I started visualizing images of my eventual come-back at the ring and stimulating my self-conscience by watching a plethora of boxing videos on YouTube.

Bam! Bam! What a knockout! The contender of the blue corner knocked out the boxer from the red team with flawless combinations. And the winner by KO is at the blue corner—Dimitry Salchev!

The rest of the day, no one did any additional medical exams. The doctors merely monitored the interaction of the Medtronic device.

*****

On Thursday, November 22, at around ten in the morning, a young Mexican nurse handed me the discharge papers. Her body type alleged that she loved eating grande burritos and enchiladas. She politely explained the instructions for my next visit, which was calendared a few days before Christmas. I Ubered myself to office digpot. Later, I spent a few bucks by hogging chicken kebab with rice and vegetables. I pictured coming back in the ring before I crashed on the couch like a perished wapiti sprawled on the tarmac somewhere in North Canada. Thanksgiving 2018 became alonegiving, and that was fine.

*****

Saturday, the twenty-fourth, I cruised to Annetis for the first time after the pacemaker procedure. Everyone out there was happy to see me, especially Ennio. The Italian boss was concerned about my health condition. He had witnessed how I almost fell on the floor for several times.

"How you feeling, kiddo?" Ennio tapped my shoulder. His smile was hooked on his face. Often, I felt like Ennio was my own uncle. He watched my back sporadically.

The Italian capo put my name on the work schedule. It was drastically better dashing orders with Medtronic. Initially, I recommended working just for a few hours a day. Two weeks later, I ran massive business orders containing more than twenty pizzas.

James and I labored like teammates of tennis doubles. Multiple times, I was buying him bagels or sausage McMuffins for brunch. We often shared lunch like biological brothers. I was portraying my appreciation of what he had done for me when my heart condition was acute. Nevertheless, I couldn't screw around with James.

After work, he transformed into a hellion. James was pushing his luck. Several times, he came hammered to Annetis. The reek of alcohol could be sniffed from a distance. Ennio was compelled to send him home. Regardless, James took for granted Ennio's compromises and continually appeared intoxicated at work. Ennio had no choice. He pulled his plug off. James was the ace-high employee for accepting orders over the phone, and Ennio knew that. Alas, the reaction of Ennio was, "Just another pawn kicked out of the checkerboard."

*****

I decided to cancel the appointment that was scheduled a few days before Christmas. The reason why was my health insurance. At that time, I couldn't comprehend the philosophy of those insurance providers. I was lost in my dark thoughts, and a prisoner in my own mind. I was overwhelmed by every traumatic month in 2018.

I was stuck at another mental breakdown. The murky storm in my head was hovering again. At that time, I wanted to leave this world. No one would care if I just disappeared. I was not accepted in any society except maybe boxing. But many can tell that boxing is a lonely sport. At that time, I wasn't homesick. I didn't even care what could happen to my country, or what could happen to me.

I took for granted how God had saved my life. Instead of praising the Lord, I wasted my time pondering about what I had been going through, and that just suppressed me even more. My jinx had started with frostbite in January, then the boxing contamination, the Geo hooptie, then open-heart surgery, the pacemaker implant, and yes, Klara. Her interaction struck me emotionally and spiritually.

One day, she asked me before we destroyed our whatevership.

"Why can't we just be friends?" Because you can't always get what you want Klara! Three months after she ditched me, I still doted and adored her. Dude! You are chopped liver and she is water under the bridge. You must forget her. Yeah, that sounds appropriate, but how can I forget her? Delete her number!

There are two most efficient ways to forget someone. First, delete everything that links you with that person: social media, photos, gifts, etc. Second, find someone else. It has always been working for me. So that was what I did. I erased everything that connected me with Klara. It didn't matter whether I would see her or not.

Both of us had to take in different directions. Klara wasn't my future. If so, there was no use talking about something that didn't link to my future. Her image had been buried deep down in my subconscious. That was jotted on the notepad of the Master of the Universe. I believed the Lord had more opportunities to render.

*****

Christmas of 2018 was one of the most boring days in my life. WHY? The pizzeria was closed. Ennio had to send all of his employees to spend the holiday with their families. I spent Christmas at the desolate dungeon of office digpot.

There were no Christmas decorations or anything related to Santa Claus. Nada! The murky storm in my sick head had grown darker. I avoided speaking with anybody, even with my own family. Gazing at the picture box and gulping Smirnoff Ice was my only target. I didn't value the present (the pacemaker) that the Lord Almighty had rendered.

What a pinhead. The same picture was broadcasting on New Year's Eve. It was like someone had blown the flame in the candle of my life. There weren't any future targets that had been set to pursue in a long term. It was just another day wasted in the dungeon of office digpot. I didn't get the memo when the clock's hand passed midnight on December 31. It wasn't making any difference to me. However, I was relieved that the year of 2018 was over.

*****

Two weeks after the first day of 2019, I drove back home from work. Jaded, I burst in at office digpot. My squinted eyes were closing slowly. It was a long day at work. Snow flurries had piled up on the streets. Dashing through the snow became harder. It was colder than a well digger's ass, a frigging dumb brick. After five minutes of roaming outdoor, my nut sack metamorphosed into ice cubes. The coolest feature of the Wehrman dwelling was that each unit on the basement level had been installed with a heat-flooring system. It could be so frigging hot that I walked around freeballing. The clock on my smartphone displayed half-past eight when, suddenly, a sound of knocking on the door rumbled.

"I'm coming," I barked, trying to find something to put on. I tried to peek through the peephole, but the door viewer was blackened. Chiz, someone had put their finger on the peephole! Who the heck is pranking me?

"Who is it?" There was no answer. It made me upset. I yanked the door, and I saw James cackling like a funky hyena.

"What up, James?" I asked like a salty crackhead hankering smack. James continued grinning.

"Yo, 'sup, dawg! I've just stopped by to say hi," James grumbled. His voice resembled a female rapper.

"Not much, bro! Just chillin'." I leered at James, and still figuring out what he wanted.

"Yo, dawg, I found a restaurant called Jonny's Place in Arlington Heights. They hired me to do the phones. Come work with me, dawg. I am telling you, the cash flow is mad there."

"Yeah? I know that joint. They have good food. Can't give you a straight answer right now. Let me think about it!" I blurted out. James kept blabbering about the bid in an aggressive and grandiloquent manner.

It took me twenty minutes to kick him out peacefully. James left, and that was the last time I saw him. James was a good kid, but he swerved into grim pathways which I tried to keep away from.

Later, I heard that he had been booted out from a few sports bars where we used to pal around.

*****

In the middle of January, the business at Annetis slowed down. One tiresome day at work, a big stocky man in his fifties, clothed in a tattered attire, burst straight into the pizzeria. He looked like he just got checked out from a nuthouse.

The man approached the register and said,

"Hello. Is Ennio here? I'd like to speak with him." The stocky man asked

John, who was yawning at the register. It turned out that the chunky man was Bulgarian as well. His name was Kurt. He used to work at Annetis a long time ago. Kurt had two lung surgeries. As we chatted, Kurt and I found that we had something in common. He was a funny gasbag; he never stopped talking. It was mission impossible to ask him a question. After a while, I finally chimed in.

"So, Kurt, where are you working?" Kurt rolled his vulture's eyes to make sure there wasn't anyone near to hear him (which was funny to me because we were clearly the only ones who spoke Bulgarian in the pizzeria). Then, he leaned closer and whispered in Bulgarian.

"Boy, if you need a job, call me." He slightly stepped back. Kurt stared at me as if he was ready to wrestle me.

"Gotta hike, kiddo. See you soon!" Kurt blurted and left the pizzeria. Bemused, I was chewing over. I'll be damned. What in the name of God was this man talking about? Does he want to stitch me up? Those thoughts pursued me for a while.

*****

The Medtronic pacemaker had such a positive influence on improving the function of my heart. It made me contemplate getting back in the boxing field. I couldn't wait to fight someone. It didn't matter who. But you can't just hop in the sea if you cannot swim.

I had to travel through a long journey into the process of restoring my athletic shape. On Friday, January 11, my boy Erik Sobczak brought me as a guest at LA Fitness. It was a convenient gym, especially for cardio and lifting weights. Also, a few kickboxing bags were dangling like hanging corpses on a gibbet.

My first training was horrible. I could merely walk fast on the treadmill. Despite my terrible training, I was blissful to have the chance to sweat and be able to do any exercise in general. Erik walked around the gym as if he owned the whole place. His character had a positive influence on me.

The guest pass allowed me to visit LA Fitness only several times, then I had to pull out the greenbacks. I wanted to speak with the office manager.

We discussed a possible membership. The supervisor was a sanctimonious chink, a hench in his twenties who perceived himself as a grandson of Bolo Yeung. Anyhow, his offer was a one-year contract and an excessive amount of dough per month. There was no way that I would agree with those circumstances.

I was a strapped mother flower. God forbid if I stampeded to the hospital again and I had to cancel the contract; they would charge me extra fees—uh-uh. So I returned to my dog pack at Oakley Fight Club. Everyone there was joyful to see me. Papa Bomb stepped closer and said,

"Welcome back, kid."

The exuberance in my pupils wasn't camouflaged. As I started my training at Oakley, some chappie told me that Don would come to spar on Thursday. I missed Don, even though I wasn't sure how he would react to seeing me. We hadn't spoken to each other since I had left the flat in Albany Park.

The last Thursday of January, I drove the Nissan to Oakley. When I burst in, my pupils peered at Don. He eyed me like a hawk. Da Bomb wasn't grinning. It was a knife-edge moment. Surveying him, I couldn't figure how he would respond. Here we are. He is coming. Will he start fighting or not? There is only one way to find out. Don stepped closer, spread his arms, and gave me a brotherly hug.

"How you doing, Don? I thought you would jump on me for a fight," I blurted out, relieved.

"Nah, champ, I still love you. I am just mad at you." We chatted a smidgen. The former IBO champ revealed that he was doing fine. He lived with an Italian beauty named Julia. A week later, I saw him again at some Chinese restaurant in Elmwood Park. We buried the hatchet and straightened everything out by shaking hands like grown-up brothers. Don was getting too busy with his chick. That was why I spotted him once in a blue moon. Da Bomb was like a bat. You would never know when he could show up.

*****

On the first Friday of February, Ennio sent me to Hyatt Regency in Rosemont. It was a huge order containing a dozen of the large pizzas. I could only carry four cardboard boxes. Each box had space for only one pizza.

Padding through the lobby, the weight of those boxes became cumbersome. It turned out to be a problem. My biceps barely could hold those boxes. Dude, don't drop them. Come on, old fart. You can do it. Push harder. Don't be a frigging p'ssy. Perspiration dripped from my forehead. Ah, duck! Can't hold them anymore. Got to put those boxes on the floor. Otherwise, they will start to tip.

I placed the boxes on the floor. I sat on the guest's bench. Panting, I was ready to puke. The stabbing pain in my heart was being ruthless. Oh geez. I almost dropped them. Thank God! I didn't. Ennio would freak out. The price of those pizzas would cost a bundle. On a regular basis, I could hold those boxes steady without any concern. Unfortunately, the aortic valve was getting worse. I didn't need a cardiologist to confirm that report.

The pain beyond my chest had spoken out loud and made it clear what would have happened at the next episode. Somehow, I managed to complete the order. The most important was that there were no flipped pizzas in those boxes. The pain in my heart struck in every single beat. My body become weak.

Shortness of breath bugged me periodically. The drowsiness and nebulous vision brought an obnoxious headache. My face was grimacing as if I had just lost all my money on poker game. Puttering back to

Annetis, I was thinking. Got to share this story with Ennio. He must know. Gasping, I walked straight to him.

"Ennio, I can't make those large orders anymore. I was lucky that I didn't drop them. Next time, I might not be that lucky," I declared. The IL capo just nodded. He wasn't joyful, but he was happy that I revealed my burden. Ennio wasn't a chump. He comprehended the simple fact that he needed another driver. The Italian boss gave me an option to take light orders with inconsequential price, which meant earning less money.

Around nine in the evening, I called Kurt. He wanted to meet me at Jewel Osco's parking lot, who had already told me that he was a clean ass or that he wasn't involved in any sort of outlawed hustle. When I met Kurt for the first time, he had reflected a quirky and peculiar demeanor, but I wanted to see what offer he could furnish.

I roared into the parking lot where Kurt had been waiting in his 1990's Toyota Camry. The two vehicles were parked parallel in the desolate parking lot of Jewel. It was close to midnight in the first days of February. A deputy might think we were dealing with drugs. We didn't goof around with anything illegal. Kurt showed me a few online platforms of food delivery named DoorDash, Postmates, and Uber Eats. Some blokes mentioned Uber Eats, but I hadn't heard anything about the other entities. I thought at that time they weren't notorious, or I'd just didn't know about them.

Kurt spoke to me contemptuously, as if he had dug out a side hustle from which cash was flowing like we were selling smack on 80 percent profit. His phony demeanor pissed me off. It got me bent out of shape just by listening to his bossy voice. Despite that, I tried to play the role of a cool guy by pulling myself together. I thanked Kurt for the opportunity that he revealed. God bless his heart. It took around ten business days to check my background. Then, I got approved for DoorDash and Postmates.

Uber Eats raised the red flag. When I burst in at the Uber office, they said, "Mr. Salchev, your TVDL driving license does not cover our policy. I am sorry." In other words, they kicked my buttocks out because I was a frigging alien holding a license for people with expired visas. It was what it was.

Ennio scheduled my name only part-time or when it got dynamic and in high demand. On Tuesday, February 19, the cashier checked me out from Annetis. Straight away, I swiped on the DoorDash app for the first time. It was around six in the evening. It was dark outside as if I lay in a closed coffin.

At the next instant, the DoorDash app sent me an order request from Portillo's. The brown Nissan rushed on Lawrence Avenue. I was speeding as if the bluebottles were chasing me for a brutal felony. That order had lots of items. I placed all of the products in my car. Then, I started driving, and at the first light, a large diet Coke spilled out on my toes. Ah, crap! What an airhead. Dammit!

Dude, cool your jets. Go inside and get another Coke! My first order with DoorDash had been completed successfully. Regardless, my wet shoes became sticky because of the Diet Coke. Ha! Dude, this gig is dope! I am an independent contractor. I choose when, how long, and where I can dash. Parenthetically, I had the freedom that I'd been looking for. That was a comfortable way to earn an acceptable wage.

Being an independent contractor was one of my dreams. The feeling of being independent at work could be translated as a fulfilled gratification, like a man being spiritually and emotionally satisfied by his wife. The distinction of the working progress between Annetis and DoorDash was bigger than Godzilla. Thus, I decided to work the whole week with DoorDash and only on Sundays at Annetis. Ennio was informed that I was looking for another job. He also knew I was flexible.

There was a huge elephant in the room that I tried to hide even from myself: the fact that I canceled my appointment at Loyola. I was aware of what was approaching. Just another morass was knocking on my door. Therefore, I needed to be prepared financially. The more I thought about it, the twitchier I became. That was why I saved all of the dough that I had earned.

The rapper Offset said, "Stay clean and the money comin' in," in his track "Quarter Milli." According to my daily journal, that is precisely true. Cashing money in the nested egg was a wise method. The feeling of premonition bugged me incessantly. Only God knew what was coming.

*****

Two weeks after my first order from DoorDash, my happiness was wiped out. Another thought wedged into my mind. DoorDash and Postmates weren't dynamic enough to catch enough greenbacks. I decided to switch the working location.

DoorDash platform allowed to enroll preliminarily for each separate zone. I had chosen the Lakeview and Lincoln Park area. My target was to work in the evenings, mostly Friday and Saturday. I was astounded. The orders there were in high demand. No one shared that gossip, not even

Kurt. He wasn't interested in dashing through the city. Chi-town was blooming, and I hoped to get laid with a bonny lass out there. The broads were bumping like ants in an ant colony.

I sneaked around, collecting bread here and there. The brown Nissan cruised around like a bumblebee on a beehive. Every yuppie living in Chicagoland went wild on the weekends. When they got hammered, they were all chomping at the bit for munches. That was great for the business but wasn't enough.

When I used to bust my ass at Annetis, I was making more dough. That tossed me into another mental breakdown. Since I dragged my ass back from the hospital, I wanted to go cold turkey. Drinking booze became routine. Gulping bevy after the gig had embedded in my character. I felt like an orphan expelled far away in the wilderness. The thoughts of what could happen worried me to the early hours. The wakefulness had been chasing me since July. It became annoying. The insomnia had never taken a day off. I did my research and purchased from Amazon melatonin extra strength at ten milligrams, but it still didn't knock me out.

After around seven pills and a six-pack of Smirnoff Ice, I could slumber for three to four hours. Then, I woke up again. Shit, man! That stuff isn't strong enough. Need something stronger. But what? The headache, agony, frustration, depression, mental breakdown, and chest pain were just part of a few unwilling guests living in a room in my head. It was a hodgepodge. Even if I was knackered from work, gulping bevy and popping sleeping pills, my eyes were still open.

*****

It was the night between Saturday and the morning of Sunday. I plowed on the freeway of I-90 Kennedy after finishing the food gig. I puttered straight to office digpot. Prudent like a Jamaican bootlegger, I burst into the dungeon and started gulping some booze. Rubbernecking at the idiot box, I was swimming in the pool of depression. It wasn't fun at all. Suddenly, something buzzed me on. I hollered, "I got it!"

The next day, on Sunday, I cruised to Annetis. I parked the Nissan in front of the pizzeria right next to a white 2011 Chevy Impala. A boy with a brushy and shaggy blond hair hopped out of that Chevy.

"What's up, Brendan?" I blurted out casually. Brendan was working at Annetis like me. He was an Irish chappie, grinning every time I saw him. He was the type of guy you could call dickface, and he wouldn't do anything about it. I had been dissecting that kipper since I started working at Annetis. He must be one of those potheads who smokes blunt regularly!

As we started chatting about subjects that would make most people yawn, I stepped on his toes. In other words, I cut to the chase and got straight to the point. It panned out that he was a spliff lover, precisely what I had been thinking. Later after work, I met him somewhere in Elmwood Park. Brendan gave me a big flower of cannabis. The price was reasonable. Twenty bucks for the whole chunk wasn't bad damage to my wallet.

Happy as a clam, I drove the Nissan to office digpot. I used the tobacco pipe stowed in the TV stand. When I blew the dro, I felt better. The Jamaican grass brought back the smile on my face. I was chilling out like a man set free of any issues. Also, the green grass shunned the negative thoughts into a box locked in my mind.

Stoned on reefers, I started watching sitcoms such as 2 Broke Girls, Seinfeld, Everybody Loves Raymond, and those flaky guys from Impractical Jokers. Those guys from Impractical Jokers were fire. Sometimes, they acted goofily, but they were highly educated. The fact that they made a fortune by achieving stardom from what they loved to do, to me, that was genius. God bless all of them.

Toking wacky baccy and watching comedy series helped me forget the emotional pain that had been piling up in my mind. It was a considerable state at that particular moment, which I desperately needed. It brought back the flame of the candle in my life. One of the greatest comedians of all time, Robin Williams, said in one of his visits on Johnny Carson's show: "The comedy is obviously for me. It's so much cheaper than therapy."

*****

It was Sunday evening. I cashed out from Annetis and swiftly rolled the

Nissan to office digpot. Chilling out on my couch, I was indolent like an ole lion who had just eaten his dinner. Then Mike rang unpredictably. He wanted to hang out. It wasn't a bad idea, considering that we pal around once in a blue moon. He suggested dragging my ass at his flat, which was right across the street. I decided to take the shot. When I knocked on his door, Mike brayed like a tortured donkey,

"Come in!" Stepping through the entry, I peered at Mike and his Bulgarian pal, who had a flattop quiff like David Beckham. Mike's friend had a body type of soaked cucumber and a loony grin. The name of this lad was Paul. I had met him two years ago in a revel at Motel Zero. I never had any interaction with that guy.

Mike and Paul had been slightly squiffed. As soon as they peered at me, they both jumped from the couch as if they would wallop my ass. The two of them were sincerely happy to see me. Then, Paul queried,

"How you feeling, Dimitry? You look marvelous for a man with two heart surgeries." That was a delightful compliment. I needed to hear something like that. It was very important at that time.

"I am doing just fine. Thanks, Paul." Since I got sick, everyone had quizzed me,

"How you feeling?" I always responded with fine or good. I am not the type of person who would pour out all of his burdens and start grumbling like a shrewish actress who had just lost her cast in a movie for billions of dollars.

Paul complained, and croaked like those drama queen guests in Jerry Springer's show. Paul did exactly what I craved to avoid. He was moaning about how he had been laid off from his well-paying job and how his wife was the breadwinner in his family.

In the meantime, Mike tried to cheer him up by consoling and praising him as a highly educated man. Most of the time, I didn't pay attention to what Paul was complaining about. Suddenly, I heard something that made me interested. Paul mentioned that he was working as an Uber driver with his 2004 Honda. Hold on right there, dude! Did Paul just say driving for Uber with a vehicle model from 2004? The year of my Nissan is 2006. Uber hasn't accepted my driving license, but Lyft did. What Paul had divulged fired me up emotionally, and I immediately left Mike's flat. The next day could be interpreted as quite essential.

*****

Back in June 2017, I haggled a Hyundai Elantra to a Bulgarian bloke named Von. My target was to make money on the aside by selling that vehicle. It turned out that I lost a hundred dollars. I attempted to make money in the car industry, which turned into a failure.

Anyhow, I helped Von by selling the Elantra. He desperately needed a ride to start working as a pizza delivery. Two months later, Von let the cat out of the bag. He started driving with a rideshare company named Lyft. Bemused, I asked,

"Von, does Lyft accept your TVDL license?"

"Hell yeah. I will show you how it works." Both of us went to the Chicago Lyft hub. I filled out all the required red tape and watched the tutorial videos designated to guide the new drivers. A few months later, Von let me use his vehicle, a hybrid 2008 Toyota Prius, to drive for Lyft

My first passenger was from Park Ridge to downtown. A lucrative ride; good money though. The passenger was a man close to my age. We chitchatted throughout the entire ride. When I dropped him off, I pondered. Yo, that's lit. I made money while I was driving and chatting with someone. That is amazing! I was on cloud nine. Why? Because I valued the chance to make money while holding the steering wheel.

Before that, I was digging holes and bending pipes, carrying heavy materials and machines, or schlepping as a roustabout for minimum wage. Everyone who had busted their ass in the construction business know what I am talking about.

I drove via Lyft to make some greenbacks by using Von's Toyota. It was a phenomenal method to make extra money driving through the city. Unfortunately, Von sold the Prius, and I couldn't use my Geo Prizm for the rideshare gig.

*****

Back in 2019, the first Monday of March, I plowed the Nissan for a technical inspection. My ride passed the test smoothly. Then, I headed up to the Lyft hub on North Avondale where they approved all of the paperwork.

The brown Nissan was ready to roll through the White City. My father had been toiling as a cab driver since I had known my name, and here I was, a chip off the old block. A rideshare driver is not a cab driver but is quite similar. A Mexican chum working in the kitchen at Annetis had revealed his rideshare experience on how to earn more brass for fewer hours by rolling from three in the morning until eight or nine in the forenoon.

My strategy was to drive mostly in the early hours or at night, especially on weekends. That was the easiest way to learn the blueprint of Chicago. It made a lot of sense. The method of the Mexican chum became quite lucrative. Lyft, as a side hustle, was working like a charm. Therefore, I stopped using the DoorDash platform.

Cruising around the streets by using Lyft boosted my self-preservation and the level of my English. I bent over backward, helping passengers while I enjoyed talking with them. The color of the skin didn't matter. I had amazing conversations with African Americans. Also, I enjoyed talking with anyone who had trekked in America.

Every European was like a cousin to me. Muslims, citizens from India, Hispanic guys, Asians, and hundreds of Caucasian people were enjoying the conversations along. Driving for Lyft, I learned that there are plenty of phenomenal humans from all races and countries.

*****

On Tuesday, March 19, I awoke early in the morning when even the sparrows slept at that time. The Nissan streaked through the city, to the airport, transporting the early bird commuters of corporate America. They were so many.

The turnpikes and roads were desolated. It was around five in the morning. The Nissan cruised to a dwelling located on Kingsbury for a ride request. I picked up a sweet young chick from the residential building. She had chosen the share option for that ride which, as you might have already known, could pick two or more unknown passengers from different locations.

It was an early hour, and the lady wasn't showing any tendency to chat. As a rideshare driver, I had never bothered passengers who were unwilling to talk. It was pointless and could go awry. As I cruised around the city, I had another ride request. The app displayed that the passenger was at Timothy O'Toole's Pub.

When I parked at the joint, a honky guy and his chick were slowly approaching. The guy hopped into the rear seat next to the sweet girl, and his girlfriend sat adjacent to me. At that moment, the vehicle reeked like a vineyard. Holy smokes, what the heck! Hammered passengers at five in the morning on Tuesday? Duck! Those guys remind me of how I used to be in my early twenties.

The girlfriend of the honky chap was staring at me incessantly. I realized this because I could see her in my peripheral vision. What the duck! Why is she is gazing at me. She doesn't look familiar. The girl sitting next to me never took her eyes off me. It started getting gawky.

According to the Lyft app, I had to drop the sweet lady off whom I had picked up initially. The Nissan stopped at a particular street number, and the lady quickly left the vehicle. I didn't judge her. It was tough to sit next to a stoned lad ponging of a bevy like a wretched skunk. The honky chap grunted like a bummed hippo craving for lust. He slurred to his girlfriend, "Cum on, sit next to me." The chappie tapped the empty seat next to him.

His girlfriend replied apathetically,

"Naw, I am good here!"

Then, the chappie continued slurring nebulous words to his girl. He wanted her to sit next to him, and his appeals became obnoxious. His girl cried out.

"You need to get another Lyft driver. Are you okay with that?" Wait, what has she just said? I thought.

"Where are we going? What's the address?" I decided to blow the whistle and interrupted them. I was getting champing at the bit. The brown Nissan was parked for longer than five minutes at the corner of State Street, flashing the hazard lights.

"Is that your address?" I asked the man in the back seat, pointing out the display of my dummy smartphone.

"Nooo. That's ain't corre…ct the addr'ss," the man hectored. His head jerked negatively side to side. Oh Lord, please don't let him puke in my car. His girlfriend grumbled again, and this time, she became much intense.

"Dude, you need to get another driver. Are you gonna be okay?" The girl was bossy. It was dark in the car, but I successfully checked her out. She had an on-fleek short brunette haircut, the same as Wynona Ryder in the early 1990s. She slightly resembled J. Lo. She was a fit bonny lass, younger than me, around twenty-five. Her lips were entrancing. Her body type was a bit curvy, just a tad. Let's put it this way: she wasn't scrawny. Her bosom bulged on the leather jacket that she wore. I thought they were huge.

The honky chap was suppressed by the commands of his girl. He hopped out of the vehicle, leaving the twin of J. Lo alone. She started to interrogate me as if I was a guest at her late night show. She asked all the basic questions: where I was from, what my name was, and yada yada. She said that her name was Julia. She was an American broad with Columbian ancestry.

"Hold on! Isn't that chap your boyfriend?" I asked.

"Nah, I've met him a few hours ago." What the duck is happening here?

"Wait a minute. Are you telling me that this man is not your—"

"Yeah," she cut me off brusquely. "Stop talking. This is so fucking sexy. I don't like it," she chirped furiously. What the heck is this broad talking about? Julia continued staring at me. She said quietly, totally contrary to her tone a few minutes ago.

"Can I kiss you?" What? Did she say what I've heard? Does she want to kiss me just like that? How is that possible? A lot of celebrities such as Brad Pitt, Tom Cruise, etc., wouldn't be surprised. To me, a Bulgarian Lyft driver, that was something unusual. I was confused, as if she just slapped me in the face. Let's get it. Who cares! I have a dash camera, which is recording the whole conversation.

"Sure." And we pecked vehemently. While we were smooching, a noise from opening the door of the rear side distracted us.

"A'e y'u m-y Uber driv'r?" A male voice stuttered. Julia and I turned away to survey who was speaking. It was the same honky chap. We both burst into laughter.

"Where are you living?" Julia muttered, eyeballing him.

"Rogers Park," the honky man mumbled.

"Do you know where Rogers Park is?" Julia hollered. Dude! This gal has lotta balls to scream like that. I don't give a duck. It is getting annoying! The Nissan headed up to North Lake Shore. The honky chap failed to pronounce his residential address. He could barely talk. That was how hammered he was.

"T'ke this exit. I wanna get off fr'm the car," the honky man slurred. I hit the Fullerton ramp from Lakeshore Drive.

"I'm goin' to su' L'ft. You'll see. You can't mess around with me." He wanted to sue Lyft because we tried to give him a ride to his pad. Perhaps he got mad because his lady had chosen me.

Waiting at the light, the honky chap hopped out and slammed the door pugnaciously. He stepped in front of the hood, showing me a finger, and I pointed it out to my dash camera. Smile, wanker!

"Where do you want me to drop you off?" I asked Julia.

"Home," she said.

"Okay…where is your home?"

"Just drive." There was a pause. "You don't want to come?"

I was bewildered. For a second, my face froze. I couldn't say anything. Does she want me in her place? How come! This is too easy! Something is going on here. She can't just say that to a stranger, can she?

"Answer me! Yes or no? What's taking so long? Say it! Am I too chubby for you or what?" Julia bellowed grudgingly.

"Okay. Okay, relax. Let's go." We kissed a bunch. Her alluring lips were like those of Scarlett Johansson's (I guess).

The Nissan plowed somewhere up to Portage Park. While we were rolling, I played jams such as "Sex with Me" by Rihanna; "Chi Town," a track by Phor; "Permissions" by Ro James; "When We" by Tank; and many more. Her taco was as wet as Lake Michigan. Julia was lecherous. Her passion turned me on faster than a New York minute. Perhaps she doesn't live with gangs? My inner voice asked.

Julia dwelled in a one-bedroom apartment that looked immaculate. She sprawled on her bed naked and whispered,

"Bag it up and take me now or leave!" she bawled surly, and I jumped on her like that would be my last hunka-chunka. Gosh, her titties' worth a million dollars! After thirty minutes of boning, we passed out.

Two hours later, she woke me up and grumbled,

"You should leave." Ah, I hate when the broads talk like that. In other words, she meant, "Get the duck outta here".

Before I hit the hike, I got her phone number. She gave me the cold shoulder. Anyway, I was joyful. I didn't make any decent money that day, but I got laid for free with a charming Columbian one night-standing chick. We did the wild mambo thirty minutes after we met. Isn't that insane?

When I left her apartment, I was pondering. Man, I love this job!

*****

While I was driving through the city using the rideshare gig, I was trying to get in shape at Oakley. Blowing a bit of wacky baccy before commencing training was unwise. My health condition was getting worse. During the time, I had that bad medical report while I was sparring with pro fighters, most people would have already been in the hospital.

My first round of sparring was fine. The second was horrible. The heart valve didn't function properly, and I was choking. The deficiency of oxygen made my whole body idle while sparring. It was the same result when someone would kick me in the nut sack. The pain was less, but the result was indistinguishable.

I needed a second to catch my breath. Unfortunately, that second was enough for the sparring guys to paint my visage in red. Waterfalls of blood ran down my nostrils. That wasn't a big surprise. What puzzled me at that time was that I couldn't get back in an athletic shape.

Days and weeks through March and April, I jogged on the treadmill to bring back my speed. Alas, I couldn't jog longer than a few minutes. While I was exercising, my subconscious was screaming. Come on, you old geezer. Move your arse!

Regardless of what my mind had ordered, my heart was pumping irregularly and I had to stop jogging. Otherwise, I would stumble on the ground like a foolish fartknocker. The failure of bringing my athletic speed had gotten me bent out of shape. Once again, the murky storm of depression arose in my head.

The letdown threw me into a dark pit and instilled a hatred growing in my subconscious. The human brain is like a vehicle's steering wheel and all the electronics, and the human heart is the engine. You can't go anywhere if the engine of your car broke down. My life was going down to the tubes. I was getting seriously aggravated. Boxing was everything to me. I used to breathe boxing gloves and sweat from sparring six times in a week. Boxing crept into my world by bringing the ultimate combination of calmness and supreme power. Also, it became a faith and a religion that had developed a strong mind-set and composure in my portfolio.

I wasn't prepared to bear with the fact that I couldn't box anymore. It was like something inside of me was dead already. That statement bothered me. The kismet had tossed me a raw deal. It was tough and painful to deal with heartache. Regardless of this frustration, I had to brazen it out. I was forced to pull the plug of my main pastime, and that caused me to swim in an ocean of anxiety. It discouraged my ambition to live.

In the early days of May 2019, I canceled my membership at Oakley. Depressing thoughts urged me to guzzle more booze night after night. I was back in the world of drinking alcohol.

One particular evening, I was guzzling bevy with indifference. An hour later, I pressed a Glock 17 against my temple and pulled the trigger. Do it! Bam! Dimitry fell onto the leather couch. His brain was halfway exposed. A lake of gore had poured from his head. His eyeballs remained open like the ones of a stuffed deer head, hanging on the wall in a hunter's house. The shot roared through the entire dwelling of Wehrman.

It was not a huge loss; just another oaf kicked the bucket. That was the whole scene pictured in my mind while I was pouring a Smirnoff Ice, then taking a melatonin and blowing dro till I passed out. The following morning, an unpleasant hangover woke me up and did melt the bitterness, just a tad.

*****

On the weekends after work, I palled around with my boy Erik Sobczak. Sporadically, I hauled my ass to his California ranch located in Chicago. Erik had introduced me to his buddies who were heavy winos. We had a ball. It was fun to hang out with them.

For the past few weeks, I was antsy about what could happen on my next visit at Loyola. I needed to hang loose. On Friday, the first day of May, the brown Nissan parked at Erik's house. As we chatted, he said,

"Follow me. I'll show you something." We crept through the stairway leading to the basement. At his laundry room, Erik pulled out a valise. Two guns were hiding there. One of them was a .357 Magnum and a 9mm.

"Dude, this is lit! How long have you owned those weapons?"

"It's been a while," he uttered.

"Yo! I have never shot with a real firearm. Do you know any shooting range nearby?" my words were spoken swiftly like a jazzed boy on his first trip to Disneyland.

"Yeah, man, I know a few places around here."

"Dude! Let's go this Sunday. What do you think?"

"What time?"

"Noon?"

"Yeah, noon is fine," Erik replied.

On Sunday, Erik cruised his black Mercedes to pick me up. We headed up to a place named Midwest Guns & Pistol Range located in the outskirt called Lyons. When we burst straight into the building, I was in awe. Wow, I've never seen so many guns in one place. It's frigging amazing!

A friendly hillbilly had checked the IDs. We purchased around 150 bullets. With a hundred of Erik's stash, we had roughly 250 cartridges. We went to the shooting zone where the noisy bastards were blasting the gunshots. Erik went first.

When he started shooting, I was flabbergasted. This fringing batka is shooting like a police officer! The word batka could be translated as douchebag in Bulgarian. Then, he conducted a short lecture on how to use his firearms. The .357 Magnum had a powerful kickback. I had to clench steady using both hands. I heard a story of a bimbo trying to shoot with that weapon. She thought that wasn't a big deal. When she pulled the trigger, the recoil was so powerful that it broke her nose. The .357 was a boisterous mother flower. I could hear the nasty sound even while using the shooting headphones.

The 9mm was lighter but tireless. That pistol had seventeen rounds in each clip. Great weapon, easy to use. My shots weren't as precise as the batka's, although, I could hit the shooting target. After half an hour of shooting, Erik declared,

"Dude, I'll go outside for a quick puff. Will you be fine on your own?"

"Yeah, for shizzle, my nizzle." I was portraying face, saying. "Dude, are you kidding me? What do you think can happen?" Erik left the shooting range. Now is the time! An insurmountable voice had whispered in my eardrums. Don't stay idle like a Queen's Guard. You wanted a chance. Here, I am giving the chance that you've been asking for. DO it! The voice in my sick head gave the order.

I loaded the .357 Magnum and pointed it at my temple. DO it! There was a ponderous pause, DO it, I said. My finger was slowly patting the trigger. NOOO! You frigging airhead. Are you numbnuts! What's matter with you? Put that gun on the tray. What are you doing? Why are you tempted to kill yourself? 'Cuz a chick that you've liked put you in the friend zone? Who gives a damn? She doesn't deserve you as a man! Put that gun down, you nutcase.

The two different voices spoke to me as if a little devil and angel were sitting on each side of my shoulders. Of course, I listened to the latter whisper. It was pointless. I placed the firearm on the board. Why should I end my life for some derogatory, shrewish person who had always criticized me? The greatest warrior never surrenders. She is under the bridge, and whatever I do is none of her business.

I still had feelings for Klara, but those emotions had been colorless. The whole nine yards that linked to her had been erased and it did work. I had no other intentions or zeal to meet the fiddle girl again. Klara was water under the bridge, and I didn't have any interest to meeting her. Why? Because I didn't have anything to say to her. Hey, Klara, how have you been? Are you doing okay? Fine. Well, listen, I got to go 'cuz I can't look at your frigging face anymore. Have a great life. Bye! God bless her heart. She did a lot for me, without any question. I wish her nothing but bright days.

"What up, dude?" the batka asked, reeking of horrendous tobacco.

"Nothing, man! Waiting for you." Actually, it happened a lot. It was quite a lurid and crucial moment in my life, a moment when I reinstated my strong common sense. At that instant, I announced to myself, "You are going to be okay. You will go to the hospital, and everything will be fine. You will live healthy again. You will have a loving family. You will enjoy the great spirit of your life". I felt those words came as a promise from the master of the universe. Joel Osteen wrote, "A setback is simple setup for a great comeback."

This thought of mine always made me ponder,

"In front of God, I shall confess the mess which brought me huge stress. I guess life is like playing chess: Any move could slip you either to success or to the lethal mattress."

When Erik dropped me at Wehrman, I was in awe, happy like a man who had just become a father.

*****

A week after I fired with Erik's guns, my mind reached a firm decision. I am going to the hospital, and I will whack this crap off. I've done it once, and I will do it again. The Lord send me guidance, and now is the time. He had also restored my confident mind-set. I wanted to get it done. I wanted to live again.

On Thursday, May 9, an Uber dropped my ass at the ER of Loyola. It was ten in the morning when the caretaker ushered me to the ICU. A male Hispanic physician, wearing an upscale haircut like Justin Bieber's and stocky body resembling Jason Statham, pussyfooted through the drapes. He said.

"Hello, Mr. Salchev. I am Dr. Matias. I'd like to check your heart. Just a second."

He pulled out a stethoscope and started listening to my heart. His grimacing face alluded to what could be the next step. I took a deep sigh. Then the doctor continued,

"You have a strong murmur, Mr. Salchev. Tomorrow, we will schedule a transesophageal echocardiogram (TEE) to check the function of your heart, okay?"

I only nodded, and he departed. After the TEE test had been processed, a few doctors tromped in the ward. All of them stared at me with compassion. One of them, resembling Mark Ruffalo, stepped over and uttered,

"Mr. Salchev, based on observation of the TEE, we have concluded that you need another open-heart surgery."

"Another open-heart surgery?" Fired up by the shocking news I almost shrieked.

"Yes, I'm sorry. I know we had spoken about the procedure called TAVR. Unfortunately, it's too late for this procedure. Your heart shrank, and we must execute another open-heart surgery."

After the crew of sawbones left, I was chewing over the recent seismic updates. Another frigging open-heart surgery! What the duck are you expecting? A boxing reward? Since you had been snorting white chalk after Klara dumped you. I am not surprised! It's my mistake. There is no space for an excuse, and now, I will pay the price for my foolish behavior.

I didn't brazen it out very maturely, and I had to face the consequences. I had pushed my luck way too far, and I screwed up. An eventual open-heart surgery could be translated as an unpleasant venture. I put my life in danger. Who would know what the odds were?

Two hours later, a gorgeous lady in her late thirties swaggered to the unit. Her broad grin could be spotted from a distance. Her golden hair was glowing like a rainbow. Her foxy muzzle was enthralling. She was a social worker. She clarified that Loyola couldn't perform the upcoming surgery because I didn't have insurance. She handed me papers presenting Cook County Hospital. The lady elucidated that since I lived in the same county, I could visit that hospital. I thanked her, emitting a pure gratitude. It was a blessing when someone gave you straightforward directions. Two hours later, an Uber dropped me off at Wehrman.

Loyola is an amazing hospital. They had saved my life twice already. Alas, I couldn't stay there any longer, not until I straightened out the obstacle with my health insurance. The closest location of Cook County was at Austin Health Clinic Center.

In the second week of May, I pussyfooted through the walkin's registering cubicles of Austin Health Center. I needed to spoke with an internal medicine physician who would render a referral to see a cardiologist. Holding the referral, I rang John H. Stroger Jr.'s hospital to schedule an appointment with a specialist. The operator shared that the nearest available date would be open by the end of August. When I heard that, I almost fainted on the floor. Ah crap! How the duck could I wait two more months!

"Sir, if you don't feel good, the fastest way to get in the hospital is through the ER," the operator advised. Well, for the past twelve months, I had been visiting the ER about six times. My common sense suggested sticking to my plan and waiting for the next two months.

My strategy was to visit the cardiologist who could set me up a referral to be admitted to the non-intensive care unit until the doctors sorted out how to proceed. Besides, I needed to save more money. I decided following up with the next appointment. I will be fine! It made me nervous, thinking about the imminent surgery. Who would not be?

*****

While I was trying to make a game plan for my health, in the meantime, my birthday was coming. The surgery is inevitable, so screw it! Let's loosen up the string tightened around my neck and get wild. I will call my boy, the batka, and ask him to have my birthday party at his place. He wouldn't mind it.

The batka agreed to organize my birthday party at his house. On June 8, Saturday, a year after my first surgery, I was blessed to have the chance to commemorate my birthday. The weather was gorgeous. The revel was hitting its climax. Many of my buddies stopped by, and later, we gallivanted to some nightclubs. We were scarfing cheap scotch at a joint with a name that couldn't be defined. Then my subconscious spoke. Enjoy your time drinking and snorting, you frigging goofball, 'cuz soon you won't have chances like that. Enjoy! We ended up the night at a gentlemen's club named Scores. I was gawking at the peelers like a hungry coyote.

"I can't be a master of the domain. Can't take it anymore," I uttered to Boohba in office digpot, and looked forward, hooking up with any available trollop. An hour later, a Columbian hoochie mama pussyfooted to the office digpot. She was a breathtaking gal in her mid-twenties with curly brunette hair. I couldn't take my eyes off her tits. When I grabbed them, it felt like a bag of marshmallows or a balloon filled with water. The hooker said they were real, but who cares. Her visage was sexy, like a top model's. The hunka-chunka had the ultimate gratification. She was the only hoe who had given me genuine pleasure. She said her name was Claudia, but only God knows what her real name was. Besides, I didn't give a damn. Claudia filled my appetite, and around five in the morning, I nodded off like a tired turtle.

*****

After the wild shindig, I decided to throw the towel and go cold turkey. Perhaps one of the best decisions that I have made in my life was to avoid the ravenous thoughts of my old friend, the coco. I must direct my mind to something entirely different, but what? Cannot box anymore! Not before the imminent surgery. Eric talked about a man named Corey Wayne. He had written a book called How to Be the 3% of Man.

The script is designated to help you how to understand women. When I was reading the paperback, my mind got blown. This book is Gucci! It's frigging awesome! I breathed the ink of that book. For the length of a month, I read it around fifteen times because I wanted to possess and own the entire material.

That book gave me all the answers that I had been asking myself. It also reaffirmed my composure in chatting with girls in general. I did not completely agree with the entire manuscript, although, it threw me a bone in a very crucial moment in my life. Rolling via Lyft was a great way to meet chicks. Thrilled with the procured acknowledgment, I tried to practice what I learned.

At the end of June, I picked up a female passenger from O'Hare. It was Friday, around six in the evening. The girl was heading up to Hyde Park. The rush hour was at the higher point, and the ride took an hour and a half. That gave us a plethora of time to chitchat. As soon as she hopped in the vehicle, the lady never stopped yapping. My mind was alerting. Something is happening here!

We chatted pretty much throughout the entire ride. The lady introduced herself as Alexandra. She was a brunette cutie-pie. Her eyes were enthralling. By the end of the ride, Alexandra was moaning about how hungry she was. I said,

"Let's go eat something 'cuz I am hungry too." Alexandra goggled as if I had just said, "I will give you ten grand to date me tonight."

She was bewildered at the top of the hill.

"But...uh... I'm not dressed," Alexandra stuttered.

"Well, you look great to me," grinning, I asserted

"Oookay then." She wasn't sure what to say. She had to agree with my proposal. We headed to Bar Louie, which was right next to her dwelling. Three hours later, I ended up sprawled at her bed. Her studio looked chaotic. There were clothes thrown haphazardly at the entire place, and it was frowsy and slovenly. It looked like a nasty hobo shack.

Her rear bumper was bigger than the state of Illinois. Alexandra was a messed-up chick, and after she gave me hoochie-woochie, I had to give her the cold shoulder. I never got back to her phone calls. Hopefully, my wife won't kick me out of the condo because I'm sharing this story with you.

Driving back to office digpot, my thoughts were. This book works! Tomorrow, I will practice what I've just learned.

The entire month of July, I tried to speak pretty much with all of my female passengers who were willing to communicate. At the end of the month, I collected ten phone numbers. I was flummoxed. They all shunned me without any response. Well, who cares? I was learning. Corey Wayne wrote, "If a girl dumped you, don't take it personal."

*****

It had been six months since I started driving with Lyft. I mastered my driving abilities while I was rolling across the entire city. Operating my vehicle became as comfy as watching a movie and spreading my legs on the leather couch in office digpot. Hypothetically, one of the best ways to acknowledge any part of the city was to shuttle via Lyft.

My father told me once, "You must always watch your vehicle, or someone will smash in you." I tipped my hat on his advice. It became quite helpful. I had to look for the blind spots. Other drivers could cut me off by switching the lanes. Also I was incessantly checking the cars behind me, the one each side and the one in front. Driving through the city, you had to be cautious and watch for bicycles and pedestrians. The cyclists would not watch you. They would think. Ha! He is a driver. He should see me! Yeah, but if you were not alert for your life, no one could protect you. The government might give you a check, but it would not bring back your lost leg or arm. Knock on wood!

When I first came to Chicago, I asked myself, "Why are the people here honking so much?" Today as a rideshare driver in Chicago, I'm still asking the same question.

Rolling on the roads of Chicago, I saw many impatient drivers, cyclists, and pedestrians who would not obey the traffic rules and often cross on red lights. Chicago is a fast-paced city, the baby version of New York. I'm asking, "Is it worth risking your life for running a red light?"

My strategy was always keeping distance from other vehicles, especially when the roads had been jammed, and never speeding unnecessarily. There were a lot of reckless chauffeurs, especially on the weekends. A load of douchebags was waiting on a green light for more than ten seconds, swiping on their smartphones.

To make money by driving with Lyft or Uber, you have to be very patient, especially when you have passengers in the vehicle. Also, you cannot be screaming and talking trash while some schlepper makes inept blunder by cutting you off when he switched lanes.

As a rideshare driver, I had to operate smoothly and avoid all of those potholes. In some streets of Chicago, they were bigger than my ass. Rolling in downtown or any area in the city, I had to be slow (not like a snail), but generating equilibrium pace.

Regularly, a bunch of loony pinheads would speed in the city with their sports cars. "Where are you going, mother flower? See you at the light, asshole!" Most of the time, they waited next to me at the traffic lights. Many of them gave me the dirty look for whatever reason.

Speeding your vehicle often leads you to make risky decisions. It happens to all of us. We should minimize those moments for the sake of our lives. In my driver's retrospect, I always tried to be tolerant and let others go first. Chicago drivers always wanted to be first, and that was fine with me.

Many drivers need to understand that we must share those roads, streets, boulevards, etc. When we speed up our vehicle, we are pushing our luck getting into car accidents or even worse, ending up in caskets. I might sound annoying, but I had lived and suffered enough to value life and praise God.

Once you hop in your vehicle, you are sitting on the chair, circled by assembled and welded pieces of metal. Cars may be worth an arm and a leg, but what is the cost of a smashed vehicle? I am not telling you how to drive or trying to give a lecture. That is your choice. I am just sharing my experience behind the steering wheel.

Gradually, I became an undisputed five-star driver—not 4.99, which had been displayed as five stars to users. Five stars meant that on weekly reports, I didn't have even a four-star review. Lyft drivers were independent contractors. However, when a passenger embarked in my vehicle, he became my boss till the ride was over.

I would turn the AC on and off; roll the windows; and put the baggage in the trunk, or grocery products, walkers, etc. There were some exceptions. For instance, I drove a man in his forties. The GPS guided me to take a one-way street, and I hit it. Then, the man asked, "Do you mind if you make a U-turn 'cuz I don't know that street?" My eyeballs boggled as if he was speaking Chinese to me. How can I make a U-turn on a one-way street while I am in the middle of the road already? Who does that?

"Sir, I am afraid I cannot make a U-turn here because it's illegal, and we could run into an accident. I am sorry. It's my bad. Next time, I will take whichever road you prefer." The man wasn't happy. I tried my best to drop him off at his destination. In the end, he gave me a tip. Sometimes, passengers requested to perform U-turns in risky streets. It was a challenge that I took, but not on one-way streets.

Some white American passengers were throwing shade at me and jeered about my English. My time was too expensive to be wasted on these people.

I couldn't let someone eat a bucket of boneless wings dipped with barbecue sauce in my car or some pothead smoke trees or drink bevy. I drove a load of plastered passengers. It was a tough assignment. It could be good and, at the same, very bad. To drive drunk people means that you have to bite the bullet and try to bear with them as much as you can. Sometimes, they started being aggressive, then you had to decide whether to continue or cancel the ride. In the end, that was my job. That was how I had been making my money, and I frigging loved it.

The brown Nissan panned out to be the Holy Grail, a moneymaker. I worshipped that vehicle. Twice a week, the car wash was mandatory. Once a month, I cruised to my auto mechanic, Gill. We became best friends, not because we needed to hang out but because the Nissan needed maintenance. Making thousands of miles required protection, such as oil, brakes, pads, tires, etc. It was natural, like how a man would go to take a dump.

Gill was an outgoing and dexterous person. He had never attempted to stitch me up. That was why I always work with him. We did a lot of business together. He trusted me. Sometimes, I didn't have enough money to pay him. Regardless, he did the labor because I always paid him back.

*****

On Sunday, August 4, Eric Sobczak and I headed to a dating event organized by a web portal called Chicago First Dates. That event started at a bar named Burwood Tap located in Lincoln Park.

I loved those events. I always had a chance to encounter new friends, which could lead to boning. When we walked in, that joint was bursting at the seams. A bunch of single guys and chicks were chatting.

We sat by the bar spread at the end of the joint. Holding a glass of Jameson on the rocks, I had started to fish those female mackerels. After a few minutes of mingling, I bumped in on a Mexican gal. She was dishy. Her hair had a bronze color, and her tan was the color of a chocolate. Her body was enthralling. I liked her a lot. That was why I tried to implement what I had learned from Corey Wayne.

We chatted for a while. As soon as she gave her phone number, she left the bar. The reason why was that she was hitting the curb and that she was getting out of hand by speaking oddly and mixing Spanish with English. Some Mexican guy helped her to keep balance, and they both left.

A few minutes later, I bumped into another gal. She was a Chinese beauty with an athletic body, dressed up like a Japanese senior in high school. Her name was Mia. We yapped for about ten minutes. Then, I introduced my boy Erik to Mia, and they haven't stopped talking since. My mind said. Yeah! Okay, whatever. Who gives a damn? There are many more to score.

Out of the blue, another Asian started talking to me about something difficult to understand. Her black dress was marvelous, accentuating her slender body. Her visage was round like a hoop. She said that her name was Lei. She was a chatterbox. Her front door never closed. She pursued me like a puppy following his master.

It turned out that Mia and Lei were besties. By nine thirty, Erik slid off, and I chitchatted with Lei and Mia for around half an hour. They jotted my phone number and took the hike. Joyful as a freshman after losing his virginity, I cruised to office digpot.

Four days later, I decided to contact Lei. Also, Erik divulged that Mia had reached out to him. I took Lei for a few dates. Lei revealed that she was a scientist. She did a bunch of research at the University of Chicago. Her education was in medicine, specializing in gastroenteritis. What an irony! I have two heart surgeries, and now I am dating a doctor! After the second date, I took Lei to office digpot. When she saw the incision in my chest, she almost fainted.

"What the heck happened to you?" she asked, nonplussed. The following hour, I had to spill out all of my burdens. Usually, I would not disclose my health condition to someone who I just met. But we were dating, and she had already seen me naked.

The wild mambo was funky, kind of peculiar. It was like I was humping a dead fish. The Asian scientist would never know that I had installed a hidden camera, recording our sexual relationship. Two weeks after we started seeing each other, Lei promised to sort out why I hadn't been able to sleep since my first surgery. A few days later, she asserted that I had a severe heart failure. Also, I was overwhelmed by everything I had been going through and about what was coming next.

*****

August of 2019 was a tough month; the business was slow. My driving stamina didn't look good. Intermittently, I had to stop my vehicle somewhere into a safe zone to turn off the Lyft app because I needed to hold my breath. Those urgent intermissions riled me up. I couldn't drive people while I wasn't capable of operating my vehicle.

The heart failure forced me to work fewer hours, which meant less money. However, I felt blessed to be poor in one of the richest countries in the world. While I was having shortness of breath, I remembered how I drove Mr. George to a sports bar somewhere in the city a few weeks ago. We had a blast discussing the hindsight of boxing events and the variation of pro boxers. Then, something popped up in my mind. I recalled a specific moment when Papa Bomb said,

"I am thinking to write my own book!"

At the next second, I felt how my countenance changed drastically. My eyes opened widely. A voice hollered in my sick head. Holy smokes! Why don't cha write your memoir? That instant was of pure epiphany. Jazzed by the enlightened idea, I embarked on this project. I had never known any editors or publishers. That didn't mean I should quit. God gave me the zeal and intensity to write this book.

*****

On Saturday, the twenty-fourth, I stopped by Erik's house to see what he was up to. The batka was drinking Rakia. Also he was listening to Bulgarian folk music called chalga. He loved that chiz. I found his euphoria extremely amusing. I had never seen any American enjoying the traditional Bulgarian music as much as he did. The batka said,

"Come on, man. Do you want something to drink? Beer, Rakia, anything you want."

I looked at him and thought. Should I drink or not?

"I don't know, man. I shouldn't drink. Okay, whatever. Give me a beer. Only one, though." Thirty minutes later, I drank four bottles of Modelo. We chuckled a bunch. Then Erik offered,

"Let's go to Turtle's house. He is having a party tonight."

"All right, dude. Let's roll."

Around fifteen minutes of driving, Erik parked his Mercedes on the side street next to Turtle's house.

"Why is it so quiet?" I asked Erik.

"Who the fuck knows? Let's go!" As we burst straight into his house, we saw Turtle working in one of his hot rod cars. That was his job. He tinkered on vehicles for fifteen hours a day. Turtle was a friendly and savvy guy. He was born in the U.S., but his ancestry came from South America. I met him at Hyper when we sparred.

"What up, guys?" Turtled quizzed, baffled to see us.

Erik and I exchange a glimpse. Then, the batka uttered,

"Man, I thought that you were having a party here?"

"Nah, I cancelled it. I am busy with this car." Then Turtle looked at us like Arnold Schwarzenegger acting in the movie Terminator.

"Okay, you mother flowers. Give me ten minutes. I'm taking a shower, and we are going out," Turtle asserted. He could work more than fifty hours per week. When we would talk about Saturday night, he was down for anything. We were of the same breed. Ten minutes later, I peeked at Turtle, who was processing a freebase on his round table.

"What are you doing up there, Turtle?" I asked. He looked at me with a face displaying, "What the hell do you think I am doing?"

"Don't do it! Don't cha even thinking about it. I know you've had two heart surgeries!"

"Yeah, but I am going to the hospital anyway, so let me take a look at what you've got."

KABOOM! I hovered two chubby rails as fast as Bruce Lee could kick. Then, I closed my eyes. AH, what a relief! The pain is gone! At that time, I thought it was fine, but today I can say it was absolutely wrong.

Erik and I hopped in the Mercedes and gallivanted to a few joints. Turtle had gone somewhere in that night. I didn't have a clue where he went. Driving around the city, Erik offered,

"Let's go to the Serbian place in Lincoln Park."

"Oh man. The place we got in a fight last year?"

"Yeah, come on. Just for a few drinks. It will be fun."

"Are you nuts? Dude, I am not sure if that is a good idea." After a quick pause, I continued, "Well, whatever. Who gives a damn? Let's go." Ten minutes later, we burst straight into the Serbian restaurant. That place was fascinating. It was packed with a bunch of young Europeans who were having fun. Every employee was amiable. The service was friendly. The prices were reasonable and the atmosphere was delightful. A drop-dead gorgeous gal wearing an upscale dress had us seated at the very end of that bistro. We both guzzled a Serbian moonshine version of Rakia. I chugged those shots like a Russian squaddie on his first vacation for the past year.

A few Serbian guys occupied the table next to us. One of them had a body like a hippo. The other two were scrawny. Out of the blue, the waitress toted us two more shots of Serbian Rakia.

"We haven't ordered those," I exclaimed to her, baffled.

"It's from the guys next to you!" I looked at them, and the big hippo rose his hand holding a glass and said, "Cheers."

At the next moment, we started chatting with those Serbian guys. They were very friendly. The next moment, I opened my eyes, and I was very confused. I was in the brown Nissan parked on the driveway of Erik's house. What in Jesus name happened! Why am I sitting in my car, holding a glass with beer? The last thing I remember was when I spoke with that big hippo and… What the heck happened?

A horrible feeling transfixed my entire body. It was the same feeling when you did something wrong, but you couldn't remember what it was because you had blacked out. I looked at the rearview mirror, and I saw that my left cheek was swollen. I checked my shirt, and it was soaked with blood.

Where is this blood coming from? What time is it? It was daylight already, somewhere around forenoon. That was my presumption. Where is my phone? In the next minute, I searched the entire vehicle. Unfortunately, there was no sign of my phone. I tried to get into Erik's house, but it was locked. That wasn't a good sign. He never locked his house on weekends, not when he was inside. I must find out what happened last night. And my phone…ah man, I lost my phone. Now I need to find a Metro PCS store working on Sunday. Good luck, you frigging dipstick!

I rolled on Mannheim Road. After a few minutes of cruising, I bumped into a Metro PCS store where I purchased another Android for a decent price. Thank God! All of my contacts had been saved in my Gmail account. Leaving the mobile store, I immediately rang Erik.

"Yo, Erik, what happened last night? Are you all right? I don't remember anything."

"Yeah, man, I am fine. Come to my house, and I will explain." When I cruised to his house, he said,

"Man, you were a wreck! Like Jack the lad, you know. You started fighting with the guys who were buying us drinks."

"Fighting? You mean like a real fight?"

"Nah, just screaming at them. I had to close the check, and we left the restaurant. You were screaming on the streets like an insane crackhead. Then you started being aggressive on me, and you stood in a boxing stance. You threw a cross and hit me right here"—he showed me the right side of his ear—"then I swung a hook and knocked you out cold. I had to drive you to my house and left you outside. I couldn't let you in my house, not like that."

"Dude, I am terribly sorry. I don't know why I acted like that. There is no explanation for my attitude. I literally don't recall anything. I apologize."

"It's all good, man. I know you've been going through a lot. It could happen to anybody."

Erik was staring at me with his quirky eyes. I felt disgraceful and ashamed because of what I did. I couldn't remember anything. I blacked out really bad. It was against all sorts of ethics. That forced me to a conclusion. No more drinking! At least, no more chugging and mixing multiple liquors like that. I had been to that resto bar twice, and both of them panned out to be a mess.

I had no intentions of doing some clumsy blunders like that. Why should I? I loved that place. It was a wonderful joint. We were supposed to grab a few drinks and have a blast, not to argue with everyone out there. Where was this anger coming from?

My behavior was out of hand, categorized as unacceptable. There was no excuse, and I was so grateful and lucky that we didn't wind up in a worse position (getting arrested, for example). The thought of the upcoming surgery haunted me incessantly despite disguising myself from my friends and pretending that nothing was going on.

*****

Lei and I roamed to the Italian festival spread across a few blocks in Little Italy. It was a sweltering day in August, and we had fun. On that day, she grumbled something vague that I couldn't comprehend. It had been four days since I saw her, and she didn't return my phone call, which was unusual.

Her silence was speaking loudly. Something is going on here. She always gets back on the horn. Her phone is glued to her palms for fifteen hours a day. She has those wireless phone chargers buried in her purse everywhere she goes. That was what my mind deciphered. I knew that something would snap in the near future. I had to step on her toes and make her spill the bean.

For some undefined reason, she got bent out of shape about something. I didn't do anything wrong. The only thing that I had done was to listen to her and ask questions. There was something that Lei wanted to tell me, but her insecurities implied that she wasn't ready to talk.

On August 26, Lei and I headed up to Stroger Hospital for the following appointment with a cardiologist. The moment I had been waiting for the last two months. The name of the doctor was Malhotra. Lei was phenomenal. She spoke to the cardiologist as if they were colleagues. Lei revealed a profound report describing my heart issues to Dr. Malhotra.

The cardiologist announced,

"He needs to have an echocardiography exam. I must know what I am dealing with. The exam can be scheduled in the following two months.

"Okay," I said like a confused yokel. No frigging way. Can't wait for another two months. I had no choice. I must go to the ER. When we left the hospital, Lei didn't stopped talking about the next appointment and yada yada. She didn't have a clue of what I had already been thinking.

We both headed to the Wehrman building, and I gave her Boohba. Lei didn't mind taking care of Boohba. She loved her. Someone needed to keep an eye on my lizard while I was at the hospital, and Lei was an appropriate option.

On Friday, August 13, Lei and I rolled to Milwaukee to spend a quiet weekend away from the city. I needed a short break before I would pussy-foot to the ER of John. H. Stroger Hospital. Then God knows what would happen. We booked a room in Comfort Inn located in West Park Place. During the baby vacation, both of us didn't have any argy-bargy.

We wandered to the Milwaukee Zoo. It was the first time I had been in a zoo since I was ten. That was an enormous zoo. We spent an hour and a half exploring the entire park. There were so many animals that I snapped more than three hundred pictures. I am not the type of guy who likes to take pictures. The bottom line was that we had a ball.

Lei never stopped talking about those animals. I felt like I was dating Amazon's Alexa. Lei was the most intelligent girl I had ever dated. There was no question about that, and I couldn't be angry for what she was, period. I kept thinking about what she had to tell me. It was a matter of time when she would let the cat out of the bag. This theory was based on my psychological report.

Chapter 33

It was Friday, September 13. I attempted to work using the Lyft app. An hour later, the shortness of breath got worse, and I stopped working. Around seven in the evening, I headed to the batka's crib to speak with him about something fundamental. When I burst into his house, the Chalga music was blasting out loud like a live karaoke event.

"What's crackalackin', man! You want a beer?" the batka mouthed.

"Nah! Listen, I need to ask you for a huge favor."

"Yeah, man. Go ahead."

"Tomorrow, I need you to drive me to the ER of Stroger Hospital." My face was as solemn as some congressman who had been charged with child molestation.

"Sure, man. No problem. What time would you like to be there?" Then, I whispered something that made Erik burst into laughter.

*****

Around half-past eleven, the batka had picked me up from Wehrman. We headed to a plaza located on Cumberland Road. A few minutes later, Erik had tucked his Mercedes into the parking lot.

"It's this door out there. I'll be at Dunkin." Erik had pointed out a door at the corner of that plaza. I pussyfooted in, an Asian lady as short as a first-grade student in her late fifties welcomed me.

"Here, this doa," she chirped, emitting a strong Asian accent. I went through the door. There was a tiny unit. Inside, there was a bed for massages. Two minutes later, a Japanese gal in her mid-twenties came to me.

"Hi. Take your clothes off," the Asian chick uttered. She said that her name was Yo-Yo. She had a black off-shoulder dress. Yo-Yo washed me everywhere and gave me a sweet massage. After that, we did the hunka-chunka. Her body was priceless. Her breasts were as breathtaking as a highly paid porn star. Yo-Yo had won the award for the queen of lollipops. It was something that I needed on the way to the emergency. Thirty minutes later, Erik and I were on I-290 Eisenhower. The batka dropped me off at the ER of John. H. Stroger Jr. Hospital. There it is! The moment that I had been waiting for finally came. A feeling of premonition kicked in at my jugular veins around the scruff area.

I slowly pussyfooted through the sliding door of the entrance. Everyone in the ER was moaning, groaning, grunting, and coughing. I was the only one who grinned because of the recent visit with Yo-Yo. My grin didn't last long. It gradually faded in the first twenty minutes when the heart failure made me feel sick again.

An African American man in his early forties wobbled a few feet away from me. He looked like he had received a few hard blows from Julian Jackson. Somehow, he remained balanced. His eyelids were barely open, and I could only see his eyeballs. He couldn't talk properly, just growling like a hungry raccoon. He looked literally like a zombie. Perhaps, he was a speedball lover, a junkie overdosed by using smack. I had been seeing those zombies passing through some bad neighborhoods in the city of Chicago. I had been waiting at the ER for seven hours straight. No water, no food. Nothing.

"Dimitry!" a nurse hollered my name. Hallelujah! I was waiting at the ER from one to eight in the evening. I was breathless, trying to catch up with the fast pace of the nurse. A drop-dead gorgeous chick wearing a gold ponytail approached me. She was an ER physician. She pulled out her stethoscope and listened to my heartbeat.

"Oh my God! Hey, Brad, come here for a moment!" A young man stepped over and started listening to the beats of my heart. At the next moment I opened my eyes, I was lying on the medical stretcher with my hands and legs tied to the sidebars.

"WHERE AM I? WHY AM I TIED?" I bellowed hysterically. A bunch of doctors and nurses loomed in front of me like cruel bats.

"Hello, Mr. Salchev. You are at Rush Hospital. Don't worry. Everything will be fine. We are here to take care of you," a man wearing a funky quiff had uttered.

"Why am I at Rush?" What the heck is going on?" I grumbled impatiently like a cranky woman having her period.

"You are very sick, Mr. Salchev. We will help you," the same male said while another physician leaned forward and poked me in my forearm.

*****

I woke up holding the steering wheel of a truck. It was dark and early in the morning. My guess was that it was around six. I was more perplexed than you are while reading this sentence. I had goosebumps. It was the same feeling when you were around the age of ten and you involuntarily scratched your father's favorite car and you hope that he would not find out. What the heck am I doing here? I'm supposed to be at the hospital, not driving. Wait a minute. Am I driving? Nah, you numb head. You can't be rolling. Who would give you that permission? You can hardly walk.

*****

I awoke lying on the medical stretcher in an unknown medical ward. The room was painted all in green like I was at the Chicago Botanic Garden. A fetchingly brunette nurse who looked like Sandra Bullock sat closely. She observed me cautiously. Lifeless, I could barely shift my head.

"Where am I? Who are you? What the duck am I doing here? Why is nobody answering me?" Nonplussed, I was questioning. Unfortunately, no one responded. It felt like I was talking to the wall. There were around ten doctors and assistants who circled me like a group of strangers, looking at me shocked as if I had just slipped and stumbled upon the iced pathway.

*****

Worn out, I rose to the cabin of the same truck, which seemed to be parked next to the hospital. It was the same hour in the morning when I woke up the first time. The fatigue had frozen my body into complete idleness.

"Help! Is anybody here?" I howled, panicked.

"Stop yelling! I'm coming!" a female with an Ebonics accent yapped. She was a sweet black lady pushing her forties. The woman opened the door. She yanked my hand, and...

*****

I opened my eyelids gradually. Holy smokes, I am at the same hospital where some doctor had revealed it was called Rush.

"Let me get out of here. Lose those ropes. I didn't do anything wrong," I bawled while desperately attempting to loosen that waxed strings. Gosh! They tied my hands and legs so hard.

"Mr. Salchev, as I said earlier, you are very sick. Don't worry! You will be fine. Just stay still please," the same doctor said by using a sedative voice.

"I can stay still, but why have you tied me up? What did I do wrong? I am not a criminal. Why are you treatening me like I am some hoodlum? Answer me for Christ's sake!"

*****

Walking through the medical hallways, I opened a sliding door. It was dead quiet. The only sound I could hear was my footsteps. All of a sudden, a noise blared. I was gravitating to that noise, which portrayed a fusing or flowing water.

That noise came from a medical compartment a few feet nearby. I warily crawled into that gloomy room, and my eyes widened. I couldn't believe what I saw. I had never seen something like that, not even in my nightmares. A human body of a man without the head and arms was floating in a huge container filled with red liquid. My guess was that this body had been kept in that container to prevent it from decomposing. His pudge was bigger than a Halloween pumpkin. What the duck is that? Are they doing biological experiments here!

"Hey! What are you doing down here? You are not supposed to be in this room!" another female African American wearing gushy specs grumbled.

*****

The next moment, I roused up in front of the steering wheel of the same truck. Ah man, I hate that truck. Will this crap end soon?

"Is anybody here? Hey! Help!" Two black ladies crept in. One of them was the same girl wearing those gushy specs. They started to undress my gown.

"Hey, what are you guys doing?"

"You are sweating!" the older woman replied. I was sweating as if I was working out at the gym. Then, I got up and looked around. The truck was the same type as those from UPS where you could stand up inside the cabin. What the duck am I doing here?

"May I get a patient room like everybody else?" I asked. The black ladies leered at me for a second.

"You will, soon." That was the last line I heard before I dozed off.

*****

A nefarious hellhound loomed in my subconscious. His eyeballs were murky like those filled in with black-ink tattoos. That fiend smiled at me, exposing his sharp teeth. Get the hell out of my head. You hear me? Get out, you ugly mother flower.

This hellish creature didn't stop grinning. His beam was enthralling yet dreadful and direful at the same time. It was something that shouldn't be named. Get out! Get out! Get the duck out! You hear me! Ah! Regardless of what I had yelled, the hellhound kept chuckling repeatedly. I didn't know how this cur pussyfooted into my head.

He popped up like an image of a boob tube. It latched to my mind like a virus floating inside of computers. I couldn't physically touch the thing that shouldn't be named. It was like he had connected in my head via Bluetooth device. Get out!

*****

A weird clattering noise roused me. I looked around. I was lying on a medical stretcher in a non-intensive care unit at Stroger. God, I must have been dreaming, was I? How long have I been here? What day is it? My phone displayed, Monday, September 16. Most likely, I had been having bad nightmares.

A few hours later, a crew of physicians entered into my room. A man in his late forties stated,

"Hello, Mr. Salchev. How are you feeling? My name is Dr. Ray Sawaqed. I'm a cardiovascular surgeon. I've heard that you are a boxer?"

"Yeah, I was training before I got sick." That was my brief answer. Dr. Ray stared at me with his sly, vulpine pupils. He then spoke nobly.

"We need to do a TEE and MRI image to make sure of what's going on with your valve. As soon as we have the results, we will schedule open-heart surgery. I suggest we should implant a mechanical valve because of your young age. In that scenario, it wouldn't be necessary to have any more heart surgery for the rest of your life. A mechanical valve requires taking a medication such as a blood thinner as long as you live. Also, it means that you cannot box if you are taking a blood thinner. Let's presume, for instance, someone punches your head. The strike will cultivate a Blood Clot in your head, which will cause severe damage in your brain. That could lead to a stroke and put you in a critical condition, which could lead to the end of your life. On the other hand, if you decide. We can implant a bioprosthetic valve, which will last no longer than fifteen years. With this bioprosthetic valve, you will be able to box. However, I wouldn't recommend inserting a bioprosthetic valve. The reason why is the huge risk after any open-heart surgery, and you have already had one which was made not too long ago. A year, if I am correct."

"Yeah, I had open-heart surgery in June last year."

Dr. Ray waited for a second, then continued his prolonged standpoint.

"To have another bioprosthetic valve means that by the age of seventy, you may have two or more open-heart surgeries. That type of surgery is one of the most complicated in the medical field. It is hard to find a doctor who will take accountability to perform another surgery if you already had been transplanted multiple times. Of course, that's your decision. We will do whatever you decide."

While he was speaking, Doctor Ray had already caught my iffy expression.

"Take your time, Dimitry. We won't execute any surgeries this week, okay? It was nice chatting with you. See you later." Dr. Ray smiled and left the medical unit. His smile was charming, almost indistinguishable from the movie star Pierce Brosnan. Dr. Ray was one of the most intelligent and shrewd people I had ever met. His sharp, wisecracking intellect had provided beneficial information. Dr. Ray mentioned that he was executing around two hundred heart surgeries per year. Furthermore, he had more than twenty years of experience practicing vascular procedures. Pondering what he said, the toughest conundrum struck my mind. What should I choose? I cohere to boxing like a latch mounted on a door. I love this sport. I can't just quit. Those decisions could not be taken as quickly as a snap of the fingers.

*****

In the evening of the same day, Lei came over. Her face looked concerned. We chitchatted about the surgery. She lowered her head, and stared at the floor. Her demeanor had alluded that she must tell me something essential.

As an alpha male, I stepped on her toes and forced her to clear out what was harassing the Asian professor. After a few minutes of talking gibberish, the Asian scientist let the cat out of the bag. Her response was prolonged and hard to understand. Regardless, I got her point. She explained that we weren't at the same intellectual level and that there weren't any sparks amid our souls. It wasn't a huge surprise. What bemused me was the simple fact that my skeptical thoughts were accurate.

"I didn't want to tell you that before the surgery," Lei said.

"It doesn't matter if it's before or after, Lei. I've got the memo. Then why were you hanging out with me?" I queried, just out of the curiosity.

"I dunno. I just wanted to give it a shot."

That was fair. Besides, the hunka-chunka was awful. No vehemence. Just shoved the golf stick in the hole. Those were my thoughts while I was listening to her excuse. It was like the kismet was laughing sardonically on my face. Why?

In 2018, I had heart surgery, then I met Klara. She dumped me. In 2019, I bumped into Lei. She jilted me, then I had another heart surgery. How many more are coming? Lei did whatever had to be done for the best of her life, and I respected her decision. There were no hard feelings. That moment, we broke up with love. Lei left the medical room like a friend of mine.

*****

On Tuesday, the transportation employee hauled another patient into the medical room. It was a huge man in his sixties. His biceps were as big as Silvester Stallone's. It looked like this man could bend a rigid pipe using his bare hands. His name was Adrian, and he was from Russia.

Adrian just had surgery on the shin of his leg. Two or three people were required to keep him in proper equilibrium, especially when he needed to use the toilet. Adrian didn't speak any English at all. He had trouble communicating with nurses and medical personnel. When the doctors attempted to talk to him, they dragged a monitor stand that linked them to an official interpreter. The rest of the time, he had issues intermingling with medical workers. I decided to throw him a bone and started providing a basic interpretation service. My Russian was horrible, although I could understand what he was saying. And since I had already read a few books in English, it wasn't arduous to make a simple interpretation.

I tried to be helpful as much as I could. Adrian worshipped me as if I was his grandson. He had a bunch of different visitors daily, and they all heard about me. Adrian gave orders to his friends, and they brought me all types of food such as bananas, soups, and even meals. I had so much food that even a horse wouldn't be able to nosh all at once.

They took him for another surgery, and I had never seen him since. I prayed to the creator of the universe for him, and I hoped he was doing okay. Adrian was a mensch. God bless his heart.

*****

I had been writing this book while lying on the medical stretcher. The nurses give me the look saying, "What the heck is this guy doing?"

"The work can't wait!" one of them declared.

"Yeah. A man shouldn't stop working on his dreams." That was my response, tossing her mind in perplexed contemplation. A man named Frederick Douglass said, "Once you learn to read and write, you will be forever free." Those words spoke loud enough of what he had meant.

After the TEE, the doctors required another CT scan, in which the medical employee flushed an additional contrast in the IV system to elaborate better picturing. Then, they placed me in an MRI tube where images of my chest were made. After all of those tests were completed, the crew of sawbones led by Dr. Ray crept into the medical room.

Doctor Ray enthusiastically announced,

"Hello, Dimitry. How are ya? The results of the TEE reassured me that the surgery is inevitable. There is something I need to know." I nodded, listening to him. Dr. Ray continued, "Why did you need a pacemaker?" His quiz made me to think about a proper answer.

"It was my fault." My brief reply wasn't helpful. I was cutting the details. Dr. Ray wanted to know more. He put me on the spot. Alas, I didn't tell him anything. Why? If I tell him how I was tooting coco, he most likely would perceive me as a skid row bum. At that time, I thought it would be inappropriate.

"Well, Dimitry, have you decided what type of valve we should implant?"

"I haven't made my last call yet. Do I have more time?"

"Sure. Besides, you don't have to stay here at the hospital. We will schedule the surgery for next Tuesday. I will let you go home for the weekend, and Monday morning, I want you to be here. Sounds good?"

"Yes, big boss," I said, and Dr. Ray left the room. An hour later, another wave of physicians pussyfooted into the medical unit. They fetched high-class technology.

"Hello, Mr. Salchev. We are the cardiac electrophysiology team. Our purpose is to check your pacemaker before your surgery. Okay?" a big stocky man wearing a shabby haircut that looked like a crows' nest stated. They were meticulous while examining the function of Medtronic. Ten minutes later, the doctors were gone.

✳✳✳✳✳

On Friday, September 20, Val responded to my call. Thirty minutes later, he came to Stroger to give me a lift to the office digpot. On the way back, we stopped at the Blossom Café to munch something. We chitchatted there for a while.

When we finished, I left a big, fat tip to the waitress. On the weekend, I was resting at the dungeon, idling like a 1,400 pound elephant. I was thinking about the surgery. It threw my mind into a state of heebie-jeebies. My sick head was thinking to call a hoochie mama and release the piled pressure, but then I removed that flaky idea. Save your money, you frigging schlepper.

Lying on the couch, I stared at the ceiling, looking for hope. You will live a long and happy life. You are going to make it. God is with you. He knows his job. You need to show up on Monday at Stroger, and they will take care of you. You had that kind of surgery before, and you will prevail this obnoxious obstacle. The Lord has more plans for you. He is the best doctor in the world. He has the power to create miracles, and you are one of them. You will make it. You hear me?

The voice in my head had bawled like an austere conservative dictator and former premier of the Soviet Union, Joseph Stalin. Regardless of those motivational words, I was restless and perturbed.

I couldn't sleep. My mind was overwhelmed with thoughts about what could happen. Popping a bunch of extra-strength melatonin pills was the only way to fall asleep. However, there weren't many hours of sleep.

*****

On Monday, September 23, early in the morning, my stingy subconscious forced me to creep onto the blue line. I looked through the windows of the CTA train. The consternation that something was about to happen kept buzzing me on and on. It took a few hours to complete the hospitalization process, and around noon, I was admitted into a non-intensive care unit.

Around four in the afternoon, followed by his crew, Dr. Ray scuttled over.

"Hello, Mr. Salchev. Tomorrow is your big day. Have you decided what valve should be implanted?" Ray questioned while he was grinning charmingly. He respectfully waited for an answer.

"Dr. Ray, I am not sure if you can understand me. Boxing flows in my blood. I can't just quit. Also, this sport is the reason why I wanted to breathe again. Boxing brings me an impetus and hunger to live. It has had a monumental influence on my mind. It's my motivation to be strong, not physically but mentally. It's a pastime hiding beyond my heart and stays right here." I thudded on my left chest using my fist. I longed to show him my love for this sport. Dr. Ray stared wordleselly. He then said.

"I do understand, Dimitry. Okay, then we will implant a bioprosthetic valve." Dr. Ray had accepted my vote, thinking, "This guy must be crazy".

"I'll see you tomorrow, Dimitry." Dr. Ray said, exposing his exuberant smile. He and his crew dissipated. One of Dr. Ray's physicians remained in the medical room. She was an African American cutie-pie in her mid-thirties.

"Mr. Salchev, I deeply comprehend your passion for martial arts. I had been fighting in UFC for seven years, but I injured my knee really bad, which forced me to stop training. I was devastated like you. I didn't know what to do. Anyway, God had enlightened my future, and I found out that there are other things in this life that can bring me the same gratification as UFC. I found a zeal to become a doctor, and here I am. You should consider searching for something else, and I am sure you will find another passion in your life."

I stared at her like a brainless donkey. Holy Moses, she got the point. Perhaps she is right! I could seek through another field, for example, finishing this book!

"You are right. Do you mind telling Dr. Ray that I would like to have a mechanical valve?"

"Not at all. I will inform him. See you later," she exclaimed, flushing a rejoiced beam. For the rest of the day, I was chilling and reading some articles on social media. I texted my mom the updates. We preferred not to talk. It made her feel uncomfortable. For that reason, we avoided speaking via FaceTime.

After midnight, I couldn't sleep. The surgeons prohibited consuming any food or liquids before the surgery. I was getting anxious. All of a sudden, the image of the wicked hellhound loomed in my mind. The same ugly mother flower who had been fazing me for the past six months.

What the heck you want? My mind asked. The hellhound was chuckling as usual. This time, a voice spoke in my head. GO TO THE RESTROOM! You might not believe it, but I did what he had ordered. I crept in the john as the voice commanded and gazed at the mirror. NOW LOOK AT THE MIRROR and start beating YOURSELF. I did as the voice said and started punching my face as hard as I could. Not too long ago, my face changed and got swollen. As I looked at the mirror, my visage looked like I was stung by hundreds of bees.

YEAH, KEEP PUNCHING YOUR FRIGGING FACE. The voice whispered. Blood flowed from my forehead. I am not a pro boxer, but I can put power in my punches. My face looked as if Jermell Charlo had walloped my ass. NOW, I WANT YOU YO SHOW UP IN THE HALLWAY. LET THEM SEE HOW MISERABLE YOU ARE! Obediently, I dragged my feet through the hallway. My head was shaking left and right. On the camera, nurses could see a frenzied man shuddering his head, completely out of hand. A nurse spotted me. Then immediately, a few doctors and nurses came over to check what was happening.

"Oh my God, look at his head! Where is this blood coming from?

What is happening to him?" they asked. The voice in my head screamed DONT TELL THEM ANYTHING, LET THEM BE CONFUSED. The next moment, I couldn't utter anything. It was like my mouth was sealed with duct tape. The physicians and associates were intimidated. The terror in their eyes was perfectly evident. They were so terrified that they didn't know what to do. They were in shock. It was a dire picture.

I returned to the medical room and sat on the bed. My head wouldn't stop shaking. I made a gesture by raising my wrist, showing a sign of writing. They got my subtle signal, and someone abruptly brought me a pen and paper. Then, my hand started jotting. Everyone stared at the paper. There were a few capital letters about two inches long. It was a message:

MAKE HIM STOP!

All of them were exchanging a glimpse by having a perplexed countenance, saying, "What the heck is that?" You might presume that I am some kind of weirdo, but I was possessed by something and those terrified medical employees witnessed the pure horror at that moment. They gave me some medication that knocked me out instantaneously.

The fight with the devil is not physical. It is mental. All the negative thoughts and chips on my shoulder were coming from him.

*****

On September 24, around six in the morning, Doctor Ray woke me up.

"Do you still want to do the surgery?" he queried. I looked at him, wrecked by the blows of the solo fight. I gave him a thumbs up. Dr. Ray nodded, his countenance was something like, "That's what I've been thinking about". Someone had wrapped my head, and I looked like a mummy.

The transportation employee rolled me somewhere in the lower levels. The anesthesiologist's team approached. Someone asked,

"Does he need surgery on his face?" That was how bad my face was. In the next ten minutes, the anesthesia knocked me out, and I slipped into comatose.

*****

When I unlocked my eyelids, two guys were chatting about something. I felt knackered as if someone beat my ass using a baseball bat. The accurately pumping heart brought me joy. The resurrection feeling could be compared to one of the most jubilant moments in my life. It was the same feeling as when you became the most successful writer or when you were so relieved after you almost got into a car accident and somehow got away with it.

The master of the universe saved my life, again. Lord, I know I messed up and have not been totally loyal to you, but as soon as I leave the hospital, I will visit a priest and make a confession. I will clear my soul for what I've done. At the next second, a male nurse of Indian descent approached. His grin was as pure as the beaming of an infant. "Welcome back! How do you feel?" the man exclaimed by expressing a friendly demeanor.

"Blessed." I replied with a short answer describing my long journey. The man tacitly nodded.

"You've made it!" he stately pronounced. The Lord did what he had been planning. He sent Dr. Ray to save my life. "Where is Dr. Ray? I need to thank him."

"He went to Indiana for a business convention. He will be back on Monday. The rest of his crew will come to check on you as soon as they can," the male nurse responded while checking my vitals.

"What day is it?"

It's Thursday, September 26, at noon around one thirty," the man politely replied. Slowly, I exposed my chest (like a male stripper) to observe the incision, which became ten inches long. It looked like I had just come back from Vietnam. There was a bundle of stapled stitches on my chest.

It's done. The worst nightmare had gone. Now, it's time to heal. Everything will be just fine. An hour later, the crew of sawbones tramped into the ICU. All of them were glad to see me. A man wearing a butch haircut stepped closer. He said,

"Hello, Mr. Salchev. I am happy to see you again. How do you feel?"

"I'm blessed." My answer widened his smile. A pause occurred, then I asked.

"Please, tell me about the surgery."

"The surgery took us sixteen hours. We tried to implant the mechanical valve. The size of your heart valve is nineteen, which is the smallest. It didn't match. That caused us to work extra hours, and we placed an animal tissue valve on top of your artificial valve."

"From which animal is that valve?"

"A cow, Mr. Salchev."

"A cow? That means I will have to eat more steaks, right?" They all cracked up. I had been bantering with all of the physicians, not because I wanted to demonstrate my comedic talent. I intended to say funny jokes to cool my jets and keep me away from unpleasant thoughts. The surgeons left the medical unit, and I sank in complete serenity.

On Friday, I woke up early to chat with mom. She was happy to hear my voice and vice versa. At the end of our conversation, she sounded much relieved. Imagine how a mother would feel for her son being located thousands of miles away, surviving after his third heart surgery at the age of thirty. The love of my mother had never disappeared.

Around noon, the hunger disturbed my tummy. I asked the nurse to bring something to eat. It was the same male nurse who had taken care of me the day before. He toted a clementine. It wasn't much but enough. I ate a piece of that fruit. Then, a severe warmth struck my head. Sweat drips flowed upon my forehead.

"Excuse me, would you bring some paper towel, please?" I muttered, and the man swiftly fetched a couple of towels. The perspiration didn't stop. Actually, it accelerated. The sweat dripped from my forehead as if I was under the head of a shower. It was like I was working out at the highest speed in the boxing gym.

"More. I need more," I said worriedly, trying to sort out why I was sweating so much. I sat on the bed, sweating as if I had been running forty miles already. The nurse came back holding many towels. He kept wiping my head and soaked all the sweat. The weirdest part was that I was sweating, but I didn't feel hot anymore. The male nurse jerked in the intensive care unit in a panic.

"Man, you are sweating!" he exclaimed and goggled at me as if he had never seen something like that before.

No cap! Why do you think I've called you? To see your pretty face? The voice in my head cried out.

"I will be right back!" the man almost hollered while leaving the ICU. He was running as if some murderer was chasing him while holding a knife. Twenty seconds later, the unit was filled with a swarm of attending doctors. The terror in the room floated like a ghost. Suddenly, I realized that I couldn't move.

WHAT THE HECK! COME ON! MOVE YOUR HANDS. DAMMIT. I pushed all of my power to jerk my pinky finger, but the nerves refused to obey. My whole body got a 100 percent paralyzed. Terrified of the dreadful situation, I became mute. I couldn't say anything. In front of my eyes, the physicians shifted left and right, trying to figure out what was happening. My neck got paralyzed as well. I couldn't tell how many physicians were rushing into the room. Some were wearing business suits that cost more than a thousand dollars. Is that it? This is the end of my life. This is how I will leave this world. No, Lord, I don't want to leave. Please, Lord!

"Boy, do you hear me? Do you know where you are? Do you know your name? Do you know which year it is?" One of the physicians wearing the expensive suit had blurted. I was aware of what he was asking. Unfortunately, I became literally voiceless. I couldn't even hum. My eyelids were paralyzed as well, I couldn't keep them open anymore. My eyes were closed, and the drapes at the theater of Dimity's show had rolled down. Thanks for watching! Is that it? Am I dying? Is that how my life ends?

"CODE BLUE, ROOM 1127. I REPEAT, CODE BLUE, ROOM 1127," a voice hollered through the speaker somewhere in the hospital.

What the heck! Where is that room? I couldn't see anything. I became blinded. I was consciousness, and I could only hear doctors' voices. That's it! I am leaving this world. Goodbye, Mom. Goodbye, Dad. Goodbye, Sunny. Goodbye to all of my friends and people whom I've met. I will miss all of you.

"CODE BLUE, ROOM 1127. I REPEAT, CODE BLUE, ROOM 1127."

What is this code? Room 1127 is your room, you nitwit!

"Boy, we must give you anesthesia. In that case, you will sleep till we make sure that you are fine." A male voice with a white American accent echoed. He sounded panicked. I started to count the seconds like a kid in preschool. My heart stopped beating like a broken watch. At that moment, I realized that I was not breathing at all. No inhales, no exhales. I had never thought that could be possible, even for a few seconds.

One hundred and forty-two... At the next moment, a 100-percent-paralyzed Bulgarian man fell into a deep sleep.

*****

Brian Houston said, "What seemed like the end was only just the beginning." That was exactly what happened to me. We all had to cross the bridge of pain. How long does it take to cross that bridge? It's up to the Lord Almighty.

One of the greatest horror authors, Stephen King, said in one of his books (The Stand), "The end of life is never pretty." I would add, "It's creepier than the scariest movie and book that has ever been written or filmed in this world."

Ernest Hemingway wrote, "The world is a fine place and worth fighting for..."

One of my quotes portrayed the foundation of my mindset: "Wherein you see falling stones, there you can build castles."

*****

That was the first book of my memorial. Stay tuned because the story of my life continues. The second book will be released soon.

Author's Note

I would like to express my appreciation to Dr. Edwin, McGee, Dr. Smit Vasaiwala, and Dr. Ray Sawaqued for saving my life from certain death. Also I would like to thank all the medical responders and nurses and physicians for their dedicated work. Without you, I wouldn't be here sharing the greatest chance to be here on earth. God bless America and all of you.

About the Author

Dimitry Salchev was born and raised in Bulgaria. His passion for learning and speaking English grew when he was in grade school. He will write and type till his hands can no longer move. Today, Dimitry has nothing to do with the person described in this book. He is free from drug and alcohol use. His only addiction is writing and reading in English. He loves to laugh and laughs to love. He will never stop being creative, and friendly just the way God created him. The Lord has helped him to pass through many unpleasant bridges. He won't stop declaring how grateful he is. He is a human as you are..

Lightning Source UK Ltd.
Milton Keynes UK
UKHW012240060223
416577UK00010B/719/J